THE STORY CURE

Also by Ella Berthoud and Susan Elderkin

The Novel Cure

The stories that shape our children's lives are too important to be left to chance. With *The Story Cure*, bibliotherapists Ella Berthoud and Susan Elderkin have put together the perfect manual for grown-ups who want to initiate young readers into one of life's greatest pleasures.

Inside you'll find a remedy for every hiccup and heartache, whether between the covers of a picture book, a pop-up book, or a YA novel. The cures will take you back to old favourites such as *The Borrowers* and *The Secret Garden* as well as to modern, soon-to-be classics by Michael Morpurgo, Malorie Blackman and Frank Cottrell-Boyce. You'll find dozens of helpful lists, such as the right reads to fuel obsessions – from dogs to dinosaurs, space to spies – and the best books to read to siblings of different ages at bedtime. Wise and witty, *The Story Cure* will guide any small (or smallish) person you know through the trials and tribulations of growing up, and help you fill their bookshelves with adventure and delight.

THE STORY CURE

An A–Z of Books to Keep Kids Happy, Healthy and Wise

ELLA BERTHOUD and SUSAN ELDERKIN

CANONGATE
Edinburgh · London

This hardback edition first published by Canongate Books in 2017

First published in Great Britain in 2016 by
Canongate Books Ltd, 14 High Street, Edinburgh EH1 1TE

www.canongate.co.uk

1

British Library Cataloguing-in-Publication Data
A catalogue record for this book is available on
request from the British Library

ISBN 978 1 78211 529 8

Typeset in Archer by
Palimpsest Book Production Ltd, Falkirk, Stirlingshire

Printed and bound in Great Britain
by Clays Ltd, St Ives plc.

For our own strange and marvellous creatures:
Morgan, Calypso, Harper, Kirin

CONTENTS

INTRODUCTION

Between 'Once upon a time' and 'happily ever after' is a land we've all been to. Strange and marvellous things happen there.

Sometimes they're things we don't normally get to do – like riding on the back of a dragon, or finding the golden ticket to the chocolate factory. Often they're things we want to do but are too scared or sensible – like running away from home. And sometimes they're things we wouldn't want to happen to us at all, but we're very curious to know what it'd be like if they *did* – like being orphaned, or stranded on a desert island, or raised by a badger, or tragically turned into a rock. By the time we come back, brushing the dust off our hats, a new, worldly look in our eye, we alone know what we've seen, experienced, endured. And we've discovered something else, too: that whatever is going on in our actual lives, and whatever we're feeling about it, someone else has felt that way too. We're not alone, after all.

When we suggested, with our first book *The Novel Cure*, that reading the right novel at the right time in your life can help you see things differently – and even be therapeutic – the idea was surprising and new. That children's books can do the same for children won't surprise anyone at all. Parents, godparents, grandparents and kindly uncles – not to mention librarians, English teachers and booksellers (who are, of course, bibliotherapists in disguise) – have long been aware that the best way to help a child through a challenging moment is to give them a story about it, whether they're being bullied at school, have fallen in love for the first time, or the tooth-fairy failed to show up. The best children's books have a way of confronting big issues and big emotions with fearless delight, their instinct to thrill but also, ultimately, to reassure.* No rampaging toddler ever feels quite so out of his depth after *Where the Wild Things Are*. No pre-teen girl so alone with her questions after *Are You There, God? It's Me, Margaret.*

* There are notable exceptions, of course: fairytales in their darkest forms, Hilaire Belloc's *Cautionary Tales for Children* and Heinrich Hoffmann's *Struwwelpeter* . . . all of which help to keep psychiatrists in business.

In this book, you'll find the very best children's books to give to (or read with) the kids in your life – whether they're three or thirteen, love books or avoid them, can't sit still, want more toys, have nits or nightmares, or are desperate for more independence. For many of us, a favourite book from childhood is among our most treasured possessions – not just any copy, but the actual copy we owned, defaced with wax-crayon scribbles and with the pop-up bits torn off. For Susan, it's a copy of *Go, Dog. Go!* by PD Eastman, with its endless litany of dogs, big and little, spotted and plain, driving in open-topped cars, or sleeping in the biggest bed you ever saw, then leaping out in a blaze of colour and light when it's time to wake up. Each time it was read – or, rather, pored over, because this book is all about the detail in the pictures – there was the chance of sharing a new, hidden joke with the author: the one dog that has his eyes open in the middle of the night, or is still snoozing at daybreak. For Ella it's her copy of *Tarzan of the Apes* by Edgar Rice Burroughs – the first in a series of twenty-four Tarzan adventures which she gulped down, one after the other, their yellowed pages teeming with the screeches and calls of the jungle. And, in the margins – sometimes running over onto the text – her own colourful attempts at sinuous snakes and bright-winged parrots and leaping monkeys. Potent time capsules, they seem to contain not just who we were, but who we dreamed we would one day be.

Which books our own children hang on to from their childhoods is anyone's guess – but they'll surely be of the physical, tangible kind. Tablets are brilliant for beaming up a book in an instant; but engaging the senses of touch and smell, as well as sight, makes it so much easier to get lost in a book.

That's when we get transported. That's when we go to the land.

So, if you're sitting comfortably, let's begin.

HOW TO USE THIS BOOK

This book is for grown-ups in the exciting position of choosing books for children – parents, carers, grandparents, friends, teachers, librarians or distant aunts wishing to send a cuddle (or a cautionary tale) from a distance.

It's arranged like a medical reference book. Look up the 'ailment' – be it boredom, bras, or not wanting to go to bed – and you'll find a 'cure' in the form of a story, or two.

Bearing in mind that reading skills and habits develop differently for every child, we've organised our 'cures' by category rather than age, using the abbreviations PB for Picture Book, ER for Early Reader, CB for Chapter Book and YA for Young Adult fiction. You'll be able to find books the right level for a child simply by scanning for these initials.

Though each abbreviation correlates roughly to a certain age group (see the table which follows), we recommend that you – and the children you're reading with – roam freely among the categories. Some kids are reading chapter books by six, and many still love to hear a favourite picture book being read aloud long after they've learnt to read by themselves. Challenging subject matter is flagged up within the descriptions. Some ailments – such as being bullied, moving house, and sibling rivalry – span all ages, and therefore we cure with all categories. Others are more age-specific – such as acne, losing your favourite toy, and first kiss – requiring a cure from just one category. Sometimes we mix the categories up: a resonant picture book can be just the ticket for a hard-to-reach adolescent; and of course chapter books – that golden treasure trove – clamour as much to be read aloud as alone, making them great for the shared bedtime read.

In all cases, our cures span well-known and lesser-known stories, classic and contemporary, those written by authors from near and far away, books that are part of a longer series (where necessary, we name the series in brackets), and books that stand alone; but they're always* fiction. Sometimes they come as a list – The Ten Best Audiobook Series for Long Car Journeys, for instance, and The Ten Best Bedtime Reads for the Very Little (see p.341 for an Index of Lists). There are ideas for dealing with common reading ailments too, such as being too fidgety to read, or the competition from screens (see p.340 for an Index of Reading Ailments). And because many childhood ailments can be as challenging for the accompanying adult as for the child, we've included some Cures for Grown-ups, too (indicated with this symbol). These cures also take the form of children's books; this is a book about children's stories, after all, and a good book is a good book,† whoever it was written for.

AGE	SYMBOL	DESCRIPTION
6 and under	PB	PICTURE BOOKS. Designed to be shared with a pre-reading child, picture books are a child's introduction to the very notion of a book, conjuring stories by appealing to all the senses. Hang on to them: many make great beginner readers, and the best ones are multi-layered enough to interest children for many years to come.
5–8 (or beginner readers)	ER	EARLY READERS. Featuring large type, simple words and illustrations, these are books designed with the beginner reader in mind.
8–12	CB	CHAPTER BOOKS. These can range from relatively simple to quite sophisticated. Give them to a child to devour in private, or enjoy reading them aloud together, depending on reading ability and whether or not you can bear to miss out on the story.
12 plus	YA	YOUNG ADULT FICTION. This thriving category in children's publishing reflects the preoccupations of adolescence. Expect relatively complex and perhaps hard-hitting storylines. Of course, many teens will be ready for adult novels as well; please refer them to our companion volume, *The Novel Cure*.

* Well, *almost* always.

† As CS Lewis said, 'A children's story that can only be enjoyed by children is not a good children's story in the slightest.'

A–Z OF AILMENTS

'Stories . . . entertain and teach; they help us both enjoy life and endure it. After nourishment, shelter and companionship, stories are the things we need most in the world.'

Philip Pullman

about, what's it all?

[PB] *You Are Stardust*
ELIN KELSEY, ILLUSTRATED BY SOYEON KIM

[YA] *The Boy in the Striped Pyjamas*
JOHN BOYNE

For some of us, it's the question we've been waiting for. Finally an excuse to get up on the soapbox and hold forth about the meaning of life, the universe and everything. For others among us, being asked to explain where we came from and where we go next as we're mashing up bananas can at best catch us on the hop and, at worst, provoke an existential crisis all our own.

Those wishing to approach the answer from a scientific point of view will appreciate the blend of biology and wonder in *You Are Stardust*. With simple words, accompanied by photographs of homespun dioramas by Korean artist Soyeon Kim, it takes us from our beginnings as atoms shooting out from an exploding star to living, growing organisms with constantly renewing cells. The emphasis is very much on being part of the great cycle of life – and on just how much we have in common with the rest of nature. Did you know, for instance, that the water inside our bodies is as salty as the ocean? Or that when we sneeze we expel air faster than a cheetah sprints? Or that bats and sperm whales get their friends to babysit? Of course, an inevitable part of being a living organism is that, along with everything else, we will one day die. But then the great cycle starts again. We are left with a sense of wonder at the miracle of it all – and the need to look after both our fragile planet and the precious ecosystem that is 'planet You'.

As children get older, the question becomes, more fundamentally, one of how to live a good life. *The Boy in the Striped Pyjamas* tells the story of nine-year-old Bruno, who has moved with his family from Berlin to a desolate place called 'Out-With'. It's only gradually that we learn his father is the commander of the notorious Nazi prison camp.

Bruno hates his new home. There's a huge garden, but he has no one to play with. And why is it that the people on the other side of the fence – fathers, grandfathers, children, none of them girls – go around wearing striped pyjamas all day? Bruno fondly imagines that these people are having a wonderful time, riding their bicycles and enjoying their meals communally. Only the reader knows how horribly far this is from the truth.

When one of these pyjama-clad figures comes up to the fence one day, he finally makes a friend. He and Shmuel talk to one another through the fence, and Bruno brings him food. Later, when grilled by a Nazi officer who visits their house, Bruno finds himself denying that Shmuel is his friend – and we see the terrible complicity he's unwittingly embracing. But Bruno, in his innocence, also sees no reason not to stick by his friend when they embark on their awful, final adventure.

This book challenges the reader to ask what they know about right and wrong, what they know about human nature, and what they know about themselves. Bring it into your own household, and use it to establish the human values of justice, fairness and respect.

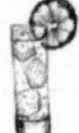

CURE FOR GROWN-UPS PB *The Three Questions* **JON J MUTH**

If you are indeed having an existential crisis, see this handsome picture book, inspired by a short story by Leo Tolstoy. Featuring a giant panda delivering Zen-inspired wisdom, it's as potentially life-changing for a grown-up as for a child.

SEE ALSO: **death, fear of** • **god, wondering if there is a**

abuse

PB *A Family That Fights*
SHARON CHESLER BERNSTEIN, ILLUSTRATED BY KAREN RITZ
(continued)

It won't always be apparent that children exposed to abuse in the home – be it physical or emotional – are struggling. Children develop all sorts of coping mechanisms to help hide their shame or make themselves feel safe. Professional help should always be sought where abuse is suspected, but sharing a book that

[PB] *The Words Hurt*
CHRIS LOFTIS, ILLUSTRATED BY CATHERINE GALLAGHER

[YA] *Learning to Scream*
BEATE TERESA HANIKE

[YA] *The Perks of Being a Wallflower*
STEPHEN CHBOSKY

reflects what may be going on* might give a child who has suffered abuse some relief – and even begin to open the door to a conversation. Knowing that someone cares, and can be trusted to listen and give support, is crucial – and books are a way to create a safe and patient space.

On the surface, *A Family That Fights* is about an ordinary sort of family – one that 'goes to movies, bakes cookies, plays games and builds snowmen'. But this one also includes a father that 'fights with his hands'. The range of things that can and do happen in this family are explored in careful detail: the mother becomes nervous when the father is due to come home; the child feels angry with the mother for pretending everything's fine. The black and white pencil drawings capture pent-up emotional states with great sensitivity.

For verbal abuse, go to *The Words Hurt*, in which an angry father – a victim of abuse himself – unleashes regular torrents of criticism on his son, Greg. At night, Greg lies in bed wondering if other kids' dads get so furious when they're late for school, and whether cleaning your room is every family's 'VERY SERIOUS rule'. There's always just enough truth in what his dad is saying that Greg's left wondering if perhaps he deserves the yelling. It's only when his best friend Joe and Joe's parents witness one of the outbursts – the tell-tale blush burning on the father's cheeks as he rapidly loses control – that Greg finally finds an ally. That the father immediately acknowledges what a bully he's become and admits to needing help is rather too good to be true; but the fact that this family faces the abuse together, with the love between father and son soon flowing back in, provides a positive, hopeful model. In cases of abuse, children need assurance that asking for help won't just make things worse.

The possibility that a grown-up close to the child may know of the abuse but turn a blind eye is explored in the gut-punching *Learning to Scream*. Since the age of seven, Malvina has visited her grandparents every Friday and taken a bath with Granddad. Underneath the bubbles, Granddad touches 'his little Malvina' and makes her touch him too – while Gran waits outside with a towel, complicit. Now thirteen, Malvina has developed the habit of disappearing inside her head during these bath times, deciding that 'he can do whatever he wants as long as he doesn't touch my thoughts'. She tries to tell her father and her brother about what's happening, but can't seem to get the words out. 'He kisses me,' is all she manages to say, and they call her 'little miss don't-

* When tackling serious ailments, always read a book through to the end yourself before sharing it with a child. The picture books recommended here are written to capture what it can be like to experience violence in the home and unless the content bears some resemblance to the child's own experience, it may disturb more than reassure.

touch-me', as if she's simply prudish. To compound matters, her grandmother's dying words to Malvina are a request to keep her mouth shut. 'Granddad can't help it,' the old lady says. 'Promise me you won't leave [him] in the lurch.'

It's when she meets a boy her own age and starts wanting a normal, healthy relationship that Malvina comes to understand exactly how wrong what's been going on has been. She wonders what her new friend Screwy would think of her if he knew the truth, and practises whispering to him: 'You've got to help me.' In the end it's her grandparents' neighbour, Mrs Bitschek, who realises that Malvina has something to say – though she has to kick her under the table to make her say it. As this story makes chillingly clear, sometimes even close family can stand between an abused child and the help they so badly need.

At the heart of *The Perks of Being a Wallflower* lies the revelation that sometimes abuse can take years to come to light. Fifteen-year-old Charlie is the sort of boy who would rather observe from the sidelines than take an active part. A wannabe writer who suffers from bouts of depression, he's nervous of starting high school – and when we find out that his best friend committed suicide at the end of the previous school year, it seems explanation enough for his mental state. But then he meets Sam, a girl he likes, and during their first kiss he's assaulted by disturbing flashbacks. At first he ignores them; but they come back even more strongly. The discovery of the trauma in his past is shocking to all parties, including the reader; but Chbosky handles it delicately, with Charlie shown to be in control of how much is revealed. Teens will see that, with the trauma now uncovered, Charlie's recovery has begun.

SEE ALSO: **bullied, being** • **bully, being a** • **foster care, being in** • **heard, not feeling** • **trauma** • **violence**

academic, not very

SEE: **good at anything, feeling like you're no**

acne

Spot the Difference
JUNO DAWSON

Though in fact caused by a virus, the popular misconception that acne is a result of lack of cleanliness only adds to the misery it inflicts. Until recently, it featured in fiction only to express an inner ugliness. Thankfully, Juno Dawson has now brought us a heroine who we love – and who overcomes its stigma.

Sixteen-year-old Avery is known as 'Pizzaface' at school. Her previous best friend, Lucy, dumped her to be with the 'A-list' – the girls who sit smugly within their bubbles, perfecting their hair, skin and nails. Her best friend now is Lois, who, with her button nose and Taylor Swift bob, might have made the A-list too, but for her one tiny arm. She is known as 'T-rex'.

Then Avery is given a new drug that clears up her acne completely. Suddenly everyone can see her for the beauty she is. Swiftly courted by the A-list, she abandons Lois, acquires a boyfriend, Seth, and – feeling unstoppable – decides to run for head girl. But just as the battle for the position of head girl is about to reach its climax, Avery is told to stop taking the anti-acne drug: it has severe side-effects that are only now being understood. She makes her election speech with a paper bag over her head – 'Imperfect, but content' in her skin – standing not for her looks but for who she is and what she believes in. We never know which way the vote goes – and for kids reading this story it doesn't matter. The empowering point has been made.

SEE ALSO: **adolescence • confidence, lack of • zits**

ADHD

SEE: **fidgety to read, being too • short attention span**

adolescence

Everything's in flux for teens in these testing years – their body, their beliefs, their sense of self and their relationships with everyone else. No one should be expected to go through it without some fictional allies to hand.

THE TEN BEST BOOKS FOR ADOLESCENCE

- CB *Dogsong* **GARY PAULSEN**
- YA *Go Ask Alice* **ANONYMOUS***
- YA *The Chocolate War* **ROBERT CORMIER**

* This moving story about a teenage girl who becomes hooked on drugs after unwittingly taking LSD at a party – originally claimed to be taken from an actual diary but since acknowledged by its author, psychologist Beatrice Sparks, to be a work of fiction – contains explicit material. Full of compassion for the angst of adolescence, we recommend it as a cautionary tale about the dangers of drug use; but be sure your teen is ready.

[YA] *Dear Nobody* BERLIE DOHERTY
[YA] *The Princess Bride* WILLIAM GOLDMAN
[YA] *The Farthest Shore* URSULA K LE GUIN*
[YA] *All Our Pretty Songs* SARAH MCCARRY
[YA] *Remix* NON PRATT
[YA] *The Square Root of Summer* HARRIET REUTER HAPGOOD
[YA] *The Scar Boys* LEN VLAHOS

SEE ALSO: **acne • alone, wanting to be left • arguments, getting into • astray, being led • bargaining, endless • body hair • body image • body odour • chores, having to do • clumsiness • dating • different, feeling • embarrassment • exams • friends your parents don't approve of, having • gaming, excessive • gay, not sure if you are • good at anything, feeling like you're no • happy ever after, had enough of • hormones, raging • innocence, loss of • laziness • moodiness • obstinate, being • periods • screen, glued to the • sulking • trashing the house while your parents are out • understood, not being • wet dreams • zits**

adoption

[CB] *The Hen Who Dreamed She Could Fly* SUN-MI HWANG, ILLUSTRATED BY NOMOCO

Once upon a time, adopted children were sat down at a random moment in childhood and delivered the 'oh, by the way, you're adopted' bolt from the blue. Thankfully, we've moved on since then, drip-feeding the knowledge from the beginning. Picture books are a great way to help do this, as well as reiterating the message that adopted children are planned and deeply wanted. Which stories strike a chord will depend on the particular circumstances of the adoption: find those that best fit the picture from the list that follows.

As adopted children get older, they generally ask more questions about their birth parents and may try to seek them out. This brings a flood of new and complex emotions for both the child and the grown-ups who adopted them. A story which shows it's normal to have mixed feelings about your adoption is *The Hen Who Dreamed She Could Fly* by the South Korean author Sun-mi Hwang. Sprout is an egg-laying hen who harbours a dream – not to fly, in fact, but to become a mother. So, together with her friend Straggler, a duck, she escapes the barnyard and makes a new life in the wild, foraging for

* Best enjoyed after having read the previous two titles in the Earthsea cycle.

food and doing her best to avoid the ever-hungry weasel. When she stumbles on a nest in a briar patch containing a 'large and handsome', still-warm egg, she sits on it through the night. By morning she can feel the tiny heart beating inside the shell.

When the little duckling – as it turns out to be – emerges, Sprout's happiness is moving to behold. With her baby, Greentop, in tow, she struts proudly past the animals in the barnyard, impervious to their taunts. 'Sure, he's a duck, not a chick. Who cares?' she says to herself. 'He still knows I'm his mum!' When, all by himself, Greentop learns to swim, then fly – spending entire days wheeling over the reservoir – Sprout is happy for him, even though she's left on the ground. One day, Greentop senses something approaching the reservoir – something that will cover the entire sky and fill the air with its honking . . . and he begins to tremble with a mixture of excitement and impending loss . . .

This fable-like novella is about many things – the desire to be a parent, and the need for a child to be who they are. But what we remember most is the over-arching love Sprout feels for her baby. Sprout knows that the best way to love her son is to understand him – even if that means acknowledging he's different to her and may have to go away at some point and find out who he is. Give this to kids as they begin to ask questions about their birth parents to show that you understand.

THE TEN BEST BOOKS FEATURING ADOPTION

- PB *The Teazles' Baby Bunny* SUSAN BAGNALL, ILLUSTRATED BY TOMMASO LEVENTE TANI
- PB *The Most Precious Present in the World* BECKY EDWARDS, ILLUSTRATED BY LOUISE COMFORT
- PB *The Nanny Goat's Kid* JEANNE WILLIS, ILLUSTRATED BY TONY ROSS
- CB *Anne of Green Gables* LM MONTGOMERY
- CB *Wintle's Wonders* (later renamed *Dancing Shoes*) NOEL STREATFEILD
- YA *Kimchi & Calamari* ROSE KENT
- YA *Find a Stranger, Say Goodbye* LOIS LOWRY
- YA *Girl Missing* SOPHIE MCKENZIE
- YA *Saffy's Angel* HILARY MCKAY
- YA *Daughter of Smoke and Bone* LAINI TAYLOR

CURE FOR GROWN-UPS PB *Horton Hatches the Egg* DR SEUSS

This story doesn't represent birth parents who give up a child for adoption in the most charitable light, but at times of extreme exhaustion, or when you get the 'You're not my real mother/father anyway' line hurled at you, the depiction of the faithful Horton will be a comfort. Having agreed to sit on an egg laid by Mayzie – a lazy bird who'd rather soak up some rays on Palm Beach and delegate the incubation job to someone else – Horton keeps his word, protecting the egg through rain and sleet, and sitting there even when the tree bends beneath his weight, when icicles form on his trunk, and when a hunter takes aim – Seuss's endlessly inventive illustrations bringing all these travails to life in the way that only he can. When the chick finally hatches and Mayzie has the audacity to claim it as hers after all, we're in no doubt who the rightful parent is. Whenever you – or your child – need reminding, adopt Horton's rallying cry as your mantra: 'I meant what I said/And I said what I meant . . ./ An elephant's faithful/One hundred per cent!'

SEE ALSO: **anger** • **different, feeling** • **feelings, not able to express your** • **parents, having**

adventure, needing an

When there's none to be had at a child's own back door, send them on one in a book.

THE ~~TEN~~ THIRTY-NINE* BEST BOOKS FOR TAKING YOU ON AN ADVENTURE

PB *The Snail and the Whale* JULIA DONALDSON, ILLUSTRATED BY AXEL SCHEFFLER
PB *Rosie's Walk* PAT HUTCHINS
PB *The Book about Moomin, Mymble and Little My* TOVE JANSSON
PB *Not a Box* ANTOINETTE PORTIS
PB *We're Going on a Bear Hunt* MICHAEL ROSEN, ILLUSTRATED BY HELEN OXENBURY
CB *Down the Bright Stream* BB
CB *The Wonderful Wizard of Oz* L FRANK BAUM
CB *Circus Mirandus* CASSIE BEASLEY
CB *The Magic Faraway Tree* ENID BLYTON

* Adventures are to chapter books as gin is to tonic. How could we restrict ourselves?

CB *The Child's Elephant* RACHEL CAMPBELL-JOHNSTON
CB *The Mouse and the Motorcycle* BEVERLY CLEARY
CB *The Saturdays* (Melendy Quartet) ELIZABETH ENRIGHT
CB *The Snow Merchant* SAM GAYTON, ILLUSTRATED BY CHRIS RIDDELL
CB *The Mouse and His Child* RUSSELL HOBAN
CB *Biggles Goes to War* CAPTAIN WE JOHNS
CB *The Phantom Tollbooth* NORTON JUSTER
CB *Sparks* ALLY KENNEN
CB *Stig of the Dump* CLIVE KING, ILLUSTRATED BY EDWARD ARDIZZONE
CB *Island of Thieves* JOSH LACEY
CB *Where the Mountain Meets the Moon* (and *Starry River of the Sky*) GRACE LIN
CB *The Story of Doctor Dolittle* HUGH LOFTING
CB *The Children of the New Forest* CAPTAIN FREDERICK MARRYAT
CB *The Apothecary* MAILE MELOY
CB *Ribblestrop* ANDY MULLIGAN
CB *Five Children and It* EDITH NESBIT
CB *Amazon Adventure* WILLARD PRICE
CB *The Firework Maker's Daughter* PHILIP PULLMAN
CB *Mortal Engines* PHILIP REEVE
CB *Miss Peregrine's Home for Peculiar Children* RANSOM RIGGS
CB *Haroun and the Sea of Stories* SALMAN RUSHDIE
CB *The Invention of Hugo Cabret* BRIAN SELZNICK
CB *Amazon Summer* (Amy Wild) HELEN SKELTON
CB *The Egypt Game* ZILPHA KEATLEY SNYDER
CB *Kidnapped* ROBERT LOUIS STEVENSON
CB *Treasure Island* ROBERT LOUIS STEVENSON
CB *Stuart Little* EB WHITE
CB *The Swiss Family Robinson* JOHANN DAVID WYSS
YA *The Last Unicorn* PETER S BEAGLE
YA *The Westing Game* ELLEN RASKIN

SEE ALSO: **bored, being** • **family outings** • **summer holidays**

alcohol

SEE: **drugs** • **peer pressure**

allergies

[PB] *The Princess and the Peanut*
SUE GANZ-SCHMITT, ILLUSTRATED BY MICAH CHAMBERS-GOLDBERG

[YA] *Shadow Jumper*
JM FORSTER

There's nothing fun for kids about having an allergy. Not only do they have to make sure they don't come into contact with whatever triggers a reaction – be it pollen, poodles or peanuts (see: worrying) – but they have to deal with the effects on their social life and close relationships as well. A child with severe allergies can end up feeling cut off from all the fun and more fragile than everyone else (see: different, feeling; friends, finding it hard to make). Sue Ganz-Schmitt's delightful twist on the classic *Princess and the Pea* fairytale is doubly welcome, therefore, for bringing levity to the issue – and showing that allergies can actually make you rather special. When a wet and soggy waif turns up at the palace door claiming to be a 'real princess', the queen decides to put her to the test in the usual way. But they're out of peas in the palace, so she plants a peanut under the mattresses instead. By the next morning, the poor princess is crying out for an EpiPen. The king and queen react impeccably, throwing out all the peanut-contaminated foods in the palace larder, and the love-struck prince swears to give up his beloved peanut-butter-and-jam sandwiches if she'll accept his hand in marriage. Three cheers for the allergy that brought the happy pair together!

Older kids will appreciate *Shadow Jumper*, the story of fourteen-year-old Jack who was born with photosensitive skin – an allergy to sunlight. His condition is so severe that he can't go outside without covering every inch of himself with creams or clothes – and, as a result, spends most of his time inside, ultra-pale and alone and feeling like a vampire. At school, he can't join in with sports or break times, which means it's hard to make friends. But like any other kid his age, he wants to have fun and take risks.

So it is that he goes up to the rooftops at dusk and jumps daringly from shadow to shadow. He knows he's dicing with death – and not just because of the danger of falling. Even in the twilight, it would only take a glancing contact with the evening rays for him to come up in an angry, fizzing rash.

When, on the rooftops, he meets Beth – an angsty teenager who, with her white make-up and dark eyeliner, looks almost as freakish as him – he feels an instant connection. Together they set out by night bus to find Jack's missing father, breaking into the lab where he works – and so begins a gradual awareness of the issues with which they both have to contend. It becomes apparent that Jack's condition worsens under stress and improves when he's calm and happy; and as he opens up to the important people in his life, his skin starts to heal. This is a story that encourages teens to share the challenges they face with others. After all, how can one's needs ever be effectively met if other people don't know what they are?

SEE ALSO: **different, feeling • fussy eater, being a • worrying**

alone, wanting to be left

[PB] *The Cloud*
HANNAH CUMMING

[PB] *All Alone*
KEVIN HENKES

[YA] *The Knife of Never Letting Go*
PATRICK NESS

Sometimes it helps to be alone. Away from the mêlée, a child can experience their emotions without having to pretend they're OK. But sometimes a child would rather be rescued from their funk, if only someone would notice. Such is the case for the child with the angry charcoal scribble hovering over her head in *The Cloud*.

While all the other kids in the art class are filling their canvases with spaceships and giant yellow chicks, the canvas of the girl with the cloud remains resolutely blank. No one dares approach her. But then a girl with a delightfully wonky-eyed portrait on her canvas walks boldly through the charcoal scribble and talks to her. It takes her several attempts, but eventually she engages the cloud girl – and soon they're combining their skills to make pictures together. The more they produce, the smaller the black cloud gets, until – puff! – it's gone, and a big, sunny smile appears on the cloud girl's face instead. Use this sensitive book with a prickly child and, ideally, their peers. Its message of patience, persistence and acceptance will help show everyone how he or she might be drawn out.

Sometimes a child wants to be alone because they've cottoned on to the fact that you can feel more truly alive when you're by yourself. Kevin Henkes introduces this concept with impressive minimalism, setting the sketchy figure of a boy against semi-abstract watercolour landscapes in *All Alone*. 'Sometimes I like to live alone, all by myself,' it begins – the choice of the verb 'to live', rather than 'to be', immediately elevating us to the level of poetry. When the boy walks in the woods by himself, he can 'hear more and see more'. He notices the way the trees sigh in the wind. He feels the heat of the sun on his skin. Many adults never learn to enjoy being alone like this. Use it to introduce solitude as a positive concept, and you'll give a child a key to contentment in life.

For older children, wanting to be left alone takes on new, hormonal angles which are hard for the grown-up to interpret and even harder for the adolescent to explain (see: adolescence; hormones, raging). The bedroom door stays shut for hours on end and excuses are given for not joining in with family activities.

Todd, the hero of *The Knife of Never Letting Go* – the first in Patrick Ness's excellent Chaos Walking trilogy – feels the need to escape the company of others more than most, living as he does on a planet where everyone can, literally, hear one another's thoughts. Surrounded day and night by 'All the Noise that men spill outta themselves, all their clamour and clatter' which comes 'at you and at you and at you', it's not surprising that Todd has started taking long walks on the lonely marshes with his dog, Manchee, to try and find some peace. Even here, he still has Manchee's thoughts to contend with, though they are somewhat basic in content and expression ('Need a poo, Todd'; 'Hungry, Todd.')

While he's trying to limit his exposure to Noise, and avoid whatever it is the older men have in store for him – a vague menace lurking around his imminent transition to 'manhood' – he stumbles across something unexpected. No women have existed on this planet since a virus wiped them out; and yet, here on the marshes, Todd finds cause to question this assumption . . . Teenagers will relate to Todd's need for privacy – and also to the joy of one day finding someone with whom to share their innermost thoughts.

SEE ALSO: **different, feeling • friends, feeling that you have no • friends, finding it hard to make • heard, not feeling • loner, being a • moodiness • trauma**

anger

PB *When Sophie Gets Angry – Really, Really Angry . . .*
MOLLY BANG

CB *Dogsbody*
DIANA WYNNE JONES

YA *Breathing Underwater*
ALEX FLINN

Over time, we learn to control the primal urge to shout, scream or hit – but it's not a skill we're born with. And if a child is exposed to peers, older siblings or grown-ups who express their rage inappropriately, or who never express it at all, a story can be a brilliant way to bring healthy role models into the house. *When Sophie Gets Angry – Really, Really Angry . . .* shows what happens during an outbreak of red-hot temper – and a way of calming oneself down.

At first glance, the deceptively simple illustrations might be the handiwork of a child with a fat brush and poster paints: here is Sophie and her sister, with flat circles for faces, dots for eyes, and a red daub for the mouth. But their artfulness soon makes its impact. When her sister snatches her toy gorilla and so triggers her anger, Sophie's face takes up the whole page, huge and *there*. And when her anger erupts, Sophie's entire body sizzles with a jagged, red outline. When she runs out of the house, everything else starts to sizzle too – the slammed door, the trees, a squirrel – as if absorbing her projected upset. In time her anger starts to burn itself out, and her outline dims to orange. But it's only when she finds an old beech tree – its gnarled branches spiralling up with a cool, blue aura – that it ebbs away completely. By the time she goes back inside her outline has faded to yellow, matching the rest of her family's outlines – all of whom are now quietly getting on with other things and are glad to see her back. This story shows that anger is natural – and that it's possible to deal with it by yourself without hurting other people's feelings.

Children too old for tantrums and too young for hissy fits will find much to relate to in the magical, thoughtful *Dogsbody*. Sirius, the immortal Lord of the Dog Star, has lost his rag all too often. Now, he's been accused of murder – and the celestial judge banishes him to Earth. Here, he must inhabit the body of a dog and find the 'Zoi', a weapon shaped like a ball, before he can return to his super-luminary state.

Sirius is humbled in various ways – first by enduring the horror of being unwanted; and then by becoming the pet of a poor family who mistreat both their animals and their children. Luckily he's rescued by Kathleen, who loves the dog wholeheartedly, calling him 'Leo' – an imposition Sirius puts up with. Life is still not easy – Kathleen lives with an abusive aunt; and the search for the Zoi is hampered by Sirius's doggy nature, which has him following his nose, literally, after all sorts of diversions from the path. Sirius still gets angry in his dog form – his eyes flashing green when he does – but it's usually short-lived and in response to injustices suffered by Kathleen rather than himself. And when he finally returns to life as a shimmering, green star, he is far less inclined to rage and rant, having learnt to accept a few home truths.

Inappropriate outbursts of rage are explored in an eye-opening fashion in *Breathing Underwater*. On the surface, Nick Andreas has it all – a rich dad, a cool car provided by said rich dad, good looks and good grades. He's also got a girlfriend, Caitlin. Told from Nick's point of view, the story begins as Nick – having lost his temper and slapped Caitlin, leaving her badly bruised – complies with a court order to write five hundred words a week in a journal and attend an anger management course with other aggressive teens. At first Nick comes across as a sympathetic character. But gradually we start to see what really happens between him and Caitlin. When Caitlin wants to enter a talent contest for her singing, Nick won't let her. Caitlin enters secretly – convinced that when he sees her from the audience fulfilling her dream, he'll be thrilled. But the moment the recital is over, Nick takes her outside and hits her until she blacks out.

We abhor Nick's actions, but by now we also know what he has had to endure at the hands of his own father, who has constantly criticised him and left him feeling worthless (see: abuse). When Nick begins to see how unacceptable his behaviour is, and that he needs to find ways to be a good boyfriend – and a good man – we root for him. For teens who find expression in their fists, or aggressive words, this story shows where the anger might be coming from – and how getting help will be like finally coming up for air.

CURE FOR GROWN-UPS PB *The Day Leo Said I Hate You!*
ROBIE H HARRIS, ILLUSTRATED BY MOLLY BANG

Children generally let us know when they're angry in blunt and basic ways – such as hurling the 'I hate you!' line. Even the most quick-witted grown-up can find themselves lost for words when this happens – and feel hurt even though they know it's an unconsidered sentiment provoked by a fleeting emotion. This book contains some good ideas on how to respond.

SEE ALSO: **arguments, getting into** • **betrayal** • **sulking** • **violence**

animals, being unkind to

CB *James and the Giant Peach*
ROALD DAHL, ILLUSTRATED BY QUENTIN BLAKE

YA *Incident at Hawk's Hill*
ALLAN W ECKERT

What makes otherwise angelic children want to stamp on ants and slice worms in half? Perhaps it's the rare chance to lord it over others (see: beastly, being). Or perhaps it's because they haven't yet learnt to feel empathy for the suffering of others (see: feelings, hurting someone's). If you catch a child near you torturing insects, intervene with *James and the Giant Peach*.

When unhappy young orphan James – who, by the way, is on the receiving end of beastliness from humans himself – finds himself inside a giant peach, he's alarmed to discover he's sharing it with a variety of giant insects, including a grasshopper, a ladybird, a spider, a centipede, an earthworm and a silkworm. He's convinced they're going to eat him – but they're quick to reassure him. 'You are one of *us* now,' they tell him. 'We're all in the same boat.'

This turns out to be true in more ways than one as, having started off in James's aunts' garden, the giant peach starts to roll downhill, toppling off the cliffs of southern England and floating out to sea in what is at times an exceedingly perilous adventure. And, as happens in stressful circumstances, the true colours of each of the characters begin to emerge. The grasshopper is wise, the spider hard-working, and the earthworm always hovers on the verge of despair. The lazy centipede, who is forever asking James to help him lace and unlace his forty-two boots*, turns out to be an even bigger pest than everyone suspected – although James is prepared to forgive a lot in return for his rascally sense of humour. All in all, the insects are shown to be as various in personality as humans are themselves – and indeed much more likeable than Aunt Sponge and Aunt Spiker, James's two wretched aunts who were, thankfully, flattened to death by the peach at the start. The ants in your garden will breathe more easily after the kids have read this story. Your rellies may not.

The possibility that animals might experience feelings just as we do is explored with an admirable lack of sentiment in *Incident at Hawk's Hill* – a story that may transform the attitudes to animals of everyone in the household. Set on the prairies of Canada in the late 19th century, it is the story of six-year-old Ben, the youngest of four siblings and the only one their hard-working settler father, William MacDonald, doesn't understand. 'There's just no communicating with him,' William complains to his wife. Ben's strange habit of mimicking the animals and birds around the farm makes his father wonder if the child is even quite normal.

One day, wandering over the emerald-green grasslands, Ben comes face to face with a large female badger – a ferocious predator, quite capable of killing a wolf – who hisses and bares her sharp teeth. Awed and alarmed in equal measure, Ben hisses back; but when he realises the badger is more interested than frightened, he 'chitters' and grunts instead. Soon she's letting him approach her, accepting a dead mouse from his hands, and even allowing him to touch her. When Ben goes home for lunch that day, he is all aglow with the encounter.

Some time later, Ben gets caught in a lightning storm and, frightened and shoeless, takes refuge by backing down a burrow. It turns out to belong to the same badger, recognisable by the notch on her ear; and so begins an extraordinary few weeks in which they share the burrow and care for one another, Ben becoming increasingly badger-like in his behaviour and movements, and the badger increasingly zealous in her protection of the small boy. Told with a keen naturalist's eye, this story shows that even wild animals may have a lot

---

* Yes, you read that right. The centipede would like others to believe he has the full quotient of a hundred feet, as his name would suggest. But, as Dahl clearly knew, most centipedes in fact do not.

ANIMALS, BEING UNKIND TO

to teach us about loyalty and respect for others. No teen will treat animals thoughtlessly after reading this.

SEE ALSO: **beastly, being** • **bully, being a** • **in charge, wanting to be**

animals, fear of

My Family and Other Animals
GERALD DURRELL

In our atomised and increasingly urban world – where most of us live a long way from the beginnings of the food chain and have no use for animals in our daily lives – it's no surprise that children can develop a fear of fur, claw, wing and whisker. Such children will learn to love small beasts more easily if they meet them first in books.

My Family and Other Animals – a memoir* which reads like fiction – is the most entrancing story of living with animals we know. Set on the sun-kissed island of Corfu, it tells of a young Gerald Durrell – known as Gerry – as he discovers a natural affinity for all creatures, from the lowliest insect life to a pelican, brown rats and a dog. As he roams the island gathering specimens for his zoology collection – kept in a dedicated room in the house – we observe, over his shoulder, crab spiders as they change colour to match their surroundings, and black caterpillars that are in fact baby ladybirds. We watch him adopt a tortoise (Achilles) and a pigeon (Quasimodo), who become his constant companions. A young owl (Ulysses) also spends months in his pocket. Gerry's protectiveness over these creatures is humbling: finding a nest of earwig eggs one day, he erects a sign that reads 'BEWAR – EARWIG NEST – QUIAT PLESE'. Telling of an idyllic, lost world in which moonlit bathing among porpoises was a regular evening event, no one can read this book without marvelling in a whole new way at the wonders of the natural world. Out of its pages many a young botanist, zoologist or eco-warrior will be born.

SEE ALSO: **scared, being**

anorexia

SEE: **eating disorder**

---

* We did say our cures were 'almost' always fiction.

ants in your pants, having

SEE: **still, unable to sit**

anxiety

[PB] *The Invisible String*
PATRICE KARST, ILLUSTRATED BY GEOFF STEVENSON

[CB] *The Bubble Wrap Boy*
PHIL EARLE

[CB] *Watership Down*
RICHARD ADAMS

Being entirely dependent on others, babies have good reason to be anxious, and reassuring, familiar stories – such as *Guess How Much I Love You, The Runaway Bunny, Thomas the Tank Engine* and *Frog and Toad** – create safety and comfort at the end of every day. When levels of anxiety continue into toddler-hood and beyond, throw in *The Invisible String*. This simple picture book introduces the idea that we're all attached to those who love us by an invisible string, and that whenever a child misses their grown-up, the grown-up will feel a corresponding tug on their heart.

Constant, low-level anxiety can be debilitating, shutting off opportunities and generally getting in the way of living life to the full. It can also be contagious. Fourteen-year-old Charlie Han in *The Bubble Wrap Boy* suffers from anxiety passed down from his mother. She still keeps a stair gate at the top of the stairs, and she won't let him go to the cinema in case he chokes on a piece of popcorn. So when Charlie discovers he has a spectacular talent for skateboarding, it's an exciting moment for the overprotected boy. And to call it his mother's worst nightmare is the understatement of the year.

Suddenly, Charlie – who has always been mocked at school for being small, and for being best friends with 'Sinus' Sedgley, so named for his enormous nose – finds himself admired for his cool, new hobby. He can fly; he can turn in the air – and he feels like the king of the world. But then his mother catches him at it and launches into a tirade in front of his peers, which is pretty much Charlie's worst nightmare. But there's more humiliation to come. Once his mother has reduced him to a laughing-stock, a group of boys swathe him in bubble wrap and, thus mummified, leave him to walk home.

It takes the root of his mother's anxiety to be revealed for Charlie to break free of his own. By the end, the Bubble Wrap Boy has become a graffiti legend.

---

* By, respectively, Sam McBratney, illustrated by Anita Jeram; Margaret Wise Brown, illustrated by Clement Hurd; the Rev. W Awdry; and Arnold Lobel.

This triumphant, liberating story – great for the grown-up too – is best enjoyed by kids with a sheet of bubble wrap to pop as they go.

The long-eared, twitchy-nosed inhabitants of *Watership Down* – a story which stands up well to the test of time – will feel like kindred spirits to tweens and teens with an anxious streak, constantly on the alert for danger as rabbits are. As long as they can hear the blackbird singing, the rabbits know it's safe to graze. But the second the blackbird's song turns to a distressed squawking, the rabbits startle, sniff the air, then bolt like blazes in the other direction.

When a sign goes up in their field announcing a new building development, Fiver senses that something 'very bad' is going to happen – and he tells his brother, Hazel. Hazel has learnt to listen to his brother's presentiments; and that very night they split ranks with the heads of the warren and lead any other rabbit that will listen to a new, safe home. Fiver's sixth sense saves the rabbits again and again on their journey – and ultimately brings them to the high, dry downs where they can see for miles around.

Many of the rabbits are prone to panic; but they also make the most of the strengths bestowed on them by Fritha, their creator, in the stories of long ago. 'Digger, listener, runner,' the incantation goes – and whenever they're threatened by one of their 'thousand enemies', they put their skills to use, digging burrows, listening for danger, and running to safety. Give this story to the nervous child in your midst and prompt them to notice their own special strengths. They may not be able to stop their anxiety, but their strengths will help them to live more successfully with it.

SEE ALSO: **depression** • **worrying**

apocalypse, fear of the

Teens worried about the end of civilised life as they know it will find comfort – and a great role model for how to survive – in *Robinson Crusoe*.* The apocalypse may be a long time coming, though, and imagining worst-case scenarios with the help of a good dystopian novel will keep them on their toes as they wait, while also encouraging them to appreciate what they've (still) got.

---

* By Daniel Defoe.

THE TEN BEST DYSTOPIAN READS

- [CB] *The Giver* LOIS LOWRY
- [CB] *Pax* SARA PENNYPACKER, ILLUSTRATED BY JON KLASSEN
- [CB] *Floodland* MARCUS SEDGWICK
- [YA] *The Handmaid's Tale* MARGARET ATWOOD
- [YA] *The Death of Grass* JOHN CHRISTOPHER
- [YA] *The Hunger Games* SUZANNE COLLINS
- [YA] *The Stand* STEPHEN KING
- [YA] *Station Eleven* EMILY ST JOHN MANDEL
- [YA] *Uglies* SCOTT WESTERFELD
- [YA] *The Day of the Triffids* JOHN WYNDHAM

SEE ALSO: **anxiety** • **planet, fearing for the future of the** • **worrying**

appendicitis

SEE: ***The Novel Cure***

arguments, getting into

[PB] *The Quarreling Book*
CHARLOTTE ZOLOTOW, ILLUSTRATED BY ARNOLD LOBEL

[CB] *Ordinary Jack*
HELEN CRESSWELL

[YA] *The Book of the Banshee*
ANNE FINE

Not all arguments occur because someone's in a bad mood, but it certainly makes an argument more likely. In the brilliant little *The Quarreling Book*, we see how bad moods can be passed, like fire, from one person to the next. It all kicks off when Mr Brown forgets to kiss Mrs Brown before he leaves for work. Mrs Brown then snaps at son Jonathan when he comes down for breakfast, who in turn snaps at sister Sally, who snaps at her best friend . . . and so on until, inevitably, it's somebody's dog that gets it in the teeth. The good-natured dog, of course, just thinks it's all a big game, which starts a counter-domino-effect of good moods going in the opposite direction. Arnold Lobel's black-and-white illustrations capture the changing moods with the tiniest of lines – a mouth turned down on one side, a hurt eye widening. Read this one to the whole fractious family; then go and buy yourselves a dog.

APPENDICITIS

If your child seems determined to pick fights, at least make sure they do it with a sense of humour. The extended family in Helen Cresswell's wonderful *Ordinary Jack* and the other Bagthorpe Saga books are great role models for inveterate quarrellers, with mealtimes usually beginning with everyone talking at once and ending with the slamming of doors. The elderly matriarch, Grandma, is the ringleader, liking nothing better than throwing a pointed jibe, and she's disappointed when it fails to stick. Mr Bagthorpe and his brother-in-law, Uncle Parker, have so many 'first-class rows' that Jack suspects they enjoy them, too – and he's noticed that many of their interchanges turn up 'pretty well word for word' in his father's TV scripts. Luckily, Grandpa's tendency to make sudden, irrelevant statements – finishing a train of thought he started in his head – tends to throw an argument off course before it can get too savage. And if that doesn't work, five-year-old cousin Daisy's newfound habit of playing with matches underneath the table does (see: pyromania).

Dare we cast the aspersion that teenagers are frequently the cause of arguments in the home (see: adolescence; hormones, raging)? To help both teens and their haggard grown-ups get through these rocky years, bring in the hilarious *The Book of the Banshee*. Written by one Will Flowers from the 'Front line' of family life, it opens with the announcement that his sister Estelle has 'curdled' – i.e. become a teenager – and that suddenly it's like sharing a home with an apprentice witch. The arguments begin at 7am, with diatribes about why school is pointless, and take up so much of everyone's time and energy that Will ends up having to leave the house without his lunch money – and with only a hastily put-together piccalilli or salad-cream sandwich instead. The day ends with more arguments, these ones about why she can't wear what she's wearing and why she can't stay out till 1am.

Meanwhile, Will finds a strange sort of comfort in a First World War memoir called *The Longest Summer* by a man named Saffery. In it he finds remarkable parallels between his own home life and Saffery's experiences on the Front lines of northern France. When Will's father comes upstairs to have words with Estelle, it's just like the brave lads going over the top. And when Will's little sister Muffy tucks her head into Will's dressing gown in fear of Estelle, it's as if she fears being hit by shells flying overhead. Before long, the military atmosphere has ratcheted up to such a point that Will decides he must take a proactive stand. He gains valuable ground and self-respect in the process; but he also learns that the battles Estelle – and in fact he, too – are now fighting are helping them sculpt themselves into the separate, interesting adults they will one day become. Arguments are excruciating, but they also mark an important rite of passage.

SEE ALSO: **anger** • **bargaining, endless** • **bath, not wanting to have a** • **bed, not wanting to go to** • **best friend, falling out with your** • **blamed, being** • **parents who are splitting up, having** • **sulking**

astray, being led

ER *Sam and the Firefly*
PD EASTMAN

CB *The Invisible Girl*
KATE MARYON

Many a grown-up frets that the cherubic, innocent child in their care might be led astray by the depraved and delinquent one in someone else's. If you introduce a child early on to the possibility that they may one day have a friend who takes off in an ill-advised direction – and they'll need the presence of mind not to follow – you'll be able to fret much less. A great story for the job is *Sam and the Firefly*, an early reader in which an owl named Sam, looking for a playmate, meets a zesty little firefly named Gus. Sam is impressed when the firefly shows him the shapes he can draw with his light, and soon the pair of them are scrawling their names across the sea-green Eastman sky. But then Gus gets the idea of writing 'Turn left' and 'Turn right' above the traffic lights for a laugh. Sam knows that Gus has over-stepped the line and tells the young firefly so – holding his ground even when Gus calls him a spoilsport (see: loser, being a bad). Sam is the perfect role model for how to stand firm against your wayward friends – without, in fact, having to lose them as friends.

The older children are, the harder it sometimes is to resist the influence of others. Gabriella in *The Invisible Girl* is a shy eleven-year-old – so shy, in fact, that she feels invisible – and when her neglectful father packs her off to Manchester to be with her mother, omitting to tell her mother that she's coming, it gives Gabriella the perfect excuse to disappear. She'd rather try to survive on the streets of a city she doesn't know than face her sharp-tongued mother.

In Manchester she finds herself more alone than ever before. Just when she's reconciling herself to having to sleep in the cathedral doorway, she meets Henny, a girl who knows a thing or two about homelessness herself – a little too much, in fact. Soon, the older girl has Gabriella shinnying up drainpipes and breaking in to people's flats; and for a while, Gabriella seems doomed to a life of crime. She's saved by her faith in her older brother, Beckett, who she hasn't seen in years, and by an innate belief that she's a good girl at heart. This is a story to help young readers maintain the courage of their own convictions rather than be swayed by the first attractive, worldly personality to come along.

CURE FOR GROWN-UPS [CB] *The Adventures of Tom Sawyer*
MARK TWAIN

One such attractive personality being Tom Sawyer, and you'd do well to acquaint yourself with his type. Though on the surface this charismatic vagabond looks like one of the bad influences described above, Tom is in fact a good egg. And although he and his true love, Becky Thatcher, do end up spending several days in a cave and almost starving to death, their adventure is well intentioned – and inadvertently leads to the discovery of a bona fide fortune. Learn to recognise the mischievous prankster who always lands on his or her feet from the doomed disaster who will take your child down with them (and see *The Novel Cure*: rails, going off the). If the child in your care is being led astray by a Tom Sawyer type, stand back and let them enjoy the ride.

SEE ALSO: **friends your parents don't approve of, having • naughtiness • peer pressure • told, never doing what you're**

attention, seeking

SEE: **praise, seeking**

autism

Just as there are a variety of behaviours associated with autism, there are a variety of ways to respond to it. Encourage an empathetic, non-judgemental response in the children you know with a story, or two, which gives a flavour of what it might be like to experience the world via an autistic brain. Then read the stories yourself.

THE TEN BEST BOOKS FOR UNDERSTANDING AUTISM

[PB] *Looking After Louis* LESLEY ELY, ILLUSTRATED BY POLLY DUNBAR
[PB] *My Brother Charlie* HOLLY ROBINSON PEETE AND RYAN ELIZABETH PEETE, ILLUSTRATED BY SHANE W EVANS
[CB] *The London Eye Mystery* SIOBHAN DOWD
[CB] *Rules* CYNTHIA LORD
[CB] *Memoirs of an Imaginary Friend* MATTHEW GREEN

- [CB] *Smart* KIM SLATER
- [CB] *Loser* JERRY SPINELLI
- [YA] *Mockingbird* KATHRYN ERSKINE
- [YA] *Marcelo in the Real World* FRANCISCO X STORK
- [YA] *The Curious Incident of the Dog in the Night-time* MARK HADDON

SEE ALSO: **different, feeling • routine, unable to cope with a change in the**

awkward

SEE: **shyness • tall, being**

AWKWARD

B IS FOR . . .

baby, being a

We've all been there – some more recently than others. See our lists below.

THE TEN BEST BOOKS FOR BABIES

- [PB] *The Baby's Catalogue* **ALLAN AHLBERG, ILLUSTRATED BY JANET AHLBERG**
- [PB] *Each Peach Pear Plum* **ALLAN AHLBERG, ILLUSTRATED BY JANET AHLBERG**
- [PB] *Forever* **EMMA DODD**
- [PB] *Ten Little Fingers and Ten Little Toes* **MEM FOX, ILLUSTRATED BY HELEN OXENBURY**
- [PB] *Mother Goose* **KATE GREENAWAY**
- [PB] *Peek-a-Who?* **NINA LADEN**
- [PB] *Faces* **JO LODGE**
- [PB] *Brown Bear, Brown Bear, What Do You See?* **BILL MARTIN JR, ILLUSTRATED BY ERIC CARLE**
- [PB] *Tickle Tickle* **HELEN OXENBURY**
- [PB] *On the Night You Were Born* **NANCY TILLMAN**

THE TEN BEST PICTURE BOOKS FOR RHYTHM AND RHYME

- [PB] *The Witch with an Itch* **HELEN BAUGH, ILLUSTRATED BY DEBORAH ALLWRIGHT**
- [PB] *Mister Magnolia* **QUENTIN BLAKE**
- [PB] *Five Little Monkeys Jumping on the Bed* **EILEEN CHRISTELOW**
- [PB] *Hairy Maclary from Donaldson's Dairy* **LYNLEY DODD**
- [PB] *The Snail and the Whale* **JULIA DONALDSON, ILLUSTRATED BY AXEL SCHEFFLER**
- [PB] *Oh, No!* **CANDACE FLEMING, ILLUSTRATED BY ERIC ROHMANN**
- [PB] *Chicka Chicka Boom Boom* **BILL MARTIN JR AND JOHN ARCHAMBAULT, ILLUSTRATED BY LOIS EHLERT**
- [PB] *Little Rabbit Foo Foo* **MICHAEL ROSEN, ILLUSTRATED BY ARTHUR ROBINS**
- [PB] *Sing a Song of Bottoms* **JEANNE WILLIS, ILLUSTRATED BY ADAM STOWER**
- [ER] *Green Eggs and Ham* **DR SEUSS**

THE TEN BEST TOUCHY-FEELY BOOKS

- [PB] *There Was an Old Lady Who Swallowed a Fly* PAM ADAMS
- [PB] *Fuzzy Fuzzy Fuzzy!* SANDRA BOYNTON
- [PB] *The Very Hungry Caterpillar* ERIC CARLE
- [PB] *Feely Bugs* DAVID A CARTER
- [PB] *In My Tree* SARA GILLINGHAM AND LORENA SIMINOVICH
- [PB] *I Love to Eat* AMELIE GRAUX
- [PB] *Pat the Bunny* DOROTHY KUNHARDT
- [PB] *Animal Kisses* BARNEY SALTZBERG
- [PB] *Wet Pet, Dry Pet, Your Pet, My Pet* DR SEUSS
- [PB] *That's Not My Puppy* FIONA WATT, ILLUSTRATED BY RACHEL WELLS

SEE ALSO: **small, being** • **understood, not being**

baby talk

SEE: **grow up, not wanting to** • **small, feeling**

babysitter, not liking your

Sometimes a bad babysitter just needs a mentor or two. Leave a stack of these stories around the house and ask the babysitter to read them aloud to the kids. The children will thank you for it.

THE TEN BEST BABYSITTERS IN THE BUSINESS

- [PB] *Benjamin McFadden and the Robot Babysitter* TIMOTHY BUSH
- [PB] *Good Dog, Carl* ALEXANDRA DAY
- [PB] *Be Good, Gordon* ANGELA MCALLISTER, ILLUSTRATED BY TIM ARCHBOLD
- [PB] *How to Babysit a Grandma* JEAN REAGAN, ILLUSTRATED BY LEE WILDISH
- [PB] *No Babysitters Allowed* AMBER STEWART, ILLUSTRATED BY LAURA RANKIN
- [CB] *Kristy's Great Idea* ANN M MARTIN
- [CB] *Mrs Noodlekugel* DANIEL PINKWATER, ILLUSTRATED BY ADAM STOWER
- [CB] *Mary Poppins* PL TRAVERS
- [CB] *The Mysterious Howling* (The Incorrigible Children of Ashton Place) MARYROSE WOOD, ILLUSTRATED BY JON KLASSEN
- [YA] *The Manny Files* CHRISTIAN BURCH

bad loser, being a

SEE: **loser, being a bad**

bargaining, endless

[PB] *Don't Let the Pigeon Drive the Bus!*
MO WILLEMS

With some grown-ups, a 'no' is final. But with others there's a small chink of doubt in the 'no', and if a child is quick about it (and they always are) they'll stick the end of a chisel into this chink and start wiggling until the 'no' gives way. If this sounds familiar, pull out *Don't Let the Pigeon Drive the Bus!*, one of the first books to bring the child into the story – and make them the responsible one. The experience will change them forever.

When the bus driver asks the reader to keep an eye on his bus while he goes away – and not, on any account, to let the pigeon drive it – no child, fluffed up with self-importance as they by now will be, can resist. The pigeon gets straight to the point. 'Hey, can I drive the bus?' he asks, innocent as you please. When the child says 'no', the wily pigeon deploys every tactic in *The Children's Handbook of Manipulation** to get an affirmative answer, from compliance-through-distraction ('Hey, I've got an idea. Let's play "Drive the bus!"') to bribery ('I'll be your best friend!') and emotional blackmail ('I have dreams, you know!'). Never was a simply drawn pigeon (round head, round eye, two stick legs) more expressive than when Willems lowers the shutter of the pigeon's eyelid to fit a simmering, tight-lipped 'Fine.' Most children find this book so absolutely hilarious that any attempts at bargaining thereafter will quickly slide into a parody of the bargaining pigeon – and become a lovely, happy shambles.

SEE ALSO: **adolescence**

bath, not wanting to have a

[PB] *I Don't Want to Have a Bath!*
JULIE SYKES, ILLUSTRATED BY TIM WARNES
(continued)

Every parent should keep a clutch of nakedly pro-bathing propaganda under the bathroom sink for when their sticky infant, smeared with jam, glue, sand, glitter, orange juice and beetroot purée needs convincing that having a dunk in a bathtub

* Only available to the under-18s.

[PB] *The Pigeon Needs a Bath!*
MO WILLEMS

[PB] *Bathwater's Hot*
SHIRLEY HUGHES

is a good idea. A stalwart staple is *I Don't Want to Have a Bath!* from the appealing and brightly illustrated Little Tiger series, in which the mischievous bundle of orange-and-black stripes cavorts with each of his animal friends in turn, getting muckier and muckier in the process. It's quite plain to the little tiger that being dirty is synonymous with having fun – and who would want to put an end to that? And then, thankfully, he meets an animal who won't play with him *unless* he's clean . . . Soap dodgers take note! *The Pigeon Needs a Bath!*, featuring the argumentative pigeon of *Don't Let the Pigeon Drive the Bus!* fame (see: bargaining, endless), is guaranteed to contain more objections to bathing than your recalcitrant toddler could ever come up with by themselves, and effectively makes them all redundant. And the enticing illustrations in *Bathwater's Hot* make the idea of being wrapped in a warm, fluffy towel at the end impossible to resist.

CURE FOR GROWN-UPS [CB] *The Witches* ROALD DAHL, ILLUSTRATED BY QUENTIN BLAKE

Clever-clogs kids of chapter-book age will, of course, counter your request that they take a bath with the argument that, in Norway witches can smell a clean child more easily than a dirty one – and that regular baths put you at greater risk of being 'squelched'. (And, as you know, witches must squelch at least one child per week if they're to avoid getting grumpy.) Rather than suffer the lecture, keep your copy of this terrifying but brilliant story under lock and key – and only bring it out once the boy narrator and his cigar-smoking grandmother have finished turning every witch in the world into a mouse.

SEE ALSO: **body odour** • **hands, not wanting to wash your** • **swim, inability to** • **told, never doing what you're**

beards, horror of

[PB] *The Runaway Beard*
DAVID SCHILLER, ILLUSTRATED BY MARC ROSENTHAL

Unless they have been raised in close proximity to one, small children frequently burst into tears at the sight of a beard. A razor is one way of dealing with it. Another is to bring out this surreal board book, which comes complete with fake beard with which, in turn, to scare the hirsute invader off.

The beard in the story – a luxuriant, fulsome, black one – has for years been happily settled on the lower half of Dad's face. But when Dad – deliciously drawn in the style of Popeye – decides to shave it off, the beard makes a last-minute run for it, leaping off his face and landing, alarmingly, on the face of the baby. When Mum chases it away with her broom, the beard tries in vain to find a new place to settle – even at one point attaching itself to a reproduction of the *Mona Lisa*. And then the children's bald uncle walks through their door . . . Nothing that is shown to be so ludicrous can possibly hold menace again.

SEE ALSO: **grannies, having to kiss** • **nightmares**

beastly, being

[ER] *Horton Hears a Who!*
DR SEUSS

[PB] *Rotten Island*
WILLIAM STEIG

If you're trying to convert a child inclined to be beastly into one that's sweet and loving, give them a dose of Horton, Dr Seuss's empathetic elephant.* Horton is enjoying a splash in a cool jungle pool when he hears a noise and, in the absence of any other suitable source, concludes that it must have come from someone living on a speck of dust, invisible to the naked elephant eye. The other jungle animals think he's gone completely nuts when he saves the speck from the water; but for Horton, this is the start of a great deal of worrying about this small 'Who' – who, it turns out, is not just one person but an entire community of 'Whos', complete with Who mayor. Once the beastly child has glimpsed the detailed community of Whos, hard at work trying to patch up their battered planet after a careless bird let it drop mid-flight, they, too, will start to worry about the Whos and, by extension, others (see: worrying). As Horton says, 'After all,/A person's a person. No matter how small.'

If this fails to inspire compassion, allow your out-and-out beast to sport with their own kind with *Rotten Island*, psychedelic home to a vile bunch of critters with extra limbs and unpleasant personalities. There's nothing on Rotten Island but bad weather and violent volcanoes – all drawn in satisfyingly scratchy outlines and sloshed with garish colours. Until, that is, a flower dares

* Who also features in Dr Seuss's *Horton Hatches the Egg* (see: adoption).

to show its pretty face. A joyous celebration of ghastliness running amok, this book will satisfy the demand for beastliness in your household – and maybe even wear it out.

SEE ALSO: **animals, being unkind to • contrary, being • manners, bad • naughtiness • share, inability to • sibling rivalry • tantrums • told, never doing what you're**

bed, fear of what's under the

PB *Bedtime for Monsters*
ED VERE

Unidentified creaks, wardrobe doors left ajar and, of course, that dark space beneath the bed . . . Turn the fear on its head with *Bedtime for Monsters,* which first acknowledges the fear ('Supposing there *are* monsters . . .'), then looks it square in the face ('He's coming to find you – RIGHT NOW!'). Finally . . . well, who can be scared of a monster, however big and green, going 'Ring a Ding Ding' on his bicycle?

SEE ALSO: **anxiety • dark, scared of the • scared, being**

bed, having to stay in

CB *Marianne Dreams*
CATHERINE STORR

Every bedridden child needs a copy of *Marianne Dreams,* capturing as it does so perfectly the associated feeling of being alone in a slightly unreal other world, marooned from family life. We never know exactly what's wrong with Marianne when, on her tenth birthday, she develops a high fever and has to go to bed. She's both 'horrified and fascinated' when the days become weeks. She's visited each day by Miss Chesterfield, a governess, who tells her about the other children she teaches in their own homes, including Mark, who is ill with polio. But what really helps pass the time is the stubby pencil she finds in her great-grandmother's old sewing box, which brings whatever she draws to life in her dreams.

The first time it happens, Marianne dreams she's walking across a lonely prairie – when there, before her, is the house she drew earlier with the pencil. It's a simple house with a square façade, four windows and a door. She tries to get in – but there's no handle, and no knocker. Two days later, she picks up her drawing again. This time she adds a knocker – and a boy's face at the window; and the next time she visits the house in her dreams, she meets the boy as well.

At times the story that follows feels like the hallucinations of someone slipping in and out of a fever. The boy in the house has polio, and is called Mark – just like Miss Chesterfield's student. He's also as sulky and irritable about being stuck in bed as Marianne is herself. Soon Marianne is so preoccupied with getting Mark back on his feet that she stops grumbling about how long it's taking her to get back on hers. This story shows a child how the mind can travel to surprising places, even if the body can't. And that one way to get better might be to focus on someone – or something – other than themselves.

SEE ALSO: **bored, being** • **cheering up, needing** • **loneliness** • **rainy day**

bed, not wanting to go to

It's hard to go to bed when it's still light outside and you've got energy left to burn – especially when other people in the house are still up. Make the duvet seem more appealing with a story that shows other lively creatures winding down.

THE TEN BEST BOOKS FOR TEMPTING A CHILD TO BED

- PB *The Going to Bed Book* SANDRA BOYNTON
- PB *I Am Not Sleepy and I Will Not Go to Bed* (Charlie and Lola) LAUREN CHILD
- PB *The Boy Who Wouldn't Go to Bed* HELEN COOPER
- PB *Night Cars* TEDDY JAM, ILLUSTRATED BY ERIC BEDDOWS
- PB *I'll See You in the Morning* MIKE JOLLEY, ILLUSTRATED BY MIQUE MORIUCHI
- PB *It's Time to Sleep, My Love* ERIC METAXAS, ILLUSTRATED BY NANCY TILLMAN
- PB *I Like it When . . .* MARY MURPHY
- PB *Good Night, Gorilla* PEGGY RATHMANN
- PB *I Don't Want to Go to Bed!* JULIE SYKES, ILLUSTRATED BY TIM WARNES
- PB *Sleep Tight, Little Bear* MARTIN WADDELL, ILLUSTRATED BY BARBARA FIRTH

SEE ALSO: **naughtiness** • **nightmares** • **over-tired, being** • **sleep, unable to get to** • **told, never doing what you're**

bed, wanting to go to before someone else

[PB] *Goodnight Already!*
JORY JOHN, ILLUSTRATED BY BENJI DAVIES

Being desperate for bed when your friends or family are all revved up and raring to party can be painful, whether you're a toddler, a teen or, frankly, a grown-up. No one likes to miss out or be seen as a party-pooper. But no one likes being tortured either; and when the pressure to stay up becomes too hard to bear for someone in your household, bring out *Goodnight Already!*, the story of a sleepy bear and his way-too-bright-eyed duck neighbour, zinging on caffeine and in need of some attention. Bear's pain is written in the bags beneath his eyes – and, not surprisingly, he becomes somewhat grouchy after a while. We, too, want to strangle and indeed roast the duck for being so insensitive and selfish, especially when the bear's head and shoulders start to droop. All of which will persuade the sleepyhead near you that it's OK to be tired before everyone else and to go to bed without further ado.

SEE ALSO: **alone, wanting to be left • over-tired, being • sibling rivalry • stand up for yourself, not feeling able to**

bed, wetting the

[PB] *Do Little Mermaids Wet Their Beds?*
JEANNE WILLIS, ILLUSTRATED BY PENELOPE JOSSEN

[ER] *Max Archer, Kid Detective: The Case of the Wet Bed*
HOWARD J BENNETT, ILLUSTRATED BY SPIKE GERRELL

[CB] *Goodnight, Mister Tom*
MICHELLE MAGORIAN

For the child just beginning to go nappy-free, waking up with wet sheets now and then is inevitable. As long as there's a good-tempered grown-up in the house, a stack of spare sheets in the airing cupboard and a bottle of gin beneath the ironing board, everything is likely to be all right. Those who make a nightly habit of it will be reassured to know that the little girl in *Do Little Mermaids Wet Their Beds?* is a nightly bed-wetter, too – even though she can already dress herself, write her name and even ride a two-wheeled bike. She hates the horrid plastic sheet her mum puts on her bed. Just as she's about to develop a hang-up about wetting her bed, she has a dream that makes her realise it's no big deal and, for the first time, wakes up dry (though, to the bewilderment of her mother, wearing a soggy coat . . .).

For older bed-wetters, we prescribe *Max Archer, Kid Detective* – the brainchild of an American paediatrician (see: tummy ache). Max is a street-wise-yet-sensitive trilby-wearing dude in the mould of Chandler's detective, Philip Marlowe. Having suffered from bed-wetting himself until he was eleven, Max now helps others kick the habit on a paying basis. When he takes on eight-year-old Billy as a client, Max gives him his usual spiel: these are the causes of bed-wetting, and here are some ways to help your body wake itself up if your bladder becomes too full. The snappy prose skims the embarrassment off all this talk of bodily functions, and the clear explanations and suggestions allow the child to assume responsibility for their issue themselves.

If bed-wetting persists in older children, it may be an indication of emotional upset, trauma or abuse – as it is for Willie in *Goodnight, Mister Tom*. A wartime evacuee, Willie arrives in the village of Little Weirwold malnourished and with his underwear sewn to his shirt. Though eight years old, he wets his bed every night and expects to be beaten for it. Tom Oakley, the elderly man who takes him in, shows great tact in his handling of the wet sheets; and as Willie discovers what it is to be treated with kindness and patience rather than hostility and suspicion, he gradually escapes the habit. Magorian writes with such hope, such positive energy and light, that one feels the real possibility that Willie will recover from the life he led with his over-zealous, religious mother and could even achieve his dream of becoming an actor one day. Sharing this encouraging story with a bed-wetting older child may help initiate discussions about what their underlying trigger may be.

Of course, for children just discovering the mixed pleasures of growing up, it may be that something else is going on . . . (see: periods; wet dreams).

SEE ALSO: **abuse • baby, being a • embarrassment • trauma**

bedroom, having to share your

SEE: **alone, wanting to be left • share, inability to**

bereavement

SEE: **death of a loved one**

best friend, falling out with your

[PB] *Gossie & Gertie*
OLIVIER DUNREA

[PB] *My Best, Best Friend* (Charlie and Lola)
LAUREN CHILD

[CB] *Roller Girl*
VICTORIA JAMIESON

Having a best friend is a high-stakes game. Bliss while it lasts; torment when there's a bust-up. Prepare toddlers to ride the ups and downs by introducing them to Gossie and Gertie. These two yellow goslings do everything together: splash in the rain, dive in the pond, play hide-and-seek in the daisies. They even wear the same boots (Gossie's red, Gertie's blue). But then one day one of them decides not to follow the other, but to go in the opposite direction . . . A lovely little board book* for reassuring a child that even when your shadow wants to branch out, it doesn't mean the friendship's gone awry.

My Best, Best Friend begins with Lola and Lotta doing everything together. They swap their fruit at lunchtime, and whenever Mrs Hanson says 'Get into pairs', they don't have to think twice about who to choose. But then a new girl, Evie, arrives and Mrs Hanson asks Lotta to look after her. Those downward-looking eyes of Lola's really capture how bad it can feel to be left out for a while. Happily, she and Lotta re-establish their special connection just as Evie finds a new bestie, too.

The transition from primary to secondary school offers a child the chance to shuffle their deck of friends. But deciding where they belong can be nerve-wracking, especially for girls. Will they and their friends go girly, geeky or sports-crazy? Or will they, as many of the boys seem able to do, try to remain neutral and independent? For those left in the lurch when their old friends leap elsewhere, bring in the graphic novel *Roller Girl*.

Nicole and Astrid are 'still best friends' when the story opens, with Astrid's impressive mum in the habit of organising an 'Evening of Cultural Enlightenment' for them both on Fridays – often one that takes them out of their depth. We see them snoozing at the opera, standing blank-faced before a piece of abstract art, and laughing in all the wrong places at poetry readings. But this particular night she takes them to something unexpected: the Roller Derby. The players bowl Astrid over with their punky hair, tattoos and make-up – as well as their other-worldly, streetwise names (Scrappy Go Lucky, Scald Eagle, Pandemonium) – and she signs up for Roller Derby camp on the spot. She takes it for granted that Nicole will come too, and she's gutted when Nicole says she's already signed up for ballet camp.

Roller-skating turns out to be much harder than it looks, and Astrid spends

* The Gossie & Gertie books are also available as early readers.

most of the first few days on the floor. On top of it all she has to walk home by herself, not having wanted to break the news to her mum that Nicole isn't doing the camp with her. One day, she takes the plunge and skates home – and so begins her gradual transformation from Astrid, a girl with no particular 'thing' of her own except for being Nicole's best friend, to the fit, fearless 'Asteroid', coasting the city streets with her new friend, Zoey. Sometimes, friendships simply run their course.

SEE ALSO: **arguments, getting into • betrayal • feelings, hurt • forgive, reluctance to • friends, feeling that you have no • friends, finding it hard to make • loneliness • stand up for yourself, not feeling able to • umbrage, taking**

betrayal

PB *Lilly's Purple Plastic Purse*
KEVIN HENKES

CB *The Lion, the Witch and the Wardrobe*
CS LEWIS

First it's worth checking to see if the child in question really has been betrayed – or if they just think they have. For Lilly, the mouse in Kevin Henkes's classic picture book, it's the person (or rodent) she adores most in the world that has betrayed her – or so she believes. Lilly thinks so highly of Mr Slinger, a dude of a teacher who winks and says 'Howdy' each morning, that she does everything she can to be like him. One day she comes to school wearing a pair of movie-star sunglasses, just like his, and carrying a brand new purple plastic handbag that plays a tune when opened. She knows Mr Slinger will love her accessories as much as she does. But Mr Slinger doesn't care for the jaunty tune singing out every five minutes in class, and confiscates both glasses and bag. Furious, Lilly draws Mr Slinger on a 'Wanted' poster . . . The teacher handles the situation beautifully; and watching Lilly go from outrage to humility as she realises *she's* the one that needs to apologise is very helpful for children who have made the same mistake.

A betrayal of a real and shocking kind lies at the heart of the *The Lion, the Witch and the Wardrobe*, the magical portal into the spellbinding Narnia series.* Of the four siblings sent to the big house in the country to escape

* Even though it is, chronologically speaking, the second book in the series. We believe the series is, like *Star Wars*, best experienced in the order in which the books were created, which is as follows: 1. *The Lion, the Witch and the Wardrobe*; 2. *Prince Caspian*; 3. *The Voyage of the Dawn Treader*; 4. *The Silver Chair*; 5. *The Horse and His Boy*; 6. *The Magician's Nephew*; 7. *The Last Battle*.

the Blitz,* the youngest, Lucy, is the first to find her way through the fur coats and into the snowy forests of Narnia. There she meets a Faun called Mr Tumnus, who invites her for tea. None of her siblings believe her when she tells them where she's been – after all, according to their sense of time, she's only been gone a few minutes. So when, on her next visit, she finds that Edmund has followed her there, she's excited and relieved. 'The others will have to believe in Narnia now that both of us have been there. What fun it will be!' she cries. But back in the house, Edmund – sick and guilty from eating so much of the White Witch's Turkish Delight – claims to have no idea what she's talking about.

This first betrayal is followed by a succession of others as, thoroughly hooked on Turkish Delight and keen to lord it over his elder brother, Peter, as King one day, Edmund becomes the evil queen's spy. The shock of Edmund's treachery is compounded by the contrast with Peter's admirable loyalty. 'We'll still have to go and look for him,' Peter says, as he realises the grave danger Edmund has put them all in. 'He is our brother after all, even if he is rather a little beast.' In Narnia, as in the real world, family and friends come first. Kids who have been betrayed will be inspired by Peter to react by being big, not bitter.

SEE ALSO: **feelings, hurt** • **umbrage, taking**

bicycle, learning to ride a

PB *Duck on a Bike*
DAVID SHANNON

Those first shaky attempts at life on two wheels are hard enough without having to deal with the fears or taunts of those watching from the sidelines, too. It's apt, then, that *Duck on a Bike* – in which Duck decides to have a go on an appealing little red bicycle – focuses more on the responses of the other animals in the farmyard than on how Duck's doing himself. 'He's going to hurt himself if he's not careful,' frets the sheep. 'You're still not as fast as me,' taunts the horse. But after the initial wobbles, Duck soars past them all gleefully, managing not to let them spoil his fun. Read this to a child, then let go of their saddle with a cheery smile.

* If you are reading this book chronologically, you will have become aware of the impact the Blitz has had on British children's literature – and therefore, bibliotherapeutically speaking, on those of us who were weaned on it. Where would we be without these stories set in big country houses, full of mysterious discoveries, and with parents conveniently out of the way?

THE TEN BEST BOOKS FOR KEEPING KIDS ON TWO WHEELS

- PB *Bear on a Bike* STELLA BLACKSTONE, ILLUSTRATED BY DEBBIE HARTER
- PB *Mrs Armitage on Wheels* QUENTIN BLAKE
- PB *Super Grandpa* DAVID M SCHWARZ, ILLUSTRATED BY BERT DODSON
- PB *Along a Long Road* FRANK VIVA
- PB *Eric's Big Day* ROD WATERS
- ER *Julian's Glorious Summer* ANN CAMERON
- CB *Five Go to Billycock Hill* ENID BLYTON
- CB *Hero on a Bicycle* SHIRLEY HUGHES
- CB *The Green Bicycle* HAIFAA AL MANSOUR
- YA *The Burning City* ARIEL AND JOAQUIN DORFMAN

SEE ALSO: **confidence, lack of • pain, being in**

birds and bees, wanting to know about the

SEE: **sex, having questions about**

blamed, being

CB *The Ghost of Thomas Kempe*
PENELOPE LIVELY

Being blamed for something that isn't your fault is a lonely business, and a child in this predicament will appreciate the solidarity of ten-year-old James in *The Ghost of Thomas Kempe*. When his family move to a cottage in the Oxfordshire countryside, James is soon aware that something very strange is going on. His dog barks at thin air, cups crash to the floor for no reason – and now he has found a note, scrawled in spidery writing with his own red pen: 'I like not this quille.' It goes on to tell James how to solve the mystery of his father's missing pipe.

James doesn't have a particularly good track record behaviour-wise, so it's not surprising when the blame for these mysterious goings-on gets pinned on him. And when the same antiquated scrawl turns up on the blackboard at school ('I have been about the towne and I am much displeased . . .'), the teacher jumps to the same conclusion. But when the meddling poltergeist that is Thomas Kempe – a 17th-century apothecary with some loose ends to tie up – starts scrawling 'wyches' over doorways and setting fire to houses, James knows he needs to find a way to send Kempe packing once and for all. Kids who find themselves cast as the scapegoat unfairly will find this story cathartic – and a catalyst for being proactive about proving their innocence.

SEE ALSO: **fair, it's not** • **lying** • **punished, being**

boarding school

Some think it's all sleepovers and tricks on the teachers. Others that it's all cold showers and no hugs. Cheer up your reluctant boarder with the stories on our first list below – and sober up a wannabe midnight-feaster with those on the second.

THE FIVE BEST BOOKS FOR REMINDING YOU HOW LUCKY YOU ARE TO BE AT BOARDING SCHOOL

CB *First Term* (Malory Towers) **ENID BLYTON**
CB *What Katy Did at School* **SUSAN COOLIDGE***
CB *Harry Potter and the Philosopher's Stone* **JK ROWLING**
YA *The School for Good and Evil* **SOMAN CHAINANI**
YA *Spud* **JOHN VAN DE RUIT**

THE FIVE BEST BOOKS FOR PUTTING YOU OFF GOING TO BOARDING SCHOOL

CB *Tom Brown's Schooldays* **THOMAS HUGHES**
CB *Back Home* **MICHELLE MAGORIAN**
CB *Midnight for Charlie Bone* **JENNY NIMMO**
CB *Witch Week* (Chrestomanci) **DIANA WYNNE JONES†**
YA *What I Was* **MEG ROSOFF**

SEE ALSO: **bed, wanting to go to before someone else** • **homesickness** • **loneliness**

* Best enjoyed after the first book in the series, *What Katy Did.*

† Best enjoyed after the first two books in the series, *Charmed Life* and *The Magicians of Caprona.*

body hair

[PB] *Hair in Funny Places*
BABETTE COLE

[YA] *'Are These My Basoomas I See Before Me?'* (Confessions of Georgia Nicolson)
LOUISE RENNISON

[YA] *Kimchi & Calamari*
ROSE KENT

To explain to a younger sibling the strange and alarming new hair sprouting on the body of an older sibling, bring in the trusty Babette Cole. Not one to beat around the bush,* she'll tell them everything they need to know without anyone getting embarrassed.

Older girls should put themselves in the hands of the great Louise Rennison, the doyenne of all the joys and horrors of changing bodies; while boys will find solace in the frank and touching diary of 14-year-old Joseph Calderaro in *Kimchi & Calamari* who, having been set a school assignment to research his ancestry, wonders which genes will dominate – his smooth-skinned Korean or his hairy Italian?

SEE ALSO: **adolescence** • **body odour** • **hormones, raging**

body image

[PB] *Cinderella's Bum*
NICHOLAS ALLAN

[YA] *Staying Fat for Sarah Byrnes*
CHRIS CRUTCHER

Most children start off having lots of fun with their bodies – but it only takes one insensitive comment for all that to change. If self-consciousness arrives early – or looks like it might be passed down from an older sibling to a younger – we recommend *Cinderella's Bum*, featuring as it does a big sister who doesn't like her bum, and a little sister who can't see anything wrong with it. 'I think it's lovely,' the little sister says, beaming up at her sister's backside admiringly – while her big sister scowls at herself in a full-length mirror. The little sister proceeds to point out that well-padded bums come in handy for 'crash landings' and sitting on a throne – and anyway, why not focus on a body part that you *do* like instead? That the big sister has actually been attempting to squeeze herself into the wrong swimming costume all along makes for a lovely twist.

Young Adult fiction tackling this sensitive issue must tread a careful line, portraying the positive potential for change without inadvertently triggering a crisis (see: eating disorder). Chris Crutcher manages to do this with grace in his intriguing *Staying Fat for Sarah Byrnes*. Chubby Eric and his friend

* Pun intended.

Sarah Byrnes put a school newspaper together as a way of getting back at those who have made them the butt of their jokes. They call it 'Crispy Pork Rinds' – Eric being the 'pork'; Sarah, who has terrible burns on her face and body, being the 'crispy'; and rinds because they're 'the parts that are left . . . that nobody pays attention to'. Their self-described bond as 'terminal uglies' brought them together in first grade; but over the years they've realised they have more important things in common, including their sense of humour and a passion for words. When Eric discovers a talent for swimming, they begin to drift apart – especially as he starts to lose weight as a result. Out of solidarity with Sarah, he tries to keep the pounds on so he can remain the freaky fat friend of the freaky charred girl. But his metabolism betrays him, and he decides the next best way to 'stay fat for Sarah' is to refuse any invitation that doesn't include her too. When, in their final year at school, he discovers that Sarah's burns were not caused by an accident as she's always claimed but inflicted deliberately by her father (see: abuse), Eric realises that it's not a person's issues that define them but the way they deal with them. This story shows children that it's their attitude towards their body that matters, not their body itself – whatever its imagined failings might be.

SEE ALSO: **eating disorder** • **overweight, being**

body odour

PB *The Smelly Book*
BABETTE COLE

No one responds well to being told they smell. But *The Smelly Book* – a delightful romp in words and pictures through all things rotten, rancid and pongy, from fish to feet and stinky cheese to piles of trash – will establish some standards for which smells are nice and which are not. Make it part of a child's library from the start and it'll provide you with a useful context for some gentle ribbing (while you hold your nose) later on. Did these whiffy socks fall from *The Smelly Book* . . .? Babette Cole's characteristically energetic ink-and-wash illustrations bring a much-needed lightness of touch to the whole malodorous subject.

SEE ALSO: **bath, not wanting to have a** • **hands, not wanting to wash your**

bookworm, being a

READING AILMENTS

FIND FICTIONAL FELLOW-OBSESSIVES

One minute all they want to do is play with their friends. The next their face has been replaced by the cover of an open book. Your previously sociable child has become a silent semi-presence, blind and deaf to the goings-on in the actual world. They walk to school without looking at their feet; they fork food into their mouth sight unseen; and when they come home, they're a guided missile locked on their reading nook. Your child has been bitten by the bug.

But that doesn't mean they're not being social. Ensure they meet people of like mind in the books they read by scattering some of the titles in the following list in their path. Here they'll find characters who, like them, devour books – and not just the words and the stories, but the paper they're printed on. Here they'll meet people who inhabit books, lose themselves in books, live through books and have their lives invaded by the characters in their books. Even as a bookworm they can be surrounded by soulmates. One day they will emerge from their chrysalis with new wings, enriched by their understanding of narrative, psychology and the world.

THE TEN BEST BOOKS ABOUT BOOKWORMS

- PB *Beware of the Storybook Wolves* LAUREN CHILD
- PB *Charlie Cook's Favourite Book* JULIA DONALDSON, ILLUSTRATED BY AXEL SCHEFFLER
- PB *The Incredible Book Eating Boy* OLIVER JEFFERS
- PB *The Fantastic Flying Books of Mr Morris Lessmore* WE JOYCE
- PB *The Boy Who Loved Words* RONI SCHOTTER, ILLUSTRATED BY GISELLE POTTER
- CB *The Wishing Spell* (The Land of Stories) CHRIS COLFER
- CB *Matilda* ROALD DAHL, ILLUSTRATED BY QUENTIN BLAKE
- CB *Inkheart* CORNELIA FUNKE
- CB *Story Thieves* JAMES RILEY
- YA *The Book Thief* MARKUS ZUSAK

BODY ODOUR

boots, being too big for your

[CB] *Shola and the Lions*
BERNARDO ATXAGA, ILLUSTRATED BY MIKEL VALVERDE

Children who think they are particularly wonderful inspire a mixture of admiration and horror. Their confidence will no doubt take them far, but one can't help notice the disparity between the size of their ego and the size of, er, *them*. Basque author Bernardo Atxaga visits this idea in his story about the inflated Shola. When a well-travelled friend visits Shola's human owner, Señor Grogó, and shares his tales of African kings and voracious wild animals, he leaves a book behind: *The Lion, King of the Jungle*. Shola laps it up, recognising herself in the description of the powerful, noble beasts who hunt for their food rather than suffer the indignity of being served ready-made mince (aromatic and alluring though mince is). Off Shola then heads to the jungle – er, park – to track down her next meal. Unfortunately all she finds is rotten food from the bins, a rather terrifying Burmese cat, and an impertinent duck. Slowly, she begins to see the truth for what it is and goes home to Señor Grogó, who, fortunately, has the mince still waiting. Valverde's quirky line-and-watercolour drawings perfectly capture the contrast between Shola's view of herself and the real her – a small and somewhat unimpressive white dog. Those with a bit of Shola in them will be nudged very gently into the appropriately sized boots.

SEE ALSO: **bossiness** • **in charge, wanting to be** • **precociousness**

bored, being

[PB] *Harold and the Purple Crayon*
CROCKETT JOHNSON

[PB] *Journey, Quest* and *Return* (Journey)
AARON BECKER

In these days of electronic devices – eagerly waiting to occupy the slightest unfilled moment – it's rare to catch sight of a bored child wandering disconsolately from room to room, complaining to whoever will listen that 'there isn't anything to do' and occasionally kicking the cat. In the circumstance that you find one, seize the opportunity to re-set expectations with the ultimate paean to making something out of nothing, *Harold and the Purple Crayon*.

It's over half a century since Crockett Johnson's onesie-clad toddler went for a walk in the moonlight and, realising there was no moon, drew one into existence. He draws the path he's walking on and everything it leads him to – including, eventually, his room and his bed, when it's time to go to sleep. The fetching shape of the toddler as he reaches up to the far corners of the page with his crayon pulls us ineluctably in; as does the fact that the crayon is presented as just an ordinary crayon. Bring this classic out for entertainment-challenged kids of all ages, together with pens and a pad of white paper – or, even better, a wall – and encourage them to invent what they will.

Older kids can graduate to Aaron Becker's sumptuous graphic trilogy, beginning with *Journey*, which plays on the same idea. A little girl sits on the steps of her sepia-tinged house, fed up. We can see a man at a computer upstairs, a woman stirring something on the stove downstairs, and a sister lying on the sofa engaged with – you guessed it – a screen. When the little girl's attempts to lure each of them out to play come to nothing, she drifts to her room and slumps on her bed. But then she notices a stick of crimson chalk . . .

The wood she finds through the door she draws on her wall is enchanting: lanterns swing from the branches and a river threads between the trunks. At the end of a dock, she draws a crimson boat that carries her downstream to a city full of spires and domes. Uniformed guards welcome her in with waving arms. Architectural complexities abound as we follow her across a raised canal, complete with locks, down which city-dwellers are propelled in Venetian-style gondolas, shaded by fringed parasols. Waterfalls cascade from great heights. When her canal ends, mid-air, it catches her out – but she quickly draws a hot-air balloon as she falls . . . The absence of words makes this picture book and its sequels gloriously untaxing for the irritable brain, while there's enough detail in the watercolour fantasyscapes to warrant a careful poring-over of each page. A cure for boredom in itself, Becker's work is also brilliant for launching kids into their own inner landscapes.

boring relatives, having

SEE: **bored, being** • **grannies, having to kiss**

CURE FOR GROWN-UPS CB *Harry and the Wrinklies*
ALAN TEMPERLEY

If you're the boring relly, do everyone a favour and read this hilarious romp. When Harry spots his two 'decrepit' great-aunts on the station platform, he thinks, '*Please* let it not be them!' One is thin and tall with a large straw hat and looks like a standard lamp. The other is short, plump and looks like a pink meringue. But Harry is in for a big surprise. Aunt Bridget and Auntie Florrie – with whom he has come to live – immediately suggest they drive home by way of the aerodrome. 'Seat belt fastened safely?' Auntie Florrie asks, before snapping a switch beneath the dashboard of the ancient Mercedes. A powerful roar throbs to life and, as the car gathers speed on the disused runway, the speedometer edges up: 90, 95 . . . 130 . . . Harry feels the leather press against his back as the wind slams in and the countryside turns to a blur. 'Lovely! Blow the cobwebs away!' cries Aunt Bridget.

Afterwards, Harry's two wrinkly aunts take him home for a nice glass of sherry (he's ten), and show him his tower room at Lagg Hall, the stately home they share with various other 'prehistoric' folk. As Harry luxuriates in the space, the woods and the dog, it soon becomes clear that these two old biddies are far from innocent and are, in fact, incapable of being dull. Read this, and you won't be dull either.

bossiness

CB *The Willoughbys*
LOIS LOWRY

Bossy children will squirm in the presence of twelve-year-old Tim, the eldest of the Willoughby children in this delightful parody of literary children's classics. The Willoughbys are an 'old-fashioned family'; and as befits an old-fashioned eldest boy, Timothy makes all the decisions for his siblings, ten-year-old twins 'Barnaby A' and 'Barnaby B', and six-year-old Jane: what game they'll play, what the rules are, how they will behave in church and whether or not they will like the food on their plates. According to Timothy's design, they each start the day with fifty points, which are then deducted if they do anything he doesn't approve of. The other children are so much in his thrall, they even ask if they can ask a question.

You can see how he got to be this way. The kids are landed with terrible parents who have a poor opinion of their offspring. Tim, they say, is 'insufferable', the twins are 'repetitive' and Jane – well, they seem to be unaware that they have a fourth child at all. The children have begun to realise they'd be better off without their parents, and when Mr and Mrs Willoughby, having reached more or less the same conclusion about their children, abscond on a global adventure, hiring a nanny (see: babysitter, not liking your) and putting the house on the market (see: moving house), the four siblings prepare hopefully for imminent orphanhood (see: orphan, wishing you were an). Meanwhile, Tim puts himself in charge.

Luckily, their firm and capable nanny sees how to help, first relieving Tim of his point-system duties, then finding a way to integrate households with their near-neighbour, Commander Melanoff – who also takes in Ruth, the abandoned baby they found on their doorstep. Under Melanoff's influence, Tim pulls himself up 'by [his] bootstraps' and although he doesn't lose his bossiness completely (he goes on to become a lawyer, after all) he does become nice enough to win the heart of baby Ruth once she grows up.

A story best enjoyed by those well versed in the classics it parodies,* use it to initiate a discussion on the issue of bossiness. Would Tim have become bossy if his parents had taken more of a role in their children's lives? What's the difference between being bossy and being a leader? Do you think anyone really enjoys being bossy?

SEE ALSO: **boots, being too big for your** • **in charge, wanting to be** • **precociousness** • **share, inability to** • **told, never doing what you're** • **unfriendliness**

brainwashed, being

A Wrinkle in Time
MADELEINE L'ENGLE

The potential for the mass seduction of the young via digital media is a disturbing phenomenon, and today's teens must wise up to the self-serving propagandists of our time if they want to hold on to their own ideals and identities. Madeleine l'Engle's cult classic will help them do so.

When the mysterious Mrs Whatsit and her friends whisk siblings Meg and Charles Wallace off on a quest to find their missing father – an eminent physicist at work on 'tesseracts' – their mother, also a scientist, doesn't stand in their way. It's a journey that takes them through time and space to a planet that's controlled by a larger-than-life being – a giant, bodiless brain called 'IT'. The hypnotic pulse of IT – removing all responsibility and angst, but also one's ability to act of one's own accord – has everyone trapped in its thrall, their father included. Charles Wallace, a boy possessed of such a luminous, unusual intelligence that he's considered by all but his family to be an idiot, is confident his own brain will be strong enough to resist; but he proves as fallible as his father. It's up to Meg to find the way out of IT's overpowering influence – and the key turns out to be not a high IQ but something she carries in her heart. Teens should take note of Meg's revelation. When everyone around them is succumbing to the will of another, this newfound knowledge will help keep them securely grounded.

SEE ALSO: **astray, being led** • **peer pressure**

---

* *Pollyanna, The Secret Garden, Heidi, Anne of Green Gables, Jane Eyre, Silas Marner . . .*

bras

YA *Bras, Boys and Blunders in Bahrain*
VIDYA SAMSON

Acquiring a first bra can be fraught for a teen or pre-teen girl. Get it too early, and they might be mocked; get it too late, and they might be mocked even more. Vidya Samson's hilarious spin on the subject is a welcome de-stresser.

Veena is a fifteen-year-old Indian girl living in Bahrain whose mother has a meltdown at the very mention of the word bra. Such is Veena's inexperience generally, she is yet to actually speak to a boy – even though she gazes rhapsodically at the gorgeous Rashid between classes. And when it's time for 'The Talk' in sex education, Veena is one of the few for whom it's all genuinely news.

Effortlessly clever, but lacking in the street wisdom that could come along with motherly advice, Veena decides she has to tackle the problem of her flat chest herself – and asks her best friend, Unita, to come shopping with her. When they find the answer – an affordable, padded bra – there's still the problem of when to start wearing it. How do you go from being 'flat as a pancake' to needing a bra overnight? Veena's first attempts to put the bra on in a toilet cubicle at school are hilarious, and she ends up working out a mathematical equation for how to do up the hooks behind her back. When she suddenly erupts in terrible boils, she assumes it must be an allergy to the socks she's stuffing in, or the bra itself – and confesses all to her mother. It turns out to be chicken pox (see: chicken pox).

Veena's bra-related torments and her gradual realisation that there are boys other than Rashid who might appreciate her for more than her sock-magnified curves will help teens relax about whether or not they get the underwiring right.

SEE ALSO: **embarrassment** • **flat-chested, being**

broken limb

SEE: **bed, having to stay in** • **pain, being in**

brother, having a

SEE: **sibling, having to look after a little** • **sibling rivalry**

bruises, cuts and

[PB] *Nurse Clementine*
SIMON JAMES

Keep a copy of this in the medicine cabinet, along with the plasters, Savlon and Wasp-Eze. The fetchingly drawn story of a little girl whose grown-ups buy her a nurse's outfit and a first-aid kit for her birthday ('You can call me Nurse Clementine from now on!'), it'll provide an excellent distraction while you clean and disinfect the wound. Clementine's approach to on-the-spot care is to wrap the hurting part copiously in bandages, adding a firm instruction to keep them on for a week. When there's no one left in the family requiring treatment, she wonders what on earth to do with herself. And then, thankfully, her brother gets stuck up a tree . . . The pen and wash illustrations – majoring in cream, peach and the gentlest of apple greens – are as soothing to the eye as is the sight of a top-to-toe bandaged little brother to Nurse Clementine at the end.

SEE ALSO: **cheering up, needing** • **pain, being in**

bullied, being

[PB] *One*
KATHRYN OTOSHI

[ER] *It Was a Dark and Stormy Night*
ALLAN AHLBERG, ILLUSTRATED BY JANET AHLBERG

[CB] *Jane, the Fox and Me*
FANNY BRITT, ILLUSTRATED BY ISABELLE ARSENAULT

Being bullied is a grim ordeal and one which every grown-up hopes their child will be spared. If it does happen, it's helpful to have some stories to hand which offer practical solutions as well as solace. *One* captures the complex group dynamics involved in bullying with striking clarity by casting splodges of colour as the characters, set against spanking white spreads. 'Blue' is quiet – not outgoing like orange, or regal like purple, or sunny like yellow; and Red, a 'hot head', likes to pick on Blue. When Red taunts Blue, Red gets bigger; and though sometimes the other colours comfort Blue, telling him what a nice colour he is, they don't ever dare say it in front of Red . . . It's hard to triumph over a bully by yourself, and how Red is brought into line by the power of the group provides an inspiring model. Read it to the bullied, to those on the sidelines, and also to the bully themselves. After all, what Red really wants is a friend, just like everyone else.

A bully can often work their way into a position of power without anyone noticing. If this happens in a classroom, share *It Was a Dark and Stormy Night*. A bunch of moustachioed brigands have kidnapped eight-year-old Antonio and carried him off to a secret cave. There they demand he tell them a story – being, actually, a bunch of overgrown kids. Brave Antonio takes a big breath and launches in with 'Once upon a time', but he hasn't got much further before the brigands interrupt with their own ideas of what should happen next – none more so than the Big Chief himself, who wants to be the hero and sulks when he's not. The brigands know better than to argue with the Big Chief and they let him have his way. But when Antonio gets to the bit where the brigands share the treasure out equally among themselves, and the outraged chief insists that he would take all the treasure himself, they begin to shuffle uncomfortably. Never has the unfairness of their situation been pointed out to them so clearly. Antonio soon has them turning on their chief for his domineering, bullying ways, upsetting the stewpot in all the commotion. Get a discussion going about how sometimes it takes an outsider – or the right story – to overthrow the narcissistic bully in a group.

The misery of being ostracised by a gang is captured with great sensitivity in the Canadian graphic novel *Jane, the Fox and Me*. Teenager Hélène is persecuted by the hip clique at her Montreal school. 'She smells like BO,' they write on the washroom door. No one will sit beside her on the bus, and though her mother stays up all night making her a new dress (last year's fashion, alas) Hélène finds she can't bring herself to confide in her. When a school trip is announced, everyone is thrilled. But for Hélène the idea of being cooped up with 'forty kids . . . not one of them a friend' is pure torture.

Sensibly, Hélène escapes into a book at camp – *Jane Eyre* – where she finds another lonely girl, but one who grows up 'clever, slender and wise' nonetheless. When Jane finds Mr Rochester ('how wonderful, how impossible', thinks Hélène, wise to easy romanticism), only to lose him again, Hélène is about to tear up the book in despair. But just then a dark-haired girl she's never noticed before walks into her tent – and changes everything. It's only when colour starts to splash the pages that we realise how monotone Hélène's world has been until now; and how quickly joy, when it sees its chance, rushes in. A fine fictional example of bibliotherapy at work, this gem of a book is the ideal cure for a teen getting back on the road once bullying has come to light.

SEE ALSO: **anger • anxiety • good at anything, feeling like you're no • heard, not feeling • loneliness • loser, feeling like a • mistake, frightened about making a • nightmares • parents who can't talk about emotions, having • role model, in need of a positive • run away, urge to • sadness • scared, being • self-harm• sleep, unable to get to • stand up for yourself, not feeling able to • stuck • suicidal thoughts • trusting, being too • worrying • wrong, everything's going**

bully, being a

Many things can make a child into a bully, but only two things can really cure them: learning to see things from the point of view of their victim, and understanding why they might feel the impulse to be a bully themselves. Stories are a great way to develop empathy and instil self-knowledge. Take your pick from the following list.

THE TEN BEST BOOKS FOR UNDERSTANDING BULLYING

- [CB] *Playground* 50 CENT
- [CB] *Cloud Busting* MALORIE BLACKMAN
- [CB] *Blubber* JUDY BLUME
- [CB] *Judy Moody Was in a Mood* MEGAN MCDONALD, ILLUSTRATED BY PETER H REYNOLDS
- [CB] *I Am Sort of a Loser* (Barry Loser) JIM SMITH
- [CB] *The Ant Colony* JENNY VALENTINE
- [CB] *The Butterfly Club* JACQUELINE WILSON, ILLUSTRATED BY NICK SHARRATT
- [CB] *Cookie* JACQUELINE WILSON, ILLUSTRATED BY NICK SHARRATT
- [YA] *By the Time You Read This, I'll be Dead* JULIE ANNE PETERS
- [YA] *Crash* JERRY SPINELLI

SEE ALSO: **in charge, wanting to be** • **sibling rivalry** • **violence**

car, being in the

CB *Chitty-Chitty-Bang-Bang*
IAN FLEMING

It takes the patience of a saint to drive long distances while keeping up a constant patter intended to cajole, deflect, divert and absorb the passengers in the back seat – especially when said passengers in the back seat are keeping up a constant patter of the 'Are we there yet?', 'I'm so bored!' and 'Why do we have to go there anyway?' variety. Alternatively, it takes an audiobook. See our lists of The Ten Best Audiobook Series for Long Car Journeys that follows, and The Ten Best Audiobooks for All the Family (see p.232).

Grown-ups still angling for sainthood might like to add a group reading of *Chitty-Chitty-Bang-Bang* to their pre-journey prep. As well as being the creator of 007's spike-producing, missile-firing vehicles, Fleming was also responsible for coming up with the children's equivalent. Chitty-Chitty-Bang-Bang is the sort of car that gets kids thinking about cylinders, pistons, flashing lights, horns – and all the things a modified car might be able to do.

Commander Caractacus Pott, eccentric inventor and father to eight-year-old twins Jeremy and Jemima, can finally afford to buy a family car after making the best-selling Crackpot Whistling Candy (a sweet that cleverly turns into a whistle). The old, twelve-cylinder racing car has seen better days, but after several weeks spent doing her up in the garage, he rolls her out for the family to admire. Jeremy and Jemima fall in love with the big round headlights immediately – and the horn that makes a 'deep, polite' and 'threatening' roar. Strangely, some of the instruments on the dashboard seem to have appeared by themselves . . . No matter: two loud backfires later, the car is charging at full pelt down the motorway.

This being England, they're soon stuck in traffic and both car and passengers start to overheat. Just then, a sign saying 'Pull' lights up on the dash.

The Commander hesitates, not knowing what it will do, but then the sign changes to 'Pull idiot!' and he obeys. Lo! the mudguards swivel out, and back . . . and . . . well, you know the rest. Experienced as Fleming originally wrote it, *Chitty-Chitty-Bang-Bang* will inspire your passengers to bring their imaginations – and hand-made buttons, levers and wings – on board to vamp up the family wheels. The driving experience will never be the same again.*

THE TEN BEST AUDIOBOOK SERIES FOR LONG CAR JOURNEYS

- CB *The Famous Five* ENID BLYTON, READ BY JAN FRANCIS
- CB *How to Train Your Dragon* CRESSIDA COWELL, READ BY DAVID TENNANT
- CB *Skulduggery Pleasant* DEREK LANDY, READ BY RUPERT DEGAS
- CB *Chronicles of Ancient Darkness* MICHELLE PAVER, READ BY SIR IAN MCKELLEN
- CB *His Dark Materials* PHILIP PULLMAN, READ BY THE AUTHOR
- CB *Harry Potter* JK ROWLING, READ BY STEPHEN FRY
- CB *A Series of Unfortunate Events* LEMONY SNICKET, READ BY TIM CURRY
- CB *The Hobbit* and *The Lord of the Rings* JRR TOLKEIN, READ BY ROB INGLIS
- YA *The Hitchhiker's Guide to the Galaxy* DOUGLAS ADAMS, READ BY STEPHEN FRY
- YA *The Maze Runner* JAMES DASHNER, READ BY MARK DEAKINS

SEE ALSO: **bored, being** • **sick, being**

care, being taken into

SEE: **foster care, being in**

carer, being a

SEE: **unwell parent, having an**

carrots, refusing to eat your peas and

SEE: **fussy eater, being a**

* And yes, you get your halo.

cast-offs, having to wear

[ER] *Old Hat New Hat*
STAN AND JAN BERENSTAIN

[YA] *Pigeon English*
STEPHEN KELMAN

Inculcate affection for pre-loved clothes – baggy-kneed, broken-zipped, and secreting dubious things in the corners of their pockets – with *Old Hat New Hat*. In this story, the Berenstain bear we know and love tries on every weird and wonderful hat in the shop, from the turban to the one with the propeller on top. Then he spies a tatty old trilby with a patch and a drooping daisy. It's the one he came in with, of course. Old is *so* the best.

It's harder to convince older kids that wearing second-hand clothes is cool, but perhaps not impossible. Set on a council estate in Peckham, *Pigeon English* tells the story of Harri, a young Ghanaian immigrant trying to make his way in the local gang culture. 'Have you got happiness?' they ask him. 'Yes!' 'Have you got happiness?' 'Yes!' By the time he finally gets what they're saying,* his street cred has taken a bashing. But how can he ever hope to climb back up the ladder when his mother buys him cast-off trainers at the charity shop?

It gradually dawns on Harri that it's what's inside his trainers that he should be focusing on: a natural athlete, he can run faster than any of his peers. This moving story speaks to kids about many issues, including immigration (see: outsiders, distrust of), bullying (see: bullied, being) and peer pressure (see: peer pressure). But in the end it's about seeing things in perspective. Acknowledge with the kids of your ken that it sometimes feels crucial to be seen wearing the right things. But that it's even more crucial to keep their eye on the bigger picture.

SEE ALSO: **peer pressure** • **things, wanting** • **worrying**

celebrity, wanting to be a

[CB] *The Strongest Girl in the World* (Magical Children)
SALLY GARDNER

[YA] *Rockoholic*
CJ SKUSE

With the current rash of TV talent shows, kid-hosted YouTube channels and the measuring of popularity by the number of likes and followers one has, it's hardly surprising that modern children angle for celebrity status. *The Strongest Girl in the World* shows that hitting the big time doesn't necessarily lead to

* 'A-penis'.

contentment. When a friend gets his head stuck between the school railings (see: stuck), eight-year-old Josie discovers she has the power to bend metal. Experimenting with her new-found capabilities, she finds she can also lift tables, people, and even a double-decker bus. It doesn't take long for someone to spot her money-spinning potential, and she and her family are soon being whisked off to New York by the sleazy Mr Two Suit to find fame and fortune. They find it; but, after much excitement, sensible Josie decides she'd rather live a quiet, happy life after all. Readers will love Josie's adventurous spirit – and her ultimate choice.

An eye-opening exploration of celebrity from both the idol and the fan's point of view is to be found in *Rockaholic*, in which teenage Jody is so obsessed with her rock idol, Jackson (from the fictional band The Regulators), that she's listening to him on her headphones at her own grandfather's funeral. When she kidnaps Jackson by accident – he having mistaken her Curly Wurly for a knife, no doubt as a result of the hallucinogens coursing through his veins – she and her best friend find themselves driving him to Jody's house. The next thing she knows, her number-one fantasy man is unconscious in her bed, naked – and she's washing him with baby wipes.

It turns out that Jackson loathes his fans and finds it pathetic that they spend their hard-earned cash on his concert tickets. In fact, he pours so much vitriol on Jody's dream that she's moved to push him off a bridge. No sooner has she done so than she has the dubious epiphany that if she can only help Jackson detox from the 'blackberries' he takes, he might turn out to be the god she imagined him to be after all . . . Thus begins the hilarious account of Jackson's descent into the troughs of normality, which sees him being transported in a wheelie bin to Grandpa's converted garage, going through cold turkey and being fed meals by Jody through the cat flap. High comedy, yes; but this story also sheds touching light on the topsy-turvy life of a fan, how much their gods mean to them, and how sometimes it takes a serious dose of life (and death) to help someone see what was staring them in the face all along.

SEE ALSO: **precociousness** • **princess, wanting to be a** • **spoilt, being**

chatterbox, being a

ER *Little Miss Chatterbox* **ROGER HARGREAVES**

A great number of challenging personality traits can be slipped into a conversation with a child via the relevant Hargreaves character.* From being messy to being scatterbrained, from being lazy to being mischievous – you name it, there's a Mr Man (or, now, a Little Miss) whose *raison d'être* is to model that feature and invite a discussion about it. One of our favourites for curative purposes is Little Miss Chatterbox, the sister of Mr Chatterbox. If Mr Chatterbox can talk the hind leg off a donkey, Little Miss Chatterbox can talk all forty-two legs off a centipede.† In the course of this story, she gets fired from four jobs – bank teller, waitress, hat shop attendant and secretary – for talking too much; and, one by one, Mr Happy, Mr Greedy, Little Miss Splendid and Mr Uppity are all left in a state of shell-shocked silence. The job she finally gets (we won't spoil the surprise) is exactly the sort of brain-numbing punishment we would wish for her – except that she doesn't notice it's a punishment at all. The chatterbox in your midst will surely notice how unhappy the other characters become in this story, and with luck – *ahem* – they'll not notice how pleased you look when they stop talking to read it.

SEE ALSO: **questions, asking too many**

cheering up, needing

PB *Guess How Much I Love You*
SAM MCBRATNEY, ILLUSTRATED BY ANITA JERAM

PB *Winnie-the-Pooh*
AA MILNE, ILLUSTRATED BY ERNEST H SHEPARD

After tears, there needs to be comfort. *Guess How Much I Love You* – a book more or less guaranteed to get a grown-up choked up, which is in itself a comforting spectacle for a child – is our favourite picture book for the job. Little Nutbrown Hare, 'who was going to bed', wants his Big Nutbrown Hare to guess how much he loves him – then tries to show him how much by spreading his arms as wide as he can. Of course, Big Nutbrown Hare can make his arms go wider, and his feet go higher; and as they continue to try and out-big the other with the size of their love, we get to see Little Nutbrown's quivering whiskers and eager little tail take it all in: '"Hmm, that is a lot," thought Little Nutbrown Hare.' With their soft, white tummies and their delicate, worn-looking ears, these hares are about as irresistible as children's book characters get – and the quiet rhythm

* If it didn't occur to you till now that there was a reason you were given *Mr Slow*, we apologise for breaking it to you so abruptly.

† Yes, you read that right a second time. If you don't know what we're talking about – or if a child in the vicinity really has taken the legs off a centipede, either by talking too much or some other way – see: animals, being unkind to.

of the prose will soothe and lull. That Little Nutbrown Hare never gets to hear the true extent of Big Nutbrown Hare's love introduces your child to the gratifying concept that sometimes a grown-up's love is just too big to describe.

Children who have, in some way, brought their upset on themselves will feel much better for getting to know Winnie-the-Pooh, loved as he so evidently is despite – and even because of – his foolishness. When Pooh gets stuck in the entrance to Rabbit's burrow, he only has himself to blame. Full of the honey and condensed milk he wolfed down at Rabbit's, without even having been invited to breakfast in the first place, his girth is now greater than the front entrance of the burrow. With his 'North end' poking into the woods, and his 'South end' still in Rabbit's kitchen, he's unable to move either in or out.

At first, Pooh tries to pretend there's nothing wrong – that he's 'just resting and thinking and humming' to himself. Then he gets cross and tries to lay the blame on someone or something else – in this case, Rabbit's front door for not being wide enough. Sensibly, Rabbit doesn't argue, but goes to fetch Christopher Robin – the equivalent of a grown-up in these stories. Christopher Robin gently chides Pooh for being a 'Silly old Bear', but in 'such a loving voice' and with such complete acceptance of his friend's follies that everybody feels 'quite hopeful again' straight away.

It's Rabbit who suggests they read aloud to Pooh while waiting for his stomach to deflate (although, ever the opportunist, he also suggests that he use Pooh's back legs as a towel rail while he's there). His kind suggestion (or perhaps it's the prospect of no meals for a week) tips Pooh over the edge and, a tear rolling down his cheek, he asks to be read a 'Sustaining Book, such as would help and comfort a Wedged Bear in Great Tightness'.* If you respond to a child's upset in much the same way as Christopher Robin does – gently chiding but in a loving voice and showing you love them just as they are – you'll do a good job of cheering them up. Then choose the 'Sustaining Book' with this story in it – or one of our laugh-inducing reads in the list that follows.

THE TEN BEST BOOKS TO MAKE YOU LAUGH OUT LOUD

- ER *My Friend's a Gris-Kwok* MALORIE BLACKMAN, ILLUSTRATED BY ANDY ROWLAND
- ER *Stinkbomb & Ketchup-Face and the Badness of Badgers* JOHN DOUGHERTY, ILLUSTRATED BY DAVID TAZZYMAN
- ER *The Hundred-Mile-an-Hour Dog* JEREMY STRONG, ILLUSTRATED BY NICK SHARRATT

* If we were keeping a running count of fictional examples of bibliotherapy to be found in children's literature, this would be number two, and we are still only on C. Now that the point has been made, we'll stop counting.

- [CB] *Arabel's Raven* (Arabel and Mortimer) **JOAN AIKEN, ILLUSTRATED BY QUENTIN BLAKE**
- [CB] *The Legend of Spud Murphy* **EOIN COLFER**
- [CB] *Hoot* **CARL HIAASEN**
- [CB] *You're a Bad Man, Mr Gum!* **ANDY STANTON, ILLUSTRATED BY DAVID TAZZYMAN**
- [YA] *Me and Earl and the Dying Girl* **JESSE ANDREWS**
- [YA] *'. . . Startled by his Furry Shorts?'* (Confessions of Georgia Nicolson) **LOUISE RENNISON**
- [YA] *Fangirl* **RAINBOW ROWELL**

CURE FOR GROWN-UPS [PB] *Lost and Found* **OLIVER JEFFERS**

Of course, when a child is upset, you need to find out what the matter is, too. This is easier said than done. When the boy in *Lost and Found* finds a dejected penguin at his door, he wants to help. But he jumps to the premature conclusion that the creature needs taking back to the South Pole and the penguin doesn't know how to explain that it's something else. When they get there, the penguin is even sadder than he was before. Think of this silently suffering penguin when you're faced with an upset child and don't rush the diagnosis stage.

SEE ALSO: **stuck**

chicken pox

[PB] *Goldie Locks Has Chicken Pox*
ERIN DEALY, ILLUSTRATED BY HANAKO WAKIYAMA

Sometimes a writer stumbles on a rhyme that's just too good not to be used – which is perhaps how *Goldie Locks Has Chicken Pox* came to be. Bringing a host of other fairytales into the mix, and with Fifties-inspired artwork mirroring the spots of Goldie's pox in the Locks family's polka-dot wallpaper, this delightful picture book covers the disease in all its vile stages, from the question of who Goldie could have caught it from (cue a phone call to the three bears) to trying not to scratch, and being taunted by a sibling who – hurrah! – gets his comeuppance in the end. Full of funny visual riffs (look out for the father's dude-ranch shirt), this book should be applied along with the calamine lotion.

SEE ALSO: **bed, having to stay in** • **bored, being**

choice, spoilt for

[PB] *Millions of Cats*
WANDA GA'G

Should it be the lemon cupcake with the jelly bean on top? Or the chocolate cupcake with the Smartie on top? Or the green cupcake with the vanilla icing and hundreds and thousands on top? It's easy to see how what starts as a treat can segue into a trauma in today's over-abundant world. What a relief, then, for a child to find an old man struggling to make up his mind in the rhythmic classic *Millions of Cats*. When the old man's wife says she'd like a cat in the house, the old man goes out to find one. He walks a long way – over the black-and-white woodcut hills and under the black-and-white woodcut clouds – and finds not just one cat, or even a dozen cats, but 'Hundreds of cats,/Thousands of cats,/Millions and billions and trillions of cats.' Of course, no sooner has he chosen one – a pretty white cat – than he sees another that's just as good. And then another – and so it goes on, each cat seeming just as beautiful as the last. The situation resolves itself in a way that is somewhat sinister – perhaps more to grown-ups than to children – but happily obviates the need for the couple to make a decision themselves.* Making the perfect choice might not be as important as being pleased with your first choice, the story suggests – or the choice that chooses you.

SEE ALSO: **spoilt, being**

chores, having to do

[CB] *The Adventures of Tom Sawyer*
MARK TWAIN

[CB] *Mrs Piggle-Wiggle*
BETTY MACDONALD

Chores are a bore as far as kids are concerned, especially when they could be lounging around doing nothing or building a den in the woods. When Tom Sawyer is confronted with the vast acres of Sahara-brown fencing that he must whitewash one Saturday morning, all joy drains from him. Then along comes Ben Rogers, impersonating a steamer and looking like he's about to make fun of Tom for his unenviable task. That's when Tom has his master-stroke of ingenuity. Instead of bemoaning his plight, he makes the job sound appealing. 'Does a boy get a chance to whitewash a fence every day?'

Soon Ben is begging Tom to let him have a go – even giving him his

* If you really want to know, he brings home all the cats and they eat each other up – leaving just one homely, frightened and presumably very full kitten.

apple for the privilege. By the end of the afternoon, Tom has earned himself twelve marbles, 'part of a jew's-harp, a piece of blue bottle-glass to look through, a spool cannon, a key that wouldn't unlock anything . . . a tin soldier, a couple of tadpoles, six fire-crackers, a kitten with only one eye' (and that's only some of the things) from other children eager to share the job. More importantly, he's been able to spend the day watching other people do his work. The definition of work, he realises, is what you're obliged to do, while play is what you want to do. Let Tom's example be an inspiration to all grown-ups when trying to get kids to muck in.*

For younger children, your go-to woman is Mrs Piggle-Wiggle, the inspirational quasi-witch who has been more or less single-handedly training American kids to be good, responsible citizens since the late 1940s. A batty woman with a hump and hair down to her knees, Mrs Piggle-Wiggle has a way with kids, and all the local parents send their offspring to her whenever they need curing of being a slow eater or of answering back. She takes a similar approach to Tom Sawyer on the subject of chores, ensuring that children want to do them rather than feel they have to. There are several books in this series, and you'll find a great cure for being a show-off in *Hello, Mrs Piggle-Wiggle* (which comes with illustrations by the great Hilary Knight), while *Mrs Piggle-Wiggle's Farm* (with illustrations by Maurice Sendak) contains an excellent cure for children who neglect their pets. Give them to a child to read – or read them yourself and take notes.

SEE ALSO: **cook, reluctance to learn to** • **job, wanting a Saturday** • **laziness** • **pocket money, lack of** • **told, never doing what you're**

cigarettes

SEE: **peer pressure**

clinginess

SEE: **confidence, lack of** • **grow up, not wanting to**

---

* Let it also be a tip-off for kids not wanting to fall into the grown-ups' trap.

clumsiness

[PB] *Clifford the Big Red Dog*
NORMAN BRIDWELL

[CB] *Redwall*
BRIAN JACQUES

All kids start out clumsy – just watch a three-year-old trying to pour milk on their breakfast cereal if you're in any doubt. Clifford, the big red dog, is clumsy too in a wet-nosed, incompetent way which stems partly from his being the size of a house, and partly from an over-abundance of zeal. A kind and affable creature with big, cartoony eyes, Clifford never means to make a mess. But when he digs a hole, he can't help uprooting an entire tree. And when he chases a car, he can't help coming back with the whole vehicle clamped between his jaws. The fact that Clifford's owner Emily Elizabeth loves her pet however inadvertently destructive he is,* is what makes these books reassuring as well as fun.

For older readers who still can't seem to look where they're going, Matthias, the young mouse-hero of *Redwall* – the first of an engrossing, twenty-two-book-long series about the inhabitants of an ancient abbey – is forever doing clumsy things when we first meet him. Flip-flopping around in sandals that are too big for him, he trips over his words as well as his feet: 'Er, sorry, Father Abbot . . . Trod on my Abbot, Father Habit.' The Abbot can see that this bungling young mouse has something special about him – and when the mice and their faithful badger Constance have to defend themselves against the evil one-eyed rat, Cluny the Scourge, and his army of vermin, it is Matthias the mice look to for leadership. Matthias's clumsiness hasn't left him by the end of this story: he still manages to go sprawling over a tree root when rushing back for his final showdown with Cluny. But by then it's a sign of his eagerness to do battle, too. Youngsters who suffer from this ailment might take note of the Abbot's advice and move through life a little more slowly. Or they can notice how endearing Matthias's clumsiness makes him and embrace theirs, too.

SEE ALSO: **adolescence** • **lose things, tendency to**

cold, having a

SEE: **adventure, needing an** • **cheering up, needing**

---

* Yes, grown-up, that's your standard.

coming out

SEE: **gay, not sure if you are**

concentrate, inability to

SEE: **fidgety to read, being too • short attention span**

confidence, lack of

Tar Beach
FAITH RINGGOLD

Whether they've been overshadowed, undermined, ground down by criticism – or never seemed to have any in the first place – children suffering from a lack of confidence need an exhilarating metaphor that helps them break free, and the encouragement to believe in themselves. They'll find both in *Tar Beach*, a story inspired by the author's memories of lying on the roof of her family's apartment in Harlem on hot summer nights.

While her parents play cards with the neighbours, eight-year-old Cassie Louise Lightfoot rises up into the sky. The only witness to the girl's magical flight is her baby brother, Be Be, 'lying real still on the mattress, just like I told him to'. The simple, bold illustrations, reminiscent of Chagall, draw us into Cassie's imagination as she soars over the George Washington Bridge, beyond the skyscrapers and up to the stars. Up here, she feels like everything she can see belongs to her – including the new Union building, which her father is helping to build but can't belong to because he's 'colored, or a half-breed Indian, like they say' – and in a way it does. Along the bottom of each page we see the stitched-together squares of the original quilt made to tell this story, a craft handed down to Ringgold from her southern ancestors.

With its legacy of slavery and discrimination, the metaphor of flying from one's constraints packs a mighty punch. Cassie tells Be Be that he can do it, too – but first he has to want to go somewhere: 'I have told him it's very easy, anyone can fly. All you need is somewhere to go that you can't get to any other way.' Encourage an unconfident child to imagine doing whatever it is they wish they could do. Believing they can do it is the first step. Once they believe that they can, they will.

SEE ALSO: **body image**

constipation

There's something immediately appealing about comic strips, with their eye-catchingly large faces, speech bubbles, undemanding storylines and private asides shared with the reader. Keep a stack of them in the loo for occupying sluggish moments.

THE TEN BEST COMIC-STRIP BOOKS TO KEEP IN THE LOO

- CB *Garfield at Large* **JIM DAVIS**
- CB *Asterix the Gaul* **RENÉ GOSCINNY AND ALBERT UDERZO**
- CB *The Adventures of Tintin* (series) **HERGÉ***
- CB *Hildafolk* **LUKE PEARSON**
- CB *The Complete Peanuts* **CHARLES M SCHULZ**
- CB *Thereby Hangs a Tale* (Calvin and Hobbes) **BILL WATTERSON**
- YA *Moomin: The Complete Tove Jansson Comic Strip* **TOVE JANSSON**
- YA *Nausicaä of the Valley of the Wind* **HAYAO MIYAZAKI**
- YA *Akira* **KATSUHIRO OTOMO**
- YA *20th Century Boys* **NAOKI URASAWA**

SEE ALSO: **tummy ache**

contrary, being

PB *Pierre*
MAURICE SENDAK

As perfectly proportioned for little hands as this book is – one of the four books in Sendak's diminutive Nutshell Library box set† – so is its impact perfectly disproportional. 'I don't care!' says Pierre to everything his parents say until they decide, understandably enough, that they've had enough of this contrary little boy and go to town without him. So when a lion comes along and wonders how Pierre would feel about being eaten, and gets the same response, no one is there to protect him.‡ We're not suggesting that children will be convinced

* We particularly love *Tintin in Tibet, Prisoners of the Sun* and *Red Rackham's Treasure.*

† The other titles in the series are *One Was Johnny, Alligators All Around* and *Chicken Soup with Rice.* All are great.

‡ For those who are concerned by this: although this is a cautionary tale in the tradition of Heinrich Hoffmann's *Struwwelpeter* and Hilaire Belloc's *Cautionary Tales,* the story doesn't end at the point where the lion eats Pierre. There's another bit after that. Sendak has updated the form for fragile, contemporary nerves. Psychiatrists can focus on those suffering from the after-effects of *Struwwelpeter* instead.

by the moral of this cautionary tale and never utter the words 'I don't care' again,* but it may convince those on the small side that if they want to make an impact disproportionate to their size, the best way to do so is not by being contrary but by being amusing, like this book.

SEE ALSO: **arguments, always getting into** • **beastly, being**

cook, reluctance to learn to

PB *Zeralda's Ogre*
TOMI UNGERER

CB *The Star of Kazan*
EVA IBBOTSON

Turning children into capable cooks is an essential part of parenting. But a busy grown-up who finds it a grind putting food on the table seven nights a week is, frankly, not the best advert for it. A far better role model is Zeralda. The daughter of a peasant farmer, Zeralda loves to cook, and knows how to 'bake and braise and simmer and stew' by the time she's six. She and her father have never heard of the ogre who terrorises the nearby town, looking for children to eat. So when her father is too sick to take their produce to market one day and sends Zeralda instead, she has no idea that the ogre she finds on the side of the road, starving and with a sprained ankle, had been aiming to eat *her*. The tender-hearted girl cooks up a great feast† there and then, using all the ingredients she was supposed to sell at the market. It's the best meal the ogre's ever eaten, and he invites Zeralda to come and be his personal chef, swearing off children for ever. Ungerer's large-scale pen-and-wash illustrations, showing Zeralda looking fondly at her cookery book and sticking out her tongue as she bastes the suckling pig, are full of the generous spirit of this book, and the limited palette of black, white, taupe and orangey-red make the package as mouth-watering as Zeralda's food. If anybody can plant a love of cooking in a child, it's Zeralda.

Children of chapter-book age who are showing no signs of expanding their repertoire beyond toast and a fried egg will find inspiration in *The Star of Kazan*. When three eccentric professors agree to bring up a foundling called Annika, they do so on the proviso that she make herself useful. This she does, learning to cook, clean and indeed take care of all the domestic duties involved in running a large Viennese house in 1908. When, at twelve, she's given the responsibility of cooking the Christmas carp – a dish she must prepare

---

* In fact – ahem – this book might introduce the phrase into their vocabulary. Sorry about that.

† Foodies will no doubt want to know the menu, so here it is: cream of watercress soup, snails in garlic butter, roast trout with capers, and a whole suckling pig.

following the recipe passed down to Ellie, one of the maids who found her – the stuffing alone requires a whole morning to prepare. Annika is hollow-eyed with worrying about it all. She knows she must add nothing to the recipe, and leave nothing out, but at the last moment she daringly adds a dash of nutmeg to the dish.

Her three professorial 'uncles' (one of whom is, in fact, an aunt, but that's another story) all pronounce the carp delicious. Only Ellie puckers up her mouth. 'What have you done?' she cries. 'Mother would turn in her grave!' But in the silence that follows, Ellie realises that Annika has in fact improved upon the recipe and her pucker turns into a smile. In her best handwriting, Annika adds 'a pinch of nutmeg will enhance the sauce' to the sacred recipe – and thus a cook is born.

SEE ALSO: **chores, having to do** • **fussy eater, being a** • **granted, taking your parent for** • **spoilt, being**

cows, fear of

SEE: **animals, fear of**

creepy crawlies, fear of

SEE: **animals, fear of**

cross

SEE: **anger** • **moodiness** • **tantrums**

cyber-bullying

SEE: **bullied, being**

D IS FOR . . .

dark, scared of the

[PB] *Sleep Tight, Little Bear*
MARTIN WADDELL, ILLUSTRATED BY BARBARA FIRTH

[PB] *The Dark*
LEMONY SNICKET, ILLUSTRATED BY JON KLASSEN

[ER] *The Owl Who Was Afraid of the Dark*
JILL TOMLINSON, ILLUSTRATED BY PAUL HOWARD

Most children are scared of the dark at some point – although because it's not so much the darkness itself that is feared as the horrible things that might be lurking within it, it's often not until the imagination is fully fired up that the fear kicks in. The minute it does, bring out the irresistible *Sleep Tight, Little Bear*. When Little Bear says he can't sleep, Big Bear has to put down his book just as he's getting to the good bit* and go and see what's wrong. Lying on his back and holding onto both his feet in the way that children do when they're a bit embarrassed to admit to something, Little Bear says that he doesn't like the dark. 'What dark?' says Big Bear. 'The dark all around us,' says Little Bear, and you can practically see him rocking back and forth on the page. Big Bear goes off to find a lantern and its glow banishes the darkness a little; but there's still darkness in the corners of the cave. And as Big Bear comes back with bigger and bigger lanterns, we feel his mounting tiredness. Meanwhile we watch Little Bear go through all the stages of restlessness and overtiredness (see: over-tired, being), captured with marvellous accuracy by Barbara Firth. Deeply comforting, this charming and ultimately soporific book will soothe both grown-up and child during these extended bedtimes and last just long enough that the little bear in your charge may also fall asleep before the end.

* A painful plight that deserves a story cure in itself, except that that would prolong the interruption.

'The dark lived in the same house as Laszlo . . .' is the beguiling start to *The Dark*, a picture book by Lemony Snicket (pen name of Daniel Handler, best known for his chapter book series, *A Series of Unfortunate Events**). By introducing the dark as *a something*, Snicket separates it from those things it might be concealing, showing us that in and of itself darkness is not a threat. Laszlo, the little boy in this book, gets to know the dark. It has its own favourite places to hang out: behind the shower curtain, in the closet and in the basement. And when he actually engages with the dark, Laszlo finds it to be a surprisingly understanding and helpful thing. In amongst the muted beiges and pale blues of Jon Klassen's lovely gouache illustrations, the dark makes its presence felt in a solid matt black. By the end, we're seeing the dark as a something too, but, from now on, a friendly something.

For children on the verge of reading, or now reading themselves, introduce Jill Tomlinson's charming Plop, the baby barn owl with 'knackety' knees in *The Owl Who Was Afraid of the Dark*. Plop has decided that he's too afraid of the dark to be nocturnal. 'You *can't* be afraid of the dark,' says his mummy. 'Owls are never afraid of the dark.' 'This one is,' points out Plop. His mother decides to send Plop out each day with the special mission of finding something out about the dark. Only then should he make up his mind, she says. So Plop tumbles out of the nest each day and meets a succession of people and animals who each tell him something about darkness from their point of view. From the little boy who's looking forward to fireworks, he learns that the dark is 'exciting'. From the old lady who wants to forget her wrinkles, the dark is 'kind'. From the girl anticipating a visit from Father Christmas, the dark is 'necessary'. One by one, the arguments add up to a compelling case. We defy any child not to see darkness in a positive light, so to speak, by the end.

SEE ALSO: **anxiety** • **bed, fear of what's under the** • **nightmares** • **worrying**

dating

YA *A Ring of Endless Light*
MADELEINE L'ENGLE

For wisdom on how to look after yourself in the dating game, give teens the fourth novel in Madeleine l'Engle's series about the Austin family.† Vicky is nearly sixteen when, over the course of a summer at

* For which, see: orphan, wishing you were an.

† While we encourage kids to read the whole wonderful Austin Family Chronicles, this one also stands alone.

her grandparents' New England holiday home, she dates three very different boys. There's Leo, the boy next door, who is vulnerable, caring and puppyish. Then there's the splashy, reckless Zachary, who gives her a strange feeling in the pit of her stomach – but drives too fast and takes her up in a plane without a licence. Lastly there's Adam, who works with dolphins. Vicky handles her dates with impressive delicacy, experiencing exhilaration with Zachary, intellectual and spiritual understanding with Adam, and emotional intimacy with Leo when he tragically loses his father. Teenagers date differently now to when this story is set, but the need to test out different sorts of partners – without causing offence – remains the same. Young readers will find answers to such issues as how to say no when you need to; who you can trust; and how to work out which person, if any, you really like.

SEE ALSO: **choice, spoilt for • dumped, being • first kiss • first love • virginity, loss of**

daydreaming, being accused of

CB *Charlotte Sometimes*
PENELOPE FARMER

Once upon a time, dreamy types caught gazing out the window were rapped over the knuckles and written off as fantasists at best and woolgatherers at worst. Happily, psychologists now recognise daydreaming for the creative pursuit it is. In fact, experts think daydreaming might be the neurological equivalent of filing – and that daydreaming children are simply those with a lot to process. Thirteen-year-old Charlotte's tendency to let her mind drift in the haunting *Charlotte Sometimes* can certainly be explained in this way. After her first night in her new boarding school, Charlotte wakes up to find she's travelled back in time. She's still at the same school, but she's now a girl called Clare and the year is 1918. Twenty-four hours later, she wakes up as Charlotte again. Charlotte and Clare – both motherless, both with a younger sister – spend alternate days as each other with, at first, no one noticing but them.

Life quickly becomes very challenging. When Clare is set homework in 1918, it's Charlotte who has to hand it in the next day; and when Charlotte agrees to be Susannah's best friend in 1963, she must find a way to update Clare. As the horrors of the First World War invade both their lives, the day-to-day stresses mount. Soon teachers and friends are complaining that Charlotte's attention always seems to be elsewhere – and there's only the reader to empathise. Full of the small details that children notice – such as Charlotte's first, surprised sight of freckled legs on one of her roommates; or the tired 'stretched' feeling she gets in her eyes when she's overwhelmed – this story will show the daydreamer in your midst that time staring into space is time well spent.*

CURE FOR GROWN-UPS [ER] *Mr Daydream* ROGER HARGREAVES

If you're unconvinced, read how Jack is whisked off by the cloud-shaped Mr Daydream during class and taken on a quick world tour. They go to Africa, Australia, the North Pole and the Wild West before Jack is snapped back to reality by the sound of the teacher calling his name. Who *wouldn't* rather travel to those places than be in a classroom?

SEE ALSO: **about, what's it all? • adventure, needing an • bored, being • short attention span**

deafness

In the early years, picture books with strong, bold illustrations, featuring characters with expressive faces – allowing kids to 'see' the story, if not hear it – are imperative. Once a child is reading themselves, they'll need the company of others who know what it's like to deal with prejudice, hearing aids and trying to lip-read the expressionless Mr Spock on TV.†

THE TEN BEST BOOKS FOR DEAF KIDS

- [PB] *Voices in the Park* ANTHONY BROWNE
- [PB] *Pumpkin Soup* HELEN COOPER
- [PB] *Freddie and the Fairy* JULIA DONALDSON, ILLUSTRATED BY KAREN GEORGE
- [PB] *The Deaf Musicians* PETE SEEGER AND PAUL DUBOIS JACOBS, ILLUSTRATED BY R GREGORY CHRISTIE
- [PB] *The Time It Took Tom* STEPHEN TUCKER, ILLUSTRATED BY NICK SHARRATT
- [CB] *El Deafo* CECE BELL
- [CB] *Mundo and the Weather-child* JOYCE DUNBAR
- [CB] *Whisper* CHRISSIE KEIGHERY
- [CB] *Feathers* JACQUELINE WOODSON
- [YA] *Miss Spitfire* SARAH MILLER

* While reminding grown-ups that the daydreaming child in your midst may in fact need some help doing the filing.

† Read *El Deafo*, then you'll know more about what it's like, too.

SEE ALSO: **different, feeling** • **friends, finding it hard to make** • **heard, not feeling** • **understood, not being**

death, fear of

[PB] *Drop Dead*
BABETTE COLE

[PB] *Badger's Parting Gifts*
SUSAN VARLEY

[CB] *Tuck Everlasting*
NATALIE BABBITT

[YA] *Ways to Live Forever*
SALLY NICHOLLS

For some, it's a gradual dawning. For others, the realisation that we're all going to die one day comes in a sudden shock of understanding. Grown-ups often shy away from exploring the after-tremors. But the more you can keep a child company as they grapple with their questions – where do you go when you die? who will die first, them or you? is it possible to die before you're old? – the better their chances of reconciling themselves to the inevitability of death, and living a life not overly shadowed by the fear of it.

A light touch is very welcome, of course, and for that look to Babette Cole, fearless doyenne of picture books that dare to go where others fear to tread.* In *Drop Dead*, a brother and sister ask their grandparents why they're such 'bald old wrinklies'. Their good-humoured elders explain that they weren't always like this and proceed to take their grandchildren on a whistle-stop tour of their lives – which, by anyone's standards, have not been dull. Cole's lively illustrations show the pair of them careering downhill in their runaway pram as babies, racing their motorbikes at sixteen, experimenting with cigarettes at eighteen, dancing on the rooftops at twenty-one, and leaping off the backs of horses as a stuntman and film star in their respective, glamorous careers (having both failed to get steady jobs as scientists). Old age has seen them start to shrink, forget things and wear false teeth – but they still have the occasional OAP adventure (parachuting with their Zimmer frames, for example). And even though they've dodged death many times in their lives, they will go 'bonk' eventually. Everyone's left with a smile at the end.

Another way to soften the shock is to explore how we continue to feel the presence of our loved ones in our lives after they've died – as shown in *Badger's Parting Gifts*. Dependable and kind, Badger is missed terribly by his friends. But then, one by one, they recall something special about him. Mole remembers how Badger once made him a mole paper chain. Frog

* For other fearless Babette Cole books, see our cures for: body hair; hands, not wanting to wash your; parents who are splitting up, having; sex, having questions about.

remembers how Badger taught him to skate. Their reminiscences, brought to life with intricate watercolour illustrations, fill the mourners – and us – with happy affection for this wise, generous friend. Whether you prefer to tell a child that the dead hover nearby, continuing to wish us well, or that they live on through the gifts they leave behind, this book will bring something warm and positive into the conversation.

For slightly older children, the profound *Tuck Everlasting* makes a case for death as a positive force in our lives. When ten-year-old Winnie stumbles upon a radiant boy named Jesse Tuck sitting under a tree, she asks him how old he is. 'I'm one hundred and four,' comes the unexpected reply. Winnie brushes off his remark – as she does Jesse's insistence that 'something terrible' will happen to her if she drinks from the stream beneath the tree. But when Jesse's older brother Miles and mother Mae turn up and proceed to hijack Winnie, tossing her on the back of their horse and racing back to their house with her, she begins to take their stories more seriously. She discovers that the stream beneath the tree is a magic stream and the whole family of Tucks became immortal when they drank from it, stuck at the same age forever. Knowing how hard it'll now be for Winnie to resist drinking from the stream herself, they are determined to persuade her not to – and they have till morning to do so. Only Jesse, yearning for a friend with whom to spend his endless life, takes the opposite stand.

The arguments against immortality are posed in a way that's direct and easy for children to grasp: life is dependent on death for its shape and meaning, they say, and one gets weary being alive forever. It's the lonely, sad figure cut by Pa Tuck that's most convincing. 'If I knowed [sic] how to climb back on the wheel, I'd do it in a minute,' he says. 'You can't have living without dying . . .' Whether Winnie will drink from the stream herself at seventeen and become Jesse's eternal mate, or age and die like everyone else, makes this book impossible to put down. Is it better to live fully, but briefly, or to exist forever, unchanging? Her decision is one that readers will never forget.

Many teens prefer not to think about death at all, for these are the years of invincibility. But events around them may force them to. Sam, the eleven-year-old hero of the heart-wrenching *Ways to Live Forever*, has leukaemia and knows he's going to die sooner rather than later. Turning his curiosity on death itself, he writes endless lists – lists of questions, such as 'How do you know when you're dead?' and lists of ways to 'live forever', such as 'Become a vampire' and 'Marry a Greek goddess'. He even writes lists of things he'd like to happen when he's dead, such as his sister inheriting his bedroom and his parents not being too sad.

We defy anyone to read this story without a lump in their throat. Sam is more courageous than either his parents or his sister, and his sense of humour holds out beyond his passing, written into the notes he leaves behind. He wants his family to be a little bit sad, but not so sad that they can't remember him without being devastated; and it's this, the art of being happy despite the knowledge that death awaits us and everyone we love, that this story inspires teens to master.

SEE ALSO: **about, what's it all? • anxiety • death of a loved one • death of a pet • life-threatening illness • worrying**

death of a loved one

Nothing is harder than the death of someone we love,* whatever our age. Seeing a fictional character going through a parallel loss – whether of a grandparent, parent, sibling or friend – can offer a safe way to explore the complex and bewildering emotions and help support a child through the different stages of grief. In all cases, it is vital to read a book closely yourself before sharing it with a bereaved child.

THE TEN BEST BOOKS TO HELP DEAL WITH BEREAVEMENT

- [PB] *Everett Anderson's Goodbye* LUCILLE CLIFTON, ILLUSTRATED BY ANN GRIFALCONI
- [PB] *The Paper Dolls* JULIA DONALDSON, ILLUSTRATED BY REBECCA COBB
- [PB] *Cry, Heart, But Never Break* GLENN RINGTVED, ILLUSTRATED BY CHARLOTTE PARDI
- [PB] *Are You Sad, Little Bear?* RACHEL RIVETT, ILLUSTRATED BY TINA MACNAUGHTON
- [CB] *River Boy* TIM BOWLER
- [CB] *A Greyhound of a Girl* RODDY DOYLE†
- [CB] *Two Weeks with the Queen* MORRIS GLEITZMAN
- [YA] *The Thing about Jellyfish* ALI BENJAMIN
- [YA] *My Sister Lives on the Mantelpiece* ANNABEL PITCHER
- [YA] *Batman: A Death in the Family* JIM STARLIN, MARV WOLFMAN AND GEORGE PÉREZ

---

* Except, perhaps, having to face the possibility of one's own death (see: death, fear of; life-threatening illness).

† And also: *Her Mother's Face* by Roddy Doyle, illustrated by Freya Blackwood.

CURES FOR GROWN-UPS [PB] *The Heart and the Bottle* OLIVER JEFFERS
[CB] *Pockety* FLORENCE SEYVOS, ILLUSTRATED BY CLAUDE PONTI

The loss of a grandparent or parent for one generation is the loss of a parent or partner for another. For the grown-up who has had to put their grief on hold while looking after others, we offer Oliver Jeffers's moving story about numbness – and becoming un-numb. For the grown-up who has lost their life partner, we offer *Pockety,* the beautiful story of a tortoise coming to terms with the loss of her soulmate, Thumb.

SEE ALSO: **anger** • **depressed parent, having a** • **depression** • **sadness**

death of a pet

SEE: **pet, death of a**

depressed parent, having a

[YA] *Broken Soup*
JENNY VALENTINE

[YA] *15 Days Without a Head*
DAVE COUSINS

Kids in this situation are likely to find themselves baffled by the neglectful behaviour of their parent. Reading a story featuring a grown-up behaving in a similar way – with the illness described and named – may turn on a lightswitch in their head.

When, in *Broken Soup,* fifteen-year-old Rowan's elder brother Jack drowns in a tragic accident, her stricken parents respond in different ways: her father by walking out, her mother by taking to her bed. This leaves Rowan to look after her eight-year-old sister, Stroma, and attempt to keep a semblance of normality. Rowan does her best, bringing her mother food, and trying not to bother her too much – because when her mother does emerge, she's moody and unpredictable. When she meets Harper, an easy-going American boy travelling the world in a revamped ambulance, she has something else to think about apart from her miserable mum. Meanwhile, the girls' father hovers on the edge, doing his best to avoid the remnants of his family and the emotions that come with them (see: parents who can't talk about emotions, having). But when their mother makes a failed suicide attempt, their father finally sees that his family needs him and steps into the breach. Rowan finds that her complicated family is actually rather wonderful. Teens will appreciate the illustration of how even a capable girl like Rowan can't be expected to manage it all alone.

Another coper – a boy this time – is fifteen-year-old Laurence in *15 Days Without a Head*. Laurence's mother, a single parent, has taken on two jobs to make ends meet, one at the chippy down the road, and one as a cleaner. This means she has to get up at 5am, leaving Laurence to get his six-year-old brother, Jay, to school before going to school himself. Sometimes his mother doesn't make it out of bed at all – or doesn't make it back from the night before till two days later – in which case Laurence has to do her cleaning shift too and never gets to school at all. So when she fails to come home one evening, it's not a huge surprise.

But once 'Whensday' becomes 'Blursday' and Blursday becomes 'Lieday', things start to get desperate. Stomachs are complaining, cockroaches are crawling around the kitchen, and the teachers are beginning to comment on Laurence's propensity to fall asleep at his desk (see: daydreaming, being accused of; over-tired, being). Eventually Laurence is so desperate for cash that he dons one of his mum's dresses and a wig and totters down to the post office in a pair of her shoes to try to withdraw money from her account. How the brothers bring their mother back from her self-imposed exile we will not reveal, but this tragicomic story shows that while trying to pretend everything's OK is admirable, depression is generally too big a problem for anyone to solve by themselves.

SEE ALSO: **parents, having • parents, too busy • parents who are splitting up, having • sibling, having to look after a little • unwell parent, having an**

depression

PB *The Red Tree*
SHAUN TAN

PB *Sylvester and the Magic Pebble*
WILLIAM STEIG

PB *Virginia Wolf*
KYO MACLEAR, ILLUSTRATED BY ISABELLE ARSENAULT

Painful as it is to think of children suffering from serious depression, it does happen. If you know a child who seems to be in a dark, locked-in place, attempting to cheer them up with jolly stories will probably just leave them feeling more isolated and out of sync with the world. Show them they're not alone – and that you're prepared to hold their hand in this dark place – by sharing stories that don't attempt any simple fixes but reflect back how they might feel, and show that there's light at the end of the tunnel.

The Red Tree is about a little girl who wakes up with the feeling that she has nothing to look forward to and that nobody understands. Shaun Tan's skilful illustrations capture the atmosphere of depression in ways that perhaps only images can: being stuck inside a thin-necked bottle and left on a pebbly beach in the rain, for instance; or standing on a chair in an empty field with a jumble of letters spilling, unheard, to the ground. There are no pat solutions, but the story ends on the image of a red tree sprouting from the floor of the little girl's bedroom, its glow lighting up her face. At last, there's a glimmer of hope, life, colour . . . and her face bears a little smile.

The author and illustrator William Steig believed that art, including children's books, helps us to know life in a way that 'still keeps the mystery of things'. His own books very much live up to this. What meaning we're intended to draw from the events in *Sylvester and the Magic Pebble* is not clear, but by the end we know we've shared something about how trapped and helpless we can all sometimes feel. Sylvester, a young donkey, loves to collect unusual pebbles and one day he finds a flaming red one, round as a marble. To his delight, he discovers it's a magic pebble: as long as he's holding it, his wishes come true. He rushes home to show his parents – but on the way he comes face to face with a hungry lion and, in a panic, he wishes himself into a rock.

As soon as the words are out of his mouth, he realises his mistake. The pebble is now lying on the ground beside him but, as a rock, he has no way of picking it up; and without touching the rock, he cannot wish himself back to being Sylvester. Indeed, as a rock he is completely powerless – he can't shout for help, or even let his parents know he's *him*.

It doesn't take long before he plunges into despair. With nothing else to do, Sylvester spends most of his time asleep, surfacing for brief moments only to remember all over again his seemingly endless plight – a state that shares much with depression. The pictures, in simple, bright colours, show the rest of the world going on without him, blue skies or grey. For a whole year, Sylvester is trapped (see: stuck). We feel not just for Sylvester, but also for his parents, whose grief Steig presents without sentimentality: they have lost their boy; nothing could be worse. But they haven't forgotten what he was like, and they haven't stopped loving him – and it's their love, in the end, that leads them back to him. This book shows that however trapped and unlike themselves a child may feel, their special grown-ups still love them and want nothing more than for them to get better.

Siblings and friends of depressed children may find it hard to understand the change in the behaviour of their brother, sister or friend – and how to tread the fine line between intruding too much and leaving too much alone. In *Virginia Wolf*, a picture book inspired by the relationship between the depressive novelist and her artist sister, Vanessa, we see what it's like from a sister's point of view. 'One day my sister Virginia woke up feeling wolfish,' it begins – and there, in a lovely bedroom full of books, we see a pair of wolf's ears sticking out from under the duvet. In this lupine state, Virginia finds even the sound of the birds too loud – and can't bear the bright yellow of Vanessa's favourite dress. Soon, her mood is bringing everyone else in the house down, too: 'Up became down . . . Gloom became doom.' Vanessa doesn't give up trying to think of ways she can help, and eventually her artistic skills come to the rescue. Happily, there's no second 'o' in this Virginia's last name, allowing us to separate her in our minds from her real-life counterpart who, in the end, was less fortunate. Not only does this Virginia stop feeling wolfish but she becomes so much better she feels rather 'sheepish' . . . Isabelle Arsenault's delicate artwork, taking us from the smudged darkness of depression to an optimistic garden vision of 'Bloomsberry', complete with floating petals and leaves that say 'hush' in the wind, brings with it the assurance that the dark mood in the house will eventually lift and a depressed sibling or friend will return to being themselves.

SEE ALSO: **anxiety • heard, not feeling • indoors, spending too much time • sadness • screen, glued to the • suicidal thoughts • understood, not being • worrying**

detention

SEE: **punished, being**

diary, catching someone else reading your

SEE: **alone, wanting to be left • betrayal**

die, where do we go when we?

SEE: **about, what's it all? • god, wondering if there is a**

different, feeling

Giraffes Can't Dance
GILES ANDREAE, ILLUSTRATED BY GUY PARKER-REES

Elmer
DAVID MCKEE

Wonder
RJ PALACIO

The Chrysalids
JOHN WYNDHAM

Perhaps they're taller than everyone else, or they're left-handed, or they speak with a lisp. Perhaps they live in a TV-less home, or in a treehouse, or with a dozen parakeets. If a small child you know feels different from others, read them the delightful *Giraffes Can't Dance*.

Gerald the giraffe cannot for the life of him dance; and every year at carnival time, when everyone else is shaking their booty, he's left feeling awkward and apart (see: tall, being). When he tries to join in on his long, gangly legs, the others jeer; and Gerald retreats into the jungle to look at the moon and mope (see: alone, wanting to be left). There he meets a cricket who tells him that everyone can dance – but that 'Sometimes when you're different, you just need a different song.' For children mocked for their difference (see: bullied, being), the vision of Gerald strutting his stuff in his own unique way can't fail to raise morale. Tell your child that 'normal' is nothing more than what everyone happens to be used to – and 'different' just means the next new thing.

Sometimes what makes a child different turns out to be their strongest asset – and they just need the chutzpah to carry it off. Take Elmer the patchwork elephant. With his gorgeous hide of coloured squares and tendency to play the clown, Elmer is adored by the other elephants. But Elmer doesn't like being different. One day he runs away and rolls himself in grey berry juice – then goes back to find out what it's like being ordinary. It's obvious to even the littlest child that Elmer's coat is special – and Elmer sees it too, in the end. Kids brought up on *Elmer* will associate difference with being more delightful than being the same as everyone else.

Few of us will ever have to deal with feeling as different as ten-year-old August in the extraordinary *Wonder*. We're never told exactly what August's face looks like, but we know he was born with a cleft palate, that he has a hole in the roof of his mouth, that he doesn't really have ears, and his eyes are further down his face than they're supposed to be. 'Whatever you're thinking,' he tells us on page one with a mixture of honesty, bravery and humour we come to know well, 'it's probably worse.'

So far, August has been home-schooled by his mother, but now he's facing his first day of school (see: home-schooling; school, being the new kid at). Both August's parents and his older sister Via (a lovely model of supportive sisterhood) have their hearts in their mouths as they watch him go in on the first day – a 'lamb to the slaughter', in his father's words – and we do, too. Everyone's fears are largely borne out. The other kids either stare at August or look then quickly avert their eyes – and even Mrs Garcia wears an overly 'shiny' smile. One of his classmates, Julian, makes a cruel reference to the deformed Darth Sidious in *Star Wars*. But when Jack, a popular, funny boy, comes and sits in the empty seat next to him, our hearts swell. Jack isn't afraid to ask August why he can't get plastic surgery. 'Hello?' says August, pointing to his face. 'This *is* after plastic surgery!' Jack claps his hand to his forehead and laughs hysterically. 'Dude, you should sue your doctor!' he says, and soon the two of them are laughing so hard that the teacher has to ask them to switch seats. Finally, August has found a friend to whom his difference doesn't matter.

August's troubles are not over, though – and we watch him face a slew of trials, from falling out with Jack (see: betrayal) to feeling bad about taking his anguish out on his ever-understanding mum. But his extraordinary ability to put his hurt aside and be the one to bring humour into the situation wins him the respect of the entire school in the end. We defy kids to remain dry-eyed when Mr Tushman, the principal, picks out a certain pupil as the one whose 'quiet strength has carried up the most hearts' during the course of the year. Children who feel different will be moved and inspired by how much August has to deal with, and children in the vicinity of someone else who feels different will come away determined to 'always . . . try to be a little kinder than is necessary' from now on.

Teenagers keenly aware of what marks them out will love discovering *The Chrysalids*, set as it is in a future where people are expelled for being different. Mutations have become rife as a result of a nuclear explosion and anyone who deviates from the norm as described in the 'Sunday Precepts' ('each leg shall be jointed twice and have one foot, and each foot five toes, and each toe shall end with a flat nail . . .') is deemed a 'Blasphemy'. David, our eleven-year-old hero who grows up during the course of the story, becomes aware that his ability to communicate telepathically is a mutation, and, terrified, does his best to hide it – not least from his own father. All over the walls of their house are quotations proclaiming 'BLESSED IS THE NORM' and 'IN PURITY IS OUR SALVATION'.

When David meets Sophie, a girl with six toes, he is slowly drawn into life on the 'Fringe'. Here, his gift for telepathy is useful – and he begins to enjoy it at last. David's journey from his home in Waknuk, surrounded by zealots, to the shining city he has seen in his dreams and his telepathic 'thought-shapes', is a difficult one – but once there, he finds he can fully embrace his uniqueness. His eventual realisation that he's one of the 'New People', destined to bring hope to humanity, will give heart to all teens in the process of discovering themselves.

SEE ALSO: **adolescence** • **autism** • **bullied, being** • **disability, coping with** • **friends, finding it hard to make** • **heard, not feeling** • **loneliness** • **understood, not feeling**

dinosaurs, crazy about

SEE: **obsessions**

dirty, not wanting to get

[PB] *Mud*
MARY LYN RAY, ILLUSTRATED BY LAUREN STRINGER

[CB] *Tarzan of the Apes*
EDGAR RICE BURROUGHS

Small children can be surprisingly anti-dirt, scrubbing at the little felt-tip mark on their hand in the manner of Lady Macbeth and recoiling in horror when you suggest they plunge their hands into the cookie dough. Give them some examples of how getting dirty can be really, really *nice* – in the 'mud, mud, glorious mud' way made famous by Flanders and Swann.* With its big double-page spreads slapped full of paint, the 'gooey, gloppy, mucky' magnificence of mud is generously celebrated in *Mud.* The narrative shows a child getting stuck right in as soon as the ground thaws after winter, squishing the mud between his clasped hands so that it oozes between his fingers. Delicious! He's barefoot, too.

For older children who don't want to get stains on their Converse, it's time for a dose of *Tarzan* – punchy prose, breathless storylines and the acknowledgement of the deep desire lurking within us all to swing through the trees on a vine.† The stories begin with Tarzan's birth in the east African jungle, where his parents have been shipwrecked. When they die, he's adopted by a tribe of great apes – in particular a she-ape named Kala, who takes pity

* By the way, you can find this ditty in the lovely collection *Here's a Little Poem*, edited by Jane Yolen and Andrew Fusek Peters, and illustrated by Polly Dunbar.

† Tarzan's ability to speak English and teach himself to read and write using the books he finds in his parents' hut may strike modern readers as a tad unrealistic. The racial stereotypes must also be taken with a healthy dose of grown-up explanation.

on the scrawny, hairless monkey. As we watch this simian boy grow up, desperately trying to be part of his clan but slowly discovering what sets him apart, we're treated to Burroughs's musings on what it means to be a savage versus a civilised human being. Tarzan's relationship to dirt lies at the heart of the exciting overlap. At night he sleeps embraced by the hairy Kala, and in the day he covers himself with the large, enveloping leaves of the 'elephant's ear'. His ablutions are jungle-drawn, of course, so Kala cleans his wounds with her tongue, and he swims in the river whenever he wants to see the colour of his skin again. In adolescence he has a moment of shame when, catching sight of his reflection in the river, he is shocked by his tiny nose and general hairlessness; and to make himself look more like his playmates, he cakes himself in mud. It's too itchy to keep on for long, but we can see that mud is his friend and it makes him feel better for a while. Encourage children to revel in the clean dirt of the great outdoors, discover their own inner beast, and worry about what's under their nails only when they come in from the jungle for tea.

disability, coping with

PB *Susan Laughs*
JEANNE WILLIS, ILLUSTRATED BY TONY ROSS

PB *Seal Surfer*
MICHAEL FOREMAN

CB *Knife*
RJ ANDERSON

YA *Accidents of Nature*
HARRIET MCBRYDE JOHNSON

Perhaps no group has been as inadequately or as cruelly represented in children's literature as those with physical or mental disabilities. Thankfully this situation is now changing, with disabled characters starting to appear in leading roles with the same range of personality characteristics as we'd expect in non-disabled characters. For children coping with a disability and those in their peer group, *Susan Laughs* offers the all-embracing message that someone with a disability is no different from anyone else in any other respect. Like all children, Susan laughs, sings, swims and enjoys a piggy-back ride from time to time – as well as feeling all the usual emotions. It's only on the very last page that we discover she uses a wheelchair as well.

Michael Foreman's *Seal Surfer*, with its beautiful illustrations of the coast, focuses on the things that a disabled boy can do, rather than the things he can't. We never know exactly what his disability is, except that he uses a wheelchair and sometimes crutches. We do know that he's freer and happier in the water than on land. Lying on his tummy on his board, the boy spends whole days riding the waves with his friends.

One day, he and his grandfather witness a seal pup being born. As the boy watches the pup grow up, a special bond forms between them – and when he gets into trouble in the water, the seal comes to his rescue. The final image of the boy, now grown himself and sitting by the sea with his own grandchildren, is full of optimism. Give this to children with a disability to inspire them to find the medium in which they excel.

An ancient, fairy-inhabited oak tree at the end of someone's garden may not seem a likely setting for a Young Adult story featuring disability issues, but *Knife* – the first in the Faery Rebels series – tackles the subject in a bold, refreshing way. The 'oaken folk' have been steadily depleted of their magical powers and vitality over the last few hundred years as a result of a virus known as 'the silence'. They do their best to avoid humans too, believing them to be an additional threat to their survival, but when Knife – a young and feisty hunter fairy – notices a young man moving around the garden in a large silver throne on wheels, she's intrigued. She discovers that Paul was all set for a brilliant career as a rower before losing the use of his legs in an accident; and when he attempts to drown himself in the pond, Knife temporarily assumes human form so that she can drag him to safety.

Paul doesn't thank her at first – he had wanted to be left to die. But as he and Knife get to know one another, enjoying conversations about art and creativity, he begins to appreciate life again. They even discover an intriguing form of interspecies love. The segues from fantasy to reality are handled well; as is the deft dismissal of the tired trope that those with disabilities may be more likely to see their lives as not worth living. When faced with the choice of regaining his full mobility but losing the love of Knife in the process, Paul chooses to remain disabled. That having a perfectly functioning body is not a pre-requisite for happiness is the joyous message, here declared convincingly and without sentimentality.

Accidents of Nature offers a harder-hitting exploration of what it's like to be disabled, through the eyes of seventeen-year-old Jean. Jean, who has cerebral palsy, arrives at Camp Courage in her wheelchair, dropped off by her loving parents. Her mum and dad have always contrived to keep things as 'normal' for Jean as they can, making light of her disability and ignoring it whenever possible. But at the ten-day camp she meets Sara, who has a very different approach. Sara calls the place 'Crip Camp', and she names Jean 'Spazzo'. Suddenly it is as if Jean has been awakened from a dream: how can she be truly herself if she doesn't embrace her difference?

Together, she and Sara plot to overthrow the regime at the camp, calling on all the 'crips' to come together and 'stomp out normalcy'. When they take over the talent contest, the camp coordinators are horrified, and the 'norms' in the audience – the mums and dads and sisters and brothers – squirm with discomfort. But for the girls their political coup is a triumph. By reclaiming these pejorative terms, they've helped to remove their slur. Jean is left elated and, for the first time, proud of her differences.

SEE ALSO: **different, feeling** • **frustration** • **understood, not feeling**

disappointment

[PB] *Zen Shorts*
JON J MUTH

[CB] *Journey to the River Sea*
EVA IBBOTSON

Most childhoods are littered with disappointments: closed ice-cream shops, no-show playmates, the wrong birthday present, or none at all (see: presents). Often there's nothing to be done except swallow the disappointment and move on. The story-within-the-story in *Zen Shorts* – featuring Stillwater, the giant Zen panda* – will help.

Michael, the eldest of the three siblings who live next door to Stillwater, worries about climbing trees. Quite reasonably, he suggests it would be bad to fall out and break a limb. 'Maybe,' is Stillwater's unexpected reply. In explanation, the panda delivers – in 'a slight panda accent'† – a Zen fable about a peasant farmer. When his horse runs away, the farmer's neighbours bemoan it as terribly bad luck. 'Maybe,' shrugs the farmer. When his horse turns up the next day with two wild horses in tow, the neighbours tell him how lucky he is, after all. 'Maybe,' he says. When his son falls off one of the wild horses and breaks his leg, he gives the same response. The broken leg turns out to indirectly save the young man's life. 'I get it,' says Michael. 'Maybe good luck and bad luck are all mixed up. You never know what will happen next.' This lovely epiphany, clear enough for children to understand, will not only dislodge the disappointment but open up the possibility of rescuing the moment itself.

Learning to bounce back from setbacks and make the best of things is surely one of life's most valuable skills. Maia, the heroine of *Journey to the River Sea*, models the skill to a T. When, still mourning the death of her parents, she is sent to live with distant cousins on a rubber plantation in Brazil, Maia has great hopes for her exotic new home. She can't wait to be

---

* Who we meet in other John J Muth books, including *Zen Ties* (see: old people, not appreciating).

† Reproduce *that*, grown-up reader.

surrounded by luxuriant jungle, colourful parrots, butterflies 'the size of saucers' and wise natives who can heal with plants. Most of all, she's excited about her new family, the Carters, whose twin girls, Beatrice and Gwendolyn, are her own age.

The rainforest lives up to all her expectations. But she could not have been more wrong about the Carters, who are ignorant bigots so afraid of catching something from the wildlife around them that they live in a haze of Lysol. It transpires that they had only taken Maia in for the money. 'It's not quite like I thought it would be, is it?' Maia says to her tough-but-true governess, Miss Minton, with heartbreaking understatement. But instead of allowing the disappointment to push her into despair, Maia gathers up her courage, pokes her head out the window and hears a familiar, whistled tune . . . Her discovery of a life even more full of wonder and unexpected friendship than she had hoped for leaves readers with the conviction that disappointments may, in fact, be new adventures in disguise.

SEE ALSO: **cheering up, needing**

distracted, being

SEE: **daydreaming, being accused of**

divorce

SEE: **parents who are splitting up, having**

dog, wanting a

SEE: **obsessions • pet, wanting a**

dreams, bad

SEE: **nightmares**

dress by yourself, refusing to

[ER] *The Story of Babar*
JEAN DE BRUNHOFF

Small children come in two varieties. There are those who can't wait to do everything by themselves, and those who see no reason to give up being carried, dressed, fed and washed by the various members of their domestic staff. If you feel it's high time a child started taking an interest in choosing and putting on their own clothes, introduce them to the sartorially savvy Babar.

When Babar's mother is shot by hunters, the frightened baby elephant runs away and finds himself in a town full of people and streets and buses. Immediately noticing a gentleman in a top hat and pin-stripes, he decides to equip himself with a fine suit – revealing an impressive ability to tune in to the mores of his new habitat. Quite by chance, he meets a rich old lady who offers to bankroll Babar's new wardrobe. The pride with which Babar models his eye-catching new pink shirt, emerald green suit, derby hat and spats is impossible not to absorb. Babar, it seems, is at heart a creature of sophisticated sensibilities, with tailoring needs to match. If you can cope with the gun-toting hunters and marrying-your-own-cousin-type eccentricities (this book dates back to 1933, after all), install a bunch of Babar books on the shelves and watch your own snappy little dresser evolve.

SEE ALSO: **contrary, being** • **granted, taking your parent for** • **laziness** • **spoilt, being**

drugs

[YA] *Junk*
MELVIN BURGESS

Every teenager will be offered drugs at some point unless they're kept locked in a tower. Give those you know an informed platform from which to step away from, or into, the world of stimulants with the eye-opening *Junk*. Together with Burgess's later *The Hit*, it does an impressive job of portraying the dangers in ways that readers will not quickly forget.

Teenager Tar has good reason to run away from home. His parents have physically abused and neglected him all his life (see: abuse). At fifteen he finally breaks free, moving into a squat in Bristol with some good-natured anarchists. When his girlfriend Gemma, just fourteen, joins him – looking for a 'big fat slice of life' – her impulsive nature soon sees them hooking up with the charismatic, junk-loving Lily. Lily introduces them both to heroin, first smoking it, then shooting up. The experience doesn't bring them euphoria so much as a natural-seeming pool of calm. Without either of them really noticing what's happening, Tar has become a dealer and Gemma a regular user.

Burgess's genius stroke is to provide understandable motives for all the characters involved and evoke our sympathy for each in turn. Though we follow events largely from Tar's and Gemma's points of view, we also see through the eyes of the tobacconist, Skolly – who takes pity on Tar when he first runs away – Lily's boyfriend Rob, Gemma's mum, and even Tar's dad. But however much sense the bigger picture makes, the outcome remains inevitable and grim. This story shows clearly and shockingly that shooting up heroin is a life choice with a dead end.

SEE ALSO: **adolescence** • **astray, being led** • **parents, strict** • **peer pressure**

dumped, being

YA *An Abundance of Katherines*
JOHN GREEN

At best, being dumped can knock a kid's confidence and leave them in the doldrums. At worst, it can send them running from relationships forever. Colin in *An Abundance of Katherines* has been dumped by nineteen girls, no less – all of them called Katherine – and it can't get much worse than that. An ex-child prodigy famous for having starred on TV show *Kranial Kidz*, the latest dumping has prompted him to take off on a road trip with his best friend Hassan in the hope of curing his heartbreak and Hassan's inertia.

They rapidly find themselves in the intriguingly named town of Gutshot, where they find unlikely employment with Hollis, owner of a tampon-string factory (yes, you read that right). They form an immediate connection with Hollis's daughter, Lindsey – despite the fact that she's going out with a total beefcake, also named Colin. When Colin-the-first decides to develop a mathematical equation with which to predict the length of a relationship, who will be the dumper, and who the dumpee, the beautiful Lindsey thinks he might be on to something. The question is, can Colin break the cycle of being dumped himself?

Their attempts at perfecting Colin's 'Theorum of Underlying Katherine Predictability' make for hilarious reading, involving as they do lengthy ruminations on the characteristics of Katherines, such as whether they like their coffee as they do their ex-boyfriends (bitter), and whether Colin can ever date somebody with a different name. But they are also touchingly heartfelt. The male friendships in the story are as important, if not more so, than the heterosexual ones: Hassan and Colin are pretty much joined at the hip throughout the story. Hassan, who comes from a devout Muslim family, also makes an excursion into the world of romance while in Gutshot – which adds fuel to their repartee. Examining being dumped, as it does, from every angle – and then some – this cathartic story will bring new hope, comradeship and laughter to the rejected party.

SEE ALSO: **disappointment** • **embarrassment** • **feelings, hurt**

dyslexia

SEE: **reading difficulties**

E IS FOR . . .

eating disorder

Girls Under Pressure
JACQUELINE WILSON, ILLUSTRATED BY NICK SHARRATT

How I Live Now
MEG ROSOFF

Proceed with caution when choosing fiction about eating disorders. Stories featuring characters for whom self-denial is a mantra, who discuss such tactics as where and how to hide food, which foods have the most calories, and how to throw up after eating can unwittingly act as a how-to guide. *Girls Under Pressure* – a sobering account of how an eating disorder can take over a life – is for teens you already know or suspect to be using food in a negative way, or who can read it within the safety of a small group and then engage in a discussion of the issues involved.

When one of her best friends gets spotted at a modelling competition, Ellie, a happy thirteen-year-old, starts to see herself as fat. Unfortunately, her step-mother happens to have just put herself on a diet, even though she is in good shape too. From that moment on, Ellie only eats when she really can't avoid it – such as on Friday nights, when it's the family tradition to get fish and chips. Soon she's desperately trying to hide the growls of her complaining stomach, struggling to concentrate in class, and feverishly joining her friend Zoe on a daily swimming routine. It's only when Zoe – who has herself become alarmingly skeletal – fails to come back to school after Christmas that Ellie recognises the depths to which she herself could sink. The story ends on a note of triumph – and serves as an encouragement to others to choose life, too; but not before providing a lot of detail about the grim road to self-starvation.

For older teens, the story of Daisy in *How I Live Now* will strike a more subtle chord. With an unhappy broken home behind her, Daisy – an anorexic American girl who has come to stay with her eccentric English cousins on the eve of a looming third World War – is surprised and delighted to find herself met at the airport by fourteen-year-old Edmond, driving the family jeep and smoking a cigarette. She immediately feels at home among this accepting, rule-breaking crew, ensconced in their beautiful country house with goats, chickens, sheep and a mother who's mostly getting on with her all-important anti-war work. Daisy is relieved when nobody asks her why she doesn't eat. But it's soon clear that her unusual cousin Edmond can read her thoughts even when she tries to hide them. After a while she explains to him the back-story to her eating disorder: how at first she stopped eating to avoid being 'poisoned' by her stepmother, and then found she liked feeling hungry and the way it drove the grown-ups 'insane'.

Soon Daisy and Edmond are discovering a hunger for each other and, without her really noticing, food stops being a battlefield for Daisy. When Edmond's mother becomes marooned in Oslo after a failed peace summit, the children enter a phase of idyllic lawlessness. But then the British Army requisition their house for troops, sending the children in different directions, and Daisy starts to know hunger of a wholly different kind . . . 'Wanting to be thin in a world where people were dying from lack of food struck even me as stupid,' Daisy tells us, realising that her cousin Piper's nine-year-old skinniness is not something to envy but a cause for concern. This passionate, powerful novel puts angsting about food into striking perspective.

SEE ALSO: **body image** • **confidence, lack of** • **fussy eater, being a** • **peer pressure**

embarrassment

YA *Eleanor and Park*
RAINBOW ROWELL

Embarrassment – and the resulting blush that advertises it – is the scourge of many an adolescent. No story sympathises more than *Eleanor and Park*, a modern-day spin on *Romeo and Juliet*. Park, the only Korean sixteen-year-old in Omaha, Nebraska, has long ago decided that the best way to survive school is to remain 'under the radar'. Red-haired, ample-bodied Eleanor, on the other hand, draws attention to herself just by stepping onto the school bus, with her crazy corkscrew curls and mismatched clothes. It's more because he can't bear the scrutiny she's inviting than out of any natural chivalry that Park offers up the seat next to him – usually vacant – and he keeps his headphones determinedly clamped to his ears all the way to school. But when, over the ensuing days, he realises this striking girl is reading his comics over his shoulder, he holds them open a bit wider, and turns the pages a bit more slowly . . . and, little by little, the two fall in love.

Their story is one that will resonate with self-conscious teens everywhere – from the initial hesitation and the *frisson* of the first touch, to the worry about who knows and what they're saying. Complicated on Eleanor's side by her feeling the need to tell her parents she's going round to a mythical 'Tina's' house, the story touches on many issues, including body image (see: body image) and racism (see: racism). But it's when Eleanor is bullied at school (see: bullied, being) that their love endears itself to us most fully. Knowing that Eleanor is embarrassed about the bright red gym suit she has to wear – a sort of mini onesie that, in Eleanor's case, barely covers her bottom – the school bully throws her real clothes down the toilet. Poor Eleanor has no choice but to walk the corridors in her onesie; and her blush is as deep as the suit is red when who should come in the other direction but Park.

Of course, seeing her in her sculpted, figure-hugging gym suit makes Park desire and love her all the more; and after that Eleanor never feels self-conscious with him again. 'Nothing was dirty with Park. Nothing could be shameful – because Park was the sun,' she tells us. Teens reading this story will learn to listen to the people that love them, not the ones who don't.

SEE ALSO: **feelings, hurt • feelings, not able to express your • shyness • wet dreams**

envy

PB *The Man*
RAYMOND BRIGGS

Sometimes kids feel that everybody else is better off than them and are left stewing miserably in a sea of envy. Briggs's wonderful graphic novel *The Man* shows them that it's not, in fact, very pleasant for the person being envied either when you feel this way.

The story tells of a boy, John, who wakes up one day to find a tiny, bearded man throwing missiles at his face. Naked and helpless, the man insists that John give him one of his socks to wear, cutting off the toe for his head and making more holes for his arms. The strange little man grumbles constantly about how little he has, envying John his house, his gadgets and all his nice things.

John does his best to help, and even uses his own pocket money to supply the man with the particular brand of marmalade he likes, but the man – who, though small, is also tyrannical* – just becomes more demanding still. It's only

* Briggs's man expresses viewpoints which at times are decidedly old-fashioned and even racist. Be sure to discuss these issues as they come up with your young reader.

once he's ready to leave that the man's eyes are finally opened to how kind John has been ('You wer mor kind to me than anny won els in the hole of my life,' he writes in a goodbye note). Kids will see that if only the man hadn't been so eaten up with envy all the time, they might have got along famously.

SEE ALSO: **manners, bad** • **moodiness**

exams

[ER] *Hooray for Diffendoofer Day!*
DR SEUSS, WITH SOME HELP FROM JACK PRELUTSKY AND LANE SMITH

[YA] *The Wind Singer*
WILLIAM NICHOLSON

Taking exams from a young age – with not just your own grades at stake but those of the whole school – is a stressful fact of life for today's kids. *Hooray for Diffendoofer Day!*, a delightful homage to Dr Seuss brought together by his long-time editor in New York and featuring Seuss-inspired words and pictures by poet Jack Prelutsky and illustrator Lane Smith, will help pop the anxiety bubble.

At the Diffendoofer school, the teaching style is unconventional, to say the least. Instead of English and maths, the kids learn listening, smelling, laughing and yelling, how to tie knots and why a hippo can't fly. Unsurprisingly, the kids love 'every single one' of their remarkable teachers. When the bushy-browed headmaster, Mr Lowe, announces that everyone has to take a test, 'To see who's learning such and such –/To see which school's the best' (think SATs), the kids are understandably anxious. If their school doesn't do well enough, it will be torn down and the kids sent to dreary Flobbertown school instead. Luckily, these kids have been taught to use their brains, not just to regurgitate facts, and they get the highest scores for miles around. Read it with a child in the lead-up to an exam and they'll be 'ninety-eight and ¾ per cent' guaranteed to succeed.

The pressure on kids in *The Wind Singer* – the second book in William Nicholson's Wind on Fire trilogy – could hardly be greater. Exams are taken from the age of two and the results determine what privileges you're given, what clothes you can wear, and where you're allowed to live. Luckily, twins Bowman and Kestrel Hath are the children of non-conformist parents who believe in poetry and the imagination more than the rules of the regime. And when Kestrel experiences a sudden revelation in the middle of an exam, she sets in motion a chain of events that will eventually bring the whole system crashing down. This empowering story will help readers put exams into perspective, while encouraging them to prepare for the challenge they pose – not just so that they do well, but so that they can move beyond them.

SEE ALSO: **anxiety • confidence, lack of • good at anything, feeling like you're no • mistake, frightened of making a • parents, pushy • school, not wanting to go to • sleep, unable to get to • worrying**

F IS FOR . . .

fair, it's not

[PB] *Looking After Louis*
LESLEY ELY, ILLUSTRATED BY POLLY DUNBAR

[YA] *Now Is the Time for Running*
MICHAEL WILLIAMS

Fairness is important to children, but it's not all that important to Life – or whoever's in charge of it. Grown-ups in the tricky position of having to explain that, sometimes, we just have to lump it will appreciate having a copy of *Looking After Louis* to hand, a picture book written to explain why preferential treatment is, on occasion, necessary. Louis, a new boy at school (see: school, being the new kid at), is 'not quite like' the other kids in the class, but the teachers never tell him off. For the little girl narrating the story it's deeply unfair that Louis can answer back in strange ways and be allowed to go and play football in the middle of a lesson – and she's not afraid to say so. Miss Owlie, her teacher, points out that she would feel pretty special, too, if she got behind Louis and supported him with his special needs. Polly Dunbar's expressive illustrations, full of her usual light touch, show us a world where unfairness rules but no longer riles.

It's not fair that fourteen-year-old Deo in *Now Is the Time for Running* has to look after his brother, Innocent, ten years his senior. Innocent has been touched since birth by an unnamed condition that makes him unable to cope in social situations. So when the rest of their family become victims of the atrocities in Zimbabwe which saw supporters of the Movement for Democratic Change (MDC) ruthlessly murdered by Mugabe's soldiers, Deo knows he has to take charge and somehow get the two of them to safety in South Africa.

To get there, they must first cross the crocodile-infested Limpopo river – the very river where the elephant got his trunk* – a hazardous enterprise that makes

* See 'The Elephant's Child' in the *Just So Stories* by Rudyard Kipling.

for one of the most gripping scenes in children's literature. On the other side they must avoid the thieves, or '*ghuma-ghuma*', known to prey on refugees. And then they must find a way to survive in a land where they are the foreigners or '*kwerekwere*', despised for taking all the jobs. Through all this running Deo has to think on his feet, cajoling and protecting the vulnerable Innocent at all times. At one point, he sings his brother a 'spirit song' from the old days to deliberately induce a fit, Innocent's eyes rolling back in his head and diverting the soldiers of the Zimbabwean government from their murderous intent.

Nothing is fair in Deo's life, but he doesn't let it affect him. Indeed, it's his ability to see what he does have and celebrate it – an attitude he has picked up from the delightful Innocent himself – that keeps him strong. Bring in this book to encourage a child to focus on what's good, instead of what is unfair.

SEE ALSO: **disappointment • loser, being a bad • sibling rivalry • sulking • umbrage, taking**

fairies, obsessed by

SEE: **obsessions**

fame, obsession with

SEE: **celebrity, wanting to be a**

family, having a different kind of

SEE: **adoption • different, feeling • foster care, being in • grandparents, living with • only child, being an • parents, same sex • single parent, having a • stepparent, having a**

family outings

PB *Zoo*
ANTHONY BROWNE

Perhaps it's the unrealistically high expectations. Or it's the effort of getting everyone out of the house on time. Or perhaps it's the inevitability of family tensions erupting among crowds and organised fun. But often family days out don't go as well as everyone hoped.

The two brothers in *Zoo*, with their pudding-bowl haircuts and sticky-out ears, are excited in the run-up to a day at the zoo. But things start to go wrong before they've even got there. First they get stuck in a traffic jam and the boys start squabbling on the back seat. Then Dad dumps his road rage on the ticket collector. And it takes them so long to find the animals they really want to see that they're tired and hungry before they've really begun. But there's also something else going on – something which was there in the family portrait on the cover, with the anxious-looking mother almost hidden behind the extra-large father in his garrulous rugby shirt and the upward tilt of his well-padded chin . . . It's Browne's bold illustrations which provide the rest of the puzzle pieces. For the child who wonders if it's just their family who has dud days out, this story will show them that's not the case. And for the grown-up trying to smile through disaster it's a reminder that, sometimes, it's better not to pretend things are OK when they're actually not.

SEE ALSO: **car, being in the • disappointment • museums, not wanting to visit • over-tired, being • parents, embarrassing • sibling rivalry • tantrums**

fan, being a

SEE: **celebrity, wanting to be a**

father, being a teenage

SEE: **pregnancy, teenage**

Father Christmas

SEE: **magic, loss of belief in**

feelings, hurt

📖 *Desmond and the Very Mean Word*
ARCHBISHOP DESMOND TUTU AND DOUGLAS CARLTON ABRAMS, ILLUSTRATED BY AG FORD

Few people can understand what it's like to have your feelings hurt as well as a black man living in a South African township during the Apartheid years. *Desmond and the Very Mean Word* was born from the experience of someone who was there: Archbishop Desmond Tutu.

When a group of white kids call Desmond a mean word (happily, we never hear what it is), Desmond's instinct is to hurl abuse back – which, the next day, he does. It makes him feel better at first, but it leaves a bitter taste in his mouth. The local priest, Father Trevor, tells him that getting the white boys back only leads to more reprisals – and that when we hurt someone else, it hurts us too. For the next few days Desmond sees the mean word everywhere: on the pages of his book, and on the face of the moon when, one night, he doesn't even feel like talking to Father Trevor. Why, wonders Desmond, should he have to take the first step when it's the other boys who should be apologising to *him*?

The answers, when they come, make for compelling reading. AG Ford's moving illustrations, which capture the buried and not-so-buried tensions in these 'bad old days' with skilful realism, show a child learning to liberate himself from his hurt feelings and turn enemies into friends.

SEE: **bullied, being • cheering up, needing • feelings, hurting someone's • feelings, not able to express your • sibling rivalry • sulking**

feelings, hurting someone's

📖 *The Snow Goose*
PAUL GALLICO, ILLUSTRATED BY ANGELA BARRETT

Sometimes a child does or says something to a sensitive friend that causes that friend to pull away. If the friend doesn't express their feelings, the child may never know what happened and why they are no longer close. Few stories evoke empathy for the hidden, unspoken suffering of others as well as *The Snow Goose*, Paul Gallico's haunting tale of love and loss set on the desolate Essex marshes.*

Artist Philip Rhayader has made his home in a disused lighthouse on these lonely tidal flats because of his love for 'wild and hunted things' – the seagulls,

---

* Although this is a picture book, it is word-heavy and heartbreak-heavy. Read it aloud to kids who you feel can cope.

teal, curlews and geese that come down from Iceland each October in great, honking skeins. He keeps a collection of tamed birds in an enclosure and makes masterful paintings of them. But he's also here because he himself feels hunted. Hunchbacked and with a claw-like left wrist, he knows that the people in the nearby town find him grotesque, and rather than be hurt every time his overtures of friendship are not returned, he opts to live apart.

One day a twelve-year-old girl, as 'eerily beautiful as a marsh faerie', comes to him with a wounded snow goose in her arms. Terrified to find herself face to face with the 'ogre', she hands the goose over and flees – but the next day she comes back to see how the goose is faring. Over the winter she and Rhayader care for the goose together, with Fritha slowly overcoming her fear of the lonely hunchback. When the goose flies away for the summer, so too does Fritha, but each winter both goose and girl return. Gradually Fritha learns the 'lore' of the birds, and Rhayader the joy of another's company – and a deep, emotional charge builds between them. It's only when, several years later, Rhayader hears of the soldiers marooned on the beaches of Dunkirk and sets sail to join in the rescue that Fritha realises how she really feels about him. Yes, this story will break your heart – for the unexpressed love between Fritha and Rhayader, and for the snow goose, loyal to the end. But there's an enduring lesson in the importance of compassion, too. Despite all the years of being shunned, Rhayader still puts the suffering of others before himself. Children exposed to this story will be encouraged to think more deeply about what might have happened when a friend withdraws. Is there anything that they might have inadvertently said to upset them – and anything that they might now be able to do to make things alright?

SEE ALSO: **beastly, being** • **bully, being a**

feelings, not able to express your

PB *The Hurt*
TEDDI DOLESKI

CB *The Peppermint Pig*
NINA BAWDEN

For the small child who takes their bruised feelings off somewhere quiet and nurses them in private, we recommend *The Hurt*, a simple but effective little story that can be as therapeutic for buttoned-up grown-ups as it is for kids (see: parents who can't talk about emotions, having). When Justin is called names by his friend Gabriel, he doesn't retaliate or tell Gabriel how it makes him feel. He just walks away, taking his wound with him. His 'Hurt' feels like a 'big round stone, all cold and hard', which he can hold in his hands. He keeps it in his room, where he adds other hurts to it – and in the simple black-and-white drawings we see the Hurt grow bigger, developing eyes and a mouth like a space hopper. Soon Justin's Hurt is taking up so much room it's squeezing him out – and that's when he finally tells his dad what upset him. For children who haven't yet discovered that the best way to deal with damaged feelings is to talk them out, this story can effect a seismic shift.

Of course it takes bravery to express one's feelings to the full – and a safe audience. Nine-year-old Poll in *The Peppermint Pig* has just the right combination of close-to-the-surface feelings and pluck to allow for ease of expression – plus a mother who's able to listen. When their father decides to seek his fortune in America, Poll, her three older siblings and their mother move in with two aunts in a Norfolk village. Here they must deal with a host of new challenges including, delightfully, the arrival of a little pig, going cheap, which runs amok in the house as their pet.

Poll's absolute refusal to let anything *not* be out in the open is there from the beginning. When her siblings George and Lily share a private look over her head, she instantly demands to be told what they know and she doesn't. When her brother Theo is bullied, she lowers her head and charges the culprit like an angry bull. And when the pig, Johnnie, wolfs down a tray of homemade hot cross buns and Poll's mother drives him out to the hen house with a broom, Poll is furious at her mother for being so cruel. 'I hate you,' she shouts, and means it, the feeling swelling inside her chest 'like a balloon'. Her mother isn't in the least flustered; Poll gets both her hot head and her bravery from her in the first place.

When her mother finds herself forced to make a difficult decision regarding a debt at the butcher's, Aunt Harriet knows that Poll will find it hard to accept. 'I don't care what you say, Emily, some children feel more than others . . .' Poll overhears her aunt saying. Poll may or may not feel more than others – but she certainly expresses more. For her healthy ability to give voice to rage and frustration, as well as happiness, Poll is an exhilarating role model for the emotionally pent-up child.

SEE ALSO: **heard, not feeling** • **shyness** • **small, feeling** • **stand up for yourself, not feeling able to** • **sulking** • **understood, not being**

fibs, telling

SEE: **lying**

fidgety to read, being too

HULA!

For some kids, sitting down to read is just too static. Teach restless readers to hula. We ourselves have mastered the art of reading while hula-hooping to great effect. Challenge them to hula for half an hour while reading and watch while they hula their way through the whole of *Harry Potter*, *Horrid Henry* or *His Dark Materials*. If the hoop doesn't take off in your household, encourage your young charges to pioneer other reading-in-motion activities: reading while dangling upside down, reading on horseback,* reading while climbing a tree and reading while paddling a canoe.

fire, playing with

SEE: **pyromania**

first kiss

YA *Angus, Thongs and Full-frontal Snogging*
LOUISE RENNISON

First kisses can be awkward. Not only do you not know where to put your tongue, but also your hands, nose and feet. All teenagers should equip themselves with this first volume of the Confessions of Georgia Nicolson series, all ten of which make ideal companions to the adolescent entering the dating game (see: dating). Fourteen-year-old Georgia gets lots of kisses from her three-year-old sister Libby. But she's pretty sure that Libby 'isn't a lesbian', so that doesn't count. Her best friend Jas has already kissed a boy and said it felt like a 'warm jelly filling', and Georgia is becoming increasingly anxious that she's the only one of her friends who hasn't yet had a go. Then Jas mentions that seventeen-year-old Peter Dyer makes himself available for kissing lessons on a first-come, first-served basis each afternoon at his house. Georgia reckons she'd rather stick her head in a bag of eels – but

* Preferably when the horse is not galloping.

he's good-looking 'in a Boyzone sort of way' and, as it turns out, they get through quite a lot in half an hour. She's not the only one who wants to pick up kissing tips: as she leaves, she sees her friend Mabs waiting for her turn on the landing . . . Georgia's teenage trials and tribulations – covering everything from boys and bras to body hair – are a compulsory demystifier for the modern teen.

SEE ALSO: **dating** • **embarrassment** • **grow up, impatient to** • **innocence, loss of** • **mistake, frightened of making a** • **scared, being** • **virginity, loss of** • **worrying**

first love

YA *Blankets*
CRAIG THOMPSON

YA *The Fault in Our Stars*
JOHN GREEN

YA *Annie on My Mind*
NANCY GARDEN

When a teen falls in love for the first time, it's the best thing that's ever happened to them. But it can quickly become the worst, because however much it may feel as if it's going to last forever, it probably won't. The right story can help kids to cherish their first love while it lasts – and try to ensure that it leaves them with mostly happy memories.

For newly stricken boys, we suggest leaving the graphic novel *Blankets* outside the bedroom door. Craig – a brooding, skinny boy with a fine, poetic nose – is bullied at home as well as at school (see: bullied, being) and has always felt at odds with the world. So when he meets Raina at Christian summer camp – both of them nervously tucking a strand of long hair behind an ear – we know how deeply he's likely to fall. Their relationship is tender and playful and honest; and though the complications of living far apart does for them in the end (and it's no spoiler to say so), they ride a number of challenges along the way, including coping with each of their challenging families. Thompson's black-and-white drawings, as full of movement as they are of sadness and the lonely spaces of the human heart, will haunt young readers just as Raina continues to haunt Craig once the relationship's over; but the memory of their love remains free of bitterness. As a love story, it offers an innocent yet meaningful model of how new love can be.

First-love stories from a girl's point of view don't come any more heart-rending than *The Fault in Our Stars*. Sixteen-year-old Hazel – sassy, dry and on 'best friends' terms with her parents – is fully aware that her cancer is terminal. So when she meets the smoky-voiced Augustus Waters at a cancer support group, we know their story is going to be intense. This may be first love but, for Hazel at least, it'll most likely be her last.

There's an honesty and wit to their interactions from the start. 'Are you serious?' Hazel asks, not missing a beat when Augustus takes out a cigarette. Augustus shrugs and explains that the cigarette is just a metaphor, and by not lighting it he's refusing to give it its power. That's when Hazel taps the window of her mum's waiting car and tells her to go on home. Hazel might have lungs that 'suck at being lungs' and be forced to wear an oxygen-feeding cannula in her nostrils at all times, and Augustus might have only one non-artificial leg (osteosarcoma having taken the other), but it doesn't stop them going to Amsterdam to meet Hazel's all-time favourite author, Peter Van Houten. Their genuine connection – and the way both sets of parents keep a respectful yet supportive distance – is one to which all teens and their grown-ups can aspire.

The love affair in *Annie on My Mind* is all the more special for being unexpected and will reassure those finding themselves falling for someone of the same gender. When two seventeen-year-old girls catch each other's eye at the Metropolitan Museum of Art in New York, it's a real Cupid's arrow moment. 'We looked at each other, really looked, I mean for the first time, and for a moment or two I don't think I could have told anyone my name, let alone where I was,' Liza recollects in a letter to Annie a year later. It takes a while for the relationship to develop, neither being sure if it's what the other wants. But at Coney Island one day, Liza puts her arm around Annie to keep her warm and, before either of them know what's happening, Annie's 'soft and gentle mouth' is on Liza's. Liza wrestles with her homosexuality, feeling it's 'sinful' – while also knowing that nothing has ever felt so right.

We infer that something has forced them to be apart – hence the need for the letter – and realise that, this being the early Eighties, they have felt the need to keep their relationship secret. But the wise words of two female teachers from their school who they've accidentally outed keep them strong: 'Don't let ignorance win, let love,' their teachers say – a philosophy we have reason to believe that Liza and Annie will follow.

SEE ALSO: **betrayal** • **gay, not sure if you are** • **innocence, loss of** • **virginity, loss of** • **wet dreams**

first sex

SEE: **pregnancy, teenage** • **virginity, loss of**

fitting in, not

SEE: **different, feeling**

flat-chested, being

Are You There, God? It's Me, Margaret
JUDY BLUME

When breasts are budding all around you, it's frankly galling to remain as flat as a pancake. Girls of eleven up wonder when their womanliness will kick in, particularly if their friends are already sporting matching bras and knickers in the changing room. Some girls, of course, will remain happily indifferent to their future bosoms, and others will positively hate them. But waiting for physical signs of adolescence to materialise can be excruciating either way.

The perfect companion to this waiting game is the American queen-of-teen Judy Blume, whose ground-breaking *Are You There, God? It's Me, Margaret,* published in 1970, paved the way for so many other YA novels dealing with the concerns of pubescence. The ultimate cry of angst over periods, breasts and boys, it tells the story of twelve-year-old Margaret, newly moved from New York City to the New Jersey suburbs. Far, now, from her beloved granny – who provided wisdom and distance from her loving but perhaps overly involved parents – Margaret starts writing to God every night, telling him about her worries. When will her breasts start to grow? Will her bust-enhancing exercises get results? Will she kiss a boy soon and, if so, how (see: first kiss)?

Fundamental to Margaret's turmoil is the question of which God she is talking to – the Christian or the Hebrew, her open-minded parents having deliberately left it up to her to choose her religious affiliation – and the story is set over the year she gives herself to decide. Meanwhile, she goes to parties where couples take turns to kiss for two minutes in a cupboard, practises with panty-liners even before she gets her period (see: periods), and pads out her bra with mounds of cotton wool. All of which today's tweens are as likely to relate to as those of the Seventies – which is why *Are You There, God?* has survived the test of time. At one point, twenty-one unattended minors at a house party start by flicking mustard at the ceiling and end by snogging each other. It's this lovely capturing of the lurches between childhood and adolescence which makes Blume so good for girls on the verge of it all.*

---

* Wait a few years before moving on to Blume's excellent portrayal of a first sexual relationship in *Forever*.

SEE ALSO: **adolescence** • **body image** • **bras** • **bullied, being** • **embarrassment** • **gay, not sure if you are** • **grow up, impatient to** • **transgender, feeling you are** • **worrying**

flies, fear of

SEE: **animals, fear of**

flu

SEE: **bed, having to stay in**

football, addicted to

SEE: **obsessions**

forgive, reluctance to

YA *The Absolutely True Diary of a Part-time Indian*
SHERMAN ALEXIE

That there is a grace and dignity to forgiveness that exalts both parties comes across with wonderful clarity in this laugh-out-loud, semi-autobiographical, cartoon-peppered story. Junior – known as 'Globe' due to his unusually large head – is skinny, wears glasses (see: glasses, having to wear) and is prone to having seizures. He also has ten extra teeth crowding his mouth – which, in his view, makes him 'ten teeth past human'. Being an American Indian living on a 'rez', he is used to being given what he calls the 'standard Indian treatment' – such as being given half the painkillers that white people get at the dentist's on the grounds that Indians feel only 'half as much pain'. His own people are generally drunk, especially his father; his sister has locked herself in the basement since leaving high school; and at school he's treated as a punch bag by kids and adults alike (see: bullied, being). Yet Junior has a lot of brains packed into his colossal head and dreams of a future beyond the rez. So when he decides to join the white boys' school twenty miles up the road – a school which will give him considerably better prospects – he knows he's in for a whole new range of torture from his fellow rez dwellers, and no doubt the white boys, too.

Sure enough, the white kids mock his name and his race – and at first Junior fights back the only way he knows: with his fists. But gradually, and with the help of his grandmother – one of the few people on the rez never to have touched a drop of alcohol – he realises he will have more power if he forgives. After all, forgiveness is something he knows about. If he hadn't been able to forgive his own country for keeping the American Indians on no-hope reservations, equipped with textbooks thirty years out of date, how would he ever have escaped one? When his father shoots Junior's dog because they can't afford the vet fees, Junior howls for days – then lets it go. When his classmates stamp on his head, Junior does a tribal chicken dance that helps him forgive them. When his best friend Rowdy spurns him for his treachery at leaving the rez, Junior slides cartoons under his door until he gets a response. If Junior and his grandmother can forgive an entire nation, teens reading this story will be moved to forgive on a smaller scale.

SEE ALSO: **betrayal** • **feelings, hurt** • **sulking** • **umbrage, taking**

foster care, being in

PB *Murphy's Three Homes*
JAN LEVINSON GILMAN, ILLUSTRATED BY KATHY O'MALLEY

CB *One for the Murphys*
LYNDA MULLALY HUNT

A child in foster care is a child on an emotional rollercoaster; and stories which reflect back some typical fostering experiences will help them feel less alone. The puppy in *Murphy's Three Homes* is moved three times before he finds a place he can stay. In his first foster home – a place full of human legs, other animals, toys and crawling babies, from dog's-eye level – nobody has time for him. In the second, the couple find him too boisterous. In the third, the couple laugh when he jumps on them with his muddy paws, but when he tips over the rubbish bin, he's frightened and runs away before anyone has a chance to kick him out. Distraught, the couple go looking for him – and they're overjoyed when they find him. Finally, some owners who are in it for the long haul . . . Murphy experiences a range of emotions in the course of the story, including loneliness, shame, anger and uncertainty – all of which we can read on his expressive doggy face. But because they're transposed onto a dog, we can explore them without attaching them too fixedly to the fostering experience. Helpful for both young children in foster care and their foster families, it's a story that emphasises the importance of being accepted, boisterousness and all.

Older kids in foster care may relate to the mixed feelings of twelve-year-old Carley Connors in *One for the Murphys*. When we first meet Carley, she can't stop shaking. Behind her is the hospital in which her mother lies recovering from a fight with Carley's stepfather, Dennis. Ahead lies her new family, the Murphys – and Carley doesn't hold out much hope for them. She's never been in foster care before, but she's not expecting it to be pleasant.

When she finds a smiling, together-seeming mother of three who seems to have time to sit and listen to anything she wants to say, Carley's not so much relieved as unnerved. Supper for Carley is usually soup eaten straight from the can, but here everyone gathers round the table while Mrs Murphy serves up homemade lasagne. For her clothes, she's used to raiding the Salvation Army dropbox, but Mrs Murphy takes her to the mall and gets her whatever she wants. Her own mother has always told her that crying's for 'suckers', but Mrs Murphy tells her it's OK to cry. And she's shocked when Mrs Murphy, who seems so strong, cries herself. The whole family, she decides, is 'freakish' and she reckons she'd feel more at home if she was made to sleep in the bath, like her mum used to make her do when they had friends to stay.

Little by little, though, Carley discovers how it feels to be appreciated, and when she's grounded for playing hooky from school she can't help smiling – no one's ever cared enough to punish her before (see: punished, being). And when she overhears Mr and Mrs Murphy arguing, and realises this family isn't as squeaky clean as she had thought, she starts to think she might just fit in after all. By the end, when her mother wants her back, Carley has a tough decision to make. This story offers a realistic model of what a loving home looks like,* and reassures readers who, like Carley, feel unworthy of belonging to one.

SEE ALSO: **adoption** • **loneliness** • **parents, having** • **sibling, having to look after a little**

friends, feeling that you have no

[PB] *Little 1*
ANN RAND, ILLUSTRATED BY PAUL RAND
(continued)

Few things are more dispiriting for a kid than the feeling that they have no friends. If this ails a child of your ken, leap in with stories that show how likely it is that a friend will suddenly appear when they're

* For another positive depiction of a loving foster home, see: nightmares.

🄲🄱 *The Wind in the Willows*
KENNETH GRAHAME, ILLUSTRATED BY EH SHEPARD

🅈🄰 *The Sisterhood of the Travelling Pants*
ANN BRASHARES

least expecting it. *Little 1* takes the intrinsic solitariness of the number '1' as a metaphor for someone in need of a playmate – and dresses him up with a pointy nose, a green striped jumper and a little triangular red cap. Despite early rejection from two rude pears in a dish – which already have each other for company, thanks very much – Little 1 shows great strength of character by continuing to approach all the other numbers in turn, even coming up with ideas of what might be in it for them. To the '8 stiff-backed books' giving '8 cross looks', he suggests 'If I stand in line,/We could then be 9.' Only when the nine frisky fish on the next page ignore him does Little 1 begin to wonder if there's something the matter with him. Luckily, a 'bright red hoop' comes rolling by just in the nick of time – and we all know what a one and a zero can make when they get together . . . Originally published in 1962, this elegant book by one of the most influential graphic designers of the 20th century has long been celebrated as an introduction to the concept of 'how many', and how numbers, together, make a ladder you can climb. It's certainly great for that, but it's also a fine demonstration of how reaching out to potential new friends can be a fraught business (see: feelings, hurt) and that it's important not to give up. That things end so well for brave Little 1 sends the encouraging message, backed up as it is by mathematical inevitability, that perseverance pays off.

Deciding to like being on your own can be an excellent temporary solution for a child who feels that they have no friends (see: alone, wanting to be left). Another is to adopt some fictional friends – ideally some who really know how to make a new friend welcome. Mole, in the eternally appealing *The Wind in the Willows*, begins the tale with no friends at all and does not particularly lament the fact. But when he feels the 'divine discontent and longing' of the spring, he leaves his hole in search of adventure (see: adventure, in need of an). Before he knows it, he's moved in with Rat and is being introduced to the life of the river.

Rat, he sees, is an energetic, social type, like the river itself – a 'sleek, sinuous, full-bodied animal, chasing and chuckling, gripping things with a gurgle and leaving them with a laugh' only to fling himself 'on fresh playmates that shook themselves free, and were caught and held again'. You can see why Mole becomes so fiercely loyal to Rat, and soon they go off on holiday with Rat's friend Toad and his canary-yellow gypsy wagon. Through his adventures, Mole grows into a more rounded and resilient individual, and by the time he's called on to defend Toad's mansion from the weasels and stoats, he's as brave and noble a friend as anyone could wish for, able to love and be loved in return. *The Wind in the Willows* shows friendship in the best possible light, and the sort of friends to look out for: those who are loyal, kind, good at sharing and exhibit a sheer exhilaration in life ('Poop poop!'). After all, finding the right friends is one of the most important skills in life.

Teens wondering how to be part of a gang will feel they already are when they read *The Sisterhood of the Travelling Pants*, the first in the Summers of the Sisterhood series. Carmen, Lena, Tibby and Bridget like to say they've been friends since before they were born, their mums having met at an antenatal aerobics class. They've always spent summers together; but now, aged fifteen, they face their first summer apart. Lena and her sister are heading to Greece to stay with their grandparents; Bridget is going to soccer camp in Mexico; Carmen will summer with her much missed dad in South Carolina; and Tibby gets the booby prize of staying at home in Bethesda, Maryland, working at Wallman's supermarket. Before they all go off in different directions, they find a pair of jeans that fits them all at a thift store and decide to share the 'pants' over the summer, each wearing them for a week, then sending them on, unwashed, with a letter detailing everything that happened while they were wearing them. It'll be their way of staying linked.

These weeks turn out to be rites of passage for all the girls. Lena falls in love with a handsome but tragic Greek boy; Bridget flirts with her much older soccer coach; Carmen's hopes for one-on-one time with her dad are dashed when she discovers he's engaged to a woman with two kids of her own; and Tibby, while making her 'suckumentary' film about the horrors of Wallman's, meets a twelve-year-old girl with leukaemia. Teens will be deeply drawn into their sagas of first love, parental let-down and loss, and feel less lonely in the company of this fictional gang. Perhaps, too, the germ of what makes a bonded gang will take root.

SEE ALSO: **imaginary friend, embarrassed about having an • loneliness • only child, being an**

friends, finding it hard to make

PB *Friends*
ROB LEWIS
(continued)

It's all very well telling a child to go and make friends, but what if they don't know how to go about it? The excellent, down-to-earth *Friends* illustrates a common mistake. When Oscar and his mother move house (see: moving house), the dungaree-clad rabbit goes in search of new playmates who share his passion for swimming. First he meets Ernie, but Ernie likes playing in the junkyard. Then he meets Zoe, but Zoe only likes wrestling. One by one, he

[CB] *Jennifer, Hecate, Macbeth, William McKinley and Me, Elizabeth*
EL KONIGSBURG

[YA] *Why We Took the Car*
WOLFGANG HERRNDORF

rejects all the rabbits in the vicinity until his mother suggests he might do better if he tries joining in with what they're doing instead, at least to begin with – a lesson many of us would do well to take to heart.

Sometimes children have friends out of school, but not in school, or vice versa, and it can be hard to bring them from one context into another. Those in this position will relate to Elizabeth in *Jennifer, Hecate, Macbeth, William McKinley and Me, Elizabeth,* who is new not just to school (see: school, being the new kid at) but also to town. Knowing no one, she has to walk to and from school by herself every day – until, one day, she sees a leg dangling out of a tree. 'You're going to lose that shoe!' she shouts, in what she hopes will be a 'stout red' sort of voice but which comes out as a 'thin blue' cry. 'Witches never lose anything,' comes the unexpected reply.

Thus begins an unusual friendship with the mysterious Jennifer, Elizabeth playing the part of apprentice to Jennifer's witch as they cast spells and make potions and predictions – but only on Saturdays. At school, they pretend not to know each other at all. It's only once they've survived a near break-up over a toad that the two feel ready to hold hands at school. Sometimes it's easier to make friends without everybody looking.

Some kids build up an aloof exterior that becomes hard for others to crack. This is the case with the hero of *Why We Took the Car*. Fourteen-year-old Mike is considered boring by his classmates – and he'd be the first to agree. Once he wrote an essay about his alcoholic mother walking around the kitchen with a carving knife and became briefly intriguing – even earning the nickname 'psycho'. But his popularity tailed off when he failed to live up to the name. When Tatiana, on whom he has a massive crush (see: first love), invites everyone to her party but him, he despairs. With his mother booked into rehab (yes, his essay told the truth) and his dad absconding on a dubious business trip, he's left alone in his fancy, air-conditioned house with not a friend in sight. He fills the time by obsessively drawing pictures of Tatiana.

In fact, Mike *has* been noticed by someone: Tschick, the new Russian guy who thinks Mike's cheap Chinese jacket with the white dragon is 'supercool'. When Tschick turns up at Mike's house in a strange car and suggests they crash Tatiana's party and give her one of Mike's portraits – and then keep going all the way to Romania – Mike is horrified. It's way too embarrassing to give Tatiana one of his drawings. But Tschick points out that 'nothing is embarrassing in a stolen Lada', and Mike can see he has a point.

They deliver the drawing to Tatiana in the Lada with aplomb, executing a perfect 180-degree turn in front of their dumbfounded classmates. Then, following their instincts rather than a map, they head to Romania. The exhilarating coming-of-age romp makes heroes out them both, albeit heroes in a spot of trouble. This story shows that it's often when you're at your lowest ebb that an unexpected buddy appears. And that you just need a chink in your armour – or a tacky Chinese jacket – to let them in.

SEE ALSO: **different, feeling** • **embarrassment** • **friends, feeling you have no** • **shyness**

friend, having a naughty

SEE: **astray, being led**

friends your parents don't approve of, having

When your child brings home friends you don't approve of, it's not really their problem.

CURE FOR GROWN-UPS [PB] *The Wonderful Adventures of Suzuki Beane*, SANDRA SCOPPETTONE, ILLUSTRATED BY LOUISE FITZHUGH

So you don't like your child's friends? Beg, borrow or persuade someone to republish this irreverent gem from the Sixties, which shows how the preconceptions of the grown-ups can get in the way of the innocent friendships of childhood. Delightfully, it's the supposedly liberal hipster parents from Greenwich Village – introduced not as Mum and Dad but 'hugh' and 'marcia' (they're too hip for capitals) by their daughter, suzuki (ditto) – who fail to 'dig' their daughter's friendship with Henry, a neatly dressed boy from the Upper East Side. We love this book for Louise Fitzhugh's sketches of suzuki's dad, hugh, looking bearded and hungover; for the excerpt from his Ginsberg-esque poetry ('In/The/Beginning/There WAS an end,' lovingly quotes his daughter); and for the intense marcia's unmotherly critique of her daughter's stick-figure drawings as 'too representational'. If you're guilty of omitting to get to know your kids' friends before disapproving of them, you'll experience a jolt of recognition at the speed with which hugh and marcia write poor Henry off as insufficiently progressive. Let your kids keep their friends, and instead boot your prejudices out on the street.

SEE ALSO: **astray, being led** • **peer pressure**

FRIEND, HAVING A NAUGHTY

frightened, being

SEE: **scared, being**

frustration

[PB] *Caps for Sale*
ESPHYR SLOBODKINA

For the child too young to be proficient at the many skills required to get through an average day, frustration is a familiar side dish. And this tale of a pedlar who loses his cool when a bunch of monkeys steal the caps stacked neatly on top of his head captures the *'Arrgh!'* feeling exactly. The pedlar – normally so calm and poised (he has to be, carrying his wares where he does) – is enjoying forty winks against a tree trunk when the monkeys play their rotten trick. Scampering back up into the branches of the tree with their stolen caps, the monkeys taunt him by copying his every move, as monkeys are wont to do. When the pedlar wags his finger at them, they wag their fingers back. When he shakes his fist at them, they shake their fists back. When he stamps his foot, they stamp their feet too. Eventually, his exasperation gets the better of him and the pedlar slams his own cap on the ground. At which point, of course, the monkeys follow suit – and the crisis is resolved. The full-page illustrations in flat, printed tan, red and white echo the timelessness of this folktale retelling. Sometimes a little expressive body language – as long as it doesn't hurt anyone or anyone's things – can be enough to vent the frustration and get the desired result.

SEE ALSO: **anger** • **wrong, everything's going**

fussy eater, being a

[CB] *Five on a Treasure Island*
ENID BLYTON

[CB] *The Kin*
PETER DICKINSON

Few things inspire such fury in a grown-up than seeing their lovingly prepared food poked and prodded, then left on the plate uneaten. Rescue the moment by bringing a light-hearted picture book to the table – see our list of the best that follows. Not only will this help avert a battle with your fussy eater (see: arguments, getting into) but, with luck, it'll entice the child to eat their peas and carrots on your behalf. And if you're not above using it, there's always blackmail . . . (see: bargaining, endless).

Unfortunately, just when you think you've got through the worst of it, your kids go to school and discover a whole new world of fussiness. If this happens, bring in some good old-fashioned attitudes, courtesy of Enid Blyton.* Descriptions of meals abound in Blyton's oeuvre: always homemade, and generally whipped up by someone called 'Cook', food is something to be gobbled up with relish. Our favourite menus are those found in the Famous Five books, in which Julian, Dick, George, Anne and Timmy the dog find themselves in a series of marvellous adventures in various parts of the English countryside on a schedule that revolves around mealtimes. These four kids and their dog can't go for more than a few hours without a hearty meal, and modern eyes will widen at their rhapsodic appreciation of a slice of homemade quiche ('Thanks *awfully*'), or a freshly picked apple. When they're trapped by a bunch of gold robbers in a cave on Kirrin Island – the island George has inherited from her parents – they somehow still manage to dig out a picnic of home-cured ham sandwiches and juicy tomatoes from their knapsacks and tuck in with gusto. Thus fortified, they swiftly come up with a cunning escape plan that snares the stupid adults in their own trap.

If the Famous Five fail to convince, try the fossilised four. In *The Kin*, a quartet set at the dawn of humankind, Suth, Noli, Ko and Mana are the last of the Moonhawks, their families having been wiped out by murderous strangers. Naturally nomadic, they roam the desert in search of a 'Good Place' where they can find food and water and safety – a responsibility that lands largely on Suth, even though he's not yet a man. Finding food is a daily concern and anything even vaguely edible goes into their mouths, be it termite, grub or caterpillar (pinching off the bitter head first, of course). For snacks, they nibble on grass seeds and raw tubers that they've hacked from the hard, dry ground with their digging sticks. When they're really lucky, they gnaw on the leathery, sun-dried leg of a fox. After living with 'The Kin' through four gripping books, a child will be positively disappointed whatever's on their plate is not wriggling.

---

* Spurned for over two decades for her un-PC take on girls, non-Caucasians and children not wealthy enough to go to boarding school, Blyton in her re-edited form has enjoyed a robust revival in the last few years. You'll still find toe-curling bits if you read them aloud – as with other children's books dating from before about 1990. You may prefer to scan ahead and edit as you go. Alternatively, use them to trigger an edifying discussion about how much attitudes have changed (e.g. 'I'm only a girl,' says Jane. Discuss.).

CURE FOR GROWN-UPS  *Eat Your Peas* KES GRAY, ILLUSTRATED BY NICK SHARRATT

The lengths to which the mother in *Eat Your Peas* will go to get the 'little green balls' into the stomach of her progeny Daisy are, frankly, embarrassing. She starts off promising ice cream and by the end has thrown in a couple of new bicycles, an elephant and, most humiliatingly of all, her right to insist on Daisy's baths and bedtimes. Bribery is never a pretty spectacle. But if you're going to wage a daily battle for a clean plate, we recommend going for the ludicrous as a tactic. Kids will put almost anything in their mouths if you make them laugh enough, and with practice and a good aim, you can even throw in a few extra vegetables while they guffaw.

THE TEN BEST PICTURE BOOKS FOR FUSSY EATERS

- PB *The Runaway Dinner* ALLAN AHLBERG, ILLUSTRATED BY BRUCE INGMAN
- PB *Vegetable Glue* SUSAN CHANDLER, ILLUSTRATED BY ELENA ODRIOZOLA
- PB *Lunchtime* REBECCA COBB
- PB *I Really Want to Eat a Child* SYLVIANE DONNIO, ILLUSTRATED BY DOROTHÉE DE MONFREID
- PB *Monsters Don't Eat Broccoli* BARBARA JEAN HICKS, ILLUSTRATED BY SUE HENDRA
- PB *Fussy Freya* KATHARINE QUARMBY, ILLUSTRATED BY PIET GROBLER
- PB *Little Pea* AMY KROUSE ROSENTHAL
- ER *Jody's Beans* MALACHY DOYLE, ILLUSTRATED BY JUDITH ALLIBONE
- ER *Bread and Jam for Frances* RUSSELL HOBAN, ILLUSTRATED BY LILLIAN HOBAN
- ER *Green Eggs and Ham* DR SEUSS

SEE ALSO: **contrary, being • cook, reluctance to learn to • routine, unable to cope with a change in the • soup, hating • told, never doing what you're**

gaming, excessive

[YA] *In Real Life*
CORY DOCTOROW, ILLUSTRATED BY JEN WANG

Playing video games only in moderation is perhaps beyond the power of a merely human child left to his or her own devices. But the graphic novel *In Real Life* addresses the compulsive nature of gaming with such insight that it will at least give them pause for thought.

Teenager Anda is just finding her feet in the world of gaming. At her new school, she and her fellow gamers are fired up about joining Fahrenheit, an all-girls gaming group introduced to them by their visiting teacher, Liza the Organiza. The game they'll be playing is Coarsegold Online – the fictional fastest-growing online game, with over ten million subscribers. Anda creates herself an avatar – a slimmer, more serene version of herself – then readies herself to 'kick ass'.

At first Anda simply slays mythical beasts and enjoys her warrior status. But then she finds herself encouraged to kill 'gold-diggers' for money. She's unnerved when real money arrives in her bank account; but, egged on by Liza the Organiza in her avatar form, she carries on. One day Anda starts chatting to one of the gold-diggers she's meant to kill and discovers that he, too, makes real money through the game – money that feeds and clothes him in his real life in China. She realises that if she kills him in the game, she'll deprive him of his livelihood.

You don't need to be a gamer to receive the full impact of this novel but, raising all sorts of questions about the ethics of what we do in the name of entertainment – and what we're prepared to overlook – it's a crucial read for gaming addicts. How do video games affect us in the real world? How might they affect others? Forcing gamers to step back and look at themselves from the outside, this book ensures that gaming will be pursued more moderately, and with added mindfulness, henceforth.

SEE ALSO: **screen, glued to the**

gang, being in a

YA *The Outsiders*
SE HINTON

Being a member of a gang can be the holy grail to children, offering as it does an exclusive identity outside the family, safety in numbers, a shared mission, and perhaps a secret password to boot. Gangs in children's books frequently start off innocent, such as the impromptu collection of ruffians in *Emil and the Detectives* by Erich Kästner and *Nicholas* by Goscinny and Sempé – and even wholesome, such as the outdoorsy gangs in Enid Blyton's Famous Five or Secret Seven books, or Arthur Ransome's Swallows and Amazons series. But as the characters get older, belonging to a gang takes on more sinister overtones, such as those in David Wilkerson's *The Cross and the Switchblade* and, more recently, Malorie Blackman's *Noughts and Crosses*, Stephen Kelman's *Pigeon English*, and *Perfect Chemistry* by Simone Elkeles. One of the very best novelists to give voice to urban gang culture is SE Hinton. Give her slim story, *The Outsiders* – which she wrote when she was just fifteen – as preventative medicine to teens for whom the idea of belonging to a gang holds allure.

Death enters the scene within twenty pages. Ponyboy, a member of the Greasers, has been drawn into a brawl with the rival Socs gang. When one of the Socs is stabbed in the back, Pony and his friend Johnny go on the run. They hole up in an abandoned church with a copy of *Gone with the Wind*, which they read with passion. Pony, it turns out, is a sensitive boy who idolises his handsome big brother, Sodapop, and reads poetry and the classics whenever he gets the chance.

Meanwhile tensions between the two gangs are escalating, and when the inevitable rumble is agreed upon and the weapons of choice – knives – announced, we know more young people are going to die (see: violence). Hinton's brilliance lies in evoking our sympathy for the members of both these gangs, even as they inflict terrible violence on each other. The blight on Pony's life as gang members lose their lives is clear to see. A more hopeful note is sounded at the end, with Ponyboy heroically rescuing a class full of children from a blazing church – and maturing into the thoughtful person who penned this story. But we know that he was the lucky one. Those who read *The Outsiders* will want to be the lucky ones, too.

SEE ALSO: **astray, being led • bullied, being • bully, being a • in charge, wanting to be • outsiders, distrust of • peer pressure • violence**

gay, not sure if you are

Some kids know they're gay from a very young age. Others take longer to work it out. Others still are confused, frightened or fascinated – and want to explore the issue. These books allow for all possibilities.

THE TEN BEST BOOKS FOR EXPLORING YOUR SEXUALITY

[PB] *King & King* LINDA DE HAAN, ILLUSTRATED BY STERN NIJLAND
[YA] *Fun Home* ALISON BECHDEL
[YA] *Rubyfruit Jungle* RITA MAE BROWN
[YA] *The Miseducation of Cameron Post* EMILY M DANFORTH
[YA] *Read Me Like a Book* LIZ KESSLER
[YA] *Ask the Passengers* AS KING
[YA] *Boy Meets Boy* DAVID LEVITHAN
[YA] *The Song of Achilles* MADELINE MILLER
[YA] *Funny Boy* SHYAM SELVADURAI
[YA] *A Boy's Own Story* EDMUND WHITE

SEE ALSO: **dating • sex, having questions about • transgender, feeling you are**

genius, being a

SEE: **precociousness**

ghosts, fear of

The shiver up the spine from the glimpse of a ghost is a delightful fear that brings children together – especially at sleepovers – and many won't want their terror of the supernatural cured at all. Take your pick from our list of the best unearthly tales – some frankly terrifying, others more homely – to fan the fear whenever you have a suitably spookable collection of kids to hand.

THE TEN BEST GHOST STORIES

Friendly Ghosts

- [PB] *Madeline and the Old House in Paris* JOHN BEMELMANS MARCIANO
- [PB] *The Little Old Lady Who Was Not Afraid of Anything* LINDA WILLIAMS, ILLUSTRATED BY MEGAN LLOYD
- [CB] *The Children of Green Knowe* LUCY M BOSTON
- [CB] *The Graveyard Book* NEIL GAIMAN, ILLUSTRATED BY CHRIS RIDDELL
- [YA] *Anya's Ghost* VERA BROSGOL*

Unfriendly Ghosts

- [CB] *The Owl Service* ALAN GARNER
- [CB] *Welcome to Dead House* (Goosebumps) RL STINE
- [YA] *Ways to See a Ghost* EMILY DIAMAND
- [YA] *Dark Matter* MICHELLE PAVER
- [YA] *The Scarecrows* ROBERT WESTALL

SEE ALSO: **bed, fear of what's under the • dark, scared of the • magic, loss of belief in • scared, being • sleep, unable to get to • sleepovers**

give up, tendency to

[ER] *Flat Stanley*
JEFF BROWN

[YA] *Hatchet*
GARY PAULSEN

Whether a child is trying to finish a cross-country race, crochet a quilt or learn the tuba, the temptation to chuck it all in when the going gets tough is hard to resist. Examples of resourceful and indefatigable heroes and heroines come into their own at such times – not only for providing a touchstone for what perseverance looks like, but also to show that the long-term rewards of achieving a goal are more fulfilling than the momentary pleasure of giving up.

Flat Stanley† never gives up, despite having good reason to. One morning he wakes up to discover he's been squashed flat by the bulletin board given to him and his brother by Mr and Mrs Lambchop for pinning up their pictures

---

* Since we dropped them from this list for lack of space, we have been haunted by *The Ghosts* by Antonia Barber and *The Time of the Ghost* by Diana Wynne Jones. Now that they've had a mention here, we hope they'll leave us alone.

† Originally illustrated by Tomi Ungerer, who captured with delightful wryness the resolutely optimistic spirit of the two-dimensional child, *Flat Stanley* has since been re-drawn for the modern market by Jon Mitchell with more rounded lines that create a less edgy but still charming effect.

and maps. Luckily, Stanley feels no pain despite now being 'four feet tall, one foot wide, and half an inch thick'; and, rather than give in to despair, he makes the most of his new wafer-thin shape. To his delight, he discovers that instead of having to open a door, he can now slide underneath it. And when his mother drops her ring through a grating, he lets himself down through the bars to retrieve it. He even dispatches himself, via Royal Mail, to California and disguises himself as a painting to prevent the theft of 'The Most Expensive Painting in the World'. In fact, Flat Stanley has been travelling the world for fifty years now, with teachers and enthusiasts sending Flat Stanleys back and forth to each other as a way to encourage their young charges to correspond. Rumour has it that Stanley can now travel in email form too . . . Thus children everywhere continue to be rallied by Flat Stanley's endless resourcefulness in the face of what could be seen as a litany of disasters.

The urge to give up is really the urge to decide to fail – failure sometimes seems easier, after all (see: loser, feeling like a). One can see the lure of it even when it means relinquishing your hold on life, as it would do for Brian, the thirteen-year-old who finds himself stranded in the vast Canadian wilderness with nothing but a hatchet in *Hatchet*. When the pilot flying Brian in a small plane from New York to Canada to visit his father – his parents having recently divorced (see: parents who are splitting up, having) – suffers a fatal heart attack mid-flight, the terrified teen manages to keep his head just enough to crash-land the plane in a lake. After two days of being eaten alive by mosquitos, vomiting up the sour berries he stuffs into his mouth in desperation and realising he has no way of signalling for help, he crawls into a dark corner of the cave and gives in to tears: 'It was all too much, just too much, and he couldn't take it.'

Later, though, he looks back at this moment as a turning point. Crying, he sees now, may feel good, but it isn't helpful. It doesn't increase your chances of survival. What *does* help him survive is his hatchet, and using the resources of his mind and body – his ability to really see, for instance, and hear, and think, abilities which also make him feel more thrillingly alive. This remarkable story inspires a child to turn their habit of giving up into a habit of resilience, perseverance and hope.

SEE ALSO: **confidence, lack of • good at anything, feeling like you're no • musical instrument, having to practise a • role model, in need of a positive • wrong, everything's going**

glasses, having to wear

PB *Winnie Flies Again*
VALERIE THOMAS, ILLUSTRATED BY KORKY PAUL

CB *Harry Potter and the Philosopher's Stone*
JK ROWLING

YA *How to Rock Braces and Glasses*
MEG HASTON

There was a time when any child who wore glasses was instantly categorised as a 'Professor Branestawm' type – that scatterbrained inventor of time-travel machines with a forehead so high he could stack all his five pairs of glasses* on it. Thanks to short-sighted heroes and heroines of recent children's fiction, some new, more positive role models have stepped into view instead.

For small children, *Winnie Flies Again* demonstrates how much better life is if you can actually *see* it properly. In a series of energetic double-page pen-and-watercolour spreads by Korky Paul, we see Winnie on her broomstick crashing into helicopters and hang-gliders and trying out a host of alternative transportation methods (bicycle, skateboard, horse) before realising that the vehicle is not the problem. Your short-sighted child may not be at risk of a mid-air collision, but point out the glorious detail they'd be missing in these illustrations if their eyes weren't in focus.

Older kids need look no further (especially if it's blurry to do so) than Harry Potter, who is, of course, the hands-down best thing to happen to glasses-wearers since the Milkybar Kid. Harry's distinctive appearance is as familiar as if we knew him personally: sticky-up hair, little round glasses 'held together with a lot of Sellotape' and, of course, the lightning-bolt scar on his forehead. The scar is nothing but a source of aggravation to his aunt Petunia while he's living with the Dursleys, and his glasses come under constant attack during the regular punch-ups with his cousin Dudley. But once Harry gets to Hogwarts and starts to understand that he's not just a wizard but an extremely famous one, his appearance takes on new associations. Suddenly the skinny boy with the scar and the glasses is the kid everyone wants to be seen with.

Harry's life at Hogwarts is not all magic and adulation. Having been brought up by 'Muggles', he has a lot more to learn about wizardry than most of his contemporaries. There are one hundred and forty-two staircases to navigate at his school (some of which lead 'somewhere different on a Friday'), complex passwords to remember for getting back to his bedroom at night, ghosts to steer clear of and the intimidating Transfiguration classes led by the strict

* 'A pair for reading by. A pair for writing by. A pair for out of doors. A pair for looking at you over the top of and another pair to look for the others when he mislaid them, which was often.' *The Incredible Adventures of Professor Branestawm* by Norman Hunter still makes for an excellent read.

Professor McGonagall to attend – classes which he finds, frankly, difficult. And he only has to catch the cold eye of Professor Snape, the sneering Potions teacher, to feel a stabbing pain in his scar. But when Harry plays Quidditch for the first time, his broom leaping straight into his hand, he realises he has found his forte. At one point he executes a fifty-foot dive, catching the ball a foot before it hits the ground (his glasses, remarkably, staying glued to his face all the while), which causes a speechless Professor McGonagall to rush him to the Gryffindor captain and see that he's signed up as 'Seeker' on the spot. By the end of the story, the whole school is talking about Harry and his fearless athleticism. Harry Potter has not only stymied 'He-who-must-not-be-named' (aka Voldemort) once again, but he has dispelled for all time the uncool connotations of glasses.

Specs-wearing girls and their friends will see glasses in a whole new light after the in-yer-face *How to Rock Braces and Glasses.* Kacey Simon is the undisputed queen bee of middle school, wearing all the right clothes and heading up a school TV channel. Though her wit has a sting, everyone wants to be her friend. When an eye infection and dental issues land her with Coke-bottle specs and a mouth full of metal, she plummets to a whole new low. Fortunately, she asks a lot of questions of herself while she's at the bottom and becomes a far more sympathetic person for it, learning to 'rock' braces and glasses along the way.

SEE ALSO: **body image** • **bullied, being** • **confidence, lack of** • **different, feeling** • **embarrassment** • **visual impairment**

god, wondering if there is a

PB *Old Turtle*
DOUGLAS WOOD, ILLUSTRATED BY CHENG-KHEE CHEE

CB *What Is God?*
ETAN BORITZER, ILLUSTRATED BY ROBBIE MARANTZ

YA *There Is No Dog*
MEG ROSOFF

Human beings start asking this question young – and many continue to ask it all their lives. Books offer a great way to explore the question while leaving a child to make up their own mind about the answer.

In *Old Turtle,* each of the elements of the natural world claim that God is made in their image. To the breeze, God is a 'wind who is never still'. To the mountain, God is a 'snowy peak'. To the antelope, God is a 'runner swift and free'. And to the tree – well, God is a She. This pantheism takes an interesting twist when Old Turtle announces the imminent arrival of a new kind of species, one who will be a reminder of 'all that God is'. Suddenly people of all colours flood the sumptuous watercolour landscapes of the central spread. They're well behaved at first, but they quickly forget their innate saintliness. Soon, it's up to the animals, mountains and trees to encapsulate God again, now finding a more unified way to do so. The illustrations are as uplifting as the words in this story, which is worth reading as much for its implicit ecological message to take care of the planet as for its encouragement to look for God in the natural world.

For a more anthropological approach, *What Is God?* provides an overview of how people think of God around the world. In some places, God is an old man with a long white beard, while in others people feel they're communing with God whenever they look up at the stars. In what amounts to a crash course in comparative religion, Etan Boritzer sketches out the world's main faiths, their holy books and their primary teachers – as well as the tendency for people of one religion to fight against those of another.* This book answers a lot of confusing questions about different faiths and lays the foundations for an accepting, all-embracing approach.

Teens who find themselves wondering how God – if He/She exists – could let so many bad things happen in the world will enjoy Meg Rosoff's irreverent satire. In this story, God is a teenage boy called Bob who, after creating the world in six days, lay down on the seventh because it was all too much effort (see: give up, tendency to). His mother Mona, a goddess, won the Earth in an intergalactic poker game and passed the job of being God to her insolent, spoiled son. Bob has flashes of brilliance – such as when he creates the butterfly – but he mostly behaves like your typical teenager, triggering earthquakes and tsunamis every time he loses his temper. Luckily, Bob has a fantastic assistant, Mr B, who runs around trying to clear up the mess Bob makes of everything – and *then* the mess the human race makes on top – while also attending to his official job of answering prayers. This he takes very seriously. Many a sleepless night is spent worrying about the fact that one man's saved iceberg is another man's famine, and he weeps copiously for those he can't help.

Meanwhile, Bob falls for a mortal girl – something which happens rather frequently, as it turns out (dark references being made to swans and showers of gold) – which leads to a spate of epic typhoons, floods and tidal waves. Then Bob's loyal companion, Eck – a 'penguiny sort of creature' – is gambled away in another poker game by his feckless mother. Poor Eck is left wondering

---

* He then takes the opportunity, surely greatly appreciated in these times, to point out how nonsensical this is, considering that most religions uphold the same basic tenet of being 'good/ To other people, just like you would want/Other people to be good to you'.

why Bob was so cruel as to create creatures who can foresee their own deaths – another question your teen might be asking, too. Fortunately, God's right-hand man, Mr B, has a master plan up his sleeve to save Eck – and the satisfying ending serves up a hearty meal of hope and faith in the miraculous. Teens are left feeling that humanity is, perhaps, capable of generous and noble acts, and even of the divine.

SEE ALSO: **about, what's it all?**

goldfish, death of a

SEE: **pet, death of a**

good at anything, feeling like you're no

PB *The Dot*
PETER H REYNOLDS

CB *Ordinary Jack*
HELEN CRESSWELL

YA *Tomorrow, When the War Began*
JOHN MARSDEN

Being overly self-critical seems almost inevitable in these high-achieving days. If a child near you tends to throw up their hands in self-disgust whenever they feel they haven't done something right, step in with *The Dot*. When Vashti finishes her art class with only a blank piece of paper to show for it, she's furious with herself. Luckily her teacher is wise to the fact that a child needs to feel good about themselves in order to be creative. She asks Vashti to draw something she can't fail at – a dot – and frames the resulting picture. Of course, seeing her dot in a fancy gilt frame boosts Vashti's spirits no end – and the fun she then has painting dots of every size and shape and colour is delightful to watch. No one can fail to notice how good a whole wall of her dot paintings looks. Read this story to a self-critical child – then find the equivalent of drawing dots in the next activity they do.

Older kids still in search of a talent to call their own will relate to young Jack in *Ordinary Jack*, the first in the ebullient series featuring the Bagthorpe family and their motley collection of rellies. Jack is the only one of the four siblings who doesn't have an obvious 'String to his Bow', whether it's playing tennis, painting family portraits, or reading Voltaire in the original. Some of his siblings have a 'Second String to their Bow', or even three or four – strings to bows being 'thick on the ground' in his family, as he puts it. He's particularly rankled when his younger sister Rosie beats him at swimming ten lengths of the pool. Luckily, Uncle Parker – the rebel of the older generation – picks up on his nephew's distress and promises to help him come up with his own 'speciality'.

The rather surprising idea he hits on – that Jack should become a 'prophet' – is typical of the wicked streak in Uncle Parker's sense of humour. 'From now on,' Uncle Parker tells him firmly, 'you will have Visions. Frequently.' And so Jack develops the disconcerting habit of staring past everyone's left ear at something only he can see and making bizarre predictions that, with a bit of well-timed assistance from Uncle Parker, seem to come true. As Jack basks in his (temporary) limelight, we see that it's Uncle Parker taking an interest in him that really makes the difference. If you have an ordinary Jack in your midst, overshadowed by high-achievers, this story may just prompt them to confide in a sympathetic relative or family friend who could play a similar role.* And if that friend or relative brings as much humour and imagination to the situation as Uncle Parker, everyone's in for an entertaining time.

Most underachievers are actually just late bloomers. When Ellie, the narrator of *Tomorrow, When the War Began* – the first in the gripping Tomorrow series – invites Homer to join her and some friends on a camping trip 'out bush', she describes him as a 'rabble-rouser'. Having grown up living next door to him, Ellie likes Homer. But he recently got into trouble for setting fire to a line of solvent on the road then waiting for cars to come along; and none of the girls at school take him very seriously.

She, Homer and the others hike to a spot so remote and hot that it's known locally as 'Hell'. Here they hang out for a few days, having the usual teenage spats and relationship intrigues. It's only when they return home to find their families have disappeared that they realise the mysterious planes with no lights that flew overhead one night had in fact been a stealth invasion. Overnight, they are forced into the role of insurgents – with neither weapons nor adults to help.

As they make their first terrifying forays into enemy territory, learning as much as they can about the encampment where their families are being held, Homer emerges as the natural leader. Always one step ahead, he stays calm, keeps them all from sliding into despair and thinks in strategic ways. 'It was getting hard to remember,' writes Ellie, as she records it all in her diary, 'that this fast-thinking guy, who'd just spent fifteen minutes getting us laughing

* Especially if you nudge that relative or family friend in the right direction by giving them a copy of *Ordinary Jack*, too.

and talking and feeling good again, wasn't even trusted to hand out books at school.' Sometimes people underachieve not because of a lack of ability but because of a surfeit of undirected intelligence. For the child who's yet to find an arena in which to excel, Homer is a great role model.

SEE ALSO: **disappointment • frustration • mistake, frightened of making a • role model, in need of a positive • sibling rivalry • war, worrying about • wrong, everything's going**

grandparents, living with

They may keep their teeth in a jar by the sink, but grandparents have a lot to offer – as these fictional children will tell you.

THE TEN BEST BOOKS FOR LIVING WITH GRANDPARENTS

- PB *Little Blue* GAYE CHAPMAN
- PB *The Wonderful Journey* PAUL GERAGHTY
- PB *Katie Morag and the Two Grandmothers* MAIRI HEDDERWICK
- ER *The Boxcar Children* GERTRUDE CHANDLER WARNER
- CB *The Diddakoi* RUMER GODDEN
- CB *Little Lord Fauntleroy* FRANCES HODGSON BURNETT
- CB *Love, Aubrey* SUZANNE LAFLEUR
- CB *Fablehaven* BRANDON MULL
- CB *A Long Way from Chicago* RICHARD PECK
- CB *Heidi* JOANNA SPYRI

SEE ALSO: **different, feeling**

grannies, having to kiss

CB *George's Marvellous Medicine* ROALD DAHL, ILLUSTRATED BY QUENTIN BLAKE

Nobody likes kissing a cheek that should be smooth but turns out to be scratchy. George's Grandma is not only whiskery but has brown teeth and a little mouth that puckers up like a 'dog's bottom'. Worse still, she's a miserable old grouch who spends all day sitting in her chair by the window, griping. Every child will thrill at the list of ingredients George puts in the pot when he decides to concoct his own fearsome brew in place of her usual medicine.* And when the evil old dame takes a swig then promptly rockets through the roof (a piece of action gloriously rendered by Quentin Blake), there'll be much celebrating. Point out to your child that the granny in their midst may be bristly, but there's an important difference between this geriatric and theirs. This one deserves George's medicine, theirs does not.

SEE ALSO: **beards, horror of • boring relatives, having**

granted, taking your parent for

All children do this, and rightly so. But if it gets *you* down, perhaps they're taking you for granted just a little too much – in which case, read on.

CURE FOR GROWN-UPS PB *Piggybook* ANTHONY BROWNE

We may have moved on from the ideal of the Fifties housewife, but the truth is that in many families there's still one person – maybe a woman, maybe a man – slaving away thanklessly at the boring domestic tasks behind the scenes and keeping everyone fed, clothed, cleaned and watered. This situation is laid out in somewhat chilling clarity in *Piggybook*, on the cover of which two smiling schoolboys and a toothily-grinning father ride piggyback on a distinctly unsmiling mother. Inside, the mother stands, slumped and cardigany, at the kitchen sink and over the ironing board, the only one in the illustrations to have no clear features: evidently, the effort of carrying everyone else has caused her to lose herself. Meanwhile, the boys and their father sing out for service at the table and loll fatly in front of the telly. The moment the mother finally cracks, leaving an angry note behind her, will elicit a bitter cackle from anyone who feels that they, too, have become a faceless drudge. The lovely twist at the end – showing that job-sharing in these days of gender equality needs to go both ways – makes this story much more than a self-pitying rant.

SEE ALSO: **spoilt, being**

---

* The ingredients include a bottle of shampoo, a jar of hair remover, a can of deodorant spray, liquid paraffin, clothes-washing powder, floor wax, flea powder for dogs, shoe polish, a tin of mustard powder, a bottle of horseradish sauce, half a pint of engine oil, sheepdip, and various veterinary pills for chickens, horses and cows suffering from gripe, gammy legs, mange, swine sickness and sore udders.

grow up, impatient to

[PB] *Molly Goes Shopping*
EVA ERIKSSON

[CB] *A Dog Called Grk*
JOSH LACEY

[YA] *Gone*
MICHAEL GRANT

This common childhood ailment is particularly painful for grown-ups to hear expressed, knowing what we know about the relative merits of youth and age. The best we can do is allow our impatient young 'uns to do things which help them feel big, while making the most of their childhoods ourselves. Meanwhile, reading them stories about other small beings eager to wield more weight in the world will show them they're not alone - and supply them with vicarious thrills.

Molly Goes Shopping is as sympathetic a story as you could wish for. Molly the pig is given a shopping list consisting of one item - a bag of beans - and sent off to the store by her grandma. Pleased as punch, she goes down the street holding the purse in her hand so that everyone can see what she's doing. Emotions run deep when so much pride is at stake, and Swedish author and illustrator Eva Eriksson's soft pastel-and-pencil illustrations brim with warmth and understanding when, the first time, Molly gets it a little bit wrong. For those taking their first steps out into the world by themselves, this story offers both solace and inspiration.

The urge to taste independence is satisfied most gloriously at the chapter-book stage, with grown-ups being killed off left, right and centre - or at the very least being dispatched to far-flung corners of the world - leaving children to their own devices. This is also the age at which children begin to focus less on what's right in front of their noses and more on what might lie beyond. For a first foray into stories with global settings, we love the wonderful Grk series by Josh Lacey, beginning with *A Dog Called Grk*. Twelve-year-old Tim - an only child whose parents are always busy (see: parents, too busy), or irritated, or both - spends his free time playing a helicopter simulator game on his computer. When, on the way home from school one day, he trips over a small, white dog with black patches, he desperately wants to keep it (see: pet, wanting a). But his parents don't want a dog's mucky paws on their leather car seats. A search for Grk's rightful owners leads them to a diplomatic residence in Kensington - the home, it turns out, of Natascha and Max Raffifi, the children of the Stanislavian ambassador to London. Suddenly we find ourselves in a plot involving a 'small, mountainous country in Eastern Europe' where the murderous Colonel Zinfandel, the Commander-in-Chief of the Army, has imprisoned the Raffifi family after staging a military coup. The next thing we know, Tim has bought a ticket to Stanislavia on his dad's computer, leaving a note suggesting that his pocket money be withdrawn for the next 183 weeks to pay for it.

The story of how Tim and the faithful Grk end up rescuing the Raffifi children is as thrilling as anything you'd find in a John le Carré novel and, with brutal dictators and their violent henchmen at large, this story will take many kids into a world of gritty realism for the first time. Yet the narrative is infused with great lightness and humour – plus the qualities Tim shares with Grk and for which the dog is named ('grk' being, apparently, the Stanislavian for 'brave, generous and foolish, all at the same time'). That the rescue involves Tim having to take the controls of a real helicopter is a lovely twist. Any brave-yet-sometimes-foolish child of chapter-book age who yearns for more independence will love the chance to live a little dangerously through Tim and Grk.

Older kids wishing their teenage years away may think twice after reading *Gone*, set as it is in a world in which everyone over the age of fifteen is mysteriously extinguished. At first, this strange interruption of the human lifecycle manifests as a kind of mass disappearance. Our fourteen-year-old hero, Sam Temple, is at his Perdido Beach school in Alabama when his teacher disappears before his eyes, along with Josh, who was sitting next to him. Then Astrid 'the genius' rushes in from her maths class, where everyone has vanished but her. It soon becomes clear that fifteen is the magic cut-off age. As soon as you hit it, you're history.

At first the teens are thrilled at their unexpected freedom – no school, no rules and no grown-ups. But as they venture outside and see the wreckage of car crashes in the street – the cars empty but still locked from the inside – and it gradually dawns on them that they've lost their parents, the excitement fades. What's more, there are baby brothers and sisters to be looked after, food to be found and cooked, and unruly behaviour to be held in check. One of the boys nominates himself as the chief of McDonald's and keeps the burgers and fries coming by following the employee manual to the letter. And then some of the teens start to develop strange new powers, such as being able to move heavy objects using only their thoughts, and setting fire to things with their eyes . . . What's more, they seem to be trapped in their town by an invisible wall. It's not long before they start wishing the clock would stop ticking. For teens who think growing up is only about getting your hands on the car keys and being able to order drinks in a bar, this story provides sobering food for thought.

SEE ALSO: **friends your parents don't approve of, having • gang, being in a**

GROW UP, IMPATIENT TO

grow up, not wanting to

Peter Pan
JM BARRIE

If, on the other hand, the child in your midst shows every sign of not wanting to grow up at all, introduce them to someone else who doesn't. When Peter Pan first flies through the nursery window of the Darlings' house clad in nothing but leaves, he still has all his milk teeth – and he 'gnashes' the little pearls at Mrs Darling fiercely. Later, Wendy discovers that Peter ran away from home after overhearing his parents talk about what he was going to be when he grew up. He's lived with the 'lost boys' in Neverland, resolutely refusing to mature, ever since.

When they fly to Neverland themselves, Wendy and her brothers discover the downsides to a world with no grown-ups. The lost boys miss their mothers, and Wendy, forced to play that role for the lot of them, discovers that maturity has its rewards. Years later, when she's a mother herself, her daughter Jane asks her why she can no longer fly. 'Because . . . when people grow up they forget the way,' she replies. 'It is only the gay and innocent and heartless who can fly.' Yes, we lose something when we grow up, but we gain something too. Has your child ever met a grown-up who wishes they hadn't learnt to love and care for others?

CURE FOR GROWN-UPS *Owen* **KEVIN HENKES**

When a child refuses to relinquish the accessories of babyhood long past that carefree state, their grown-up can find themselves in a dilemma. They don't want to deny their child the thumb/security blanket/soft toy, but at the same time they don't want their child to get teased – or end up with sticky-out teeth. Owen, a little boy mouse, refuses to be separated from his fuzzy yellow blanket, Fuzzy, and Fuzzy has become distinctly manky. When the interfering old busybody Mrs Tweezers next door starts to *ahem* about it ('Haven't you heard of the Blanket Fairy?' she asks Owen's parents, pointedly), they start to worry they should be doing something about it. Thankfully, Owen is wise to the Fuzzy-destroying ruses of Mrs Tweezers and Fuzzy lives on. But then Owen's mother comes up with a much better idea for how Owen, who is about to start school, can keep Fuzzy with him in a sociably acceptable form. Secure is the child who knows their grown-ups are on their side, thinking up cunning ways to bend the rules to their advantage – and happy is the grown-up who has managed to find a way for the child to comfort themselves when they're out in the big wild world by themselves.

SEE ALSO: **dress by yourself, refusing to • fussy eater, being a • imaginary friend, embarrassed about having an**

growing up in a house with no books

MAKE THE MOST OF THE LOCAL LIBRARY

READING AILMENTS

If you know a child growing up in a house with no books, introduce them to Roald Dahl's *Matilda* – and a friendly librarian. Matilda is a child prodigy who can talk in complete sentences by the time she's eighteen months old and read the newspaper by three (see: precociousness). At four, she starts hankering after books – but the only one in the house is a copy of *Easy Cooking*. Her parents can't understand why she'd want to read a book when she could be lounging in front of the telly or playing bingo like them. But, happily, there's a public library nearby – and Mrs Phelps, a kind librarian – and by the time she's four and three months, Matilda has devoured every title on the children's shelves and moved on to Dickens, Austen and Hemingway. Sometimes a child needs a mentor outside the family to guide them to the right books. Libraries and schools are good places to find one. Or, be one yourself and use the book you hold in your hands for ideas.

H IS FOR . . .

hamster, death of

SEE: **pet, death of a**

hamster, wanting a

SEE: **pet, wanting a**

hand-eye co-ordination, lack of

SEE: **clumsiness**

hands, not wanting to wash your

[PB] *Dr Dog*
BABETTE COLE

They may not listen to you, but they'll listen to a dog. Especially one that wears a white coat, a stethoscope round his neck, and is the pet of the incorrigible Gumboyle family, drawn in their full disgusting glory by the ever-zany Babette Cole. The Gumboyles are all guilty of bringing illnesses on themselves. They itch their bums then suck their thumbs, go out in the rain without a hat, and even smoke behind the bike sheds. Dr Dog, forced to return from a fancy lecture tour in Brazil to tend to his hapless humans, explains to each of them how they became ill or infected, whether it was sharing hairbrushes (see: nits) or failing to wash their hands. Bring him into your home and he'll lick you all into submission.

SEE ALSO: **bath, not wanting to have a • nose, picking your • told, never doing what you're**

happy ever after, had enough of

TURN THE FAIRYTALE TROPE ON ITS HEAD

READING AILMENTS

There comes a time when predictable endings no longer satisfy. See the following list for some enjoyably witty riffs on familiar tales.

THE TEN BEST FAIRYTALE RE-TELLINGS

- PB *Beware of the Bears!* ALAN MACDONALD, ILLUSTRATED BY GWYNETH WILLIAMSON
- CB *The Pied Piper of Hamelin* RUSSELL BRAND, ILLUSTRATED BY CHRIS RIDDELL
- CB *The School for Good and Evil* SOMAN CHAINANI
- CB *The Sleeper and the Spindle* NEIL GAIMAN, ILLUSTRATED BY CHRIS RIDDELL
- CB *A Tale Dark and Grimm* ADAM GIDWITZ
- CB *The Goose Girl* SHANNON HALE
- CB *Clever Polly and the Stupid Wolf* CATHERINE STORR, ILLUSTRATED BY MAJORIE-ANN WATTS
- CB *Breadcrumbs* ANNE URSU
- YA *Beastly* ALEX FLINN
- YA *Beauty* ROBIN MCKINLEY

heard, not feeling

CB *The Tiger Rising*
KATE DICAMILLO

Whether it's because no one is listening, no one understands, or because they never manage to get the words out in the first place, a child who doesn't feel heard can feel frustrated, angry and isolated. Rob, the boy in *The Tiger Rising*, has been keeping his thoughts and feelings bottled up ever since his mother died (see: death of a loved one). His father doesn't think there's any point in talking about her – she's dead, and there's nothing anyone can do about it (see: parents who can't talk about their emotions, having) – and Rob has become a pro at 'not-crying' and 'not-thinking'. Bullied at school, he has developed an itchy red rash on his legs. And when the headmaster suggests he stay at home until the rash clears up, Rob is relieved. He knows the rash will never go away – just like all the feelings he stuffs into the imaginary, overflowing suitcase in his head. But at least he won't have to face the bullies any more.

And then he finds a real, live tiger pacing up and down in a cage way out in the woods. That the tiger is his secret seems to invest him with some of the tiger's power. It helps him keep that suitcase of feelings shut, as if the tiger were actually sitting on it. But he hadn't counted on the intriguingly named Sistine, the feisty new girl at school, not letting him 'not-say' things. And he's equally taken aback by the words of Willie May, the housekeeper at the motel where he lives, who takes one look at his rash and announces, 'I can tell you how to cure that.' Suddenly Rob is overcome with a desperate need to tell somebody about the tiger – somebody who will really hear him, somebody 'capable of believing in tigers'.

Every note in this tight, lyrical tale is pitch perfect, and the caged tiger develops into a powerful symbol of emotions needing to be released. When Rob's father finally hears what his son has to say, we defy anyone to remain dry-eyed. For kids who feel unheard, the catharsis will go deep.

SEE ALSO: **abuse** • **anger** • **anxiety** • **feelings, not able to express your** • **frustration** • **loneliness** • **stand up for yourself, not feeling able to** • **stuck** • **understood, not being** • **worrying**

hearing difficulties

SEE: **deafness**

heights, fear of

Rooftoppers
KATHERINE RUNDELL

Children nervous of looking down from tall places will gain a whole new perspective from *Rooftoppers*. When the authorities decide that eccentric, unmarried Charles is no longer an appropriate sole carer for twelve-year-old Sophie, the two decide to find out if Sophie's mother is still alive. Charles took Sophie in as a baby after finding her floating in a cello case in the English Channel when the stricken *Queen Mary* sank, and he has looked after her with aplomb in his ramshackle, book-filled London house ever since. The cello case that was her raft bears the name of a Parisian instrument maker; so together they flee to Paris, before anyone can take her away.

One night, Sophie steps through a top-floor window to find herself on the roof of their apartment building – and meets Matteo, one of a tribe of outlaw French kids also intent on eluding the authorities. The tactic of these kids is to live on the rooftops, avoiding street level completely. Small, ragged and barefoot, Matteo jumps from roof to roof with astonishing agility – sprinting along the flat ones, balancing on the slanted ones, leaping over the gaps like a frog – and Sophie watches, transfixed. Soon she is following him; and while Paris sleeps beneath them, Matteo and Sophie search for her mother together.

Matteo teaches Sophie how to stay safe on the rooftops: how to spot the loose, crumbly tiles, and the tiles that make too much noise and might give them away. At one point, he helps her by-pass her fear by telling her to close her eyes and leap across a void 'the length of a pig'. 'How long is a pig?' she wonders as she takes to the air. Tell your youngster to read the story to find out if she makes it to the other side – then show them a good climbing tree.* Inspired by Matteo, they'll scramble up with new-found confidence.

SEE ALSO: **scared, being** • **sick, being**

holidays

SEE: **summer holidays**

home-schooling

CB *My Name Is Mina*
DAVID ALMOND

Nine-year-old Mina, a character who first won our hearts in David Almond's wondrous *Skellig*† and then inspired this prequel of her own, is a great advert for home-schooling. Genuinely interested in the world around her, Mina was taken

* Save the rooftops of Paris for their first French exchange.

† See: moving house.

out of school because her mother felt that her daughter's natural curiosity and creativity were being stymied there. What Mina hated most was being told to plan her stories in advance – and this book, presented as her journal, certainly bears that out, meandering as it does in whatever direction her zany and rapacious mind chooses. Printed in hand-written font and dotted with her doodlings, the narrative includes meditations on words that she loves ('NONSENSICAL! WHAT A GREAT WORD! WOW!' and 'PARADOX! What a word!'), and descriptions of 'Extraordinary Activities' she likes to do, such as making a ring with her finger and thumb through which to contemplate 'the great emptiness' of the sky. Sometimes she writes down words over and over until they lose all meaning. She knows that the kids at her old school thought she was a 'weirdo', but she doesn't care. 'They're nothing to me. I don't even look at them. Them! Huh! HUH! Nothing!' And so, while ordinary mortals sleep, Mina stays awake, sitting in her tree, drawing the baby blackbirds, wondering how big Heaven must be to fit in all the people who have lived and died in the world so far – one of them being her own father – and feeling capable of extraordinary things. Home-schoolers will feel the decision of their grown-ups to eschew conventional education affirmed after spending time with someone as quixotic as this.

SEE ALSO: **different, feeling**

homesickness

PB *A Kissing Hand for Chester Raccoon*
AUDREY PENN, ILLUSTRATED BY BARBARA L GIBSON

CB *Kensuke's Kingdom*
MICHAEL MORPURGO

For kids struggling with spending time apart from their grown-ups in the early years, we love *A Kissing Hand for Chester Raccoon*. Chester is tearful at the thought of starting Owl's night-school classes, as he doesn't want to be away from his mother. Mrs Raccoon assures him that he'll have a great time and make lots of new friends. And besides, she has a cunning idea for how he can administer her caring touch even when she's not there. Introduce this one into your child's library and it won't just be when they're little that they'll borrow the wise Mrs Raccoon's cure. The pen-and-wash illustrations are cute and comforting in all the right ways.

Part of what makes children continue to feel homesick is the lack of all that's familiar – the smells, sounds and routines of home. Remind kids that the separation is only temporary. This is not something Michael can be assured of in the haunting *Kensuke's Kingdom*. When the twelve-year-old boy is knocked overboard on a round-the-world trip with his parents, no one hears him cry out. The next thing he knows, he's lying on a beach with just his dog, Stella, a bunch of howling monkeys and a million mosquitos.

Michael knows he's lucky to be alive – but he also knows that his parents' boat, the *Peggy Sue*, will have drifted far from here by now and his parents, when they wake up, will have no idea where he is or that he's still alive. When he realises he's sharing the island with a mysterious benefactor – an elderly Japanese man who only speaks a few words of English – his loneliness is compounded. The man leaves Michael a daily ration of freshly caught fish and fruit and water, but makes it clear he wants nothing to do with Michael – even drawing a line in the sand to delineate their separate territories. Michael experiences such pangs of homesickness that he almost loses the will to live.

When, one day, he's stung by a jellyfish and wakes up in Kensuke's cave, unable to move and with the stench of vinegar in his nose, for a moment he thinks he's back home and smelling the fish and chips his father used to bring back on Fridays. In fact, this marks the beginning of Michael finding a proper home on the island. His courage as he does so will inspire a child yearning for their own family to keep their spirits up and try to enjoy their adventure meanwhile. They're not going to be away from home forever and, perhaps, if they take an interest in their new surroundings, they might even find it hard to leave when it's time to go.

SEE ALSO: **boarding school** • **boring relatives, having**

homework, reluctance to do

CB *Artemis Fowl*
EOIN COLFER

Kids who don't like doing their homework need an industrious, dedicated role model. They'll find it in Artemis Fowl. Twelve years old and suffering, along with the family fortunes, from the mysterious disappearance of his father a year ago, Artemis has given himself the gargantuan task of deciphering the ancient language of the fairies. He's convinced that the fairy book he bamboozled from a Sprite contains clues as to the whereabouts of the famed 'fairy gold' – and Artemis is determined to steal it, finding his father along the way. The Gnomish text – which looks a bit like Egyptian hieroglyphics – is dastardly difficult to decode; and most kids would give up this seemingly impossible task within a day or two. But Artemis is no ordinary child. A criminal mastermind in the making, Artemis studies for weeks on end, denying himself computer games, sunshine and the company of all but his trusty helpmeet,

Butler, in pursuit of his dubious goal. Study-shirkers will be shown a whole new *modus operandi* for getting something done. Although the heady mix of leprechauns, magic, technology and code might temporarily distract them from their homework even more, they'll emerge from the experience with a fresh understanding of what hard work really is.

SEE ALSO: **exams** • **laziness** • **parents, strict** • **school, not wanting to go to**

hormones, raging

YA *Grasshopper Jungle*
ANDREW SMITH

For the teen seeing through a haze of hormones, the world looks a little . . . well, different. They'll find it reassuring to know they're not the only one experiencing it this way. Unashamedly sexually explicit, *Grasshopper Jungle* is the surreal and oddly touching story of what happens when sixteen-year-old Austin and his friend Robbie discover that they can turn the inhabitants of their small town of Ealing, Iowa, into (wait for it) giant praying mantises. With mounting astonishment, they watch as the people they've grown up with shed their human skins and turn into voracious, mandible-wielding insects.

Six feet tall, the praying mantises are interested only in two things: eating as much as possible, and having as much sex as possible. Which, of course, are interests the boys can relate to. The fun of the story is that while Austin is aware of the apocalyptic nightmare he and Robbie have unleashed, he remains as horny as ever, and his main preoccupation is deciding who he wants to have sex with more – his girlfriend Shannon or Robbie himself (see: gay, not sure if you are). Teens flooded with both testosterone and oestrogen will enjoy being swept up in this all-consuming tsunami of desire. Think Kurt Vonnegut, with a dash of Stephen King thrown in.

SEE ALSO: **body hair** • **body odour** • **first kiss** • **first love** • **innocence, loss of** • **virginity, loss of** • **wet dreams**

hygiene, personal

SEE: **body odour** • **hands, not wanting to wash your** • **smelly friend, having a**

I IS FOR . . .

ill, pretending to be

SEE: **lying** • **school, not wanting to go to**

imaginary friend, embarrassed about having an

PB *Slightly Invisible* (Charlie and Lola)
LAUREN CHILD

PB *Dotty*
ERICA S PERL, ILLUSTRATED BY JULIA DENOS

Imaginary friends are great stand-ins for the real thing – always there, and always in tune with your own agenda. But some children feel shy about admitting to having one – afraid they (or their imaginary friend) will be mocked (see: bullied, being). Seeing one being taken seriously in fiction will help. Lauren Child's clever rendering of Lola's imaginary friend, Soren Lorenson, as a translucent, grey figure that only she (and the reader) can see is particularly satisfying – as is his distinctive Swedish name and his aversion to mushrooms. The way he fades in and out depending on whether there's someone else occupying Lola's attention adds to his integrity. He's particularly welcome when, in *Slightly Invisible*, Charlie is busy playing with his best friend Marv and they don't want Lola to interrupt.

Imaginary friends are often small and discreet – but not always. Ida's imaginary friend in *Dotty* is a hefty creature with horns, red spots and an interestingly upturned tail. When Ida starts school (see: school, being the new kid at), she takes Dotty with her on a long blue string – and is pleased to see that several other children are leading imaginary friends by strings, too – all fantastical creatures brought to zesty, joyful life by Julia Denos. As the school year progresses, though, the other imaginary friends begin to disappear – and one day in spring, her friend Katya is surprised to see a blue string dangling from Ida's pocket. 'You don't still HAVE her, do you?' asks Katya, shocked. The huge Dotty galumphs to Ida's defence – and Ida finds the proof she needed that you're never too old for imaginary friends. This spirited story with a cast of human characters as racially diverse as its various fantastical species encourages children to feel OK about keeping imaginary friendships going a little longer than might be expected.

SEE ALSO: **embarrassment** • **friends, finding it hard to make** • **grow up, not wanting to** • **only child, being an**

in charge, wanting to be

YA *Lord of the Flies*
WILLIAM GOLDING

Many children love nothing better than to follow a leader, and a confident child will enjoy assuming the leadership role. But when that child starts taking leadership too far, insisting on how things should be done and becoming cross with those who don't toe the line, leadership starts to veer towards dictatorship. In William Golding's extraordinary *Lord of the Flies*, a desert-island survival story which still very much holds its own, two boys, Ralph and Jack, demonstrate the fine line between being a leader and being a dangerous despot.

When their plane is shot down over the Pacific, the schoolboys surviving the crash are wildly excited to find themselves on their own little piece of paradise. It's immediately clear that they need a 'Chief'. Twelve-year-old Ralph, blond-haired and good-looking, has a certain 'stillness' about him which immediately sets him apart. And by the time the scattered boys have all found each other in a clearing in the jungle, Ralph has already asserted dominance over the bumbling Piggy, with his dismissive 'Sucks to your auntie!' whenever Piggy invokes this dubious authority figure. That Piggy, despite his humiliation, attaches himself limpet-like to Ralph sends a clear message to the younger boys about which one's the stronger character. But it's when Ralph puts his lips to the conch and sounds the deep, harsh note that booms beneath the palms and 'through the intricacies of the forest', causing clouds of birds to rise from the tree-tops and the last stragglers to appear from all directions, that his power is made manifest.

Then the ginger-haired Jack makes his entrance, leading a troop of marching choirboys down the beach, their bodies swathed in black cloaks and topped with white frills so that they appear, at first, to be a single, many-legged insect. In contrast to Ralph, Jack barks 'orders' and demands obedience from his choir. He's immediately competitive with Ralph, nominating himself as chief. The boys decide to take a vote, and the clear choice of everyone apart from the choir – too cowed by Jack to have opinions of their own – is Ralph.

Ralph immediately shows himself to be a decisive and eloquent leader as well as a natural diplomat, conferring back on Jack the governance of his choirboy 'hunters'. But Jack is not so easily appeased. All too soon the stage is set for a battle between democracy and a militaristic rule of fear. Hold this mirror up to tyrannical children entering their teens and they'll see that being a leader who has everyone's best interests at heart is very different to being a dictator who forces everyone else to play their game.

SEE ALSO: **boots, being too big for your** • **bossiness** • **know-it-all, being a** • **precociousness** • **sibling rivalry**

independence, wanting more

SEE: **grow up, impatient to**

indoors, spending too much time

CB *The Secret Garden*
FRANCES HODGSON BURNETT

If ever there was a boy in literature who spent too much time inside, it's Colin Craven in *The Secret Garden*. Imagining himself to have inherited his father's hunchback – an idea with which the adults in the household collude – he has spent most of his life confined to his bed, strapped into an uncomfortable back brace. Now ten years old, he is a fretful, spoilt child who refuses to see anyone beyond his tight circle of doctor and servants – and the rare, terse visits from his globe-trotting father – and is resigned to an early death. Until, that is, Mary Lennox – a cousin whose parents have died of cholera in India, and who is just as spoiled and obstinate as he is – comes to live in his Yorkshire house.

Mary herself is sickly when she arrives, with a yellow, pinched face and a similar disinclination to want to go out into the wintry garden, but boredom soon forces her feet. Outside, she discovers the joys of skipping – and also of Dickon, the freckle-faced youth who spends his days up on the moors and can name all the birds by their songs. Most importantly of all, she discovers the key to the overgrown door that leads to the secret, walled garden.

One night, the sound of sobbing leads her to Colin. Colin is entranced by Mary's description of the beautiful garden – locked and forgotten since his mother died there, soon after he was born – with its daffodils and snowdrops. Together they hatch a plan to bring the garden back to life. Mary and Dickon clear the weeds and train the roses, and Colin eventually joins them too. As he spends more time in the secret garden, Colin's etiolated body unfurls. Expose the sun-starved child in your midst to this garden from which, in Dickon's words, 'th' sky looks so high an' th' bees an' skylarks makes such a nice noise hummin' an' singin'', and let its magic work on them, too.

SEE ALSO: **laziness** • **walk, not wanting to go on a**

innocence, loss of

The Giver
LOIS LOWRY

For children approaching their teens, the world is an increasingly complicated place, filled with new pleasures and joys but also uncomfortable and distressing realities. *The Giver* – one of those unforgettable children's books which confronts difficult subjects head-on – is an essential companion to this rite of passage.

Eleven-year-old Jonas is nervous about the imminent 'Ceremony of Twelve' in which he, along with his friends in their sealed community, will be assigned the job they'll be doing for the rest of their lives. Until now, nothing unexpected or frightening has ever happened to Jonas, except when an unidentified jet flew over the community a year ago. In this sterile world, devoid of colour and minutely controlled by the Elders, each calm, ordered day is the same as the last and rules are strictly observed. Each family is allotted two children; feelings are shared among family units after supper; and anyone who transgresses three times is 'released' – along with the elderly and the underweight newborns – to a place vaguely referred to as 'Elsewhere' and from which no one has ever returned.

When Jonas is told he'll be the next 'Receiver of Memory', he has no idea what it means except that it's a great honour, and that it will bring him pain. To begin with, when he meets the bearded old man who has been Receiver up till now, he can see no reason to be afraid. Placing his hands on Jonas's back, the old man – now the 'Giver' – transmits a 'memory of snow' and, with a sharp intake of frigid air, Jonas experiences the glee of a sled-ride for the first time. Soon, he sees the world in vibrant colour and understands what is meant by 'love'. But the Giver has aged prematurely as a result of these collective memories – and soon Jonas understands why.

Profound and unforgettable, *The Giver* is about joy and suffering as flip sides of the same coin, and why it's impossible to feel one without the other. Leave it out for teens and pre-teens under siege by their emotions.

SEE ALSO: **adolescence** • **happy ever after, had enough of**

J IS FOR . . .

job, wanting a Saturday

It's never too early to start earning. But before the kids sign away their freedom, suggest they check out these fictional business ventures. Will their first taste of paid work be a great money-making wheeze – or blatant exploitation?

THE TEN BEST BOOKS ABOUT CHILDREN AT WORK

- PB *Cinderella* CHARLES PERRAULT, ILLUSTRATED BY ARTHUR RACKHAM
- CB *Just William* RICHMAL CROMPTON, ILLUSTRATED BY CHRIS RIDDELL
- CB *The Giraffe and the Pelly and Me* ROALD DAHL, ILLUSTRATED BY QUENTIN BLAKE
- CB *Smith* LEON GARFIELD, ILLUSTRATED BY KENNY MCKENDRY
- CB *The Family from One End Street* EVE GARNETT
- CB *The Water-Babies* CHARLES KINGSLEY, ILLUSTRATED BY JESSIE WILLCOX SMITH
- CB *Lyddie* KATHERINE PATERSON
- CB *Lawn Boy* GARY PAULSEN
- CB *The Amazing Maurice and His Educated Rodents* (Discworld*) TERRY PRATCHETT
- YA *Trash* ANDY MULLIGAN

SEE ALSO: **laziness** • **pocket money, lack of** • **chores, having to do** • **school, not wanting to go to**

---

* But you do not have to read the twenty-seven Discworld books which precede it to enjoy this cure.

know-it-all, being a

[PB] *Interrupting Chicken*
DAVID EZRA STEIN

[CB] *Frindle*
ANDREW CLEMENTS, ILLUSTRATED BY BRIAN SELZNICK

Know-it-all children can't help leaping in and showing off their new-found knowledge – perhaps because they're aware of just how recently they were completely clueless about everything. That this habit is irritating for others becomes all too clear after meeting *Interrupting Chicken*. The big red father chicken attempting to read a bedtime story to his little red chicken has barely cleared 'once upon a time' before the little red chicken interrupts and sums up the rest of the story in one garbled line. Cleverly, author/illustrator David Ezra Stein has the father reading from a book of fairytales, so we know where they're going, too – but that doesn't stop us wanting to hear the full story. So when the father starts toppling over from the waist in despair, we're totally on his side. With its lively pastel pictures showing the little chicken jumping – literally – into his favourite tales, this is a highly effective tool for teaching little mouths, and beaks, to say zipped.

The classroom, of course, offers an ideal theatre for know-it-alls, stocked as it is with a teacher to outwit and an audience to witness the outwitting. Eleven-year-old Nicholas Allan in *Frindle* is renowned among his peers for lobbing a flummoxing question at his teachers in the last three minutes of class – neatly absorbing the time for setting the homework assignment (see: homework, reluctance to do). He tries it out on Mrs Granger, their new teacher, who is already building a reputation for her love of the dictionary. 'Where did all the words come from?' he asks. But Mrs Granger is one step ahead. 'Why don't you find out for yourself?' she asks, setting him an extra assignment overnight.

This Nick duly does, delivering a forty-minute talk the following day about where words come from, how dictionaries work, who wrote the first one,* and how many different ways there are to use the word 'take'.† Mrs Granger is delighted – until she realises that Nick has segued into reading aloud an extremely lengthy and tedious prologue from his dictionary. The battle is on.

Nick's masterstroke is to invent a word – 'frindle', meaning 'pen' – and bring it into circulation, first by asking for a frindle at the corner shop, then encouraging everyone else at school to do the same. Soon, the word has entered the lexicon of the wider community, with unexpectedly life-changing results. This thought-provoking, word-celebrating story – with its beautiful pencil drawings by Brian Selznick – will have little know-it-alls chuckling everywhere. But its final note is one of caution. Perhaps, whenever your little know-it-all reckons they have the answer, they might like to write it down instead of blabbing it out loud – using not a pen but a frindle.

SEE ALSO: **boots, being too big for your** • **bossiness** • **in charge, wanting to be** • **precociousness** • **sibling rivalry**

* Samuel Johnson, in 1755.

† 113.

L IS FOR . . .

language, having to learn another

When Hitler Stole Pink Rabbit
JUDITH KERR

Whether it's French, Spanish, Chinese or Inuit, the idea of having to learn a new language can be a daunting prospect. In fact, most kids are natural linguists and, when immersed, tend to pick up a new tongue much more quickly than their grown-ups. *When Hitler Stole Pink Rabbit* is an ideal book to give to kids facing a move to another country, showing as it does that, though speaking another language can be hard at first, fluency comes more quickly and easily than they might expect.

We know that life is about to change for nine-year-old Anna. It's 1938 and posters of Hitler are springing up all over Berlin. Realising the growing threat to their safety, Anna's father – an outspoken Jewish intellectual whose anti-Nazi books are publicly burnt – arranges for the family to flee. In Paris, Anna and her brother Michael struggle to fit in (see: school, being the new kid at). A rather lazy boy up till now, Michael makes a monumental effort to keep up with his peers in maths and football, while Anna, who has previously thrived with little effort, becomes increasingly withdrawn. How exhausting it is to have to translate her German thoughts into French before expressing them to the teacher! Nearly every word in her dictation book is underscored with red and Anna despairs of ever speaking the language well enough to have proper friends. As her exercise books fill with doodles, she concludes she must be one of those people who are simply 'no good' at languages.

But one day, when she's been in Paris for nearly a year, everything changes. Falling into step with her friend Colette on the way to school, she is asked, 'What did you do on Sunday?' and, without thinking, she hears herself answer in French without first translating the question into German, formulating a German answer, then translating that answer back into French again. And then she does it again – and again – all day. From that moment on, it's as if she has suddenly found she can fly, and her previously sickly pallor gives way to a happy glow.

Learning to speak another language generally requires two things: intense immersion and the belief that you can do it. This story will encourage your hesitant linguist to keep persevering. One day they'll hear themselves sounding like a native without even knowing they were capable of doing it.

SEE ALSO: **confidence, lack of • different, feeling • friends, feeling like you have no • give up, tendency to • good at anything, feeling like you're no • moving house**

laziness

PB *Gift of the Sun*
DIANNE STEWART, ILLUSTRATED BY JUDE DALY

It's fine for kids to indulge in some intensive lounging when they've been working hard at school or playing sports. But when a kid hasn't been playing hard, adventuring hard or chipping in with the household chores – and yet is *still* lacking in get-up-and-go – they might need a story cure. *Gift of the Sun*, a South African folktale, illustrates the value of putting in a bit of effort.

Thulani loves to spend his days basking in the sun. The only job required of him is to milk the cow, but he finds even this too much work, and decides to sell it and buy a goat instead. When the goat eats all the seeds his wife has planted, he replaces it with a sheep. When the sheep is too much trouble to shear, Thulani swaps it for three geese. When Thulani's wife (who, by the way, has been busy all this time planting, harvesting, cooking and generally keeping their lives going) says they need some seeds to plant for next year's harvest, Thulani is finally moved to get off his backside, trade the three geese for some seeds and plant these seeds himself.

The seeds grow into magnificent, stately sunflowers, which then produce more seeds, which Thulani feeds to his hens, which then multiply so much that Thulani exchanges them for other animals. Soon he is busy trading animals and even milking a cow, and he realises he is happy in a whole new way. 'I have my best thoughts when I'm milking,' says Thulani, and he and his wife both laugh as if the whole trauma never happened. Scattered over the endpapers, the seeds become a symbol of everything we can make happen if we try – and of the joy we can find in work when we choose to do it ourselves (see, immediately: chores, having to do).

CURE FOR GROWN-UPS [PB] *Frederick* LEO LIONNI

Be aware, though, that what may look like a bone-lazy child may in fact be a child tending to seeds of a different kind. Frederick, the little mouse brought to life in Lionni's trademark rough-hewn collage, appears to all the other mice to be avoiding his fair share of the work. While they're busy gathering corn, nuts, wheat and straw to keep them going through the winter, Frederick just sits there, enjoying the heat of the sun and gazing at the view. The mice are understandably annoyed. But when, in the deep of winter, the food store runs dry and they're struggling to keep themselves warm, Frederick heats up their hearts by reminiscing about the summer and evoking the smells and colours of spring. Think twice before you berate the shirker in your midst. Perhaps he or she is a poet in the making.

SEE ALSO: **daydreaming, being accused of • homework, reluctance to do • indoors, spending too much time • walk, not wanting to go on a**

leader, wanting to be the

SEE: **in charge, wanting to be**

leaving friends behind

SEE: **moving house**

left out, being

SEE: **friends, finding it hard to make • stand up for yourself, not feeling able to**

life-threatening illness

[PB] *Jim's Lion*
RUSSELL HOBAN, ILLUSTRATED BY ALEXIS DEACON

A child facing a life-threatening diagnosis or a dangerous operation needs a very special book – one that can provide an image of strength to hold on to, and a vision of pulling through. They'll find this in *Jim's Lion,* a remarkable exploration of the psychology of healing told both in words and vivid, hallucinatory pictures.

A metaphorical tone is set from the start, opening as it does with a haunting dream sequence in which, among other things, Jim's hospital bed is devoured by a lion and he's left as a collection of puzzle pieces. We discover, when he wakes up, that Jim is to have a big operation – and is scared of being lost in his bad dreams forever (see: nightmares). Although his illness is never named, we understand that it's one from which not everyone recovers.

A kind, practical nurse is there for Jim in his moment of need. Nurse Bami tells him he has to discover his 'Finder'. To do this, he must go to a place in his head where he remembers feeling good. That's where he'll meet his Finder – and where his Finder will always be able to find him, should he ever need to be found. Jim's special place turns out to be by the sea, where he once went with his parents. It's on his second 'visit' to the seaside in his head that a lion emerges from the waves – as fierce and strong and frightening as the one who attacked his hospital bed. We are as surprised, and moved, as he is. What a creature to have on his side!

When the time comes for Jim to have his operation, the pictures take over – and, as a blood-coloured, formless beast battles with his Finder for supremacy, we realise how close to death Jim comes. The strength of the lion prevails, but the battle is tough. The story finishes with Jim coming downstairs on Christmas morning to greet his parents, 'the best present' they could ever have.

Speaking directly to the subconscious – the place where terrors lurk – this is a book that works on a deep level, reflecting and invading dreams with strong, archetypal imagery. It's also a book that requires being shared, and discussed, together. Where will your child's good-feeling place be? What form will their Finder take?

SEE ALSO: **about, what's it all? • bed, having to stay in • death, fear of • feelings, not able to express your • god, wondering if there is a • sadness • scared, being**

lights out, refusing to stop reading when it's time for

EFFECT AN ARTFUL SEGUE INTO A DISCUSSION ABOUT THE STORY

No childhood is complete without the occasional reading-under-the-duvet moment – torch in one hand, book in the other, head holding up the roof. Frankly, we'd rather not deny your kids the illicit pleasure of losing sleep in this way. But if you're determined to put sleep before stories, draw a child out of their book by asking them questions about it. Are they leaving the characters on the verge of a crisis? What do they think will happen next? Which of the characters would they most like to be? What would they ask the author if he/she were right now sitting on the end of their bed?

If the child's eyes are still locked firmly on the page after these attempts to lure them away, the book clearly has them in its thrall, and a tacit complicity may be called for instead. Leave a good torch on the bedside table as you go out.

loneliness

CB *Northern Lights*
PHILIP PULLMAN

If you think a child you know is lonely, give them a copy of *Northern Lights*, the first in the His Dark Materials trilogy. Not only will it absorb them completely – set as it is in an alternate universe in which a twelve-year-old girl, Lyra, discovers that children are disappearing and sets off on a quest to the far north to find them – but it will introduce them to the concept of the personal 'daemon'.

A daemon is an animal spirit that keeps you company at all times. It is your other half, without which you're incomplete. A daemon cannot survive without its human – and indeed when a daemon and their human are separated, they can only go a certain distance from each other before both begin to suffer. A daemon can talk, often speaking a truth their human is trying to ignore. Assuming various forms as a child is growing – shifting, minute by minute, from butterfly to dog, to owl, to mouse and so on – daemons only settle into their permanent form during the child's teenage years. Solid, tangible creatures, daemons can be cuddled, played with, held, hidden. And, perhaps most wondrously of all, daemons can feel their human's pain – just as the human feels theirs. Thus, when Lyra's daemon, Pantalaimon – still apt to change but starting to settle into its form as a pine marten – meets the golden monkey belonging to Mrs Coulter (a powerful woman mysteriously keen to take Lyra into her household) the monkey jumps on Pan and it's Lyra who doubles up in agony.

As Lyra makes her dangerous journey north to discover the whereabouts of the missing children, every daemon we meet sheds light on the human to whom it belongs. Thus, the daemon of Lee Scoresby – hot-air-ballooning adventurer – is a long-eared hare called Hester, as mild-mannered as Scoresby is exuberant. And the daemon of the powerful and ambitious Lord Asriel, who has dreams beyond the planet's boundaries, is a magnificent snow leopard. We meet humans with snakes, rats, lizards and birds of all varieties – from sea birds to kestrels. Over all of them hangs the threat of 'intercision', or the forced cutting of a daemon from their human – a fate worse than death. Ask your child, as they read the story, what their daemon would be. With a daemon you are never alone – and you are also more powerfully yourself.

SEE ALSO: **different, feeling • friends, finding it hard to make • only child, being an • school, being the new kid at**

loner, being a

PB *The Very Helpful Hedgehog*
ROSIE WELLESLEY

There's nothing wrong with being a loner. But a child who prefers their own company *too* much of the time may not realise the advantage of friends, especially when they're in need of a helping hand. This book will add weight to your case when pointing this out.

Isaac the hedgehog is curled up in the autumn leaves minding his own business when a falling apple lands on his back and spears itself on his spikes. He rolls over, rubs himself against the fence, and practically ties himself up in knots trying to get the apple off. Just when he's despairing of ever moving freely again, a donkey comes by and, delighted to see what just rolled into his paddock, munches the delicious apple up. At first Isaac thinks nothing of the donkey and goes back to his solitary life. But when another apple thuds down beside him he starts to get an idea. He and the donkey could add to each other's lives in a wonderfully symbiotic way if only they chose to look out for each other instead of just themselves.

CURE FOR GROWN-UPS *My Side of the Mountain*
JEAN CRAIGHEAD GEORGE

Consistently avoiding contact with others, even when it's offered in an honest, friendly way, can be a sign that something is wrong; and if you have a loner in your midst who doesn't leave their room except to go to school, eat and use the bathroom for weeks or even months on end, we recommend seeking professional help. But sometimes, as with the hero of *My Side of the Mountain*, a child's preference for their own company is merely a sign of rugged individualism and something to nurture, not fight. Sam Gribley hates living in the tiny New York apartment he shares with his parents and seven siblings. And when, at just twelve years old, he announces his plan to leave home, his parents know there is nothing they can do to stop him. Having read up in his local library about how to survive in the wilderness, he sets out for the Catskill mountains one day in May with nothing but a penknife, a ball of string, an axe, and a flint and steel with which to start a fire.

His first night under the stars is a disaster. But he learns quickly, and by September he has made himself a cosy nest inside a hemlock tree and is perfectly content. He cooks up meals of fish, onion soup and acorn pancakes, and for friends he has Baron the weasel, Jesse the raccoon and, most importantly of all, Frightful, a falcon he has trained to hunt. His comical conversations with this trio are a delightful part of the story, and as we watch Sam grow from cocky kid to mature young man capable of true independence we know that his instinct to escape had been good.

But what ultimately makes us feel confident about Sam is that he does, in fact, miss human company. At one point he befriends a lost schoolteacher who he nicknames 'Bando' and who in turn calls him 'Thoreau'. Bando memorably comes back to join Sam in his tree for Christmas, and Sam's father turns up too. These brief moments of companionship show us that there is nothing de-socialised about Sam; he is just a person who enjoys forging connections with animals and nature, as well as people. Being a loner doesn't necessarily have to mean there's something amiss – nor does it mean your loner will, in fact, be lonely.

SEE ALSO: **about, what's it all? • alone, wanting to be left • depression • indoors, spending too much time • laziness • screen, glued to the**

lose things, tendency to

CB *The Borrowers*
MARY NORTON

Children who have a habit of losing important things – homework, for instance, or small siblings – may in fact be suffering from another ailment entirely, of which this one is merely an unfortunate side effect (see: daydreaming, being accused of; homework, reluctance to do; sibling, having to look after a little). But if it's small things going astray – knick-knacks, pencil sharpeners, house keys – they'll benefit from being introduced to *The Borrowers*.

Every night, Pod – who lives with his wife Homily and their daughter Arrietty beneath the floorboards of a big country house – comes out to go 'borrowing': carting off small objects to re-purpose in their home 'down below'. Postage stamps become portraits of Queen Victoria to hang on their walls. Discarded letters become striped wallpaper. An open jewellery box becomes Arrietty's bed. And, the *pièce de résistance*, a knight from a chess set becomes a sculpture of a horse's head (a borrowing which, understandably, caused a 'great deal of trouble upstairs'.) Losing something is annoying – but imagining what it might have become if found by a Borrower will make a child almost pleased it has gone.

SEE ALSO: **frustration** • **toy, losing your favourite**

loser, being a bad

PB *Sally Sore Loser*
FRANK J SILEO, ILLUSTRATED BY CARY PILLO

PB *I Want to Win!* (Little Princess)
TONY ROSS

CB *SilverFin*
CHARLIE HIGSON

No one likes playing a game with someone who can't handle losing. Nip the tendency in the bud with *Sally Sore Loser* – a how-to story about a girl who throws a strop whenever things don't go her way. It's Sally's friends who sort her out, gently steering her towards playing to have fun, rather than playing to win. For those who've been over-indulged at home by game-fixing grown-ups – and who've got so used to winning that it comes as a shock when they don't – see *I Want to Win!* Even princesses need to let other people have their turn in the sun.

Who better to inaugurate older children into decent British ways than the young James Bond? In *SilverFin*, we see James starting his first year at Eton where, just twelve years old and recently orphaned, he's filled with the same first-day qualms as everyone else. Almost immediately, he finds himself in

MATCHE

competition with George Hellebore, the son of an American arms dealer, as they train for the Hellebore cup* – a test of strength and endurance that involves shooting, swimming and running. James hasn't yet developed his full repertoire of skills – social, sporting or spying – and when Hellebore junior pursues James around the school grounds for the sadistic pleasure of dunking him in the ice-cold river, James starts to see what he's up against. Hellebore's swimming is strong, and his shooting skills are the best in the school. But when it comes to long-distance running, James is better. He knows he could lick George in a fair race.

But there's the rub. Hellebore will do whatever it takes to finish first, including cheat, and James would rather not taint his conscience, or reputation, with any ungentlemanly behaviour. As the action moves to Scotland and becomes as nippy as the Aston Martin James is about to inherit, the Hellebores and their performance-enhancing serums prove no match for James's superior moral fibre. True to the spirit of Ian Fleming, Higson's young hero is a great mentor for kids to adopt. There's not even any of Bond's usual hanky-panky in sight.†

SEE ALSO: **fair, it's not** • **praise, seeking** • **sulking**

loser, feeling like a

CB *Scribbleboy*
PHILIP RIDLEY, ILLUSTRATED BY CHRIS RIDDELL

YA *Going Bovine*
LIBBA BRAY

In a culture obsessed with success, it's easy to feel like a loser – and once a kid starts beating themselves up about their lack of achievement, it can become a self-fulfilling prophecy. Young Bailey Silk in *Scribbleboy* has good reason to feel like a loser. Since his mum left (precisely sixty-four days, ten hours and twenty-two minutes ago), everything has been going downhill. The housing estate he's moved to with his older brother, Monty, and father, Skipper, is unrelentingly grey: grey concrete buildings, grey concrete walls and grey concrete pathways. Skipper seems to be under the impression he's living in a war zone, addressing Bailey as 'Trooper Two' and making him wear his school uniform even in the holidays; while Monty has shelved his ambition to go to college and taken a job at the Pizza Most Yum-Yum. So when Bailey receives a mysterious letter urging him to come to the 'Scribbleboy Fan Club', and shortly afterwards comes across a scribble on a wall in colours

* Named after Hellebore senior, who was keen to put his stamp on the elite British institution.

† Yet.

so intense that he actually passes out, things start to pick up. Little does he know it but this is the beginning of discovering that, far from being a loser, he's a vitally important link to 'Scribbleboy'.

Soon he's hanging out with Tiffany Spangle, who prescribes ice-cream flavours according to emotional need;* Ziggy, who needs Bailey's help when his wheelchair can't get up the stairs (see: disability, coping with); Ma Glamrock, who insists they boogie whenever there's a problem; and the excellent Levi and his moon-dancing mates – and Bailey's life becomes filled with colour, music and bounce. Watching him work out who was – or is – the original Scribbleboy (or could it even be Scribble*girl*?) will encourage any kid feeling lacklustre to unleash their own inner blaze of colour.

Sixteen-year-old Cameron in the surreal *Going Bovine* is your archetypal teen with a bad attitude who smokes pot in the toilets and whose idea of making an effort at school is to buy the 'Don Quixote Fake It! notes'. It doesn't help that his twin sister Jenna seems to be 'pre-majoring in perfection'. His parents have all but given up on him – and perhaps each other too – and familial communication happens via notes on the fridge.

So when he's fired from his weekend job at a fast-food burger joint for upending a tray of drinks, it seems at first as if holding down a job is just one more of the things he's failing at. Next he's suspended from school for unruly behaviour, and his parents send him to a drug counsellor and therapist. But when they find him rolling on the kitchen floor in agony, unable to control the jerks in his limbs, they send him to hospital for an MRI scan. The diagnosis shocks them all: Creutzfeldt-Jakob – or mad-cow disease – is slowly turning Cameron's brain to sponge.

What follows is one of the most surreal road trips in YA fiction, as Cameron, encouraged by a punk-rock angel named Dulcie with pink hair and fishnets (who may or may not be a hallucination), sets off to find a physicist named Dr X, an expert on wormholes and 'dark matter' (who may or may not know how to cure him). Whether it's really happening or whether it's one big hallucinatory 'figment of his spongiform mind' is something we're constantly kept guessing. But, along the way, Cameron realises something important: that however much time you've got left, life is what you make it. For desultory teens who recognise themselves in Cameron as he is at the start of the story, this is a brilliant wake-up call.

SEE ALSO: **give up, tendency to** • **good at anything, feeling like you're no** • **role model, in need of a positive** • **wrong, everything's going**

---

* An alternative practitioner after our own hearts.

losing a best friend

SEE: **best friend, falling out with your**

lost, being

[PB] *Blueberries for Sal*
ROBERT MCCLOSKEY

[CB] *The Silver Sword*
IAN SERRAILLIER

As traumatic for the child as for the grown-up who was supposed to be looking after them, getting lost is high on the list of scary things that can happen to a kid. *Blueberries for Sal*, with its slow, of-another-era pace and gorgeously detailed drawings, will make a lasting impression – shocking the reader just enough to make an effective preventative medicine. Use it to encourage small kids never to wander out of sight.

When Little Sal goes blueberrying with her mother, she drifts around the other side of Blueberry Hill without either of them noticing. Here, someone else is stocking up for the winter with her cub, too – a mother bear. While Little Sal mistakes the snuffles and twig-snaps made by the bear for those of her own mother and follows the creature unthinkingly, the little bear cub is making the same mistake on the other side. It's the mothers who notice first. Nothing ever gets really scary, but the knowledge of just how close Sal came to danger will penetrate kids and grown-ups alike. That both mothers are reunited with the right cub in the end means this works as a calming-down cure in the aftermath of getting lost (and found), too.

Getting lost near to home is one thing – but getting lost amid the chaos of a country at war is quite another. This is what happens to the three Polish siblings in *The Silver Sword*. When, shortly after their father, Joseph Balicki, is taken away by the Nazis, their mother Margrit is also captured, thirteen-year-old Ruth, eleven-year-old Edek and three-year-old Bronia are left to join the ranks of the dirty, starving 'lost children' who've been separated from their parents in war-torn Warsaw. Forced to fend for themselves, they live for a while in the basement of a bombed-out building, where Ruth resourcefully runs a makeshift school. In summer, the little family move to the woods on the outskirts of the city, where there's more food to be found. But when Edek, too, is taken prisoner, Ruth and Bronia decide to set foot for Switzerland – where, before the war started, their father told them to go should they ever become separated.

They're joined on their journey by the erratic yet loyal Jan, another lost child who carries with him a little silver sword, picked from the rubble of the Balickis' own house. The sword comes to represent the belief that their parents are alive and waiting for them at the other end. Having a pre-arranged meeting place is an excellent plan – both on a local and a global scale – and those with children in their care would do well to borrow the idea. But the real inspiration here is in the resourcefulness of the children. Not only do they find practical ways to keep themselves alive – smuggling food, persuading a Russian soldier to give them shoes for their long walk – but they also never give in to panic. Tragically, of course, not all lost children are found, and certainly the Balicki children encounter a lot of good luck and kindness on their journey. But encouraging kids to keep a cool head if ever they do get lost will boost their odds of finding their way home.

SEE ALSO: **give up, tendency to** • **scared, being**

lying

PB *Doug-Dennis and the Flyaway Fib*
DARREN FARRELL

CB *The Fib*
GEORGE LAYTON

YA *The Lie Tree*
FRANCES HARDINGE

The difference between lying and make-believe can be confusing for kids. What makes one bad and the other good? One of the best picture books for explaining the distinction is *Doug-Dennis and the Flyaway Fib,* in which best friends Doug-Dennis and Ben-Bobby go to the circus. While they're gazing at the acrobats, Doug-Dennis helps himself to Ben-Bobby's entire carton of popcorn – then says it was 'monsters' who ate it. Suddenly he begins to drift up into the air. As he comes up with increasingly unbelievable stories to explain the popcorn's disappearance, he's buoyed higher and higher on the hot air of his lies. Finally he realises that the only way to get back down to earth (and the circus he's missing) is to pop his bubble with the needle of truth. This story offers a lesson made all the more memorable for the strength of its visual metaphor.

For older readers, the brilliant short story *The Fib* shows how what starts as a seemingly harmless untruth can easily spiral out of control. Set in the north of England in the Fifties, young Gordon Banks wakes up with a heavy heart: it's football today, which he dreads. Not only is he always put in goal, but he has to wear his uncle's baggy old football kit and everyone, especially Barraclough, takes the mickey out of him for it. But in a moment of inspiration, he tells everyone that his uncle of the baggy shorts is none other than the great Bobby Charlton.

Gordon's lie, of course, takes wings in much the same way as Doug-Dennis's, and he gets caught out in the most satisfying way you can imagine – by

Charlton himself. Luckily for him, Charlton turns out to understand the agony of losing face in front of the other boys. But for the reader, the lesson is learned.

There's an even more scarring lesson for the reader to absorb in *The Lie Tree*. Faith has always cherished dreams of following in the footsteps of her father – a reverend and natural scientist. But, living at a time when women were considered less intelligent than men (see: role model, in need of a positive), she is constantly thwarted. When she and her family move from Kent to a remote Scottish island, Faith becomes increasingly exasperated by the way she is treated by her father's scientific peers; and when her taciturn father is found dead in mysterious circumstances, she decides to take matters into her own very capable hands. One of his botanic specimens, brought home from a recent expedition, is a curious tree which, she discovers, thrives on being told lies – and her father has been feeding it. Not only must the owner whisper lies to the tree, they must then spread those lies around the community. The more the lies take root, the more the tree thrives, eventually bearing fruit. If the liar then eats this fruit, a truth will be revealed relating to the original lie.

Faith decides to use the tree as a way of unmasking her father's killer – but in order to do so, she must herself start feeding it lies. As it turns out, she's rather good at this, revealing just the right snippets to just the right servants in her household. Soon, everyone is convinced that her father's ghost is at large and haunting their island community, and one servant is so terrified that she takes to sleeping in the church at night. As the tree grows stronger and stronger, Faith begins to doubt the wisdom of her plan. The powerful and poignant conclusion will give pause to those teens whose tongue tends to twist towards mendacity.

SEE ALSO: **blamed, being** • **know-it-all, being a** • **naughtiness** • **punished, being**

M IS FOR . . .

magic, loss of belief in

CB *The Last of the Really Great Whangdoodles*
JULIE ANDREWS EDWARDS

YA *Weetzie Bat*
FRANCESCA LIA BLOCK

There comes a time when a child starts to question their belief in magical things. The end to the innocent, gullible phase of childhood can give rise to a sort of grief – and not just for the child. Who better than Julie Andrews – she who once took to the skies with an umbrella as Mary Poppins – to make the case that, for all man's advances in science and technology, something valuable has been lost in this cynical age.

When siblings Ben, Tom and Lindy meet a quintessential mad professor with sparkling eyes and a purple-and-yellow-spotted scarf in *The Last of the Really Great Whangdoodles*, they have no idea he's Professor Savant, the famous cloning scientist who has just been awarded the Nobel Prize. But his scientific prowess certainly adds weight to his proposition that they come with him to Whangdoodleland to meet the 'last Whangdoodle'. These wise creatures – a little like a moose, but with horns – have almost completely died out as a result of no one believing in them any more, just like the Unicorn and the Hippogriff before them. But there's still one left – and with the right sort of mental training, one can still hope to catch a glimpse of him in the magical land to which he has retreated.

To get to Whangdoodleland, the children must learn to use their senses in a whole new way – not just seeing the grass and assuming it's green, but getting down on the ground and really looking at it. What would the earth look like to an ant or a worm? the professor asks. 'The lumps of clay would be mountains and the blades of grass would be a forest,' he says. 'Wouldn't it be a whole new countryside?' Once they get to Whangdoodleland, they do indeed find a whole new countryside – a vivid, Technicolor one inhabited by a motley collection of fantastical creatures, some more benevolent than others. Even the most sceptical child (not to mention their grown-up) will see that their lives would be more fantastic too if they re-trained their senses like this.

There's a lovely blend of the chimerical and the quotidian in the five novels of Weetzie Bat – set in California in the Eighties, but with added magic. Weetzie is a skinny girl with a 'beach-blonde flat top', pink Harlequin sunglasses and sugar-frosted eye shadow, who hates high school and everyone in it because 'no-one seems to be *living* any more'. But then she meets Dirk, with his 'shoe-polish-black' Mohawk and his red '55 Pontiac, and the two become inseparable. It turns out that Dirk is gay, and together they go looking for men – or 'duck hunting' in Dirk's lingo.

When Dirk's Grandma Fifi senses that Weetzie is sad, and gives her an antique brass urn which needs a bit of a polish, it's only a matter of time before a cloudy, turban-clad figure emerges . . . The way in which the genie grants Weetzie's wishes – making them come true in a literal as well as a metaphorical way (so that Dirk gets a 'duck' called, in fact, 'Duck', and Weetzie gets a beau called, in fact, 'My Secret Agent Lover Man', true to the exact wording of their requests) is one of the joyous aspects of this zany story. Real life rushes back in: AIDS drives Duck away for fear of loving too much, and My Secret Agent Lover Man won't have children with Weetzie because of all the suffering in the world. But, meanwhile, teens are treated to a compelling argument over the course of this fast-paced series for hanging on, whenever possible, to the magic they still sense at the periphery of their world.

CURE FOR GROWN-UPS PB *The Bog Baby* JEANNE WILLIS, ILLUSTRATED BY GWEN MILLWARD

For grown-ups in mourning, read this charming story of two sisters who find a 'bog baby' in the Bluebell Woods – a place of uncurling fern fronds and fecund insect life, beautifully conjured by Millward. They bring him home and keep him secretly in a bucket. When the bog baby becomes sickly and stops eating, the girls reveal his existence to their mother – who surprises everyone with her response. Perhaps the best way to counter a child's loss of belief in magic is to keep it alive in yourself.

SEE ALSO: **happy ever after, had enough of • innocence, loss of • praise, seeking • tooth fairy, non-appearance of the**

manners, bad

[PB] *The Elephant and the Bad Baby*
ELFRIDA VIPONT, ILLUSTRATED BY RAYMOND BRIGGS

[PB] *Madeline Says Merci*
JOHN BEMELMANS MARCIANO

[CB] *A Bear Called Paddington*
MICHAEL BOND, ILLUSTRATED BY PEGGY FORTNUM

[PB] *How Do Dinosaurs Eat Their Food?*
JANE YOLEN, ILLUSTRATED BY MARK TEAGUE

Begin by showing what *bad* manners are with *The Elephant and the Bad Baby,* in which an elephant meets a baby and takes him on a joyride through town. 'Would you like a ride?' asks the elephant. 'Yes!' 'Would you like an ice-cream?' 'Yes!' With the baby grinning happily from between the elephant's enormous ears, they go 'rumpeta rumpeta rumpeta' down the street, the elephant snaking his long grey trunk (painted by Raymond Briggs in lovely soft watercolour greys) into cake stalls, butcher's cabinets, sweet displays and fruit stalls, and helping himself without asking, let alone paying, for their smorgasbord. They're soon being pursued by several irate shopkeepers, waving their cleavers and crying, 'You never once said please!' When they arrive at the bad baby's house, the bad baby's mother charmingly invites them all in for pancakes. 'Yes please!!' they cry, revealing that just because someone's been rude to you doesn't mean you need to lose your manners in return.

If the child is a Madeline fan (and *vraiment*, who isn't), *Madeline Says Merci* will sort them out. Ludwig Bemelmans, the creator of Madeline – she who lives in the old house in Paris 'covered with vines' and goes out with her fellow orphans in 'two straight lines' – died in 1962, but his spirit, and drawings, were reincarnated in this book by a grandson he never met. John Bemelmans Marciano offers clear but gentle instruction on such subtle social niceties as the appropriate way to greet people you know in the street (a wave is fine if there's just one of them, but if it's a whole group of people you know, say 'hello' to each in turn, looking them in the eye, smiling, and possibly shaking each of their hands); what to do when the Queen comes to tea (curtsy, of course); and what to do when someone gives you a gift you don't want (exactly the same as when they give you a gift you *do* want. If in doubt, see: presents*). As the twelve little girls in two straight lines demonstrate by lapsing into energetic pillow fights, being polite doesn't have to mean being boring – and, what's more, those with good manners tend to have a more agreeable ride through life.

For evidence of this, move on to *A Bear Called Paddington.* When

* Indeed, if you were in any doubt about any of those answers, please ask your toddler (politely) if you can borrow the book when they're done.*

* *If you don't see why you need to ask politely, give up expecting good manners from your child.*

Paddington arrives in London from 'Darkest Peru', he greets the first strangers he meets – Mr and Mrs Brown – with a polite raise of his hat and a modest 'Good afternoon.' While they stand there gawping at him, he follows up with a 'Can I help you?' And when Mr and Mrs B take him to the station café for a sticky bun, he makes sure not to walk in first. 'After you, Mr Brown,' he says. It's impressive behaviour for anyone of small stature, let alone one who's straight out of the jungle. Paddington makes a bit of a mess over tea – never having used a cup and saucer before, and being a little over-excited about the sticky bun – but he's nevertheless invited back to 32 Windsor Gardens and, ultimately, offered a home. 'I expect it was because he raised his hat,' Judy tells her brother. 'It made a good impression.' We're not suggesting the younger generation need to start wearing (and raising) trilbies,* but this story does show how impeccable manners make someone hard to resist.

Talking of table manners seems old-fashioned these days, but nobody particularly likes sharing a meal with someone who burps, belches, fusses, fidgets, picks at their food, throws their food on the floor, plays with their food, glares at the food when you put it down in front of them, spits out their partially chewed food (and then draws everyone's attention to it on the side of their plate) or sticks their food up their nose. In *How Do Dinosaurs Eat Their Food?* we see a succession of dinos demonstrating these and other behaviours in detailed and hilarious ways. In the second half of the book, the same dinos are shown saying please and thank you, trying everything on their plates, picking things off the floor that they've dropped – and even holding a little finger in the air as they finish their mouthful before taking their turn to speak. These polite dinosaurs are arguably even funnier than the rude ones, and your child will probably enjoy parodying the niceties more, too. With luck, the parodies of the polite dinos will stick.

SEE ALSO: **grannies, having to kiss** • **presents** • **thank you letter, having to write a**

masturbation, embarrassment about

YA *How to Build a Girl*
CAITLIN MORAN

YA *Doing It*
MELVIN BURGESS

Being able to explore every nook and cranny of one's body is surely the right of every being lucky enough to have one – and for burgeoning teens wanting to live a sexually satisfied life one day, it's a necessity. To this end, we urge curious adolescents to read some unapologetically filthy fiction.

* Although that would be charming, too.

Girls can do no better than *How to Build a Girl,* in which a frustrated fourteen-year-old, Johanna, matures before our eyes into seventeen-year-old 'Dolly Wilde' – music journalist and self-styled 'Lady Sex Adventurer'. As well as spending much of the novel masturbating, Dolly embarks upon a lot of actual sex, graphically described (grown-ups, make sure your reader is ready). Likening her learning curve to that of a plumber working out how to be safe around a U-bend, Dolly's frank and enthusiastic exploits – which take her through Wolverhampton's bedsits and beyond – are both educational and liberating. By the end she has vowed 'never to fuck anything bigger than an eight-inch penis', never to say no to something new, and never to say yes to anything she doesn't want to do (vows which may, of course, cancel each other out, but she doesn't let that concern her). We look forward to meeting a new generation of girls who, inspired by Dolly, can share their masturbation stories without a blush.

Boys don't tend to have qualms about achieving orgasm in solitude, but they'll probably feel better about wanting to do it as often as they do after reading *Doing It.* Jonathan, Dino and Ben are all seventeen; and here, narrated from multiple viewpoints, are their thoughts about girls, sex, their parents, sex, their hot teachers, sex, their school – oh, and sex. Handsome Dino – 'possibly the most gorgeous creature in the school' (his own view, but widely shared) – is biding his time until Jackie, the 'other most gorgeous creature in the school', decides he's not a prat after all, and that she'll be his girlfriend. Jonathan fancies Deborah, who fancies him back – but he's worried what her being 'a bit chubby' might do to his status (happily, he soon gets over that). Ben, meanwhile, is having regular, steamy and increasingly demanding sex with Miss Young, a youthful but slightly unhinged drama teacher who flashed her knickers at him as a joke when he was fourteen – a sight which gave him much fuel for thought before, a couple of years down the line, he found himself being lured by her into the props cupboard.

It's Jonathan who's most keen to share details of his 'wank life'. After kissing Deborah in the park, his penis is so hard that he's positively uncomfortable – and the only thing he can do is rush home to see to 'Mr Knobby Knobster', which he gratefully does, three times in breathless succession. The refreshing frankness of this story will help boys articulate their own feelings, desires and habits – to themselves, if no one else – while girls will be given an insight into the hormonally driven mind of the adolescent male. As Sue, one of the more sensible girls in Dino's class, opines, so many girls 'think boys are like girls with knobs on – they're not'.

SEE ALSO: **embarrassment** • **hormones, raging** • **secret, having a** • **sex, having questions about** • **virginity, loss of**

materialism

SEE: **things, wanting**

maths, horror of

SEE: **school, not wanting to go to**

meltdown, having a

SEE: **tantrums**

mice, fear of

SEE: **animals, fear of**

middle one, being the

SEE: **sibling rivalry**

mistake, frightened about making a

PB *Beautiful Oops!*
BARNEY SALTZBERG

If a child thinks mistakes are a sign of weakness or failure, many otherwise fun activities – from painting a portrait to baking chocolate brownies – become fraught ones, offering as they do so many opportunities to mess up. That it's OK to make mistakes – and that mistakes can in fact be happy accidents, opening up all sorts of unforeseen possibilities – is the empowering message behind *Beautiful Oops!* With interactive flaps, turned-down corners and holes punched into its sturdy pages, this little board book shows how a rip in a piece of paper can become an alligator's smile, how a paint spill can become an elephant, and a stain from a mug of hot chocolate a drawing of a frog. Next time the child in your midst says 'Oops!', look for the opportunity to give it some legs.

SEE ALSO: **good at anything, feeling like you're no • parents, pushy • parents, strict • role model, in need of a positive**

misunderstood, feeling

SEE: **understood, not being**

monsters under the bed

SEE: **bed, fear of what's under the**

moodiness

[PB] *My Many Coloured Days*
DR SEUSS,
ILLUSTRATED BY STEVE JOHNSON AND LOU FANCHER

The causes (and effects) of our moods are myriad – and sometimes all we can do is accept them. This is very much the message of *My Many Coloured Days*, a rhyme found in Seuss's archives after his death and a great book to whip out next time a child in your vicinity is in a funk. 'Some days, of course, feel sort of Brown./Then I feel slow/and low, low down./Then comes a Yellow Day/and Wheeee!/I am a busy, buzzy bee.' With its softly painted pictures by husband-and-wife team Johnson and Fancher, the misery of a grey day is conveyed with an owl, the sadness of a brown with a bear, and the joy and lift of bright blue days with a bird. Young children are given a way to understand and accept their moods, and to share with their grown-ups the message that moods are OK. But – with the gleeful return of the yellow day – we see that moods can also change, and quickly too. Though it's aimed at kids from the pre-verbal to early school age, this book also works brilliantly with those on the autistic spectrum, and for older kids during moments of emotional extremity.*

SEE ALSO: **anger • sadness • sulking • tantrums • umbrage, taking • understood, not being**

* For more on teenage moodiness, see: adolescence; feelings, hurt; heard, not feeling; hormones, raging; violence; worrying.

moving house

[PB] *Half a World Away*
LIBBY GLEESON, ILLUSTRATED BY FREYA BLACKWOOD

[CB] *Skellig*
DAVID ALMOND

Moving house can be unsettling for children, particularly if they're leaving the only home they've ever known. And when it means saying 'so long' to neighbourhood friends, it's even harder. In *Half a World Away*, we meet Amy and Louie – friends who have, until now, only had to call out a 'Coo-ee, Am-ee' or a 'Coo-ee, Lou-ee' and the other comes scrambling through the hole in the fence. Together they play in the sandbox, dress up or lie on their backs looking at the shapes of the clouds. But then Amy's family move to a high-rise city on the water – 'half a world away' – and Louie is left all alone in his green suburbia. It's Louie's grandmother who gives him hope that if he goes outside and calls loudly Amy may still hear him; and when the clouds shaped like dragons and seahorses that he saw overhead are reflected in the window of Amy's city high-rise, we know that she has. With their soft, watery hues and tendency to move from the close-up details of toys to big, panoramic skyscapes, Blackwood's illustrations capture the sense of deep longing that both kids feel, while suggesting their continued connection.

After the sadness of what must be left behind come the prickles of excitement over what may be lying in wait. Wonder of a mysterious, eerie kind is to be found in *Skellig*, the story of a boy who moves to a new house on the other side of town. Michael's new house is 'supposed to be wonderful' but is in fact a ramshackle wreck, and he wishes they were back in their old house, close to his mates and school. To make matters worse, his parents are both distracted by his prematurely born baby sister, who hovers between life and death. But when, the day after they move in, Michael peers into the old, semi-derelict garage, full of dust-caked old furniture and rolled-up carpets, he is astonished to find a strange creature sitting propped up against the wall. Pale and filthy and covered with spider's webs, the man looks to be near death himself, but every so often he picks a dead bluebottle off his jacket and puts it in his mouth. 'What do you want?' he croaks in a voice that sounds like it hasn't been used in years.

When Michael meets Mina (see: home-schooling), an unconventional girl down the road who can quote lines from William Blake – a poet, she tells him, who saw 'angels' in his garden – he realises he's found someone who will know what to do. Together they care for the curmudgeonly being, moving the calcifying creature from the stricken garage to a place where he can rediscover his urge to live, and their friendship blossoms. Even children leaving a place and people they've loved will start to wonder what discoveries and new friends are waiting to be made in their new neighbourhood after reading this extraordinary tale.

SEE ALSO: **friends, feeling like you have no • school, being the new kid at**

museums, not wanting to visit

CB *Wonderstruck*
BRIAN SELZNICK

Museums can be places of magic and mystery, revelation and wonder. But they can also be huge, seemingly endless, and exhausting. And although some museums work very hard to lure children in, others leave it to the attending grown-up to generate the excitement and weave the narratives. Next time a museum visit is planned, prepare the kids first with *Wonderstruck*.

It's 1977, and Ben's librarian mother has died. When he finds a notebook of hers that hints at his unknown father, he decides to go in search of him and hides out in the Museum of Natural History in New York.* Here he stumbles on a diorama of wolves from Gunflint Lake – the very lake he has grown up on – which makes him feel very much at home. In fact, he's something of a museum curator himself, his collection at home including a bird's skull, a stromatolite fossil, and pieces of a meteorite.

Meanwhile, back in 1927, we meet Rose, another runaway child, this one given to building model cities out of paper. The two narratives converge and when, in 1977, Ben finds a spectacular miniature New York taking up an entire room of the Queens Museum of Art,† we soon realise who made it. Ben and the now elderly Rose walk like giants through the streets of this mini metropolis – and discover that the passions they share may be grounded in more than coincidence. Told in what has become Selznick's classic mix of text and highly detailed pencil drawings, this is a story with the power to make kids fall in love with museums and all they stand for – not just the artefacts themselves, but the stories behind the artefacts and the people who made or found them. Give it to the kids to read, then set off with your fledgling curators to form connections with the treasures they find in the museum near you.

SEE ALSO: **bored, being • laziness**

---

* Just as Claudia and Jamie hide out in the Metropolitan Museum of Art in the wonderful *From the Mixed-up Files of Mrs Basil E Frankweiler* (EL Konigsburg), a book to which Selznick pays obvious homage.

† Now known as the Queens Museum.

musical instrument, having to practise a

[ER] *Gus and Grandpa and the Piano Lesson*
CLAUDIA MILLS, ILLUSTRATED BY CATHERINE STOCK

[PB] *Lafcadio, the Lion Who Shot Back*
SHEL SILVERSTEIN

Whether it's the trumpet or the piano, learning to play a musical instrument can be painful for everyone involved at the start. Not only is there the need to keep to a regular practice schedule, but there's also the shame of facing the teacher each week when they haven't, and the hideous noises they make before they start to get any good. All of which means it's often several years before it starts to feel worthwhile or enjoyable. The delightful *Gus and Grandpa and the Piano Lesson*, an early reader aimed at just the age when the trouble generally hits, covers all these issues and more. Luckily for Gus, his understanding grandpa not only makes him feel better when he botches his first piano recital, but also finds a way to get the music 'in Gus's fingers'. Inspiring stuff.

Practice, of course, is key and a lovely demonstration of just how much someone can achieve if they really put their mind to it is to be found in *Lafcadio, the Lion Who Shot Back* – the mischievous Shel Silverstein's first published story. A long picture book that lends itself to being read out loud, it tells the tale of a lion who politely introduces himself to the man with the cap and funny long stick when all the other lions run away. The meeting goes badly for the hunter. First, he provokes the lion's ire by admitting he was planning to make him into a rug on which to toast marshmallows in front of his fire. And then he ignores Lafcadio's counter-suggestion that he go back to the hunter's house alive, and they toast marshmallows together. Lafcadio has no choice after that: he eats the hunter, then has a go at firing the hunter's 'stick'.

He can't do it at first. But he doesn't give up. After a while he manages to pull the trigger with his tail and every afternoon after that, while the other lions are sleeping, he sneaks off to practise, using his paws this time. The next time hunters come, Lafcadio shoots first – and for a while he and the other lions enjoy a happy, carefree existence, their territory now scattered with charming 'hunter rugs'. The lesson is clear to all: practise hard enough and you can master anything you want.

SEE ALSO: **give up, tendency to** • **laziness**

N IS FOR . . .

nails, biting your

Paint the vile child's nails with foul-tasting varnish, make them wear a pair of disposable plastic gloves and, if necessary, offer a financial bribe.* Then challenge them to get through a nail-biting book without succumbing to temptation. If they can do it, they're cured.†

THE TEN BEST NAIL-BITING READS

- CB *The Letter for the King* TONKE DRAGT
- CB *The Dreamsnatcher* ABI ELPHINSTONE
- CB *A Dog Called Grk* JOSH LACEY
- CB *Hatchet* GARY PAULSEN
- CB *Harry Potter and the Prisoner of Azkaban* JK ROWLING
- YA *Dead Time* (The Murder Notebooks) ANNE CASSIDY
- YA *Stolen* LUCY CHRISTOPHER
- YA *Twisted* LAURIE HALSE ANDERSON
- YA *The New Recruit* (Liam Scott) ANDY MCNAB
- YA *Unwind* NEAL SHUSTERMAN

SEE ALSO: **anxiety** • **exams** • **worrying**

---

* For guidance on how to bribe to best effect, see *The Berenstain Bears and the Bad Habit* by Stan and Jan Berenstain.

† If you're worried about this cure backfiring, remember that 'nail-biting' also means 'gripping'.

name, hating your

[PB] *Chrysanthemum*
KEVIN HENKES

[CB] *Into the Wild*
ERIN HUNTER

When, for whatever reason, a child falls out of love with their name, it can be as painful for the grown-ups who chose the fanciful appellation as it is for the child lumbered with it. The parents of the little mouse in the eponymous *Chrysanthemum* gave her that name because, to them, it expressed her perfection. And Chrysanthemum, to begin with, loves it too. But then she starts school (see: school, starting). 'It's so *long*,' Victoria, Jo and Rita – her more conventionally named classmates – say. 'It scarcely fits on your name tag.' And, of course, 'You're named after a *flower*.' Chrysanthemum is crestfallen, and though her parents try to convince her that her name is far more fascinating and unusual than everyone else's, Chrysanthemum is unimpressed. However, when the charismatic new music teacher, Miss Delphinium Twinkle, brings instant panache to being named after a flower – and reveals the name she's got in mind for her soon-to-be-born mouseling – everything changes. This lovely story shows that once you make your name your own, you can get away with the zaniest of monikers.

If, as he or she grows older, a child feels their name doesn't match who they are, they'll probably get a kick out of *Into the Wild*, the first in the Warriors series. Rusty, a young marmalade tabby, lives a comfortable, cosy life with his human owners. But for reasons he doesn't quite understand, he finds himself drawn to the cool, strange scents of the forest at the end of his garden, and one night he dares to go in. Within moments, a creature he didn't see coming has landed savagely on his back, sharp claws digging into his skin. Rusty rolls himself free, knocking the breath from his attacker's lungs – and so begins his friendship with Greypaw, one of the trainee wild cats living freely in the woods.

As it turns out, the wrestling match was a test. 'You fight well for a Twoleg pet,' says a magnificent, large grey she-cat appearing from the undergrowth and turning her piercing blue eyes on Rusty. Soon Rusty has ditched his human owners and bravely followed these savage felines to their camp deep in the woods. Here, he meets the individual members of ThunderClan, each with their own personality-defining name – Lionheart, Yellowfang, Smallear and the beautiful 'medicine' cat, Spottedleaf – and learns about the other clans from whom they must defend their hunting grounds. When he finds himself in another fight, which ends with him standing victorious in a shaft of sunlight, his orange pelt blazing, he is given a new warrior name: Firepaw. And, of course, Rusty is never Rusty again. If your name doesn't match your nature, find some friends who see you for who you are. A nickname will surely follow.

names, being called

SEE: **bullied, being**

naughtiness

[PB] *Where the Wild Things Are*
MAURICE SENDAK

[ER] *The Adventures of Captain Underpants*
DAV PILKEY

All small children are inherently feral, but some are more feral than others. And when a child's innate capacity for wildness exceeds the level considered acceptable in their household, he or she can easily earn the label of 'naughty' – and then live up to it. To avoid this happening, bring in Max from *Where the Wild Things Are*.

Max likes to dress up in a pointy-eared monster costume and hurl himself down the stairs in pursuit of the dog with a dinner fork in his hand. When this gets him sent to his room, Max looks angry enough. But in the time it takes to turn two pages, his anger has morphed into a mischievous chuckle. Soon Max is sailing across the sea in his very own boat, a picture of contentment. When he's crowned king of the wild things – a hugely satisfying collection of hairy, big-eyed monsters with horns, claws, teeth and swollen bellies, all brought to glorious life by Sendak's cross-hatching pen – he's proud to be in charge (see: in charge, wanting to be). What follows is the sort of rumpus most grown-ups would love to indulge in if they would only admit it, with much stamping and hollering and howling at the moon. And when the need to run amok is all used up, Max is just like any other tired kid, all worn out and wanting his grown-ups, food and bed. Max has no fear of the wild things, either inner or outer; and Sendak's book is delightful proof that while enjoying some feral behaviour every now and then may challenge a child's grown-ups temporarily, it doesn't mean they're wicked. Even rumpuses come to an end.

It can be helpful to consider that within every naughty child lies a creative, intelligent, fun-loving individual who doesn't really understand why life has to be taken so seriously . . . or at least that's one way to look at it. It's certainly the case with school pranksters George and Harold in Dav Pilkey's fabulous *Adventures of Captain Underpants* books. George and Harold* are always up to something – such as swapping the letters on signs ('Pick Your Own Roses'

* Named after two children's book characters that Pilkey loved as a child: Curious George and Harold of the purple crayon fame.

is rearranged to become 'Pick Our Noses') and pouring bubble bath down the brass horns of the marching band – much to the fury of their head teacher, Mr Krupp. They're also responsible for creating their very own comic books, featuring a superhero who flies through the air in his underpants singing, 'Tra-la-laaaa!'* Featuring a cast of nicely named teachers (Mr Meaner, Ms Ribble – read them out loud), kid-tastic villains (toilets with gnashing lids, zombie nerds) and with built-in 'Flip-o-Ramas'™ for some delightful low-tech animation effects, *Captain Underpants* may be just the ticket for encouraging your naughty child to dig out their own talent while they're missing out on Golden Time.

CURE FOR GROWN-UPS [PB] *Love You Forever* **ROBERT MUNSCH, ILLUSTRATED BY SHEILA MCGRAW**

If your child is so naughty you find yourself losing patience, this book will help you re-group. By day, a mother is driven crazy by her son's antics, but by night she creeps into his bedroom to watch him sleeping, her face brimming with love. Unusual perspectives – such as looking down on the son's head as he climbs upstairs – help to make this book moving instead of mawkish, and it's a nice reminder of the deep and complex ways in which we love our children, irrespective of their behaviour. It's also an inducement to plumb deep into your patience reserves. However much you show your children when they're at their most exasperating, they'll be inclined to show to you when you're old and ornery yourself.

SEE ALSO: **adventure, needing an** • **animals, being unkind to** • **bath, not wanting to have a** • **beastly, being** • **told, never doing what you're**

nausea

SEE: **sick, being**

* The fact that Dav Pilkey was himself always being sent out of the classroom for disruptive behaviour, and invented Captain Underpants while doing detention in the corridor, aged eight, surely has a lot to do with why these books ring so true.

nightmares

[PB] *Tell Me Something Happy Before I Go to Sleep*
JOYCE DUNBAR, ILLUSTRATED BY DEBI GLIORI

[PB] *Kate, the Cat and the Moon*
DAVID ALMOND, ILLUSTRATED BY STEPHEN LAMBERT

[CB] *Gossamer*
LOIS LOWRY

The first time a child says they're afraid of falling asleep in case they have a bad dream, introduce them to Willa, the adorable bunny in *Tell Me Something Happy Before I Go to Sleep*. At bedtime, Willa's big brother Willoughby takes her round the house on his shoulders showing her everything that's happy, from the chicken slippers under her bed, waiting for her feet, to the morning itself, waiting to wake her up, all painted in soothing pinks, blues and yellows. Head thus filled with positive and reassuring thoughts, she drops off happily. Adopt the same nightly ritual.

Slightly older children will enjoy having their heads filled with the imaginings of Kate, in *Kate, the Cat and the Moon*. When Kate – irresistibly drawn by Stephen Lambert with big brown eyes and a not-too-neat bob – is awoken by the '*miaow*' of a cat on a moonlit night, she discovers her inner feline. Licking her 'tiny sharp teeth' with her 'tiny rough tongue', she jumps into the night with her newfound friend. They climb to the top of a hill and, the world suddenly opening out in a surprise three-page-spread, find a sky full of the very dreams being dreamt by all the members of her family. Here's Mum and Dad in a boat on a heart-shaped lake; there's brother Pete chasing the dog; and there's Grandma dancing at the Roxy with Grandpa. If ever there was a suggestion that sleeping is not just safe but full of wonder and love, this is it.

Older children troubled by nightmares may find comfort in *Gossamer*. 'Littlest One' is one of the tiny, fairy-like creatures whose job it is to visit humans at night and stock their heads with happy dreams. Up till now, Littlest One has had an easy time collecting 'fragments' with which to fill the head of the old lady to whom she's assigned, delicately touching the photo of the man in the uniform on her bedside table, for instance, bringing her a dream which never fails to make her smile. The dog, too, is easy – Littlest One generally bestows dreams about food on him. But when the old woman takes in John, a troubled foster boy (see: foster care, being in), Littlest One knows that her job has just become much harder. This traumatised boy is vulnerable to an attack from the Sinisteeds – responsible for inflicting nightmares – and she'll need all her strength to compete with them.

The boy has very few possessions, and even fewer positive associations. But when she realises that the angry boy has begun to love the old woman's dog, a whole new dreamscape opens up. Another encouragement to observe a nightly ritual of ending the day on a positive note, this gentle chapter book will itself help to keep the Sinisteeds at bay.

SEE ALSO: **scared, being** • **sleep, unable to get to**

nits

PB *Scritch Scratch*
MIRIAM MOSS, ILLUSTRATED BY DELPHINE DURAND

The scourge of many a classroom and the one thing grown-ups dread the children in their care bringing home, nits are as hard to eradicate as they are easy to catch. For the lucky little nit in Miss Calypso's classroom, there's no shortage of thick and enticing heads of hair to make a home in – but the one it picks is particularly thrilling for the reader.* A great introduction to the dreaded little critters' insidious ability to stage a comeback if just one person stints on the treatments, this book also manages to be a story in itself with true love, no less, found at the end. All the nit-lit you'll ever need or, frankly, want.

nose, picking your

PB *Don't Do That!*
TONY ROSS

Most cautionary tales make children want to do exactly the thing they're being cautioned against. Not this one. When a little girl called Nellie sticks her finger up her nose and then can't get it out again, it triggers just the right amount of disgust to really, really, *really* put us off – while also wanting to find out what happens. Everybody has a go at trying to get Nellie's finger out, and everyone fails – even the scientist who ties Nellie's arm to a rocket and her leg to a park bench, then blasts the rocket into space (taking with it Nellie, the whole park bench, and the old man dozing on it). Nobody listens to Nellie's brother Henry, who keeps saying that *he* knows how to get her finger out – partly because each time he says it, he has some sort of alarming tool in his hand, a saw and a pitchfork among them. In fact, it *is* Henry who saves the day in the end – and in a way that isn't gruesome at all. But we can't help noticing that after all this stretching and battering, the pretty little nose Nellie sported at the beginning is not quite so small and button-like as it was before.

* The teacher's.

O IS FOR . . .

obsessions

Feed the craze.

THE TEN BEST BOOKS ABOUT BALLET

- [PB] *Angelina Ballerina* KATHARINE HOLABIRD, ILLUSTRATED BY HELEN CRAIG
- [PB] *Dogs Don't Do Ballet* ANNA KEMP, ILLUSTRATED BY SARA OGILVIE
- [PB] *The Dance Teacher* SIMON MILNE, ILLUSTRATED BY CHANTAL STEWART
- [ER] *Ella Bella Ballerina and the Nutcracker* JAMES MAYHEW
- [CB] *Summer's Dream* (The Chocolate Box Girls) CATHY CASSIDY
- [CB] *To Dance* SIENA CHERSON SIEGEL, ILLUSTRATED BY MARK SIEGEL
- [CB] *Ballet Shoes* NOEL STREATFEILD
- [CB] *Tales from the Ballet* LOUIS UNTERMEYER, ILLUSTRATED BY ALICE AND MARTIN PROVENSEN
- [YA] *Billy Elliot* MELVIN BURGESS*
- [YA] *Bunheads* SOPHIE FLACK

THE TEN BEST BOOKS ABOUT DINOSAURS

- [PB] *Captain Flinn and the Pirate Dinosaurs* GILES ANDREAE, ILLUSTRATED BY RUSSELL AYTO
- [PB] *Tom and the Island of Dinosaurs* IAN BECK
- [PB] *Yohance and the Dinosaurs* ALEXIS OBI, ILLUSTRATED BY LYNNE WILLEY
- [PB] *Harry and the Bucketful of Dinosaurs* IAN WHYBROW, ILLUSTRATED BY ADRIAN REYNOLDS
- [CB] *The Enormous Egg* OLIVER BUTTERWORTH, ILLUSTRATED BY LOUIS DARLING
- [CB] *Dinotopia: A Land Apart from Time* JAMES GURNEY
- [YA] *The Lost World* SIR ARTHUR CONAN DOYLE

---

* Based on the screenplay by Lee Hall.

YA *Jurassic Park* **MICHAEL CRICHTON**

YA *The Land that Time Forgot* **EDGAR RICE BURROUGHS**

YA *A Journey to the Centre of the Earth* **JULES VERNE**

THE TEN BEST BOOKS ABOUT DOGS

PB *Bad Dog, Marley!* **JOHN GROGAN, ILLUSTRATED BY RICHARD COWDREY**

PB *Harry the Dirty Dog* **GENE ZION, ILLUSTRATED BY MARGARET BLOY GRAHAM**

ER *Go, Dog. Go!* **PD EASTMAN**

ER *The Invisible Dog* **DICK KING-SMITH**

ER *Henry and Mudge* **CYNTHIA RYLANT AND SUCIE STEVENSON**

CB *Because of Winn-Dixie* **KATE DICAMILLO**

CB *The Call of the Wild* **JACK LONDON**

CB *Shiloh* **PHYLLIS REYNOLDS NAYLOR**

CB *Where the Red Fern Grows* **WILSON RAWLS**

YA *Fifteen Dogs* **ANDRÉ ALEXIS**

THE TEN BEST BOOKS ABOUT FAIRIES

PB *The Complete Book of Flower Fairies* **CICELY MARY BARKER**

PB *The Teeny-Weeny Walking Stick* **KAREN HODGSON, ILLUSTRATED BY SALLY ANNE LAMBERT**

CB *The Field Guide* (The Spiderwick Chronicles) **HOLLY BLACK, ILLUSTRATED BY TONI DITERLIZZI**

CB *Goblin Market* **CHRISTINA ROSSETTI, ILLUSTRATED BY ARTHUR RACKHAM**

CB *The Night Fairy* **LAURA AMY SCHLITZ, ILLUSTRATED BY ANGELA BARRETT**

CB *The Girl Who Circumnavigated Fairyland in a Ship of Her Own Making* **CATHERYNNE M VALENTE**

YA *Glimmerglass* (Faeriewalker) **JENNA BLACK**

YA *The Mystery of the Fool and the Vanisher* **DAVID AND RUTH ELLWAND**

YA *Stardust* **NEIL GAIMAN**

YA *Fablehaven* **BRANDON MULL, ILLUSTRATED BY BRANDON DORMAN**

THE TEN BEST BOOKS ABOUT FOOTBALL

ER *Great Save!* **ROB CHILDS, ILLUSTRATED BY MICHAEL REID**

ER *Boys United* (Football Academy) **TOM PALMER**

CB *The Transfer* **TERENCE BLACKER**

CB *Hannah's Secret* **NARINDER DHAMI**

CB *Leah and the Football Dragons* **PAUL MULLINS**

CB *Foul Play* **TOM PALMER**

CB *Keeper* **MAL PEET**

CB *Do Goalkeepers Wear Tiaras?* **HELENA PIELICHATY**

YA *Booked* **KWAME ALEXANDER**

YA *Bend it Like Beckham* **NARINDER DHAMI**

THE TEN BEST BOOKS ABOUT GREEK MYTHS

ER *Tales from the Odyssey* **MARY POPE OSBORNE, ILLUSTRATED BY TROY HOWELL**

CB *Atticus the Storyteller's 100 Greek Myths* **LUCY COATS, ILLUSTRATED BY ANTHONY LEWIS**

CB *The God Beneath the Sea* **LEON GARFIELD AND EDWARD BISHEN, ILLUSTRATED BY CHARLES KEEPING**

CB *The Orchard Book of Greek Myths* **GERALDINE MCCAUGHREAN, ILLUSTRATED BY EMMA CHICHESTER CLARK**

CB *The Lightning Thief* (Percy Jackson and the Olympians) **RICK RIORDAN**

CB *The Lost Hero* (Heroes of Olympus) **RICK RIORDAN**

CB *Black Ships Before Troy* **ROSEMARY SUTCLIFF**

YA *A Song for Ella Grey* **DAVID ALMOND**

YA *Troy* **ADÈLE GERAS**

YA *The King Must Die* **MARY RENAULT**

THE TEN BEST BOOKS ABOUT KING ARTHUR AND THE KNIGHTS OF THE ROUND TABLE

CB *The Lost Years of Merlin* **TA BARRON**

CB *The Sword in the Tree* **CLYDE ROBERT BULLA**

CB *Over Sea, Under Stone* (The Dark Is Rising) **SUSAN COOPER**

CB *King Arthur and His Knights of the Round Table* **ROGER LANCELYN GREEN**

CB *The Sword in the Stone* **TH WHITE**

CB *King Arthur and the Knights of the Round Table* **MARCIA WILLIAMS**

YA *The Seeing Stone* (Arthur) **KEVIN CROSSLEY-HOLLAND**

YA *Corbenic* **CATHERINE FISHER**

YA *The Sword and the Circle* (King Arthur) **ROSEMARY SUTCLIFF**

YA *Sword of the Rightful King* **JANE YOLEN**

THE TEN BEST BOOKS ABOUT MARTIAL ARTS

PB *Beautiful Warrior: The Legend of the Nun's Kung Fu* **EMILY ARNOLD MCCULLY**

PB *Ninja!* **ARREE CHUNG**

PB *JoJo's Flying Sidekick* **BRIAN PINKNEY**

CB *The Way of the Warrior* (Young Samurai) **CHRIS BRADFORD**

CB *White Crane* (Samurai Kids) **SANDY FUSSELL, ILLUSTRATED BY RHIAN NEST JAMES**

CB *Moonshadow* **SIMON HIGGINS**

YA *Girl Fights Back* (Emily Kane Adventure) **JACQUES ANTOINE**

YA *Across the Nightingale Floor* (Tales of the Otori) **LIAN HEARN**

YA *Jet Black and the Ninja Wind* **LEZA LOWITZ AND SHOGO OKETANI**
YA *Tiger* (The Five Ancestors) **JEFF STONE**

THE TEN BEST BOOKS ABOUT SPACE

PB *Man on the Moon!* **SIMON BARTRAM**
PB *Dougal and the Space Rocket* **JANE CARRUTH AND SERGE DANOT***
PB *If You Decide to Go to the Moon* **FAITH MCNULTY, ILLUSTRATED BY STEVEN KELLOGG**
PB *Whatever Next* **JILL MURPHY**
ER *Fortunately, the Milk* **NEIL GAIMAN, ILLUSTRATED BY CHRIS RIDDELL**
CB *Gloria Rising* **ANN CAMERON**
CB *Charlie and the Great Glass Elevator* **ROALD DAHL, ILLUSTRATED BY QUENTIN BLAKE**
CB *A Wrinkle in Time* **MADELEINE L'ENGLE**
YA *The Martian Chronicles* **RAY BRADBURY**
YA *172 Hours on the Moon* **JOHAN HARSTAD**

THE TEN BEST BOOKS ABOUT VAMPIRES

CB *Fang of the Vampire* (Scream Street) **TOMMY DONBAVAND**
CB *Vampire Island* **ADELE GRIFFIN**
CB *A Taste for Red* **LEWIS HARRIS**
CB *Bunnicula* **DEBORAH AND JAMES HOWE**
YA *Let the Right One In* **JOHN AJVIDE LINDQVIST**
YA *Notes from a Totally Lame Vampire* **TIM COLLINS, ILLUSTRATED BY ANDREW PINDER**
YA *The Radleys* **MATT HAIG**
YA *Vampire Academy* **RICHELLE MEAD**
YA *Twilight* **STEPHENIE MEYER**
YA *Dracula* **BRAM STOKER**

THE TEN BEST BOOKS ABOUT WEREWOLVES

CB *Young Werewolf* **CORNELIA FUNKE**
CB *Harry Potter and the Prisoner of Azkaban* **JK ROWLING**
CB *Werewolf Skin* (Goosebumps) **RL STINE**
YA *The Silver Wolf* **ALICE BORCHARDT**
YA *The Werewolf of Paris* **GUY ENDORE**
YA *Cycle of the Werewolf* **STEPHEN KING**
YA *The Wolf's Hour* **ROBERT R MCCAMMON**

---

* As a rule, we have not included out-of-print books; here we make a nostalgic exception. Ella has a copy, if you're struggling to get hold of it.

- YA *Breaking Dawn* (Twilight) **STEPHENIE MEYER**
- YA *The Wolfman* **NICHOLAS PEKEARO**
- YA *The Wolf Gift* **ANNE RICE**

THE TEN BEST BOOKS FOR KIDS WHO LOVE HISTORY

- ER *Dinosaurs Before Dark* (The Magic Treehouse) **MARY POPE OSBORNE**
- CB *The Terrible Tudors* (Horrible Histories) **TERRY DEARY AND NEIL TONGE, ILLUSTRATED BY MARTIN BROWN**
- CB *Wolf of the Plains* (Conquerer) **CONN IGGULDEN**
- CB *The Thieves of Ostia* (Roman Mysteries) **CAROLINE LAWRENCE**
- CB *The Escape* (Henderson's Boys) **ROBERT MUCHAMORE**
- CB *Wolf Brother* (Chronicles of Ancient Darkness) **MICHELLE PAVER**
- CB *I Survived the Sinking of the Titanic, 1912* (I Survived) **LAUREN TARSHIS, ILLUSTRATED BY SCOTT DAWSON**
- CB *The Lottie Project* **JACQUELINE WILSON, ILLUSTRATED BY NICK SHARRATT**
- YA *Skippy Dies* **PAUL MURRAY**
- YA *The Eagle of the Ninth* **ROSEMARY SUTCLIFF**

THE TEN BEST DETECTIVE BOOKS

- PB *Hermelin, the Detective Mouse* **MINI GREY**
- CB *Look into My Eyes* (Ruby Redfort) **LAUREN CHILD**
- CB *The Hound of the Baskervilles* **SIR ARTHUR CONAN DOYLE**
- CB *Operation Bunny* **SALLY GARDNER**
- CB *Skulduggery Pleasant* **DEREK LANDY**
- CB *Death Cloud* **ANDREW LANE**
- CB *Wild Boy* **ROB LLOYD JONES**
- CB *Precious and the Monkeys* **ALEXANDER MCCALL SMITH**
- CB *Encyclopaedia Brown* **DONALD J SOBOL**
- CB *Murder Most Unladylike* **ROBIN STEVENS**

THE TEN BEST FANTASY BOOKS

- CB *Alice's Adventures in Wonderland* **LEWIS CARROLL**
- CB *The Spook's Apprentice* (The Wardstone Chronicles) **JOSEPH DELANEY**
- CB *Stoneheart* **CHARLIE FLETCHER**
- CB *The Cry of the Icemark* **STUART HILL**
- CB *The Secret of Platform 13* **EVA IBBOTSON**
- CB *The Tree that Sat Down* **BEVERLEY NICHOLS**
- CB *Eragon* (Inheritance Cycle) **CHRISTOPHER PAOLINI**
- CB *The Colour of Magic* (Discworld) **TERRY PRATCHETT**

CB *Charmed Life* (Chrestomanci) DIANA WYNNE JONES
YA *Throne of Glass* SARAH J MAAS

THE TEN BEST GRAPHIC NOVELS

ER *Zita the Spacegirl* BEN HATKE
CB *El Deafo* CECE BELL
CB *Smile* RAINA TELGEMEIER
CB *American Born Chinese* GENE LUEN YANG, COLOURED BY LARK PIEN
YA *The Encyclopedia of Early Earth* ISABEL GREENBERG
YA *Ray Bradbury's Fahrenheit 451* TIM HAMILTON
YA *The Sculptor* SCOTT MCCLOUD
YA *The Thrilling Adventures of Lovelace and Babbage* SYDNEY PADUA
YA *The Lost Boy* GREG RUTH
YA *This One Summer* MARIKO TAMAKI AND JILLIAN TAMAKI

THE TEN BEST HORSEY BOOKS

ER *Adventures of the Little Wooden Horse* URSULA MORAY WILLIAMS
CB *National Velvet* ENID BAGNOLD
CB *The Black Stallion* WALTER FARLEY
CB *The Princess and the Foal* STACY GREGG*
CB *The Silver Brumby* ELYNE MITCHELL
CB *War Horse* MICHAEL MORPURGO
CB *My Friend Flicka* MARY O'HARA
CB *The Flame of Olympus* (Pegasus) KATE O'HEARN
CB *Black Beauty* ANNA SEWELL
YA *The Scorpio Races* MAGGIE STIEFVATER

THE TEN BEST SPY BOOKS

CB *Spy Dog* ANDREW COPE
CB *Harriet the Spy* LOUISE FITZHUGH
CB *SilverFin* (Young Bond) CHARLIE HIGSON
CB *Stormbreaker* (Alex Rider) ANTHONY HOROWITZ
CB *The Secret of the Old Clock* CAROLYN KEENE
CB *The Recruit* (Cherub) ROBERT MUCHAMORE
CB *Liar and Spy* REBECCA STEAD
YA *I'd Tell You I Love You, But Then I'd Have to Kill You* (Gallagher Girls) ALLY CARTER
YA *The Set-Up* (The Medusa Project) SOPHIE MCKENZIE
YA *The Ruby in the Smoke* PHILIP PULLMAN

---

* Also see her Pony Club Secrets books.

obstinate, being

[PB] *The Very Persistent Gappers of Frip*
GEORGE SAUNDERS, ILLUSTRATED BY LANE SMITH

Kids can show admirable strength of will when they dig their heels in – admiration that grown-ups with an ounce of sense will do their utmost to conceal. For those with particularly obstinate children in their lives, *The Very Persistent Gappers of Frip* – a fairytale for all ages, but perhaps most ideal for tweens and early teens – offers a mirror to the child and some memorable visuals to boot.

The tiny town of Frip, which consists of three leaning shacks by the sea, is overrun with gappers – which, in case you didn't know, are bright orange creatures with multiple eyes like the eyes on a potato. Gappers have a great fondness for goats. When they see one, they emit a shriek of pleasure. Unfortunately the fondness doesn't go two ways; and the shrieks enervate the goats and render the poor creatures useless, unable to sleep or produce milk. This is a problem for Frip, which depends for its livelihood on goat's milk. It's the job of the children to keep the gappers at bay, brushing them off the goats with special gapper brushes, loading them into sacks, then emptying the sacks into the sea. The gappers sink to the bottom, but three hours later they've generally suckered their way back to Frip to harass the goats some more.

In the shack nearest the sea lives a girl called Capable, who decides to do something about this deadlock situation. But first she must contend with the ferocious obstinacy of not only the gappers themselves, but also her own father. When she suggests moving away from the gappers, or finding another way of making a living, he won't even consider it. Their neighbours are just as bad. Eventually, Capable finds a way to keep her father, her neighbours, the goats and, amazingly enough, even the gappers happy. We won't reveal what it is, but suffice to say that flexibility – an underrated, under-sung quality, if ever there was one – is key. Let the idea seep into your kids by osmosis.

SEE ALSO: **bossiness** • **know-it-all, being a** • **routine, unable to cope with a change in the** • **stuck**

odd one out, feeling like the

SEE: **different, feeling**

old people, not appreciating

[PB] *Zen Ties*
JON J MUTH

[CB] *Granny was a Buffer Girl*
BERLIE DOHERTY

In theory, the very young and the very old make ideal companions. One group has an excess of energy and joy, the other an excess of calm and wisdom – which they can happily swap between them at the leisurely pace required by both. But sometimes it just doesn't work. Those who are as yet un-embittered by life can find those who are withered, toothless and quietly raging about it all disconcerting company. And those who are unsteady on their pins can find the young too unruly and loud. Neutralise the situation with *Zen Ties*. Karl, Addy and Michael – siblings we meet in other of Muth's fine Zen panda books – are mystified when their giant panda neighbour, Stillwater, announces he's going to visit Miss Whitaker. '*That* Miss Whitaker?' asks Karl, by which he means the one who spits when she talks and shouts mean things at them whenever they pass her house. Stillwater looks at them in his Zen you'll-understand-eventually way, and the children agree to go along – as unable to resist an afternoon spent in the company of this tranquil panda as we are.

At first the crabby Miss Whitaker lives up to her reputation. 'Why on earth did you bring those children here?' she squawks. But when Stillwater puts an affectionate paw around her bony shoulder, helps her with her soup and gets the children sweeping up and drawing pictures around her, the siblings begin to see that behind the harridan lies a kindly soul with some interesting life experiences. As in all Muth's books, the ripples of meaning reach the shore without ever seeming didactic.

Teens must meet Jess in the delightful *Granny Was a Buffer Girl*. It's the evening before Jess is due to leave for her year abroad and she's having a send-off supper with her close-knit family in their Sheffield home. Grandpa Jack is there, talking of his wife Bridie as though she were still alive, and Grandad Albert and Granny Dorothy. Jess is in contemplative mood – and when her grandparents start to tell stories about their pasts, she soaks it all up like a sponge. Moving from one point of view to another, we hear from the now dead Bridie, a young Catholic girl who fell in love with Protestant Jack – and his motorbike – and married him against the wishes of both sets of parents. And then the younger Dorothy, the 'buffer girl' of the title, who operated a polishing machine at the local steel cutlery factory and thought she might win the boss's son, but in the end settled for Albert, the boy next door. Jess herself remembers how, as a teen, she was left with 'difficult' Great-uncle Gilbert, married to Bridie's sister, when he was dying and couldn't speak – and how she, alone in all the family, found a way to understand what he needed to say. As the lives of the generations that came before conflate with her own, we see how they affect Jess's decisions as she prepares to leave two would-be loves behind. Most of all, this story reminds young people that their oldies were once young and full of promise themselves.

SEE ALSO: **boring relatives, having** • **grannies, having to kiss** • **unfriendliness**

oldest, being the

SEE: **sibling, having to look after a little**

only child, being an

CB *A Stitch in Time*
PENELOPE LIVELY

CB *Finn Family Moomintroll*
TOVE JANSSON

There are many great joys associated with being an only child – not least the undivided attention of their grown-ups. But there are times when an only child can be thrown too much on their own resources (see: bored, being; friends, feeling that you have no) and grown-ups and child alike yearn for the diversion of extra playmates. Eleven-year-old Maria in *A Stitch in Time* is an only child who largely enjoys her own company but feels shy and awkward around children she doesn't yet know. And, a bookish sort (see: bookworm, being a), she's not good at spontaneous and lively play. So when she and her parents take a cottage near Lyme Regis in Dorset for the summer and her parents expect her to entertain herself, she is at first delighted, then bored.

She has always enjoyed a curious tendency to talk with inanimate objects and, on their way to Dorset, Maria converses for some time with a petrol pump. When they arrive, she engages in even longer chats with the rather grumpy cat who shares their cottage. The cat questions her reluctance to play with the family of boisterous kids next door. 'You're scared they wouldn't want you,' he says. Certainly she finds the cat easier to approach than any of the siblings – though she can't help noticing that the eldest, Martin, is quieter and more thoughtful than the others. After a while, Maria does gravitate towards Martin, despite herself, but she's also intrigued by a girl called Harriet, who lived in this very cottage in Victorian times. When she stumbles across an embroidered sampler of ammonites on the beach beneath the cottage – which declares, in stitched lettering, that it was begun by Harriet Polstead, aged ten, and finished by Susan Polstead, 30th September 1865 – she wonders why Harriet stopped in the middle of making it. Did it have anything to do with the unstable chalk cliffs – or the dog which she sometimes hears barking and which no one else seems to notice?

This is a thoughtful, inward-looking story that reflects the concerns that only children often have: where they fit in in the world, and where they might be welcomed. Maria feels a kinship with Harriet and embraces the echoes of the girl's existence, but, more importantly, she begins to make a real friend of Martin, and even to feel part of his rowdy family. Those needing to be encouraged out of their own social shell will be inspired to see Harriet develop a new confidence for her teenage years, trusting herself to say the right thing at the right time, where before she might have stayed silent.

For younger children,* Moomintroll in *Finn Family Moomintroll* – the second in Tove Jansson's series about these shy, loveable trolls from the Finnish forests – enjoys all the benefits of being an only child, with none of the drawbacks. As the only son of Moominmamma (surely the most reassuring, understanding and fair-minded mother in literature) and Moominpappa (something of a let-down in comparison, but therein lies the humour), Moomintroll has a healthily robust opinion of himself and knows without a doubt that he is loved. Yet he is never lacking in playmates – due largely to Moominmamma's open-door policy. One only has to turn up on the doorstep of the Moominhouse with a suitcase to be swept up in the family's warm embrace.

All of Moomintroll's friends, it transpires, have been taken in in this way – Snufkin, the Snork and the Snork Maiden, Little My and her sister Mymble, the Hemulin, as well as Thingummy and Bob. Even the gloomy Muskrat, who spends most of his time in a hammock reading *The Uselessness of Everything*, is endured with affection. Which might explain why Moomintroll is nothing at all like the traditional cliché of the only child, who's always wanting his or her own way (see: in charge, wanting to be), doesn't know how to listen, and doesn't know how to share (see: share, inability to). Moomintroll waits respectfully for his friends to unburden their souls when they seem sad. And when Moomintroll's best friend Snufkin decides it's time to head off for another lone adventure (see: adventure, needing an), leaving Moomintroll unbearably sad, he still finds it in himself to defend Snufkin's reasons. ('One must be alone sometimes,' he says, albeit a little loftily.) When offered a wish by the Hobgoblin, he asks, without hesitation, for their party table – piled high with a glorious array of Moominmamma's homemade food – to fly to Snufkin and land before him, 'wherever he is just now!'

---

* Although, really, every age is the perfect age for the Moomins.

In short, one could not wish for a better person than Moomintroll. Only children (and their grown-ups) could do a lot worse than hold him (and his mother) up as their mentor figures.

SEE ALSO: **loneliness** • **precociousness** • **routine, unable to cope with a change in the** • **spoilt, being**

orphan, wishing you were an

The Bad Beginning
LEMONY SNICKET

Orphanhood isn't nearly as much fun in reality as it's cracked up to be in children's books. If the children in your care are under the impression that it is and seem to be wishing that their grown-ups (aka you) would conveniently cop it and leave them to their own devices, you'll need to introduce them to Lemony Snicket's deliciously menacing, mock-gothic *A Series of Unfortunate Events*. From the minute the three ill-fated Baudelaire children – Violet, Klaus and Sunny – lose their parents in a house fire in *The Bad Beginning,* the first in the series, they are beset by a catalogue of unremittingly awful events of the sort we wouldn't wish on our worst enemy. As the narrator warns us from the start, if we're interested in happy endings, we'd be better off reading something else.*

News of the Baudelaires' orphanhood is broken by Mr Poe, the dried-up banker entrusted with overseeing their care – and their considerable family fortune. When Violet (an inventor-in-the-making who ties her hair up in a ribbon whenever she's hatching an idea) turns eighteen in four years' time, she will inherit their parents' money. But for now she, bookish Klaus and baby Sunny – who likes biting things with her four sharp teeth – are to go and live with a distant relative, Count Olaf. The children think it's strange they've never heard mention of Olaf before, despite the fact that he lives in the same town; but they remain optimistic. Though when they arrive at Count Olaf's dark, run-down house with its curtains drawn, their hopes begin to wither. And one look at Count Olaf himself – angry eyes shining out from beneath a monobrow and a creepy ankle tattoo – is enough to know their lives have taken a serious turn for the worse. Soon they are swept helplessly up in the Count's insidious plan to force Violet into marrying him so that he can claim their money for himself.

Not only is there no happy ending here, but no happy beginning and 'very

* Almost any other story featured in this book will do.

few happy things in the middle', too. In fact, there is nothing remotely positive to be found in any of these books about the state of orphanhood. If, by the end of book thirteen, your child *still* wishes you to disappear, they've probably got good reason and you should, for their own sake, pack them off to boarding school forthwith (see: boarding school).

SEE ALSO: **parents, embarrassing** • **parents, pushy** • **parents, strict**

outer space, obsessed by

SEE: **obsessions**

outsider, feeling like an

SEE: **different, feeling**

outsiders, distrust of

[PB] *The Island*
ARMIN GREDER

[CB] *The Unforgotten Coat*
FRANK COTTRELL BOYCE

It's not always easy for kids to embrace newcomers wholeheartedly – especially if the strangers come from a place they've never heard of, speak a language they don't understand or wear clothes they're not used to seeing. Encourage children to be open to outsiders with *The Island,* a sobering study in how ignorance and distrust can turn into fear – and fear into cruelty. Though a picture book, this one's for kids of eight and up; it is not recommended for the very young or the faint-hearted.

The story opens with a strange man emerging onto the beach of an unnamed island, washed up by 'fate and ocean currents'. Naked and hairless, he's not nearly as threatening as the islanders themselves – big, burly men brandishing pitchforks. But the islanders are immediately distrustful, nevertheless. One of them suggests they send the stranger back out to sea, saying he probably 'wouldn't like it here, so far away from his own kind'. But another one – who, being a fisherman, knows the sea – points out that they'd be sending the stranger to his death. We turn the page to a wordless spread showing a forbidding charcoal-grey sea beneath an equally forbidding charcoal-grey sky.

And so they decide instead to keep him in a pen, as if he were an animal, and toss him some straw, before getting on with their grubby, gluttonous lives.

But the outsider has needs – for food, for clothing, for warmth – and one day he appears in town, hungry and desperate. The islanders are resentful. Why should they feed him when they barely have enough for themselves? The fisherman, his conscience pricked once more, says that now they've taken him in, he's their responsibility: they can't just ignore his needs. But the islanders have begun to panic now, and in a series of cartoon boxes we see their imaginations run away with them as they imagine him crouching, naked, on their beds at night and lurking in a dark corner with a murderous knife in his fist . . . As rumours spread and fear gains momentum, the stranger's fate is sealed. No one can miss the message that prejudice can spiral out of control and turn you into the very thing you fear if it's left unchecked. Keep it at bay in your household with Greder's expressive masterpiece.

For a lighter but still poignant take on immigration which will develop empathy in its young readers, *The Unforgotten Coat* brings to vivid life the story of two refugee brothers from Mongolia who pitch up in the Merseyside town of Bootle. Chingis and Nergei are completely at sea when they arrive at the start of the summer term. Dressed in big fur coats, they have strong ideas about the way they should be treated, which makes their classmates wary. But our narrator, Julie, takes it upon herself to be their 'Good Guide'. Gradually, the brothers open up to Julie, sharing stories of the wild, strange place they have left behind – a land where eagles are tamed with hoods over their heads, where everyone has their own horse, and where there are portable palaces made from bamboo. Julie becomes convinced the house they live in now must be a veritable Xanadu and is determined to see it for herself. Of course, when she eventually gets there, it's a depressing council flat on the tenth floor of a tower block, near a flyover, and their tearful mother – terrified that their illegal status will be discovered – slams the door in her face.

Designed in the style of a school exercise book, with lined pages and polaroid photographs, *The Unforgotten Coat* is a poignant symbol both of Julie's own naive hopes that she can help Chingis and Nergei to transition smoothly into their new lives – and of the elusive refugee dream of a more promising future. When we get to the end, we discover there's a real-life dimension to this story, making it a particularly good starting point for a discussion about one of the biggest issues of our times.

SEE ALSO: **strangers, talking to** • **trusting, being too** • **unfriendliness**

over-tired, being

Once a child has reached the point of no return, meltdown is inevitable. Grab a gin and tonic while the messy business plays out, and have one of these comfort reads to hand for when recovery mode kicks in.

THE TEN BEST COMFORT READS

- PB *The Snowman* RAYMOND BRIGGS
- PB *Borka* JOHN BURNINGHAM
- ER *Little Bear* ELSE HOLMELUND MINARIK, ILLUSTRATED BY MAURICE SENDAK
- ER *Frog and Toad Are Friends* ARNOLD LOBEL
- CB *The Secret Island* ENID BLYTON
- CB *Aubrey and the Terrible Yoot* HORATIO CLARE, ILLUSTRATED BY JANE MATTHEWS
- CB *The Silver Chair* CS LEWIS
- CB *The Sign of the Beaver* ELIZABETH GEORGE SPEARE
- YA *Never Always Sometimes* ADI ALSAID
- YA *Murder on the Orient Express* AGATHA CHRISTIE

CURE FOR GROWN-UPS PB *The Boss Baby* MARLA FRAZEE

Also grab this picture book, particularly if having small children in the house has left you fractious from over-tiredness yourself. A pitiless send-up of modern parenting, it tells of a baby who arrives into the world via the back of a limo, briefcase in hand, looking every inch the business tycoon (bald head included), and proceeds to put Mum and Dad on a round-the-clock schedule with 'no time off'. By the time the child in your care has finished their meltdown, you'll have had a good giggle over Boss Baby's iron rule and be in a much better mood for the comforting read that follows.

overweight, being

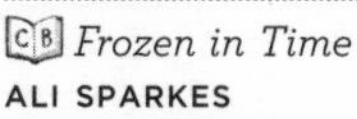

CB *Frozen in Time*
ALI SPARKES

Carrying around excess weight is a hazard of childhood these days, with over a quarter of British children now overweight, and half of those obese. The causes are hotly debated, but it is widely acknowledged that children would do well to exercise more and eat less processed food. To combat these twin ills in the kids in your lives, bring in the bracing *Frozen in Time*.

Abandoned by their parents to Uncle Jerome for the holidays (see: summer holidays), twelve-year-old Ben and his older sister Rachel are enduring a boring, sodden summer. When the sun comes out for ten minutes and their TV satellite dish simultaneously breaks, the pair venture out into the garden for the first time in weeks – and discover a mysterious chamber containing two sleeping children and their dog. It turns out the three have been held in 'cryonic suspension' – in other words, 'frozen' – since 1956.

When Polly and Freddy wake up, the four kids realise that they are in fact cousins, that Polly and Freddy lived in this very house, and that they must try and find their father who, if he's alive, is surely an old man by now. They also rapidly discover that, while they get on famously, they share some very different attitudes – to the role of women, how best to get around, and food, for a start. Faced with these two hearty cousins who think nothing of taking off on a twenty-mile bicycle ride in the country, swimming across a river in a moment of crisis, or whipping up a homemade 'hot-pot', Ben and Rachel are soon reassessing their own more sedentary lives – and so will young readers. They may even find that the Fifties lingo ('super!', 'jolly,' 'golly,' 'spiffing') rubs off on them too.

SEE ALSO: **body image** • **depression** • **stuck**

own way, wanting your

SEE: **bossiness** • **in charge, wanting to be**

pain, being a

SEE: **boots, being too big for your**

pain, being in

Once
MORRIS GLEITZMAN

One of the best cures for pain is distraction, and one of the best methods of distraction is, of course, a good story. Any of the stories in this book might offer respite from this ailment, therefore; but none more than *Once*, featuring as it does a character who himself uses stories for their anaesthetising power.

Felix has been telling himself stories all his life, but he's been finding them increasingly necessary of late. Hidden away in a Catholic orphanage while the Nazis round up his fellow Jews throughout Poland, Felix tells himself that his parents will come to get him one day, thus keeping his hope alive. Given to reading meaning into the world around him, he finds a whole carrot in his broth – a rare occurrence in these times – and tells himself it's a message from his parents, wanting him to come and find *them*. So, leaving the safety of the orphanage, he sets out on foot for his hometown, only to discover when he gets there that another family now lives in his house. When he hears gunshots around him, he tells himself a story about farmers shooting rabbits. It's only when a pit full of bodies opens its horrifying maw before him that, for a while at least, he falls mute.

But, in amongst the bodies is a child, Zelda, who's alive, and as he leads her away from danger – and the truth about her murdered parents – the stories start up again, with Felix explaining away the trucks of emaciated men and women passing them on the road: 'They're on their way to a holiday in the countryside!'

he says. When they come dangerously close to being herded onto a truck themselves, they're rescued by a kindly Jewish dentist called Barney who is keeping himself – and a cellar full of Jewish children – alive by working as a dentist for the Nazis, extracting teeth. Barney sees how Felix has been using stories to protect himself against emotional pain and, there being no anaesthetic to hand, persuades him to try them on his patients as he works. Fantastical and optimistic, featuring cakes that arrive at just the right moment and wild animals roaming through Polish jungles, Felix's stories are a huge success.

Through it all, Felix is himself kept aloft by another storyteller – Richmal Crompton, the real-life author of the Just William stories.* He prays to Crompton at night, as if she were a goddess. Without her behind him, we realise, Felix wouldn't be able to tell the stories he does, each storyteller needing the one that came before. Next time a child you know is in pain – be it of the emotional or physical variety – give them this story about the power of stories to anaesthetise, distract and soothe.

SEE ALSO: **stuck**

parents, embarrassing

YA *Socks Are Not Enough*
MARK LOWERY

The list of ways in which parents can be embarrassing is too long to provide in full. But here's a shortened version: wearing clothes that are too dressy, or trying too hard to be cool; licking their fingers, then wiping the marks off their child's face; shouting 'Cooeeee!' from across the street when their child is hanging out with their schoolmates (or, even worse, trying to hang out with their schoolmates themselves); and awful dancing. If a child you know suffers from this challenging ailment, slip this story under their door when their grown-ups are looking the other way.

When fourteen-year-old Michael walks in on his parents having a cup of tea and finds them wearing nothing but a pair of socks, his world begins to unravel. 'The Absolute Worst Moment of My Entire Life' is what he calls it in the diary he's asked to keep by Miss O'Malley, the counsellor he sees as part of a daily 'Dealing with Feelings' session at school. Michael doesn't just have issues with his parents for having made the controversial decision to live life in their birthday suits. He also has issues with donkeys, custard creams, and nudity in general. And somehow it all connects to Lucy, 'The Most Beautiful

* For our own dose of Richmal Crompton, see: job, wanting a Saturday.

Girl in Preston'. As we watch him work through it all – a process made all the more enjoyable by his interesting way with words (his counsellor's hands are huge enough to 'crush a kitten', he tells us, while her Irish lilt, in contrast, is 'gentle as a draught under a door') – we realise that everything stems from a formative beach holiday in Devon several years ago. By the end, Michael emerges as a more accepting human being, his relationship with his parents having improved sufficiently for him to forgive them their eccentricities – and his relationship with Lucy taking a new, upbeat turn. Reading this, the children in your life will realise that they haven't really got it that bad.

SEE ALSO: **embarrassment**

parents, having

CB *The Parent Agency*
DAVID BADDIEL, ILLUSTRATED BY JIM FIELD

Having parents is generally a blessing, but not always (see: parents, embarrassing; parents, pushy; parents, strict). For any kid who's beginning to wonder if they drew the short straw, this story is a must – tearing up parenthood as it does by its very foundations, only to rebuild it again with the positive elements exposed.

There are so many things Barry Bennett hates about his parents that he keeps a running list. It includes: being boring (Dad works in Ikea; Mum spends her life loading and unloading the dishwasher), deciding to name him Barry (all his friends have cool names like Jake and Lukas and Taj), preferring his twin sisters to him, being tired all the time, being strict, and not letting him play video games. But what he hates most is that they can't afford to give him the sort of birthday party he wants – one like his friends all have, such as going go-karting, or being driven around in a limousine for an afternoon. Many kids will sympathise. But when he screams 'I wish I had better parents!' very loudly one day, he's rather surprised by what happens next. First the room begins to shake, and then he finds himself in a strange city that proclaims itself, in glittery neon signs, as United Kid-dom – a city where kids get to choose their parents for themselves.

In a large municipal building, two girls with clipboards ask him what kind of parents he would like. It transpires that he can test-drive each set of parents for a day before having to make a decision, and Barry decides that the best way to judge their relative merits is to ask each of them to throw him a party. First up is Lord and Lady Rader-Wellorfs, who, as their name suggests, are fabulously rich and live in a mansion where Barry is expected to shoot at a beautiful chained grouse. Then there's Elliot and Mama Cool, who live in a tent and let Barry do whatever he likes. Then there's Vlassorina, a famous couple who have merged their names and share everything they do on 'BirdyNoise' (the Twitter equivalent). And lastly there's the super-fit Derek and Emily, who exhaust Barry with their endless exercise regimes. Amid all the parent-trialling mayhem that ensues, Barry is besieged by flashbacks of his previous life – and we can't help noticing that many of the characters in Kid-dom seem oddly similar to those at home . . . When he gets a taste of what it's like to be the favourite child, eating the first slice of birthday cake and choosing what film to watch, he starts to feel sorry for his new siblings. Lurking in his subconscious is the feeling that there are two people out there who would, actually, be the ideal parents for him, a couple he can only glimpse hazily but who, every now and then, seem to assume a more definite shape . . .

OK, so you can see where this is going – but it's a delightful ride. Children who find themselves feeling similarly critical of their progenitors will love the vicarious fantasy of choosing their perfect parents, while also experiencing the nagging suspicion that they'd miss their own if they weren't there.

CURE FOR GROWN-UPS [PB] *The Marzipan Pig* **RUSSELL HOBAN**

If your child is expressing disappointment in their parents, take your shoes off and curl up in a foetal position with *The Marzipan Pig*, a story which masquerades as a children's book but is actually an existential little masterpiece of heartbreak and loss that's best absorbed by an older, sadder soul. A marzipan pig has fallen behind the sofa and there is 'nothing to be done'. He knows it, the reader knows it, and if you dare to read this to your child, they'll know it too. 'Help!' he calls, feebly, but no one hears him, and after a while he grows hard and bitter. What a waste of all that sweetness in him! he thinks, just before being eaten by a mouse. Yes, that's right. And it gets worse. The pig's sadness and yearning passes into the heart of the mouse, who doesn't know what to do with this unexpected emotion – except that he experiences a sudden, inexplicable need to be loved by the grandfather clock. From there the emotions are transferred to an owl . . . and so it goes on. Sometimes the biggest feelings cannot be explained, are not reciprocated, and make no sense. You will never be able to tell your child how much suffering is involved in love – and how painful their disappointment in you is. But no matter. Have another G&T, let the tears splash onto the page, and allow just a tiny bit of your own marzipan skin to harden.

SEE ALSO: **anger** • **disappointment** • **orphan, wishing you were an** • **sibling rivalry**

PARENTS, HAVING

parents, pushy

The OK Book
AMY KROUSE ROSENTHAL, ILLUSTRATED BY TOM LICHTENHELD

It's one thing for a child to be encouraged and cheered on from the sidelines and quite another to be hounded by grown-ups who snap at their heels and nip them in the buttock if they show any signs of flagging. Having pushy parents can be the bane of a perfectly capable child's existence, sucking the fun out of otherwise enjoyable activities and fostering a tendency to be overly self-critical. If a small child in your vicinity is being chased in this direction, encourage their sense of being good enough as they are with *The OK Book*. Made up of an 'O' for a head and a sideways 'K' for a body, the little stick man knows he's 'OK' at lots of things – climbing trees, swimming, sharing – and not great at any of them. But who cares? 'One day, I'll grow up to be really excellent at something,' he says, imagining himself at an easel, digging a garden, or flying off into space in a rocket. It's not until the end that we realise the stick man is himself an OK written sideways. Recreate him on the pavement with a piece of chalk whenever perfectionism threatens to get the upper hand.

CURE FOR GROWN-UPS  *How to Train Your Parents*
PETE JOHNSON

If this line made you shift in your seat, we prescribe the hilarious *How to Train Your Parents*. It tells of the plight of twelve-year-old Louis, a wannabe comedian who is increasingly concerned at the odd behaviour of his 'relics' – the choice of his new school, for a start. Why have they sent him to this place where the classes are so small, and where everyone seems genuinely interested in their test results? His new friend Maddy has got it all worked out. If you encourage your parents to get more involved in their own activities (salsa dancing, for instance), they have less time to be pushy. However, it can backfire. Maddy has trained her parents so well that when she takes a day off school to accompany Louis to a comedy competition in London, they don't even notice. Indeed, they seem almost to have forgotten that she lives with them . . . This rollicking read will make you think twice about watching your kids in quite such a hawk-like fashion.*

SEE ALSO: **anxiety** • **exams** • **homework, reluctance to do** • **musical instrument, having to practise a** • **praise, seeking**

* It may also explain why they've signed you up for salsa dancing classes.

parents, same sex

PB *And Tango Makes Three*
JUSTIN RICHARDSON AND PETER PARNELL, ILLUSTRATED BY HENRY COLE

YA *The Benefit of Ductwork*
KIRA HARP

YA *Living Upside Down*
KATE TYM

Whether you're seeking to reflect back a uni-gender pairing in your own family – or open a child's mind as to what a family can look like – start with *And Tango Makes Three*, the heart-warming tale of two male penguins at Central Park Zoo. Roy and Silo yearn for a chick of their own. But, alone of all the penguin couples, they can't seem to produce an egg. As they watch the cute, fluffy baby penguins hatch around them, they become increasingly desperate – and even try sitting on an egg-shaped stone. Luckily, their keeper, Mr Gramzay, has noticed their plight and when another penguin couple lays two eggs, he slips one into Roy and Silo's nest. No baby penguin could wish for more dedicated dads than these two – or be more adorably drawn. Based on a real-life story, this is a picture book that rises beyond its agenda.

Older kids looking for a two-dad parenting model to set alongside their own will enjoy the intriguingly titled *The Benefit of Ductwork*. Up till now, seventeen-year old adoptee Andy has lived a largely uneventful existence with his two fathers, Dad and Pops. But when his dads bring home Kyle, a sensitive thirteen-year-old who's been chucked out of his home for being gay, his boat is severely rocked. Rob and Geoff, Andy's dads, are keen to show Kyle a loving family that won't judge him for his sexuality, but Andy feels threatened, convinced his parents will end up preferring the charming youngster to him. So when Kyle wears a pink T-shirt to school and gets called a 'fairy boy', Andy fails to stand up for him. It's his own fault, he thinks, and remembers how he was taunted for having two dads when he was younger, too.

Of course Dad and Pops are deeply disappointed by Andy's failure as a big brother, but when, that night, Andy overhears his parents talking via the heating duct, he realises where their priorities lie – and how much happier he'd be if he helped Kyle through this difficult patch in his life. An uplifting and thought-provoking story, it shows same-sex parents facing the same sorts of issues that all parents face, and resolving them as best they can.

For a tale of two mums, look to *Living Upside Down*. When sixteen-year-old Chloe's mother leaves her father and 'shacks up' with a woman, Chloe's internal 'normal-ometer' explodes. At first she does her best to keep her mum's new living situation a secret, not wanting to be the sort of person other people 'whisper about behind their hands'. In private, she pretends to be in a TV documentary. 'Well, Sue, I feel very philosophical about the whole thing. Dad is still Dad and Mum is still Mum. I really don't think that a person should be defined by their sexuality.' Sometimes, though, she's on the *Ricki Lake* show, launching herself at Grace for 'ruining her life', while her mother weeps in despair. In real life, visiting her mum is increasingly difficult – her mother's partner, Grace, seems bossy and unloving; and her mother appears to be intimidated by her. As the fantasy scenarios shift from TV shows to a psychiatrist's office, a court of law and a prison for young offenders – a device which allows Chloe's feelings to be explored with sensitivity and wit – we begin to realise it's not her mum's sexuality that's the issue, but the particular relationship she's in. Whether or not they have parents who buck the stereotypes, all teens will relate to Chloe's need to feel accepted at school, and anyone can benefit from the message that it's the happiness and strength of one's grown-ups' relationships that matter, not the gender of the person they're with.

SEE ALSO: **different, feeling**

parents, strict

CB *Crummy Mummy and Me*
ANNE FINE

If your kids complain that you're stricter than other parents, leave *Crummy Mummy and Me* lying around. If ever there was proof that it might be harder to have a parent who's the *opposite* of strict, this is it.

Minna's mum doesn't insist that Minna goes to school. In fact, she'd quite like it if Minna wasn't so uptight about needing to go herself – especially when it's chucking it down outside. In the mornings, Minna's the one who has to yell to her mum to hurry up. And when her mum *does* appear – wearing something completely inappropriate, such as a sleeveless dress and fishnets in the middle of winter – Minna has to send her back for a jumper. The problem, of course, is that Crummy Mummy's lax attitude forces Minna to be the responsible one – and the one left to run down to the shop when there's nothing in the fridge for tea. Once they've glimpsed the realities of life with a 'Crummy Mummy', any child will be relieved that at least, in their family, they get to be the rebellious one.

SEE ALSO: **chores, having to do • friends your parents don't approve of, having • mistake, frightened of making a • parents, embarrassing • routine, unable to cope with a change in the**

parents, too busy

PB *Not Now, Bernard*
DAVID MCKEE

CB *Coraline*
NEIL GAIMAN, ILLUSTRATED BY CHRIS RIDDELL

It's not that we're trying to induce guilt among the grown-ups. Raising a family while earning a living, keeping house, keeping fit and keeping up with your latest TV show addiction (ahem) makes for a demanding schedule. But it's important that children don't feel they're getting relegated to the bottom of the to-do list – or knocked off it completely – because of the way they are. *Not Now, Bernard* sets the record straight.

Bernard's parents have a lot of things on their mind, leaving zero headspace left for Bernard. Just sauntering into the room and saying 'Hello, Dad,' in a friendly sort of way, is too much for Dad to compute. 'Not now, Bernard,' comes the testy reply. An uncomplaining sort of chap (he's used to it), Bernard keeps his chin up, his hopes down, and tries the same line on Mum. But 'Hello, Mum' is too much for Mum as well. He'd probably give up there and then, but there's a new development. A monster has turned up in the garden who wants to eat him. And when he points this out to Mum and gets the same response, he drifts out the back door and surrenders haplessly to his fate. McKee's depiction of Bernard's benign air of neglect and the parents' infuriating insouciance are achieved with impressive minimalism. Every child who's been told 'Not now' will adore this book – in fact, probably a little too much for their grown-ups' liking . . .

If they're older, kids may identify with Coraline, whose parents both work at home but are always 'doing things on computers'. In the big, old, shared house they've just moved into (see: moving house), Coraline finds herself at a loose end. 'Explore the flat,' her father suggests, without even turning round. 'Count all the doors and windows. List everything blue . . . And leave me alone to work.' She duly goes round the flat counting the doors and windows – which is how she discovers the big brown door in the far corner of the drawing room.

Through this door she finds a flat that's almost, but not quite, like their own. And in it there is a woman who is almost, but not quite, her mother. This 'other mother' – thinner and paler and with big black buttons for eyes – has time to make a mouth-watering, golden roast chicken, and lives with an 'other father' who looks round from his computer when Coraline comes in. 'We're ready to love you and play with you and feed you and make your life interesting,' her other mother says. '*This is more like it*,' Coraline can't help thinking.

They're intensely creepy, though, and seem to want her just a little too much. And when she decides it's time to go back to her real home, she discovers that her actual parents have disappeared . . . This chilling little tale will chime with children whose parents seem to prefer their work over them; but the extent to which Coraline is prepared to go to rescue her parents shows how intensely she loves them, despite their non-availability. By the end, she's overjoyed to be reunited with 'her real, wonderful, maddening, infuriating, glorious mother' again. And this time, when she goes into her father's study, he turns round, smiles with his 'kind grey eyes', and puts his computer to sleep. Give this to a child – then read it yourself. Forgiveness is instant, once the willingness to be present is there.

CURE FOR GROWN-UPS PB *If You Want to See a Whale* **JULIE FOGLIANO, ILLUSTRATED BY ERIN E STEAD**

The pace at which small children live can seem jarringly at odds with the pace at which you have to live when you're busy. With a zillion things on your to-do list, it can be hard to prioritise playing peekaboo behind the sofa or picking out the plasticine pressed into their hair. To help you slow down, read this lovely picture book about what to do if you want to spot a whale – an exhortation to pay attention, even for those who already live by the sea. The stillness of mind emanating from the sparsely furnished page, with its patiently watching and waiting little boy, his dog and the friendly bird who decides to join them, are exquisitely captured with linoleum printing blocks on textured, watercolour paper. An active lesson in deliberate noticing, use this book to re-set your body clock to small-child time.

SEE ALSO: **bored, being** • **loneliness** • **screen, glued to the**

parents who are splitting up, having

PB *Two Homes*
CLAIRE MASUREL, ILLUSTRATED BY KADY MACDONALD DENTON

PB *Living with Mum and Living with Dad*
MELANIE WALSH

(continued)

Separation and divorce are hard on kids. For young children, reading stories which reflect their situation as much as possible will help explain and reassure. *Two Homes,* featuring a little boy, and *Living with Mum and Living with Dad,* featuring a little girl, acknowledge bruised feelings while painting a positive picture of how it might look to have two bedrooms in two different homes – and two parents who still love you just as much as they did before. The less gender-specific *Two Nests* is also great. Meanwhile, *It's Not Your Fault, Koko Bear* and the

[PB] *Two Nests*
LAURENCE ANHOLT, ILLUSTRATED BY JIM COPLESTONE

[PB] *It's Not Your Fault, Koko Bear*
VICKY LANSKY, ILLUSTRATED BY JANE PRINCE

[PB] *Mum and Dad Glue*
KES GRAY, ILLUSTRATED BY LEE WILDISH

[PB] *The Un-Wedding*
BABETTE COLE*

[CB] *It's Not the End of the World*
JUDY BLUME

* Also published as *Two of Everything.*

excellent *Mum and Dad Glue* are ideal to read with children who seem to be blaming themselves for what has happened.* For a delightfully optimistic spin, we celebrate Babette Cole's inimitable take on the subject in *The Un-Wedding,* in which two children, Demetrius and Paula Ogglebutt, sick of their problem parents who can never agree about anything, suggest that they get 'unmarried'. It's a little controversial – they ask the minister who married them to un-do the bond himself – but few can fail to be amused by the sight of the two new divorcees jetting off gleefully on their separate un-honeymoons (one plane heading to a tropical island, the other to a sheer ski slope) or the two-of-everything set-up this pair of siblings can boast in the end, even if it is somewhat wishful thinking.

Children a little older will take comfort from Judy Blume's realistic portrayal of the ending of a marriage and its effect on siblings of different ages. Written in the early Seventies, when Blume's own marriage hit the rocks, it was one of the first children's books to address divorce head-on. Twelve-year-old Karen has decided she's never going to get married – it clearly just makes people miserable. Even petty disagreements between her mum and dad seem to culminate in smashed plates, spilt milk and all-round wailing. And she can't remember the last time she had an 'A+' day. While her older brother Ted responds by retreating further into teenagehood, chuckling softly to his girlfriend on the phone, and little Amy bumbles through without seeming to notice anything, Karen feels it's left to her to try and fix things. If only she could get her parents into the same room for a few minutes, surely everything would go back to being as it was before.

With typical Blume realism, Karen's efforts are thwarted and her father does indeed move out. But she discovers compensations to the new world order. At her father's new home she meets Val, a girl her own age whose parents are also separated – making Val something of an authority on the subject. Drawing heavily from her separation bible, *The Boys' and Girls' Book About Divorce,* Val leads Karen into this unknown territory with a firm hand, impressing on her

* If they're not, you might want to steer clear. No one wants to put this idea into a child's head if it's not already there; although, frankly, many kids will be blaming themselves even if they aren't expressing it out loud.

the importance of looking after herself, and being practical at all times. By the end, Karen begins to see that divorce isn't necessarily the end of the world – it's obvious that they all love each other deeply, but in new, changing ways. And if her best friend can make her laugh, and her little sister has started telling riddles again, who knows? She may even start having 'A+' days again. This uplifting story is a great accompaniment to the seismic transition.

SEE ALSO: **anxiety • arguments, getting into • disappointment • family outings • feelings, hurt • loneliness • moving house • nightmares • sadness • single parent, having a • sleep, unable to get to • stepparent, having a**

parents who can't talk about emotions, having

PB *Hug Me*
SIMONA CIRAOLO

CB *The Boy in the Dress*
DAVID WALLIAMS

If you tend to be a bit buttoned up,* your child might relate to one of the characters in these books. Felipe's family in *Hug Me* are not the touchy-feely type – which is perhaps understandable once you know they're a family of cacti. Told with wax crayon and watercolours in desert hues, the story shows young Felipe searching for others who understand his need for a hug. It doesn't go well with the balloon, but the rock – whose parents are equally unavailable – knows exactly what it's like. Use this story to open a discussion about who is prickly and who is soft and squishy in your family – and perhaps you'll find out who your child wishes they were more able to hug than they are.

There's a strict ban on hugging in Dennis's household in the wonderful *The Boy in the Dress* – although neither Dennis's truck-driving dad nor his older brother John would ever call it that. Dennis is just aware that ever since their mum left – who, by the way, must not be mentioned – the household has descended into an emotional ice age. Dad is depressed and spends his time drinking beer and eating chips in front of the telly. John mostly teases Dennis for not being as much of a male as he is. It's only football – and his best friend, Dervish (whose mum is emotionally expressive to the point of embarrassment), who keeps him going.

One day, Dennis's dad catches Dennis with a copy of *Vogue*. It 'just ain't right', he says. It's not long before Dennis is sporting a sequined dress and high heels and showing his dad that boys can be good at football *and* like girls' clothes, too. The moment of emotional unbottling that follows will cause

* If you don't think you are buttoned-up but simply like to maintain a stiff upper lip – and frankly think the kids should, too – see *The Novel Cure*: stiff upper lip, having a.

even the most uptight members of the family to well up. Share this story between you (there's an excellent audio version, performed by Walliams himself) to pave the way for an unburdening family embrace.

SEE ALSO: **depressed parent, having a • heard, not feeling • loneliness • understood, not being**

peer pressure

[ER] *The Berenstain Bears and the In-Crowd*
STAN AND JAN BERENSTAIN

[YA] *Stargirl*
JERRY SPINELLI

The pressure to wear the right clothes, own the right phone, talk the right talk and walk the right walk is one of the major stresses of child- and teenagehood. Seeing peer pressure for what it is – a sheep mentality with arbitrary rules – is difficult when your popularity feels like it's on the line; but a timely story or two can help. For youngsters, *The Berenstain Bears and the In-Crowd* is a great start.

Sister Bear and her friends think the new cub, Queenie McBear, is the 'sharpest' cub they've ever set eyes on: not only does she wear purple stretch pants and a yellow headband (this is the Eighties, after all), but she also owns a ten-speed bike and has *pierced ears*. Sister Bear wastes no time introducing herself to this 'It' bear – and the stinging put-down she receives takes her completely by surprise. 'Sister Bear? Now what kind of a name is that? And you've got to be kidding with those clothes – a pink ruffled jumper and a *hair bow*?' We can't help but feel hurt ourselves. Mama Bear rushes straight out to buy Sister a cool pair of jeans and a designer top, but we know that something isn't quite right about this approach – and Sister Bear knows it, too. Hurrah for this unashamed celebration of Eighties fashion mistakes – and the encouragement to kids to stay true to themselves.

There's a lovely call to reject peer pressure and do your own thing in *Stargirl*. When a new girl arrives at Mica Area High School in Arizona (see: school, being the new kid at), no one knows what to make of her. One day she turns up in a Twenties flapper dress, the next a kimono, the next pioneer's buckskins. Seeming to be completely unconcerned by what people think of her, Stargirl has the charming habit of playing the ukulele at lunchtimes to anyone who has a birthday that day, and dropping her spare change on the floor just so that others can experience the pleasure of finding it.

The largely conventional majority consider Stargirl freakish, but our narrator, sixteen-year-old Leo, is drawn to her despite the challenge the association creates. His well-intentioned attempts to turn Stargirl back into Susan at first fill him with happiness, but Stargirl can't keep up the pretence of being 'normal' – and Leo is changed forever for having crossed paths with her. This story encourages an admiration of those who dare to go against the grain – and, ultimately, to express their own essential nature.

SEE ALSO: **astray, being led** • **drugs** • **friends your parents don't approve of, having**

perfectionist, being a

SEE: **mistake, frightened of making a**

periods

The Greengage Summer
RUMER GODDEN

Simultaneously dreaded and hotly anticipated, periods are the subject of widespread playground rumour for tweens; and confused notions about blood loss, cramps, and what you can and can't do when you're 'on', make it hard for girls to know what this vital sign of growing up actually entails. Mums, big sisters and other female carers can all do their bit to clarify matters, and there are several excellent non-fiction guides to help with the job.* But for a fuller exploration of the emotional changes that accompany the moment the red flag goes up – or the vicar/Aunt Fanny comes to tea – look to fiction.

We know that Cecil, the thirteen-year-old narrator of *The Greengage Summer*, 'becomes a woman' over the course of the long, hot summer in which this story is set. But this being the Fifties, nothing is ever spelled out. The First World War has ended, and Cecil's mother has decided to take her five children to see the battlefields of northern France, where so many men lost their lives. On the way the mother is bitten by a horsefly – which puts her conveniently out of action for the rest of the story – and it falls to sixteen-year-old Joss to lead the journey to the rambling hotel, Les Oeillets, where they are to stay.

Here, surrounded by beautiful orchards in which the titular greengages plop into their hands, intrigues of various kinds develop. The proprietor,

---

* Try *The 'What's Happening to My Body?' Book for Girls* by Lynda Madaras. There's an equivalent book for boys.

Madame Zizi, seems to be playing a complex love game with the enigmatic Englishman Mr Eliot. Mr Eliot, in turn, seems a little too appreciative of Joss, who is suddenly blooming into womanhood before their eyes. One fateful night there's a party. Cecil drinks champagne for the first time – and then, with everything suddenly all awry, she feels terrible pains accompanied by a vast sense of desolation. Withdrawing to a cupboard, she discovers the cause of these sensations and – having learnt from Joss what she needs to do* – deals with it, going to her older sister's drawer for the right accoutrements. With the party clattering on downstairs, she feels the loneliness of this moment sharply. Just then, Mr Eliot appears and kisses her on the mouth. He seems like an angel to her – even though she knows his purpose is nefarious.

Young readers will appreciate the blend of complicated emotions and sensations replete in Cecil in this moment – one which holds both triumph and loss, loneliness and love at its heart. Forearm tweens with this story and the rite of passage, when it comes, will be imbued with added romance and enchantment.

SEE ALSO: **body hair • body odour • grow up, impatient to • grow up, not wanting to • innocence, loss of • smelly friend, having a**

pet, death of a

PB *Goodbye Mog*
JUDITH KERR

CB *Fred*
POSY SIMMONDS

The death of a much-loved pet can be deeply shocking to a child. Sharing stories that show others going through a similar loss can help by acknowledging what has happened, giving everyone a chance to talk about the lost pet, and grieve. We love *Goodbye Mog,* in which author/illustrator Judith Kerr boldly allowed her much-loved fictional tabby to die – a move which triggered a long-echoing wave of sadness among fans. Mog is accepting of her death, but she's also curious about what will happen to the family she's leaving behind, and when she dies, 'a little bit of her' rises up from her body and stays to watch.

What does happen is that all the family cry (even Mr and Mrs Thomas), then they bury her in the garden and talk about how lovely she was. After that, nothing much happens for quite a long time. Debbie and Nicky talk about

* For an excellent explanation of the biology of periods, see the online *Menstrupedia Comic* by Aditi Gupta and Tuhin Paul, written originally for girls in India (and available from Amazon India as a paperback too).

her sometimes, remembering how she used to hang her tail in front of the telly and creep into their beds at night; and the spirit of Mog floats contentedly above them, remembering too. And then one day Mrs Thomas brings home a new kitten, a frightened, scratching creature who nobody takes to much – least of all Mog herself. But then Mog realises she might be able to help, even in her ethereal form . . . Steeped in love, the idea that the spirit of a much-loved pet might hover around just long enough to help its grieving family move on is a deeply reassuring one.

For slightly older children bring in *Fred*, a quirky comic-strip take on the demise of another cat, which brings humour and a dash of the unexpected into the grieving process. Fat, lazy and a master of the art of sleeping anywhere – from the ironing board to the top of the fridge – Fred was, as far as his owners were concerned, very much your typical sort of cat. But on the night of his death the children, Sophie and Nick, are woken by strange noises and pad outside. There, to their amazement, they find Mrs Spedding's ginger cat from next door dressed up in top hat and tails. 'Are you friends of our dear departed?' he sniffs. It turns out that Fred was no ordinary cat at all but famous throughout their neighbourhood for entertaining others with his song-and-dance routines. 'He sang, oh how he sang!' they caterwaul in fond remembrance. At the funeral service, hundreds of wailing cats belt out his songs to the moon – before running off to tuck into the funeral feast down by the rubbish bins.

The next day, the children wake up wondering if they imagined it all. But then they see hundreds of little muddy paw prints going through the house . . . With Posy Simmonds's quirky drawings bringing a mischievous touch, this book will inspire children's own memories and what-if wonderings about their much-missed pet.

SEE ALSO: **cheering up, needing** • **loneliness** • **sadness**

pet, wanting a

PB *Madlenka's Dog*
PETER SÍS

CB *The Cat Who Walked by Himself*
RUDYARD KIPLING

Most children are drawn to animals – and it's almost inevitable that, at some stage, they'll beg for a pet. Arm yourself in advance with *Madlenka's Dog*, which may, at least, buy you some time. Zooming in from outer space to New York City, and then to Madlenka's apartment in what has become Peter Sís's trademark style, we meet a little girl so desperate for a canine companion that she sticks pictures of dogs of different shapes and colours all over her bedroom wall.

One day she hears a bark – and suddenly an imaginary dog appears. Madlenka takes the invisible dog for a walk on a bright red lead – and all the friendly people on her block (some of whom will be familiar to Sís readers already) respond in delightful ways, never for a minute questioning the reality of the hound. By the time she gets back to her apartment, she has attracted a throng of multi-shaped and multi-shaded yappers, who follow her like the Pied Piper. Ask the kids why they would want to limit themselves to one real dog when they can have as many imaginary dogs as they want.

Should the child in your midst start wanting to bring home a sugar-gliding possum, a bearded dragon or a corn snake, you might want to take a different tack. Rudyard Kipling's Just So story, *The Cat Who Walked by Himself*, explains how some animals came to be domesticated while others did not. Kipling takes us back, in his storytelling sing-song narrative voice, to the time when everything was wild: 'The Dog was wild, and the Horse was wild, and the Cow was wild, and the Sheep was wild, and the Pig was wild.' Even the first Man was wild – 'dreadfully wild', in fact – and didn't even start to become tame until the first Woman came along and made him move into a nice clean cave and wipe his feet at the door. To begin with, each of the species 'walked by their wild lones in the Wet, Wild Wood'. But then the Woman has a cunning idea. Luring the animals to the cave with the light of their fire, she bargains with them, one by one. First she makes a deal with the Dog, who will hunt with the man in return for food and fire. Then with the Horse, who will work for the man in return for warm, fresh grass. Then the Cow, for the same. Finally, the Cat comes along. The woman knows that the Cat is not naturally inclined to be either friend or servant and will always do as he pleases. Besides, the cave is full of creatures now, and there isn't room for any more. So she sends him packing – but not before they've made a pact of a different and more intriguing kind. Kipling's story offers an explanation for why the range of pet options is limited* – though you might find that you've argued yourself into having an easy-to-care-for cat instead.

SEE ALSO: **friends, feeling like you have no**

phone, wanting a

SEE: **screen, glued to the** • **things, wanting**

* To ensure the efficacy of this cure, the child will need to avoid Gerald Durrell's *My Family and Other Animals*. See (or, rather, don't see): animals, fear of.

picked on, being

SEE: **bullied, being** • **stand up for yourself, not feeling able to**

picked up, waiting to be

[PB] *Owl Babies*
MARTIN WADDELL, ILLUSTRATED BY PATRICK BENSON

[PB] *Waiting for Mama*
LEE TAE-JUN, ILLUSTRATED BY KIM DONG-SEONG

Finding yourself in the unpaid role of glorified chauffeur is an unfortunate side effect of having children – tedious, thankless and, if you're running late, stressful. But for the child left waiting, it's worse, especially if they're the sort to dream up all sorts of terrifying scenarios as to where their tardy grown-up has disappeared to (see: worrying). Acknowledge the potentially scarring nature of this experience with one of these age-appropriate reads.

Few moments in literature pack as emotional a punch as the double-page spread in *Owl Babies* in which the mother owl finally returns. Waking in the night to find her gone, owl babies Sarah, Percy and Bill know that she's probably just gone hunting. But they can't help feeling anxious as they wait, and wait . . . and wait . . . Soon their heads are filled with all the dreadful notions that owl babies entertain – that she's got lost; that she's been caught by a fox – and they squeeze their eyes shut to wish for her return. When the 'AND SHE CAME' moment comes – that large, comforting wingspan swooping dramatically across the double-page spread from out of the night – you'll find yourself wanting to fill the room with the boom of your voice. You'll both enjoy the wave of security that washes over your child.

If you really were *very* late, *Waiting for Mama* may get you off the hook. This still, quiet book – first published in Korea – shows a toddler clad in a traditional Korean coat, and boasting an adorable tummy-first stance, waiting on a station platform. Smaller by far than all the other passengers, he watches while several trains fail to produce the grown-up he's hoping to see. He doesn't give up – even though not everyone he asks is friendly; and even though he waits so long it starts to snow and his nose turns red from cold. Waiting is OK, says this book: patience is an art. Be sure to scrutinise the last spread closely, lest you and your child are haunted forever.

SEE ALSO: **loneliness** • **scared, being**

pink, passion for

SEE: **princess, wanting to be a**

planet, fearing for the future of the

Most kids hear the ecological message loud and clear. These planet-saving reads will inspire, inform and keep them believing that everything they do makes a difference.

THE TEN BEST PLANET-SAVING BOOKS

- PB *Oi! Get Off Our Train* JOHN BURNINGHAM
- PB *One World* MICHAEL FOREMAN
- PB *Just a Dream* CHRIS VAN ALLSBURG
- ER *The Lorax* DR SEUSS
- CB *This Morning I Met a Whale* MICHAEL MORPURGO, ILLUSTRATED BY CHRISTIAN BIRMINGHAM
- CB *The Giving Tree* SHEL SILVERSTEIN
- CB *The Story of the Blue Planet* ANDRI SNAER MAGNASON, ILLUSTRATED BY ASLAUG JONSDOTTIR
- CB *Silver Dolphins* SUMMER WATERS
- YA *The Monkey Wrench Gang* EDWARD ABBEY
- YA *Exodus* JULIE BERTAGNA

SEE ALSO: **apocalypse, fear of the**

play by yourself, preferring to

SEE: **alone, wanting to be left** • **loner, being a**

pleading

SEE: **bargaining, endless**

pocket money, lack of

[ER] *The Milly-Molly-Mandy Storybook*
JOYCE LANKESTER BRISLEY

Let's face it: however much pocket money they get, it's never going to be enough. So rather than argue about how much it should be, help the children in your care get wise as to how to spend it. One of the most savvy approaches to getting the most for your buck can be found in a *Milly-Molly-Mandy* story set in the late 1920s, 'Milly-Molly-Mandy Spends a Penny'. When MMM (as we shall call her) happens to find a penny in the pocket of an old coat, the first thing she does is take advice from her immediate entourage – Grandpa, Grandma, Father, Mother, Uncle and Aunty. They all give her a different suggestion: put it in the bank; buy a skein of wool and learn to knit; buy a 'patty-pan' and bake a cake; buy some seeds to grow 'mustard-and-cress'; buy some sweets. Her uncle has the best idea – save it up until she gets three pennies, then buy a baby duckling. MMM takes all these ideas off into a corner of the garden to think them over. And then she makes her decision.

First she buys the mustard-and-cress seeds, sells what she grows and doubles her original investment. Of the two pennies she now has, she spends one on wool, knits a kettle-holder and sells it to her mother for another penny. That still leaves two pennies. She uses one to buy a 'patty-pan', bakes a cake in it and sells it to a passing lady cyclist for a penny. Back to two pennies again. She spends one on sweets – enough to give one to all her grown-ups and still have plenty for herself. Then she saves the one remaining penny until she has enough for the little duckling.

OK, so a penny went further in those days – but the principle is the same. MMM got to do lots of splendid things with her money – in fact, everything she'd hoped to do – by being a little canny and not spending it all at once. We suspect that many an investment banker in the City today was raised on these stories.

SEE ALSO: **job, wanting a Saturday** • **parents, strict** • **spoilt, being** • **things, wanting**

pony, wanting a

SEE: **obsessions** • **pet, wanting a**

poo and pee, fascination with

[PB] *The Story of the Little Mole*
WERNER HOLZWARTH, ILLUSTRATED BY WOLF ERLBRUCH

By the time we've reached adulthood, we prefer to pretend that our bladders and our bowels get on with their doings with little or no attention from us – which, until old age, they mostly do. But for the very young, their eliminations – and the smells, sensations, shapes and sounds that arrive along with them – loom large in the course of a day (and often for those around them, too). Indulge the fascination with *The Story of Little Mole,* which offers extensive poo exposure of an intriguing and diverse kind. When the mole brings his head to the surface one day and finds himself sporting a crown-like turd of mysterious provenance, his search for the culprit takes him around a variety of species, each with their own particular type of poo. His affronted pride – and the revenge he exacts – will bring great satisfaction to your young.

SEE ALSO: **baby, being a** • **potty training**

pornography

It's increasingly difficult to protect young adults from pornography online – an exposure which can radically affect perceptions of what is normal or acceptable within sexual relationships. Balance out unwanted distortions by encouraging teens to read fiction which portrays mutually respectful relationships and sex.

THE TEN BEST BOOKS EXPLORING LOVE AND SEX FOR YOUNG ADULTS

[YA] *Nick and Norah's Infinite Playlist* RACHEL COHN AND DAVID LEVITHAN
[YA] *To All the Boys I've Loved Before* JENNY HAN
[YA] *The First Part Last* ANGELA JOHNSON
[YA] *Every Day* DAVID LEVITHAN
[YA] *Sloppy Firsts* MEGAN MCCAFFERTY
[YA] *Jellicoe Road* MELINA MARCHETTA
[YA] *Eleanor and Park* RAINBOW ROWELL
[YA] *Fire Colour One* JENNY VALENTINE
[YA] *If You Come Softly* JACQUELINE WOODSON
[YA] *Everything Everything* NICOLA YOON

SEE ALSO: **hormones, raging** • **screen, glued to the** • **sex, having questions about**

potty training

Embracing a chilled *whoops!* attitude to accidents of the I-didn't-get-there-in-time variety, these picture books provide a child with all the info they need about bodily functions and how to best make the transition from nappies to toilets.

THE TEN BEST BOOKS FOR POTTY TRAINING

PB *Father Christmas Needs a Wee!* NICHOLAS ALLAN
PB *The Prince and the Potty* NICHOLAS ALLAN
PB *The Princess and the Potty* WENDY CHEYETTE LEWISON, ILLUSTRATED BY RICK BROWN
PB *Once Upon a Potty (Girl)* and *Once Upon a Potty (Boy)* ALONA FRANKEL
PB *Everybody Poos* TARO GOMI
PB *Sam's Potty* BARBRO LINDGREN, ILLUSTRATED BY EVA ERIKSSON
PB *Skip to the Loo, My Darling!* SALLY LLOYD-JONES, ILLUSTRATED BY ANITA JERAM
PB *I Want My Potty* (Little Princess) TONY ROSS
PB *The Potty Book for Boys* and *The Potty Book for Girls* ALYSSA SATIN CAPUCILLI, ILLUSTRATED BY DOROTHY STOTT
PB *Who's in the Loo?* JEANNE WILLIS, ILLUSTRATED BY ADRIAN REYNOLDS

SEE ALSO: **grow up, not wanting to • poo and pee, fascination with**

praise, seeking

PB *The Neverending Story*
MICHAEL ENDE

Children are programmed to seek approval – first from the inner sanctum of family, and later from their peers, teachers and the various onlookers of their lives.* Those who fail to find it – or, conversely, get too much of it showered on them in their early years – may spend the rest of their lives hungrily seeking it out. One such is the extraordinarily named Bastian Balthazar Bux in *The Neverending Story*, who, starved of praise up till now, develops such a taste for it that he hankers for it more and more. This cautionary tale shows how it nearly kills him.

A lonely boy who lives with his distracted, neglectful father, Bastian comes across a beautiful old book in an antiques store one day. It calls to him so strongly that, when the shopkeeper turns his back, Bastian runs off with it.

* Some also seek it from an omniscient being, of course (see: god, wondering if there is a).

The next thing he knows, he's living inside the book, along with Atreyu, a boy warrior attempting to save the land of Fantastica from being devoured, piece by piece, by 'the Nothing' – a metaphor for greed and the lust for power. At first, Bastian doesn't know how he can help Atreyu, but he hasn't reckoned on his talent for telling stories. Drawing on his natural inventiveness, he finds he can rebuild Fantastica, story by story – and soon becomes everybody's hero.

His heroism comes at a price. Every time he wishes back a piece of Fantastica, he loses a memory of his real life. The people of Fantastica love him more and more for what he's doing, showering him with greater and greater accolades. After a while, he begins to crave the wealth and respect his storytelling brings him – and we realise he's in danger of being taken over by the very lust for self-importance and power he was trying to fight. Will he retain enough of his memory to get back home – and remember that he once had a father? Delving deep into the psychology of storytelling and the question of why both writers and readers crave stories, this thought-provoking fantasy explores the point at which brilliance ends and egotism, or a need for attention, takes over. Let Bastian's dilemmas show kids how to enjoy praise without letting it turn their heads.

SEE ALSO: **parents, pushy** • **parents, strict**

precociousness

[PB] *Iggy Peck, Architect*
ANDREA BEATY AND DAVID ROBERTS

[YA] *Ender's Game*
ORSON SCOTT CARD

What do you do if you catch your five-year-old, mocktail in hand, discussing the finer points of astrophysics with someone six times their age at a party? Panic, probably. Or, instead, introduce him or her to Iggy Peck. Iggy is only two years old when he starts showing an eye for design and a talent for construction. His early works include a tower built of nappies (dirty ones, unfortunately) and a life-size imitation of the Great Sphinx. His sophisticated-looking parents are soon clapping their hands in delight at their clever child's creations. But his second-grade teacher, Miss Lila Greer, does not share their enthusiasm. When Iggy builds a castle out of sticks of chalk, she orders him to tear it down – architecture having 'no place' in grade two.* This, of course, sends Iggy into

* It turns out that Miss Greer's aversion to architecture has its roots in a personal trauma. When she was seven, she got lost on the ninety-fifth floor of a skyscraper and was found two days later crammed into an elevator with a French circus troupe.

a slump of lassitude and he loses all interest in school (see: school, not wanting to go to). Thus this canny picture book puts its finger on the actual problem: not the precocious child, but the grown-ups who don't know how to handle one. Show your wünderkind as early as possible that being advanced for their years is a cause for celebration – but that they (and you) might need to help the people around them adjust.

The older they get, the more a precocious child can feel set apart from their peers – and if bullying is added to the mix, the isolation will be compounded (see: bullied, being). Few children's books explore this theme more viscerally than *Ender's Game*, the gripping story of the boy genius chosen to save mankind from a deep-space alien attack. Ender is only six when the IF, or International Fleet, turn up on his doorstep and tell his parents they've come for Ender. Having monitored his every move since birth via a device inserted into his neck, they've found him to have the combination of intelligence, resourcefulness and emotional control to make him a future starship captain. 'We need a Napoleon. An Alexander . . . a Julius Caesar,' says Graff, the principal of the Battle School where Ender will be kept until he's sixteen.

As we follow Ender through Battle School – as gruelling psychologically as it is physically – we begin to see what makes him special. He doubles numbers in his head to stop himself crying at night, only stumbling when he gets to 67108864. He quickly bores of the two-dimensional video games the other 'Launchies' play, preferring those involving holographic objects hovering in the air enjoyed by the bigger boys – and it's not long before he's putting even the older boys to shame. He becomes the hero the IF need him to be* (which makes for as thrilling a read as you can find in YA fiction), but he's also desperately lonely (see: loneliness) and comes to hate himself for his talents. No one, we hope, will ever have to give up as much of their childhood as Ender does to fulfil his potential. But those set apart by brains, maturity or aptitude will appreciate the companionship – and caution – of someone who knows what it's like.

---

* Although the second book in the series, *Speaker for the Dead*, brings a whole new slant on the achievement. Read on!

CURE FOR GROWN-UPS [PB] *Baby Brains* SIMON JAMES

It's your own fault you've got a supersonically intelligent child. If you don't know why, ask your one-year-old to read you *Baby Brains*. No doubt you read aloud to your foetus every night while you were expecting, played music and modern languages to it on headphones, and turned up the volume on the television whenever the news came on. Well, Mrs Brains did, too, and the morning after she brings the newborn Baby Brains back from hospital, she finds him on the sofa reading the paper. He's still in his babygrow when he starts school; two weeks later he's accepting patients at the local hospital. It's only when he's sent into space as an astronaut that he – and his bemused parents – realise it might all be a tad premature. Emotional development has got to keep up, after all. James's adorable pen-and-wash illustrations – full of eager attitudes and protective arms – are heart-warming and humbling in equal measure.

SEE ALSO: **bookworm, being a** • **bossiness** • **in charge, wanting to be** • **know-it-all, being a**

pregnancy, teenage

[YA] *Megan*
MARY HOOPER

[YA] *Boys Don't Cry*
MALORIE BLACKMAN

Getting pregnant in your teens is no joke, and both families have a part to play in helping the couple decide what to do once it's happened. For the pregnant girl herself, Mary Hooper's Megan trilogy provides a sensitive, funny and wise exploration of the issues – from the moment of discovering the pregnancy to life with a toddler a few years down the line. It also helps to make the fact of the pregnancy a reality.

Megan thinks she had safe sex with Luke, a temporary boyfriend from school. After all, he 'pulled out'. But during a Personal Development class, she hears something which makes her sit up sharp. 'Of course, it is possible to be pregnant and still have periods . . .' her teacher is saying. Panicking, she does the maths and soon a test confirms her fears.

Her best friend Claire is sympathetic but can't help sharing the juicy secret with her friends – who, of course, pass it on. The reaction of Megan's mother is far from ideal ('How *dare* you do this to me?' followed by a threat to pack Megan off to Australia to live with her dad) and Megan is left spinning in confusion, surrounded by other people's opinions and with none of her own. As she faces each decision in turn – whether to have the child at all, whether to keep it once she's had it, where she and the child will live – it is clear that there are no easy answers. Teen readers will be hooked by the twists and turns taken by Megan's relationships and romances during this turbulent time. They'll also come away with a suitably rocky picture of what life as a teen mum might look like.

Teen fathers can end up taking a passive role, both in the decision-making process and thereafter – and not necessarily by their own choice. An eye-opening example of a young man excluded from the decision itself but who rises to the challenge of fatherhood thereafter can be found in the powerful *Boys Don't Cry*. Dante is a hard-working student waiting for the results of his A-levels when his ex-girlfriend comes knocking at the door with a baby in tow. It's soon clear that he is not only the father but is also going to be the one left holding the baby. Dante is appalled. He had hoped for starred A grades, followed by university and a career as a journalist. It's his own father – a moral, hard-line man – who insists that Dante accept his responsibility.

Overnight, Dante's life becomes dominated by walks in the park, preparing vegetable purées and changing nappies – and Blackman paints a vivid picture of the tedium of everyday childcare. But we also see a moving metamorphosis taking place, as love begins to dawn in the heart of this young man. A positive and practical person, Dante has good relationships with his father and younger brother, Adam – and these relationships prove to be fundamental to his evolution as a parent. Readers who have already woken up to the importance of birth control will take extra care with the condom after reading Dante's story, while those who find themselves in the same position will be both heartened and inspired.

SEE ALSO: **feelings, not able to express your** • **periods** • **scared, being** • **sex, having questions about** • **virginity, loss of**

presents

CB *The Little Princess*
FRANCES HODGSON BURNETT

Whether there weren't enough, there were too many, there weren't any at all, or they weren't the right ones, the giving and receiving of presents is a complex and worrisome business. Outside the family, a new can of worms opens up. How should a child respond to a present from a friend or relative if: they don't like it,* they already have it,† they might like it if only they knew what it was,‡ they like it while violently disliking the giver,§ or they violently dislike it while loving the giver?¶ And who wants presents anyway, if it means having to write thank-you letters?** There is one character in literature to whom children can look for an example of how to behave gracefully around all these issues: Sara Crewe, the heroine of *The Little Princess*.

When Sara is left in Miss Minchin's school for girls while her daddy sails away to make his fortune – or, rather, to add to his already sizeable one – Captain Crewe leaves instructions that Sara be given 'every pleasure she ask for'. But as soon his back in turned, Miss Minchin moves in, making it clear that she doesn't approve of pleasures, including the frilly, expensive underwear in Sara's trunk, or her priceless doll, Emily. Soon everyone in the school is whispering about Sara, envying and deriding her in equal measure.

Ungenerous treatment generally invites ungenerous treatment back; but not so with Sara. However mean Miss Minchin and the other girls are, Sara is never less than exquisitely courteous and polite to them in return. When her father loses his fortune and Miss Minchin moves her up to the attic to sleep with the scullery maid, Sara's peers gloat. Surely now the little princess will lose her fine ways! But Sara's composure remains intact. 'It would be easy to be a princess if I were dressed in cloth of gold, but it is a great deal more of a triumph to be one all the time when no one knows it,' she says to herself. Her detractors are driven mad by her refusal to be brought low – even when she's starving, shoeless and freezing. Indeed, it may exasperate some readers, too. But when her fortunes take an upward turn again, and she remains the same as ever, it's hard not to admire her. Introduce your children to Sara Crewe, and next time they prepare to give or receive a gift, get them to ask themselves what Sara would have done – or said – in their place.

SEE ALSO: **disappointment** • **manners, bad** • **thank you letter, having to write a**

---

* Don't see: lying.

† See: spoilt, being.

‡ Sorry, we have no idea either.

§ See: things, wanting.

¶ See: feelings, hurting someone's.

** See: thank you letter, having to write a.

princess, wanting to be a

[PB] *The Little Princess*
TONY ROSS

[YA] *The Princess Diaries*
MEG CABOT

Princess mania can set in around the age of three – and stick around all the way into teenagehood, albeit with an emphasis on attitude rather than outfits. It's a hard tiara to tumble, and many a grown-up has been driven to anti-monarchist demonstrations by the tiered frocks, frills and fripperies adored by their despotically princessy child. Thankfully, various authors have stepped in with stories that show that 'real' princesses can be much more like ordinary people than all the fuss would suggest.

The little princess in Tony Ross's fifty-odd-title Little Princess series is captivatingly filthy. Barefoot, cheeky and generally to be found wearing a white nightie below her gender-neutral crown, she is in all ways the opposite of the pink princesses in girls' magazines. Her parents look like any other couple from down the street, apart from their crowns – oh, and their castle, their cook, their maid and the presence of the Admiral (who, for reasons that never become entirely clear, wears a rubber ring around his middle). Princesses are people just like you and me, says Ross, deftly knocking the stuffing out of princessy behaviour – and, going by the scrapes that the little princess tends to gets into, they are as in need of assistance growing up as anyone else.

For girls suffering from princess syndrome in their teens – interested only in looks and pretty things, and inclined to treat their families as maids-in-waiting – we prescribe *The Princess Diaries*. Mia, fourteen years old and at high school in Manhattan, is the last person you'd think was a princess. 'I am so NOT a princess,' she tells us. 'You never saw anyone who looked less like a princess than I do. I mean, I have really bad hair . . . and . . . a really big mouth and no breasts and feet that look like skis.' However, a princess she is, and it's time for her to be groomed as the next ruler of Genovia, a fictional country 'between France and Italy'. This means leaving behind her Doc Martens and her interest in animal and minority rights – because 'Grandmère', the Dowager Princess Clarisse Renaldo, is worried Mia may provoke an international incident by her refusal to eat meat. Luckily, Mia has her head well screwed on, having been brought up by her mother in true New York bohemian style, and she knows that what really matters in life are her friends, Greenpeace, and saving the whales. This series of books is an easy read, but they do challenge girls to acquire some political backbone. Use them to nudge your child to worry more about sticking to her principles and less about the length of her nails.

SEE ALSO: **celebrity, wanting to be a** • **role model, in need of a positive**

puberty

SEE: **acne** • **adolescence** • **body hair** • **body odour** • **hormones, raging** • **innocence, loss of** • **periods** • **wet dreams**

punished, being

PB *Skippyjon Jones*
JUDY SCHACHNER

CB *Holes*
LOUIS SACHAR

YA *Ash Road*
IVAN SOUTHALL

Whether a child has been sent to the naughty step, made to cut the lawn with a pair of scissors or has lost their Wi-Fi privileges for week, a fictitious companion being similarly punished will help put their misdemeanours into perspective – and provide them with food for thought.

When the hyperactive Siamese cat in *Skippyjon Jones* is sent to his room for some 'serious thinking', it's not really a punishment at all. He finds plenty of fun things to do in there – not least bounce on his bed. Then he dresses up as a masked sword-fighter called El Skippito and runs off into the desert to join a band of Mexican Chihuahua bandits. He even finds his birthday piñata hidden in his wardrobe and cracks it open with his sword, prematurely releasing a great explosion of sweets – which of course gets him into trouble with his exasperated mama all over again. Skippyjon will strike a chord with mischief-makers of comparable size – and help divert a high-spirited child from engaging in analogous antics.

Children required to do back-breaking chores in the house or garden will learn the art of contemplation, as well as endurance, from Stanley Yelnats in *Holes*. He and the other detainees at Camp Green Lake must dig five-foot holes in the hard desert floor all day, seven days a week – in sweltering heat and with limited drinking water. This at least leaves Stanley plenty of time to think, and it doesn't take him long to work out that 'Mister Sir' has an ulterior motive for forcing the youths to dig. As he strives to endure the 'character-building' labour, Stanley starts to piece the puzzle of his own past – and that of Camp Green Lake – together. When he unearths a lipstick bearing the initials 'KB' in one of his holes, he decides it's time to choose the mercy of the desert over his sadistic gaolers, and he absconds with his friend, Zero. Hopefully your labouring child will come to a different conclusion and feel they're getting their just deserts.

The most effective punishment of all is one in which the culprit gets to feel the injury caused by their transgression themselves. By giving teens a vicarious brush with guilt of a horrifying kind, the gripping *Ash Road* works as a powerful preventative medicine. Australian teens Graham, Wallace and Harry feel like kings as they head out bush for a camping trip, unable to believe they all managed to dupe their parents into saying yes. So when a passing motorist spots them grilling sausages on the side of the road and bluntly orders them to 'Put that fire out!', their charged-up egos are affronted. That night, in an act of defiance, Graham heats up water for coffee using methylated spirits in a camping burner. It only takes one gust of the hot, dry wind for the flame to catch on the tinder-dry grass. Within minutes the boys are all up and screaming as they try to stamp out the clusters of flame with bare feet. As the fire leaps from the grass to the trees, the foliage flaring with the sound of cracked whips, the air soon becomes too hot to breathe. Appalled, they grab their things and run for their lives.

For the community of families living on the dead-end Ash Road some distance away, the bushfire is initially not a major concern. Leaving their children in the care of elderly grandparents, the grown-ups drive into town to help with the fire-fighting effort. But the bushfire spreads more rapidly than anyone anticipated and we watch in mounting tension as Graham, Wallace and Harry stumble, stricken, into one of the Ash Road houses themselves, trying to decide whether or not to admit to their guilt. With the inferno bearing down on the trapped children, the three boys writhe in discomfort as they grapple with the enormity of what they've done. The shame of these boys leaves the reader determined never to bring such a thing on themselves.

SEE ALSO: **blamed, being** • **fair, it's not**

pyromania

ER *Frances the Firefly*
DEPARTMENT FOR COMMUNITIES AND LOCAL GOVERNMENT

YA *We Were Liars*
EMILY LOCKHART

The lure of fire can be hard to resist. Thankfully, most children learn a healthy fear of it early on, but the message that fire is dangerous cannot be reiterated too often. A nicely expressed warning comes in the form of the government-published cautionary tale *Frances the Firefly*. In an idyllic insect kingdom where everyone offers up their particular skill to the community, the job of the older fireflies is to light the streets with their tail-torches. Frances is desperate to put her light to use, but her tail doesn't glow brightly enough yet. Then Cocky Roach tempts her. 'If you strike a match, you can have a tail-torch of your own, and be like the grown-up fireflies,' he says. Frances can't resist and soon she's flying up high with the match, which glows brighter and brighter – then sets her wings on fire. Soon the whole beautifully farmed forest is on fire. King Chrysalis puts it all back together again, and Frances is given a special new job teaching the little insects never to play with fire; but children reading this will see that it's better to learn their lesson from Frances than to go through a trauma like this themselves.

Up the shock factor for older kids with *We Were Liars*, which packs such a punch near the end that leaves the reader wanting to go back and re-read the whole thing again in the light of what they now know. Something awful happened the summer before last – and seventeen-year-old Cadence has spent the last two years suffering from migraines and memory loss as a result. Finally, she's coming off anti-depressants and going back to the beautiful island owned by her grandfather off Cape Cod, where she and her cousins, a privileged and carefree bunch, have spent their holidays since they were young.

As they lounge around in the sunshine flirting and reminiscing, we start to build up a picture, through flashbacks, of Cadence's burgeoning romance with Gat, a family friend; and then of the bickering between the adults over who will inherit the biggest and most important house on the island when the grandfather dies. Cadence is jolted into the suspicion that she and her cousins – affectionately known as 'the Liars' – may be to blame for something unforgivable that she had blanked from her mind. Anyone who has ever played with fire, or fantasised about doing so, will never forget the extraordinary revelation in this dark story – and do their utmost to avoid the whisper of a conflagration henceforth.

SEE ALSO: **punished, being** • **violence**

questions, asking too many

Why?
LINDSAY CAMP, ILLUSTRATED BY TONY ROSS

When it occurs to a child that they can know everything there is to know if they want to – and that they only have to ask 'Why . . .?' – it's exciting at first. But when the answers you give to their first 'why?' are themselves greeted by more 'whys?', and then *those* answers lead to further 'whys?', it can fray the nerves of even the most patient of grown-ups. This is the moment to bring in (apologies in advance) another *Why?* – a picture book with a twist that's as delightful for the questioner as it is for the one who posed the questions. When the dad in the story is driven mad by the incessant 'whys?' of his small, red-haired Lily, it's not too many pages before the previously-gentle-but-now-seriously-strung-out man resorts to the killer phrase, 'Just *because*.' Tony Ross's cross-hatched colour-pencil illustrations show a world that is comfortingly familiar – until, on an outing to the park one day, they show something that is *not*. Saying what it is would ruin one of the best surprises in picture books. But it shuts even Lily up for a while. When, eventually, she finds her tongue again, and says – of course – 'Why?', it has an effect for which we can all be grateful. Introduce this to your incessant questioner and it'll help both of you laugh.

CURE FOR GROWN-UPS  *The Little Prince*
ANTOINE DE SAINT-EXUPÉRY

It's easy to fall into the trap of thinking that you've got more important things to concern yourself with than answering a child's relentless questions. Revisiting *The Little Prince* will remind you that you may have your priorities wrong. When the narrator crashes his plane in the desert and makes the acquaintance of the 'most extraordinary small person' he's ever met, he soon ascertains that the little fellow is from another planet – and that he leads a lonely life, pulling up baobab seedlings and watching repeated sunsets. But he's busy trying to fix his plane and so when the prince asks a seemingly random question about why flowers bother to grow thorns if it doesn't stop sheep from eating them, the pilot snaps at him. They have thorns out of spite, is his testy reply.

The pilot doesn't really believe that flowers are spiteful, of course. He only said it because he has 'matters of consequence' to deal with. But now the prince wants to know what could be more important than the question of why flowers have thorns. Because what if, the prince goes on, he happened to know and love one particular flower, unique in the world. And what if a sheep could destroy it in a single bite one morning, without even noticing. Does the pilot think that's not important? At which point the narrator stops what he's doing and takes the little prince in his arms, knowing that the broken plane, his thirst and even his death are of no consequence compared to the need to answer this question, now.

SEE ALSO: **chatterbox, being a**

R IS FOR . . .

racism

[PB] *Amazing Grace*
MARY HOFFMAN, ILLUSTRATED BY CAROLINE BINCH

[CB] *Roll of Thunder, Hear My Cry*
MILDRED D TAYLOR

[YA] *Noughts and Crosses*
MALORIE BLACKMAN

The all-embracing message that human beings are fundamentally the same, wherever we come from, whatever the colour of our skin and whatever the language we speak, can be delivered to a child from the beginning through books, behaviour and words – and if it's there from the start, it will never go away. But when an awareness of discrimination in the outside world enters in, bring in *Amazing Grace*. Grace is a confident girl with an open face and big brown eyes who loves to dress up and act out stories. We see her play a whole range of parts at home, from Joan of Arc and Helen of Troy to a pirate with an eye patch and peg leg. So when the teacher at Grace's school announces they're looking for someone to play Peter Pan in the next school play, she immediately puts up her hand. 'You can't be Peter Pan,' whispers another girl. 'He isn't black.' Her ma and nana go quiet when Grace explains why she's feeling crestfallen. 'You can be anything you want, Grace, if you put your mind to it,' says Nana. Of course, she goes on to win the part and steal the show – and the transformation in the eyes of Ma and Nana as they share a look of triumph says it all. Caroline Binch's gloriously realistic watercolour illustrations show Grace as a spirited, charismatic child, and her mother and grandmother as women who know exactly what it's like to be told you can't when you can. A moving read, this story shows how people can absorb inherently racist attitudes without even being aware of it – and that it's up to all of us not to let prejudice stand in any child's way.

For chapter-book-age kids, *Roll of Thunder, Hear My Cry* – told as it is from the point of view of a black nine-year-old, Cassie Logan – offers an intelligent, if sobering, way to take a child from innocence to experience on this issue. Growing up in poverty at the height of the American Depression, Cassie is blissfully oblivious of the disadvantages and intimidation faced by her mama and Big Mama on a daily basis. Cassie's father, David, works on the railroad and comes home when he can – and it's left to the two women to bring up the four children and make a living from cotton on their family land. When the horrific news of the 'burning' of a black man begins to spread, David despatches his brother, Hammer, and a gentle giant, Mr Morrison, to keep his family safe. However, Hammer's temper – like Cassie's – is easily inflamed and risks putting the family in greater danger than if he hadn't come at all.

When, on her first trip to town, Cassie accidentally bumps into a white girl on the street and discovers that she's expected to apologise in a grovelling, insubordinate way, the terrible unfairness of 'the way of things' begins to dawn on her. And when Cassie's mother takes the children to the bedside of one of the victims of the burnings, Cassie's outrage grows. But so, too, does her fear, and the dreadful realisation that the only way to survive and hold on to their land is to suppress her anger and, in effect, herself. Essential reading, this gripping story of a loving family living amidst dire injustice well after the official abolishment of slavery in America will open the door to a discussion about the existence of racism in the modern world and impress upon a child the importance of judging others by their actions, not by their colour, race or beliefs.

For teens, we prescribe the equally essential *Noughts and Crosses*. Thirteen-year-old Sephy and her lifelong friend Callum are starting to become aware that they may be more to each other than friends – but also that something they can't yet articulate has come between them. Life is hard for Callum and his family – and has been since his mother was fired by Sephy's mother after being in service to her for fourteen years. And though he is lucky to be one of only four Noughts to be accepted into Heathcroft, the school where Sephy goes, he knows it will mark the end of the innocent years of their friendship: Sephy is a Cross, a member of the wealthy and privileged ruling class; and Callum is a Nought, the powerless underclass who were once slaves to the Crosses.

What Blackman brings to this so-far-so-familiar set-up – in a sleight of hand that overturns history and all our assumptions – is that the privileged Crosses, including Sephy, are black; and the underclass Noughts, including Callum, are white. And so we find ourselves in a world in which it's a black family – Sephy's parents, in fact – who own the seven-bedroom country house, and it's the new white kids at school who are jeered at when the previously all-black school opens its doors to accept them. In the world of *Noughts and Crosses*, the only plasters you can buy are dark brown.

Sephy, younger than Callum, doesn't yet understand why it is complicated for her friend to come to her school as a minority Nought. Nor does she understand why there is bitterness in his voice when he says he only got in thanks to his friendship with her. But when the protests outside Heathcroft trigger a wave of violent uprisings, we know that things are about to get a lot harder for both of them. The first in a gripping series, this story opens eyes and minds, challenging readers to see that prejudice can be so deeply ingrained we don't even notice it's there.

SEE ALSO: **gang, being in a** • **manners, bad** • **unfriendliness**

rainy day

Water, water everywhere . . . means a great excuse for battening down the hatches and cosying up with a really good read. These books will make everyone feel lucky to be warm and dry inside.

THE TEN BEST BOOKS FOR A RAINY DAY

- [PB] *Rainstorm* BARBARA LEHMAN
- [PB] *The Tin Forest* HELEN WARD, ILLUSTRATED BY WAYNE ANDERSON
- [ER] *Half a Man* MICHAEL MORPURGO, ILLUSTRATED BY GEMMA O'CALLAGHAN
- [ER] *The Grunts All at Sea* PHILIP ARDAGH, ILLUSTRATED BY AXEL SCHEFFLER
- [CB] *One Hundred and One Dalmatians* DODIE SMITH
- [CB] *Island of the Blue Dolphins* SCOTT O'DELL
- [CB] *A High Wind in Jamaica* RICHARD HUGHES
- [CB] *Heart of a Samurai* MARGI PREUS
- [CB] *We Didn't Mean to Go to Sea* ARTHUR RANSOME
- [YA] *The Book of Storms* RUTH HATFIELD

SEE ALSO: **adventure, needing an** • **bored, being** • **disappointment** • **indoors, spending too much time** • **summer holidays**

rape

[YA] *Speak*
LAURIE HALSE ANDERSON

The severity of a sexual attack on a child cannot be over-stated, and the tendency for victims not to tell anyone what has happened – because of shame or confusion, or for fear of how the perpetrator will react – can compound the damage even more. This is what happens in *Speak*, in which fourteen-year-old Melinda arrives for her first day of high school in Syracuse, New York, to find herself shunned by her peers, including Rachel, her former best friend. Over the summer she committed social suicide by calling the police to a house party, bringing the night to an abrupt end and causing one of her peers to be fired from his job. Only she knows what made her cry for help in the only way she could think to do – but now everyone hates her for spoiling their fun.

Even though her throat aches with the unspoken truth, Melinda finds herself unable to get the words out. 'All that crap you hear on TV about communication and expressing feelings is a lie,' she tells us with her characteristically sardonic wit. 'Nobody really wants to hear what you have to say.' And so she bites her lip till it bleeds, looks for a new friend to hang out with and watches her school grades plummet. Only her art teacher, Mr Freeman, suspects there's something she's not saying. When she finally speaks up, the release is cathartic and the sympathy and support from those around her immediate. Victims of rape and other abuse will find this story an encouragement to talk, and it will chime with any teen who needs help yet doesn't dare ask.

SEE ALSO: **abuse** • **feelings, unable to express your** • **heard, not feeling**

read to, always wanting to be

READING AILMENTS

READ TOGETHER IN COMPANIONABLE SILENCE

Sometimes kids think that once they can read themselves, they'll no longer be read to.* Subconciously, they stave off learning to read independently in case it brings these tranquil, bonding moments to an end. When else do they get the full attention of an undistracted grown-up and share a story to boot? It's important to reassure a child that just because they can read independently it doesn't mean they're too old for a bedtime story; indeed, if we had our way, everyone would be read to well into middle age and beyond. Of course you'll need to encourage a child to read by themselves, too, and to this end we suggest you transpose the physical and emotional intimacy of the reading-aloud moment to a shared silent-reading moment, too. You read your book, they read theirs – but in the same room, at the same moment, and ideally

* Sometimes their grown-ups think this, too.

with your limbs tangled up together.* There's no reason why reading in your head has to be a solitary experience. You might even like to read copies of the same book simultaneously.

read to, no longer wanting to be

READING AILMENTS

INTRODUCE FAMILY STORY-TIME

Kids who feel, conversely, that they really are too old to be read to, and wish their grown-ups would leave them to it, may need to have their interest reignited. To do this, elevate the reading-aloud experience to a whole-family ritual, with each member of the circle taking a turn to read from a well-chosen book – a few pages each for the older kids, a few lines for the younger. See The Ten Best Books to Read with Children of Different Ages (p.259) for ideas of what to read. Make a date to do this one night a week, at weekends, or on holidays, when a shared book will bond you as a family and add to the memories of your time together. After all, Christmas wouldn't be Christmas without reading either *The Night Before Christmas* or *A Christmas Carol* aloud *en famille*; and what better way to get through a three-hour jam on the M25 than a hammed-up rendering of *How to Train Your Dragon* by whichever one of you is least likely to get car-sick?† And if hamming it up to each other really isn't the family style, bring in the professionals to do it for you: see our list of The Ten Best Audiobooks for All the Family that follows.

THE TEN BEST AUDIOBOOKS FOR ALL THE FAMILY

- CB *Walk Two Moons* SHARON CREECH, READ BY HOPE DAVIS
- CB *Because of Winn-Dixie* KATE DICAMILLO, READ BY CHERRY JONES
- CB *The Ocean at the End of the Lane* NEIL GAIMAN, READ BY THE AUTHOR
- CB *The Wind in the Willows* KENNETH GRAHAME, READ BY ALAN BENNETT
- CB *George's Secret Key to the Universe* LUCY AND STEPHEN HAWKING, READ BY HUGH DANCY

* Maybe with a cat or two thrown in.

† And is also not driving.

[CB] *The Railway Children* E NESBIT, READ BY JOHANNA WARD
[CB] *A Single Shard* LINDA SUE PARK, READ BY GRAEME MALCOLM
[CB] *Treasure Island* ROBERT LOUIS STEVENSON, READ BY ALFRED MOLINA
[CB] *Charlotte's Web* EB WHITE, READ BY THE AUTHOR
[YA] *The Count of Monte Cristo* ALEXANDRE DUMAS, READ BY BILL HOMEWOOD

reading difficulties

[CB] *A Dog Called Flow*
PIPPA GOODHART, ILLUSTRATED BY ANTHONY LEWIS

[CB] *Percy Jackson and the Lightning Thief*
RICK RIORDAN

[PB] *Thank you, Mr Falker*
PATRICIA POLACCO

[YA] *brown girl dreaming*
JACQUELINE WOODSON

Primed as teachers these days are to look out for early signs of dyslexia and other reading difficulties, a recently diagnosed child will benefit enormously from being introduced to fictional friends who share their struggle with words. A good place to start is *A Dog Called Flow,* in which ten-year-old Oliver has, as yet, no name for his battle with letters – and hates school as a result (see: school, not wanting to go to). Constantly kept behind to write lines by an unsympathetic teacher, Oliver can't wait for the summer holidays. And when a farmer neighbour has puppies on offer, he adopts Flow – a black and white dog with an irresistible, off-kilter gait* – with whom he can spend his days running over the fells. Meanwhile, with the help of his potter father, Oliver practises writing his letters in clay.

One day, six terrified sheep rush past them and Oliver, having heard rumours of a huge, wolfish dog in the area, suspects the worst. Flow, increasingly agitated, insists Oliver follow him into the mists – where they find a boy who has fallen down a crag and broken his leg. Flow proves his mettle that day, and in the note he leaves the boy while they go for help ('gon of help down hill') Oliver proves his dyslexia. This story of two brains that function a little differently from others (see: different, feeling) is deeply touching and inspires a spirit both of acceptance and of asking for help.†

Slightly older kids will relate to Percy Jackson, the twelve-year-old boy who, despite being a demigod, has never managed to achieve anything higher than a C grade at school. Not only is Percy dyslexic but he has ADHD. When

* The result, it transpires, of being deaf in one ear and blind in one eye.

† Dyslexic readers will no doubt work out sooner than others why the dog is called Flow.

he tries to read, the letters seem to be 'doing one-eighties as if they were riding skateboards' and at other times his brain seems to 'skip a beat', as if a 'puzzle piece fell out of the universe and left [him] staring at the blank space behind it'. One day, looking at some strange lettering in a museum, he finds he's reading fluently for the first time in his life. And when his best friend Grover reveals himself to be a satyr who speaks ancient Greek, Percy can understand every word. Finally, he can see his 'flaws' for what they are: signs that his reading brain is wired for ancient Greek, not 21st-century English, and his body for the flight-or-fight response required of a mythical champion, not a 21st-century schoolboy. Readers will feel encouraged and exonerated by this hero who shares their struggles – and inspired to look further than their schoolbooks for success in life.*

Sometimes it requires a real role model or two to convince children that having dyslexia doesn't mean they can't fulfil their potential. For young children, bring in *Thank you, Mr Falker*, the autobiographical story of Patricia Polacco's early struggles with reading. Trisha, as she then was, longs to learn to read – books being valued highly in her family. But when she's finally old enough to go to school, all she sees are 'wiggling shapes' on the page. The other children laugh at her when she tries to sound out the words and she soon falls behind. For the next few years Trisha plays it safe and concentrates on drawing. But then Mr Falker walks into her life. This moving book, with its quirky ink-and-watercolour illustrations, is Polacco's thank-you letter to the man who gave her his time and patience – and testimony, both in words and pictures, of how well she came through.

Older children can find their role model in Jacqueline Woodson, whose personal struggle with reading is touched upon, very lightly, in *brown girl dreaming*, her fictionalised memoir. Written in luminous and accessible free verse, it tells a story of growing up African-American in the Sixties and Seventies, raised by her mother and grandparents first in South Carolina – a land of porch swings and fireflies – then in Brooklyn, New York. At first, the city is 'treeless as a bad dream'. But from the moment she goes to school, Jacqueline is excited by stories and knows they will 'be her life' one day. She marvels at her first 'composition notebook', with its blank pages smelling 'like something/I could fall right into,/live there'. So it comes as a surprise that when she starts learning to read, the words 'twist/twirl across the page' and 'When they settle, it is too late./The class has already moved on.' Woodson doesn't use a label for her problems with reading: whatever it was, the existence of this memorable book – and the many others she has written – is

* Look out for the audiobook too, brilliantly read by Jesse Bernstein.

tangible proof that it didn't stop her becoming the writer she dreamed she could be.

SEE ALSO: **bullied, being** • **frustration** • **good at anything, feeling like you're no** • **understood, not being**

relatives

SEE: **boring relatives, having**

reluctant reader

SEVEN EASY STEPS TO CREATING AN EXCITED YOUNG READER

READING AILMENTS

Before you tarnish books (and yourself) by resorting to bribery and paying a child to read, try these more creative approaches.

1. Create an enticing place to read – a cosy nook complete with beanbag, reading lamp and a shelf for a bowl of grapes. Or a wigwam, equipped with furry throw, slippers and fairy lights. Or a hammock with pillows and a mocktail wedged into a branch. Who wouldn't want to jump in?
2. Stop all the clocks, turn off the phones, disconnect the Wi-Fi – and declare a reading half-hour. Everyone in the house must take a break from what they're doing and settle down quietly with a physical book. The reading half-hour slots in nicely on a weekday before supper, and on Sunday afternoons once everyone has spent all their energy and is ready to flop. In our experience the reading half-hour becomes something everyone looks forward to once it becomes a habit. Before you know it, half an hour has become forty-five minutes and still nobody's asked what's for supper.
3. Download an audiobook and plug your reluctant reader in with a set of headphones. If it's a good one and read well (not too slow, not too fast, and in a voice you like – play an extract first), it'll give a kid the experience of being transported by a story and leave them wanting more. It'll also give them practise at focusing quietly for a longish chunk of time. Start by playing the audiobooks in the car, where there's nothing else to do. Then introduce an audiobook into the daily

routine – during snack time, or when the kids are tidying up their rooms. You'll find an increasingly wide selection available to download on www.audible.co.uk – or in CD form at your local library. (See: The Ten Best Audiobooks for All the Family (p.232) and The Ten Best Audiobooks for Long Car Journeys, (p.55.)

4. Books which have been made into movies come with a ready-made carrot: once you've finished the book, you can watch the film.* Never break the book-before-film rule, though (see: watch the film first, wanting to).
5. Up a tree, in a haystack, under the trampoline – reading accrues extra novelty value when enjoyed somewhere unexpected. Halfway up the stairs is a favourite of ours – as is in the cupboard under the stairs with a head torch.
6. Go wordless. Take your pick from our list of The Ten Best Wordless Stories that follows. With the pictures alone telling the story – and complex ones, at that – children can take a rest from deciphering words, while still developing an appreciation for character, narrative and the physical object of the book. Wordless novels are also a great way to encourage a creative approach to stories as a whole. Who says the author should be the one to decide a character's name – or how the conversation goes?
7. Keep it clean. Reluctant readers fare best when reading clear fonts against cream or tinted backgrounds, and on paper thick enough to ensure that the text doesn't show through from the other side. Pictures and short chapters are a bonus. The stories themselves must be intriguing from the first line, without too many subplots, and not bogged down with too much description or too many different characters. Of course, the book must still challenge, stimulate and address at the right level. See our list of The Ten Best Books for Reluctant Readers that follows.

THE TEN BEST WORDLESS STORIES

[PB] *Fox's Garden* PRINCESSE CAMCAM
[PB] *Flora and the Flamingo* MOLLY IDLE
[PB] *A Boy, a Dog, and a Frog* MERCER MAYER

* This, of course, also applies to books that come with apps, such as the Beast Quest series.

[PB] *Sea of Dreams* **DENNIS NOLAN**
[PB] *Wonder Bear* **TAO NYEU**
[PB] *The Lion and the Mouse* **JERRY PINKNEY**
[PB] *The Girl and the Bicycle* **MARK PETT**
[PB] *The Umbrella* **INGRID AND DIETER SCHUBERT**
[PB] *The Tree House* **MARIJE AND RONALD TOLMAN**
[PB] *Flotsam* **DAVID WIESNER**

THE TEN BEST BOOKS FOR RELUCTANT READERS*

[PB] *The Girl Who Hated Books* **MANJUSHA PAWAGI, ILLUSTRATED BY LEANNE FRANSON**
[ER] *Ferno the Fire Dragon* (Beast Quest) **ADAM BLADE**
[ER] *Ted Rules the World* **FRANK COTTRELL BOYCE, ILLUSTRATED BY CATE JAMES AND CHRIS RIDDELL**
[ER] *The Not-a-Pig* (Mango & Bambang) **POLLY FABER, ILLUSTRATED BY CLARA VULLIAMY**
[ER] *Ruby the Red Fairy* (Rainbow Magic) **DAISY MEADOWS**
[ER] *My Dad's Got an Alligator!* **JEREMY STRONG**
[CB] *Brock* **ANTHONY MCGOWAN**
[CB] *Waiting for Anya* **MICHAEL MORPURGO**
[YA] *The Recruit* (Cherub) **ROBERT MUCHAMORE**
[YA] *Tales from Outer Suburbia* **SHAUN TAN**

role model, in need of a positive

Buck the usual stereotypes with these stories of feisty, careerist girls and emotionally intelligent boys.

THE TEN BEST ROLE MODELS FOR GIRLS

[PB] *Princess Smartypants* **BABETTE COLE**
[PB] *The Princess Knight* **CORNELIA FUNKE, ILLUSTRATED BY KERSTIN MEYER**
[PB] *The Paper Bag Princess* **ROBERT MUNSCH, ILLUSTRATED BY MICHAEL MARTCHENKO**
[PB] *Zog* **JULIA DONALDSON, ILLUSTRATED BY AXEL SCHEFFLER**
[PB] *Interstellar Cinderella* **DEBORAH UNDERWOOD, ILLUSTRATED BY MEG HUNT**

* It goes without saying that *Harry Potter and the Philosopher's Stone by* JK Rowling is on this list.

CB *The Curious World of Calpurnia Tate* JACQUELINE KELLY
CB *Pippi Longstocking* ASTRID LINDGREN, ILLUSTRATED BY LAUREN CHILD
CB *Ottoline and the Yellow Cat* CHRIS RIDDELL
CB *Emily's Tiara Trouble* (Anti-Princess Club) SAMANTHA TURNBULL, ILLUSTRATED BY SARAH DAVIS
YA *Sun Catcher* SHEILA RANCE

THE TEN BEST ROLE MODELS FOR BOYS

PB *Halibut Jackson* DAVID LUCAS
PB *Made by Raffi* CRAIG POMRANZ, ILLUSTRATED BY MARGARET CHAMBERLAIN
ER *How to Write Really Badly* ANNE FINE
CB *Love That Dog* SHARON CREECH
CB *Running Wild* MICHAEL MORPURGO
YA *Ghost Hawk* SUSAN COOPER
YA *Will Grayson, Will Grayson* JOHN GREEN AND DAVID LEVITHAN
YA *Scat* CARL HIAASEN
YA *Wonder* RJ PALACIO
YA *Okay for Now* GARY D SCHMIDT

routine, unable to cope with a change in the

PB *The Tiger Who Came to Tea* JUDITH KERR

Most kids like a bit of routine; but some become so set in their ways that any deviation from the norm triggers anxiety – if not a full-scale meltdown. If this happens, see: tantrums, anxiety and anger; and, in the meantime, treat by gentle suggestion with *The Tiger Who Came to Tea*, the story of a mother and daughter who take the unexpected in their stride.

When a huge, stripy tiger turns up at the door and asks to come in for tea, Sophie's mother doesn't miss a beat. 'Of course, come in,' she says. The tiger *does* cause a raised eyebrow when he gulps down not just one sandwich but the entire plateful – although their surprise is more about manners than anything else (see: manners, bad). And there's a definite blush on the mother's cheek when the tiger doesn't just drink one cup of tea but drains the teapot directly into his mouth. When Sophie's daddy comes home and is told there's no supper, he just shrugs and they all go out for a meal instead. The unflappability of this family is impressive, and the demonstration of supreme *sangfroid* in the face of unexpected interruptions to the usual routine will at the very least plant a seed.

SEE ALSO: **autism**

run away, urge to

All children fantasise about running away at some point. Encourage the kids you know to explore the thrill vicariously – and wear out their need to make it happen for real.

THE TEN BEST BOOKS ABOUT RUNNING AWAY

- PB *Mama, Do You Love Me?* BARBARA M JOOSSE, ILLUSTRATED BY BARBARA LAVALLEE
- PB *We Were Tired of Living in a House* LIESEL MOAK SKORPEN, ILLUSTRATED BY JOE CEPEDA
- PB *The Runaway Bunny* MARGARET WISE BROWN, ILLUSTRATED BY CLEMENT HURD
- CB *Brendon Chase* BB
- CB *Bud, Not Buddy* CHRISTOPHER PAUL CURTIS
- CB *One Dog and His Boy* EVA IBBOTSON
- CB *From the Mixed-up Files of Mrs Basil E Frankweiler* EL KONIGSBURG
- CB *Mrs Frisby and the Rats of NIMH* ROBERT C O'BRIEN
- CB *The Runaways* RUTH THOMAS
- YA *Paper Towns* JOHN GREEN

SEE ALSO: **cheering up, needing • frustration • loner, being a • school, not wanting to go to • suicidal thoughts**

TEA

S IS FOR . . .

sadness

PB *Michael Rosen's Sad Book*
MICHAEL ROSEN, ILLUSTRATED BY QUENTIN BLAKE

YA *The Ice Palace*
TARJEI VESAAS

Sometimes a child is sad because something didn't go the way they wanted it to, in which case, see: disappointment; cheering up, needing – or help them find a way to fix it. But sometimes a child is sad because something really sad has happened and there is nothing anyone can do about it.

Someone who understands this feeling all too well is the much-loved children's author Michael Rosen, whose son, Eddie, died when he was eighteen years old – and *Michael Rosen's Sad Book* is the book he wrote as a response. An exploration of the state of sadness, it is a book that gives a child permission to be sad, and not to try and chase the feeling away. It explores, via portraits of Michael Rosen by Quentin Blake, the different ways sadness can look: unshaven, owl-eyed and with a despairing slump to the shoulders, or hidden behind an insane, forced grin – a look which Blake, with his energetic pen-and-wash illustrations, does particularly well. And it explores some of the crazy things we do when we're sad, from shouting in the shower to banging a spoon pointlessly on the table and saying hurtful things to those we love.

Children who act out as a result of their sadness will find it a great relief to discover that when he's feeling really bad, this grown-up named Michael Rosen acts out too – and, in fact, does things so awful he won't even tell us what they are except that the poor cat is involved. Snapshots from Eddie's short, happy life – from the baby delighting in his bubble bath to bracing father–son games of catch on the sofa – blister with love and loss. But there is hope and redemption here, too. The ease with which Quentin Blake's liberated squiggle moves from one end of the emotional spectrum to the other suggests that even the deepest grief doesn't rule out being happy sometimes – or even, perhaps, being happy and sad at the same time. Bring in this book to spread an acceptance of sadness among the members of your household. Sadness shared is better than sadness bottled up (see: feelings, not able to express your).

Teens are usually rather adept at letting their emotions run their course, and they'll find a resonant tale to echo their sadness in *The Ice Palace*, set in the author's native Norway. Eleven-year-old Siss, a popular girl, tries to welcome Unn to her group at school. Revealing the instinct that children sometimes have around friendships, the two girls know at once they like each other. But Unn, who has just lost her mother and moved to this remote mountain village to live with her aunt (see: school, being the new kid at), holds back. Eventually Unn musters up the courage to invite Siss back to her house, and in that single, brief after-school meeting, they share feelings so profound that Unn can't face going to school the next day. Instead, she goes alone to the legendary 'ice palace' which forms each year at the site of a waterfall.

Unn is drawn deeper and deeper into the individual chambers formed by the frozen waterfall, eventually taking off her coat so as to squeeze through smaller gaps between the stalactites and stalagmites of ice. Each chamber is more beautiful and mysterious than the one before. Eventually she finds a place she likes and curls up in a ball, the sun seeming to have found a way to reach and warm her through the gently dripping walls. When, the next day, Unn fails to come to school, it's Siss's turn to hover at the edge of the playground, not joining in. This dark, disturbing love story mirrors and refracts the reader's own sadness, leaving them with the feeling their own emotion has been seen and understood. Feelings need time to heal, this book says, and here is a quiet, elegiac space in which they can.

SEE ALSO: **cheering up, needing**

saying no

SEE: **bullied, being • stand up for yourself, not feeling able to • told, never doing what you're**

scapegoat, being a

SEE: **fair, it's not**

scared, being

PB *Swimmy*
LEO LIONNI

CB *Varjak Paw*
SF SAID

CB *Stormbreaker*
ANTHONY HOROWITZ

YA *Game Changer*
TIM BOWLER

Children have good reason to be scared at times, being smaller and less capable than others (see: small, being). One way to feel more brave is to do what the little fish does in *Swimmy*. Bringing homespun potato stamps to his trademark collages, Lionni introduces us to the little black fish who, alone in the 'deep wet world', marvels at the gorgeously hued creatures to be found there, including a rainbow 'medusa' (cue purple, green and fuchsia prints) and a forest of exotic seaweed. In time, Swimmy meets a shoal of little red fish – but they're too scared to leave the shelter of their rock and explore with him. Then Swimmy has an idea: if they swim in formation, they can make themselves look like the biggest fish in the sea. Share this one with a child scared of venturing out into the world without you: a gaggle of friends offers a whole new way of feeling big.

Slightly older kids nervous of the world beyond their front door will enjoy having Varjak Paw as a mentor, with his martial arts-inspired tactics and feline cunning. Varjak is a Mesopotamian blue cat who has lived inside all his life, with milk and food appearing at regular intervals, so it's understandable he doesn't want to venture beyond the cat flap. But when a host of black cats with lifeless eyes invade the security of the Contessa's house, Varjak, the smallest of his clan, decides it's time to take a look. Despite having no idea what one looks like, he goes in search of a dog – the scariest thing he can think of – with the intention of asking it to chase the invaders off.

Luckily, Varjak is blessed with the ability to communicate across the ages with his ancestor Jalal Paw, the only other cat who's ever been outside, and who now teaches him the 'Way'. Through Jalal, Varjak learns such skills as 'Open Mind', 'Slow-Time' and 'Shadow-Walking' – all of which help him to overcome his fear and cheat his opponents' expectations. Readers following Varjak's journey will discover their own form of the Way, and that they, too, can surprise not only their peers but themselves.

There's a liberating lesson to be learned from the reluctant young spy in *Stormbreaker*, the first in the Alex Rider series. When his uncle Ian dies in suspicious circumstances, fourteen-year-old Alex – raised by Ian since he was small – sets out to investigate. After narrowly avoiding being flattened by a junkyard crusher when he discovers his uncle's BMW sprayed with bullet holes, Alex finds himself invited to discuss his future with his uncle's bosses at the 'bank'. Left briefly alone in an office adjacent to his uncle's, Alex climbs out the window and, determined to gain access to his uncle's papers, scales a ledge with a sheer fifteen-storey drop beneath it.

It turns out, of course, that Alex's uncle was a spy – and has been preparing Alex to follow in his footsteps all his life. Well built, and with the body of an athlete, Alex can already ski, climb and speak several languages; but it's Alex's attitude to his fear that marks him out in the eyes of his uncle's bosses. Alex allows himself to think only two things when scaling the ledge. First, if he were in a jungle gym, he wouldn't think twice about it. And second, that he should 'just do it' rather than spend any longer thinking.

And that's what he does. 'I told you,' cries the head of MI6, Alan Blunt, watching the whole thing on a CCTV camera from another room. 'The boy's extraordinary.' MI6 co-opt his services on the spot. By the end of the story, Alex has faced death several times and in several surprising fashions, including by fast-moving cheese wire – and every time he acts before his fear has had a chance to take hold. Children will see that sometimes it's the thinking about the thing, rather than the thing itself, which stops them from being able to do it.

Older children held hostage by their fear may relate to fifteen-year-old Mike Molyneux in *Game Changer*. Mole, as his classmates call him, is terrified of going outside and spends whole days curled up in a wardrobe with his favourite escapist read, *Treasure Island* (see: our list of The Ten Best Comfort Reads, p.193). He hates himself for not being able to do normal things like travel in a car – and has been trying to come out into the light more, with the encouragement and aid of his little sister Meggie. It's only when Mole is called on to protect Meggie, not the other way round, that he is forced to overcome his fear. Nobody can read this book without feeling great empathy for Mole – and being encouraged by its gently percolating message.

CURE FOR GROWN-UPS PB *Black Dog* LEVI PINFOLD

Grown-ups have less reason to be scared, but it doesn't seem to stop us. When a huge, slobbering black dog appears outside the Hope family's house – as large as the house itself – the parents in *Black Dog* panic, switching off the lights, closing the curtains and barricading themselves in behind a home-spun fort. But the youngest member of the family, Small, has a different reaction. She steps outside to meet the dog for herself. Soon she discovers that fear can make something seem much larger than it actually is. The powerful illustrations – a combination of Bosch, Grimm and American Gothic – do not shy away from depicting the black dog as a metaphor for depression, inviting us to consider the possibility that sometimes we label something as scary when actually it's our anxiety or depression speaking. Read this picture book to remind yourself that fear may be nothing more than a habit. Act brave, even if you don't feel it – and you'll pass on that bravery to your kids.

SEE ALSO: **animals, fear of** • **anxiety** • **dark, scared of the** • **small, being** • **small, feeling** • **worrying**

school, being the new kid at

Arriving halfway through the school year is a challenge for even the most outgoing child. Stories of others in the same boat will show that nervousness is natural – and that while inductions can be bumpy, it generally works out in the end.

THE TEN BEST BOOKS FOR THE NEW KID AT SCHOOL

PB *You Will Be My Friend!* PETER BROWN
PB *First Day Jitters* JULIE DANNEBERG, ILLUSTRATED BY JUDY LOVE
PB *Marshall Armstrong is New to Our School* DAVID MACKINTOSH
PB *When an Elephant Comes to School* JAN ORMEROD
ER *Doctor Proctor's Fart Powder* JO NESBØ, ILLUSTRATED BY MIKE LOWERY
CB *The Demon Headmaster* GILLIAN CROSS
CB *Inside Out & Back Again* THANHHA LAI
YA *Boy2Girl* TERENCE BLACKER
YA *Looking for Alaska* JOHN GREEN
YA *We Are All Made of Molecules* SUSIN NIELSEN

school, not going to

SEE: **home-schooling**

school, not wanting to go to

Whether school is heaven or hell for a child depends in large part on their teachers, their friends and their attitude. You might not be able to do much about the first two, but you can definitely help with the latter. Share a tale in which someone feels the same as they do about school – and finds something to like about it in the end.

THE TEN BEST BOOKS FOR KIDS WHO DON'T WANT TO GO TO SCHOOL

PB *I Hate School* JEANNE WILLIS, ILLUSTRATED BY TONY ROSS
ER *Ms Wiz Spells Trouble* TERENCE BLACKER, ILLUSTRATED BY TONY ROSS
CB *Arthur's Teacher Trouble* MARC BROWN
CB *Ramona Quimby, Age 8* BEVERLY CLEARY, ILLUSTRATED BY JACQUELINE ROGERS
CB *Diary of a Wimpy Kid* JEFF KINNEY
CB *Aquila* ANDREW NORRISS
CB *Sideways Stories from Wayside School* LOUIS SACHAR
YA *Because of Mr Terupt* ROB BUYEA
YA *Out of My Mind* SHARON M DRAPER
YA *There's a Boy in the Girls' Bathroom* LOUIS SACHAR

SEE ALSO: **blamed, being • daydreaming, being accused of • different, feeling • exams • friends, feeling that you have no • friends, finding it hard to make • homework, reluctance to do • loner, being a • punished, being**

school, starting

From having your own coat hook to walking in crocodile formation . . . prepare a child with books which show what to expect when going to school (or pre-school) for the first time.

THE TEN BEST BOOKS FOR STARTING SCHOOL

PB *Topsy and Tim Start School* JEAN AND GARETH ADAMSON
PB *I Am Too Absolutely Small for School* (Charlie and Lola) LAUREN CHILD
PB *Maisy Goes to Nursery* LUCY COUSINS
PB *Chu's First Day of School* NEIL GAIMAN, ILLUSTRATED BY ADAM REX
PB *Planet Kindergarten* SUE GANZ-SCHMITT, ILLUSTRATED BY SHANE PRIGMORE
PB *Whiffy Wilson: The Wolf Who Wouldn't Go to School* CARYL HART, ILLUSTRATED BY LEONIE LORD

PB *Wemberly Worried* **KEVIN HENKES**
PB *Alfie and the Big Boys* **SHIRLEY HUGHES**
ER *Ramona the Pest* **BEVERLY CLEARY**
CB *Just Peachy* **JEAN URE**

CURE FOR GROWN-UPS  *If I Could Keep You Little . . .* **MARIANNE RICHMOND**

OK, so here's how the first day of school actually went. Your child said goodbye, then raced into his or her classroom with a sunny 'HELLO!' and nary a backward glance. *You*, on the other hand, were left standing there with your knuckles in your mouth and a lump in your throat. Right? A child's first day at school is a major rite of passage for a grown-up, signalling as it does the beginning of the end of being needed 24/7 – and a return to time alone with the person staring back at you from the mirror (whoever the hell *that* might be now). Allow yourself a one-day nose-dive into sentimentality with *If I Could Keep You Little*. It'll remind you that the separation is temporary, and that watching your child grow up might be hard but has its pay-offs. Then pick up *The Novel Cure* and see: family, coping without; identity crisis; job, losing your; left out, feeling; loneliness; love, unrequited; pointlessness; tired and emotional, being.

SEE ALSO: **parents, having** • **scared, being** • **school, being the new kid at** • **shyness**

screen, glued to the

PB *Press Here*
HERVÉ TULLET

ER *We Are in a Book!*
MO WILLEMS

YA *Feed*
MT ANDERSON

If there's one thing likely to come between a child and a book in the modern age, it's a screen (see: reluctant reader, for some good ways to tackle this modern plague). Alternatively, stock up on a couple of picture books which play on the idea of interactivity. Start with *Press Here*, a brilliant riff on touch-screen technology in which the reader is invited to press coloured 'buttons' (circles painted in primary colours) and so become complicit in the idea that they can change what happens on the page. Designed to appeal to three-year-olds (it's a board book), the joke is perhaps appreciated even more by kids who can read the instructions for themselves. Use it to add humour when making the case for old-fashioned paper and ink.

Follow up with *We Are in a Book!*, from Mo Willems's loveable Elephant and

Piggie series. When it suddenly occurs to the two best friends – not without a little angst – that they only exist while someone's reading the book, we can't help feeling bad for them. And when their faces, expressively drawn in cartoon style, loom large as they come up close to peer at that watching monster over there – or could it perhaps be the *reader*? – we become delightfully self-conscious. Small children will thrill at the idea that, as the reader, they play a role in the story, too.

Shock an older kid out of their screen daze by interposing a paper-and-ink copy of *Feed* between nose and screen. Hooked in by its irresistible opening line,* teens will find themselves in a future that, in many respects, seems familiar: young people are out to have fun and indulge in a lot of shopping. But Titus and his friends find their highs on the moon (in the low-grav Ricochet Lounge), the forests on Earth having been razed to make way for 'air factories', and a visit to the beach now requiring a special mask to cut out the stench of decay. Computers no longer exist outside our bodies, but as implants, with an unremitting stream of information, news and adverts being zapped directly into the brain.

It doesn't take the reader long to see the drawbacks of this 'feed'. Titus and his friends often go blank-eyed while one of them is attending to something only they can hear. Habituated to constant stimulation, they are easily bored and always looking for the next 'meg fun' thing to do or 'brag' product to buy. And the girls have become victims to the latest craze – that of rupturing their bodies to make artificial 'lesions', or open wounds, which are, supposedly, attractive. When Titus meets Violet, an unconventional girl who wears natural wool clothes and was home-schooled by her father, she seems to offer something more real, and more human – and we are pleased when Titus is drawn to her. But soon after they meet, their feeds are hacked at a nightclub and Violet's begins to malfunction. In her disintegrating state, Violet becomes desperately aware of all the sensual experiences she's never had and which would make her feel truly alive – to fly over a volcano, discover if there's any moss still left in the world, spend a night in a hotel room with Titus. But Titus, distracted by the price-slashing sales being announced in his head and lacking the humanity to know how to respond to her anguish, is reduced to baffled by-stander.

Streaming the future and its lingo right into our heads the old-fashioned way, this compulsive YA novel is every bit as addictive as a screen. By the time your teen has turned the last page, they'll have a fresh appreciation of the sensual reality we are lucky enough to still inhabit.

SEE ALSO: **gaming, excessive • indoors, spending too much time • overweight, being • short attention span**

---

* 'We went to the moon to have fun, but the moon turned out to completely suck.'

secret, having a

[CB] *The Indian in the Cupboard*
LYNNE REID BANKS

[YA] *Only Ever Yours*
LOUISE O'NEILL

If you find it difficult to resist the pleasure of spilling a secret, think how much harder it is for a child. To ease their agony, show them what fictional characters go through when they find themselves in a similar situation.

It's every child's fantasy that a toy comes to life. And when nine-year-old Omri in *The Indian in the Cupboard* puts his plastic 'Red Indian'* figure in an old medicine cabinet overnight, he can hardly believe his eyes when he opens the door the next morning to find a living, breathing three-inch Native American brave. Omri's desperate to share the miracle with someone else, but he quickly understands that if he keeps the existence of Little Bull a secret, this will be the most marvellous thing that has ever happened to him – and if the secret gets out, Little Bull will end up in a cage, and subjected to the scrutiny of scientists.

At first, Omri enjoys having a secret. With his gleaming, blue-black plait, buckskin trousers and naked torso bristling with muscle, Little Bull is a splendid thing, defiant and fierce and proud. But not telling his parents and older brothers is one thing; and not telling his best friend Patrick is quite another. Readers will enjoy watching what happens when Omri decides to bring his friend on board, demonstrating as it does the full range of pros and cons.

Teens tempted to spill a confidence in order to gain the upper hand will think twice after reading the unsettling *Only Ever Yours*. Our heroine freida (and yes, that's a lower case f, girls not being considered worthy of capital letters in this misogynistic society) is one of a pod of thirty 'eves' who were 'hatched' on the same day. Ten of them will go on to be 'companions', ten 'concubines', and ten will be shaven-headed 'chastities' with the job of teaching the new, upcoming eves. Now sixteen and in her final year, freida must compete to be chosen as one of the lucky companions – which means being slim and pretty. The girls will do anything to achieve this goal: eating the absolute minimum, vomiting up the excess, taking 'kcal blockers' and laxatives, and running on treadmills until they're so exhausted they soil themselves.

As the countdown to the choosing ceremony begins, the eves are introduced to the boys, or 'Inheritants', and freida is strongly drawn to Darwin, son of a judge and the highest ranking of the boys. And her interest is

* Not a term we'd use today, of course. For some suggestions of how to handle racist, sexist, homophobic and otherwise prejudiced attitudes in children's books of a certain era, see our footnote to: fussy eater, being a.

reciprocated. But Darwin responds to their growing closeness by telling freida a secret, and freida agrees to keep it. Shortly afterwards, when freida seems to have no friends left, she uses the secret as a bargaining tool. Within twenty-four hours, the secret is all over 'MyFace', the subject of a frenzy of video-chats. We won't reveal what happens to freida, but it's not pretty. This chilling dissection of 21st-century sexist attitudes – magnified and skewed but still oh-so familiar – is a sobering cautionary tale. News and gossip can travel just as fast and uncontrollably through today's digital channels as the futuristic ones described here.

SEE ALSO: **abuse** • **lying**

self-consciousness

SEE: **embarrassment**

self-harm

The urge to harm oneself – most commonly in the form of cutting the skin – is a serious and distressing behaviour requiring professional help. Often described as a coping mechanism, providing temporary relief from intense feelings such as anxiety, depression or a sense of self-loathing (see: anxiety; depression; good at anything, feeling like you're no), it is a habit that, as with eating disorders, can be triggered by books and other media.* Self-harm is more common than you might think;† and novels featuring characters who self-harm can be extremely useful for adults wanting to understand how and why the practice happens – and to become aware of the warning signs.

* This is one of the reasons it's a good idea for adults to be aware, as much as possible, of what their children are reading during these vulnerable years.

† Studies suggest that one in ten teenagers experiment with self-harm; and, though it's less common, the phenomena exists among children much younger than teens.

CURE FOR GROWN-UPS YA *Red Tears* JOANNA KENRICK

Of the clutch of YA novels which provide an insight into what might be going on in the mind of a self-harming adolescent, a particularly useful one – since the child concerned is so apparently ordinary – is the compelling *Red Tears*. Fifteen-year-old Emily is doing well at school, though she's anxious about her forthcoming GCSEs. Cutting herself is a way of staying in control when she's feeling the stress. She does it in secret, in her bathroom, with a carefully stored tin of razors, and she finds the process so addictive that she runs out of space on her arms, thighs and torso. There's no sudden unearthing of psychological or physical abuse in Emily's past which might neatly explain her behaviour – and there's no obvious road to recovery. It's when Emily sees the look on her brother's face as he catches her wondering where to cut next that she understands she must stop. We recommend that this book and any others touching on self-harm* are read only with known harmers, or in conjunction with adult discussion around the topic.

SEE ALSO: **abuse** • **anxiety** • **body image** • **bullied, being** • **depression** • **exams** • **good at anything, feeling like you're no** • **peer pressure** • **worrying**

separation

SEE: **parents who are splitting up, having**

sex, saying yes or no to

SEE: **stand up for yourself, not feeling able to** • **virginity, loss of**

* Other novels that deal sensitively with self-harm include: *Saving Daisy* by Philip Earle, *Wintergirls* by Laurie Halse Anderson, *How to Build a Girl* by Caitlin Moran and *Cut* by Patricia McCormick.

sex, having questions about

[PB] *Mommy Laid An Egg*
BABETTE COLE

[YA] *Forever*
JUDY BLUME

For those who can't quite face going there themselves – or to help back up your story, if your child thinks you've gone completely bonkers – Babette Cole is your woman. First she gets everyone laughing by sending up the Fifties-style parents who gave us 'sugar and spice and all things nice' (her modern-day versions include babies being squeezed from toothpaste tubes). Then she gives it to them straight: here's the hole, here's the tube, and here's some ways the two fit together. Her characteristically entertaining pen-and-ink drawings with washes of colour manage to take the embarrassment out of the subject and bring it satisfyingly into the realms of the shoulder-shrugging ordinary. We suggest reading it to kids from the moment the questions start.

It's one thing for a teen to get their head round the mechanics of the sexual act in the abstract, but quite another to feel prepared for their first sexual encounter themselves. Blume still tops the list of go-to YA authors when it comes to questions about sex – especially (but not exclusively) for girls. While novelists of the past have tended to be euphemistic,* and many contemporary writers tend to focus more on the romantic aspect of relationships, Blume's matter-of-fact writing style is well suited to demystifying sex, exploring such questions as when is the right time to start, when to say no, how you might feel, and what can go wrong both emotionally and physically. The best Blume for this job is *Forever*, exploring as it does in relatively tame language a girl's transition from fancying a boy to having a full-blown adult relationship.

Katherine is eighteen when she meets Michael and decides she's ready for the great adventure of sex. She discusses the issue openly with various people, starting with Michael himself – who, rather cringe-inducingly, introduces her to 'Ralph', which is the name he gives his penis, to start the ball

* To put it mildly. Historically, novelists have sidestepped the issue of sex to such a degree that many a first-time participant suffered an awful lot of confusion. Remember the 'rising salmon, plunging home to spawn'*; and the hand which 'began to travel down the curve of her back, blindly, with a blind stroking motion, to the curve of her crouching loins'**? Couples generally took part in some 'restless, sensuous wrestling . . .'*** which, if they were lucky, might involve 'a flower depositing pollen on a hummingbird's forehead'****, with the whole thing finally resulting in the 'hunchback in the belfry' having 'jumped' and being left 'swinging madly on the rope'.*****

**Dreams, Demons and Desire* by Wendy Perriam.

***Lady Chatterley's Lover* by DH Lawrence.

****Atonement* by Ian McEwan. Not so far in the past, that one. Ahem.

*****Maps for Lost Lovers* by Nadeem Aslam. Nor that one either. Perhaps it's just grown-up fiction that's euphemistic?

******Middlesex* by Jeffrey Eugenides. Must be.

rolling. Advice from her mother is pertinent: 'Sex is a commitment . . . once you're there you can't go back to holding hands.' Her grandmother – impressively for one of her generation – dispenses contraceptive advice via letter, while her best friend Erica, who tends to believe that sex is purely physical, encourages her to get on with it. 'It might not be a bad idea to get laid before college,' she suggests.

When Katherine and Michael do have sex – on his sister's bedroom floor – they both see it as the romantic sealing of a love that will last forever. But when their work commitments force them to spend their summers apart, Katherine starts to become aware of the relationship's limits – and finds herself attracted to someone else. Perhaps she's not, in fact, 'ready for forever'. Not as physically graphic as some contemporary YA books, *Forever* is an involving story which explores the sort of things teens are rightly concerned about.*

SEE ALSO: **first kiss • first love • gay, not sure if you are • masturbation • transgender, feeling you are**

sexuality, unsure of your

SEE: **gay, not sure if you are**

shadows, fear of

SEE: **dark, scared of the**

share, inability to

[PB] *Stone Soup*
MARCIA BROWN
(continued)

The old tales are often the best when it comes to a crucial childhood ailment like this – and Marcia Brown's 1947 re-telling of the traditional folktale *Stone Soup*, with its black, white and rusty-orange

* Grown-ups should be aware that although Katherine does take the pill to make sure she doesn't get pregnant, she isn't as conscious of the risk of STDs as modern teens need to be – Blume wrote this story pre-AIDS. If you can, get hold of one of the more recently published editions, which includes an introduction by Blume in which she emphasises the importance of using condoms to prevent disease as well as pregnancy.

CB *The Naughtiest Girl*
ENID BLYTON

images that conjure up life in a simple country village, is a classic to be read to children regularly as they learn why it's good to share. When three tired and hungry soldiers arrive at a village on their way home from 'the wars', they hope they'll be given something to eat and a place to sleep. But the peasants hide their meagre supplies from the outsiders. 'We have little enough food for ourselves,' they say, as they lower buckets of milk down wells and shove potatoes under beds. The soldiers put their clever young heads together and come up with a cunning ruse. 'Well then, we'll have to make stone soup,' they tell the villagers. This piques the peasants' curiosity – and their greed. First the soldiers ask for a pot of water over a fire – that, the peasants are happy to provide. Next they need a stone. No problem! And then they ask for a few more edible things – but only one at a time, so the villagers barely notice what they've given. Of course, before they know it, there's a lovely big pot of steaming broth – enough for everyone. It ends up being a marvellous banquet to which nobody has minded contributing. The encouragement is not to trick others into sharing with you, but to make it fun for them to do so.

Slightly older children will find inspiration in *The Naughtiest Girl*. Elizabeth is tremendously spoilt and has always done exactly what she likes. Her pretty blue eyes and angelic curls work to her advantage. So when her mother tells her she has to go away to school (see: boarding school), Elizabeth decides to be so naughty they'll send her straight home again.

She does her best to keep to her resolve. But Whyteleafe School has its own rather clever rules for teaching a child how to behave. One of them is that children must pool the food and pocket money they've brought from home so that it can be shared equally between them later. 'I'm not going to share. I shall eat them all myself,' declares Elizabeth of the tuck she brought; and she sequesters her money, too. But when her new dorm mate, Belinda, shares a scrumptious chocolate cake, Elizabeth gets none at all – not having shared her own. And when she starts to realise how unhappy Joan, one of her classmates, is – her parents never visiting, picking her up for half term, or never sending letters or treats – she discovers an urge to do something for someone else instead of herself. Bring the philosophy of Whyteleafe into your household, too.

SEE ALSO: **only child, being an** • **spoilt, being**

shock, wanting to

SEE: **swearing** • **tattoo, wanting a**

shopping, not wanting to go

[PB] *Llama Llama Mad at Mama*
ANNA DEWDNEY

No toddler worth the label likes being shunted around a supermarket – and considering that most grown-ups don't want to be there either, the likelihood of disaster is high (see: tantrums). The moment your child starts giving you the evil eye, whip out *Llama Llama Mad at Mama*. He or she will like to see baby llama suffering just as much as they are – and Dewdney's paintings of the baby llama are packed to the brim with readable human emotions. But most of all they'll like the bit where baby llama starts throwing the Cheezee Puffs out the trolley. At this point, you'll have about ten minutes to get to the checkout before it occurs to your child to follow suit.* A great way to get your shopping done in double-quick time.

SEE ALSO: **bored, being** • **routine, unable to cope with a change in the**

short attention span

READING AILMENTS

PLAY WITH SCALE

Grab them by the short and curlies with a book that is in itself a playful object. Teeny-tiny books, just the right size for small hands, have enormous appeal for small children; and absurdly over-sized books are funny just to hold open. Lift-the-flap and pop-up books, meanwhile, keep hands as well as eyes nice and busy.

THE TEN BEST MINI AND MAMMOTH BOOKS

Mini

[PB] *The Tales of Beatrix Potter* BEATRIX POTTER
[PB] *Nutshell Library* MAURICE SENDAK

* Probably safer not to buy Cheezee Puffs.

[PB] *The Story of the Root Children* SIBYLLE VON OLFERS

[ER] *Ant and Bee* (and the other books in the series) ANGELA BANNER

[ER] *Mr Men* and *Little Miss* books ROGER HARGREAVES

Mammoth

[PB] *A Lion in Paris* BEATRICE ALEMAGNA

[PB] *365 Penguins* JEAN-LUC FROMENTAL, ILLUSTRATED BY JOELLE JOLIVET

[PB] *Timeline: An Illustrated History of the World* PETER GOES*

[PB] *A Camping Holiday* (Orlando the Marmalade Cat) KATHLEEN HALE

[PB] *The Snow Princess* EMILY HAWKINS

THE TEN BEST LIFT-THE-FLAP/POP-UP BOOKS

[PB] *In the Forest* ANOUCK BOISROBERT AND LOUIS RIGAUD

[PB] *Dear Zoo* ROD CAMPBELL

[PB] *One Red Dot* DAVID A CARTER

[PB] *Where's Spot?* ERIC HILL

[PB] *Where Is Baby's Belly Button?* KAREN KATZ

[PB] *The Wheels on the Bus* PAUL O ZELINSKY

[CB] *The Wizard of Oz* L FRANK BAUM, ILLUSTRATED BY PAUL HESS

[CB] *Haunted House* JAN PIEŃKOWSKI

[CB] *Hansel and Gretel* LOUISE ROWE

[CB] *Alice's Adventures in Wonderland* ROBERT SABUDA

short, being

SEE: **small, being**

shortsighted, being

SEE: **glasses, having to wear**

* Non-fiction, yes, but a must for every child's bookshelves, if you can fit it on.

show-off, being a

SEE: **boots, being too big for your** • **know-it-all, being a**

shyness

Fuzz McFlops
EVA FURNARI

Children who spend their days hiding behind the legs of their grown-ups and who go pink at the slightest provocation may benefit from an introduction to the internationally renowned Fuzz McFlops, a rabbit who almost never leaves his burrow. The famously reclusive Fuzz spends his time writing melancholy masterpieces such as 'The Withered Carrot' and 'The Back to Front Princess'. The fact that his poems tend to have sad endings is, no doubt, a result of his traumatised bunnyhood: born with one ear shorter than the other, Fuzz was forced to wear an ungainly contraption round his head called a 'Bunny Perfection Earlongater', which served only to make him more self-conscious about his mismatchedness. One day, he gets a letter from his fan, Charlotte Passe Partout, who regularly urges him to write poems with happier endings. 'Dear Fuzz come soon swallowed piano help,' reads this latest missive. Fuzz doesn't think twice. Rushing to her aid without so much as a trim of his whiskers, he arrives at Charlotte's house to find her covered in hair-dye and waxing lotions, happily eating chocolate balls while playing the piano. But Fuzz doesn't care – and soon nor does Charlotte either. From now on these two shy creatures will face their fears together. Kids will see that not being confident and self-assured really doesn't matter. Those worth knowing will love you precisely because you're not.

SEE ALSO: **different, feeling** • **embarrassment** • **friends, finding it hard to make** • **only child, being an** • **small, feeling**

sibling, having a new

For most children old enough to clock what's happening, the arrival of a new baby sister or brother brings a tumult of emotions: fascination and excitement at first, and jealousy, disappointment and irritation later on. Show them they're not alone – and that, in the end, siblings can be a great boon once you've got used to them.

THE TEN BEST BOOKS FOR HAVING A NEW SIBLING

- [PB] *There's a House Inside My Mummy* GILES ANDREAE, ILLUSTRATED BY VANESSA CABBAN
- [PB] *Double Trouble for Anna Hibiscus!* ATINUKE, ILLUSTRATED BY LAUREN TOBIA
- [PB] *There's Going to Be a Baby* JOHN BURNINGHAM AND HELEN OXENBURY
- [PB] *Mission: New Baby* SUSAN HOOD, ILLUSTRATED BY MARY LUNDQUIST
- [PB] *Peter's Chair* EZRA JACK KEATS
- [PB] *Lulu Reads to Zeki* ANNA MCQUINN AND ROSALIND BEARDSHAW
- [PB] *The Night Iceberg* HELEN STEPHENS
- [ER] *The Smile* MICHELLE MAGORIAN, ILLUSTRATED BY SAM USHER
- [CB] *Beezus and Ramona* BEVERLY CLEARY
- [CB] *Anastasia Krupnik* LOIS LOWRY

SEE ALSO: **sibling, having to look after a little** • **sibling rivalry**

sibling, having to look after a little

[CB] *The Earth Giant*
MELVIN BURGESS

One of the biggest challenges for an older sibling typical of their place in the birth order (responsible, careful, rational) is to have a younger sibling typical of *their* place in the birth order (selfish, impulsive, instinctive) who they're expected to look after. The exasperation and anxiety of the older child in this dynamic is beautifully captured in *The Earth Giant,* providing great solace when it seems that no one understands.

When an ancient oak tree blows down in a storm, Peter's younger sister Amy has a hunch that something, or someone, needs her help. Sure enough, from the massive root ball now exposed, Amy witnesses the emergence of a female giant, grotesque but beautiful. 'Giant', as Amy calls her, cannot speak – but Amy finds that she can read Giant's feelings. Together they frolic in the field, establishing a touching bond. But Amy knows she must keep Giant's existence a secret and takes her to an abandoned theatre where no one is likely to find her, bringing her food at night while the rest of her family sleeps.

One time Peter follows her, and when he meets Giant, thrashing about in the darkened theatre in terror at this unexpected visitor, he's shocked by the enormity of what his sister has done. And when Giant is forced to flee, taking Amy with her, Peter is left in an impossible situation. Caught between his furious, grief-stricken parents who don't understand how he could have stood by while his sister was abducted by an outsized simpleton, and the suspicion that his sister knows exactly what she's doing, only the reader understands his mental torture. Older siblings will empathise, and see that they're not the only one with a difficult younger sibling to account for; while grown-ups reading this story will be nudged into looking out for the responsible, sensible sibling, for a change.

SEE ALSO: **babysitter, not liking your** • **fair, it's not** • **in charge, wanting to be**

siblings, sharing the bedtime read with

FIND STORIES THAT ARE IRRESISTIBLE TO ALL

Only children hit the jackpot when it comes to the bedtime read, curated as the reading list can be entirely with their needs and tastes in mind. But for those with siblings spanning a range of ages and who, for purposes of efficiency, must be read to as a mob, the selection process is much trickier. How to find a book that will engage those at both ends of the age spectrum, neither passing too far over the heads of the youngest listeners, nor leaving the older ones dissatisfied? Chapter books featuring characters of different ages will help, giving everyone someone to identify with; as will picture books that pack a more resonant or thought-provoking punch than the simplicity of their pages might suggest. Here's our pick.

THE TEN BEST BOOKS TO READ TO CHILDREN OF DIFFERENT AGES

- PB *Jumanji* CHRIS VAN ALLSBURG
- PB *The Three Questions* JON J MUTH
- CB *Fantastic Mr Fox* ROALD DAHL
- CB *The Jungle Book* RUDYARD KIPLING
- CB *The Lion, the Witch and the Wardrobe* CS LEWIS
- CB *The Railway Children* EDITH NESBIT
- CB *Harry Potter and the Philosopher's Stone* JK ROWLING
- CB *The Hobbit* JRR TOLKIEN
- CB *The Mennyms* SYLVIA WAUGH
- CB *Charlotte's Web* EB WHITE

sibling rivalry

PB *My Rotten Redheaded Older Brother*
PATRICIA POLACCO

CB *The Watsons Go to Birmingham – 1963*
CHRISTOPHER PAUL CURTIS

YA *Summer and Bird*
KATHERINE CATMULL

Siblings who fight – with words or fists or both – are unpleasant to be around. And when they're competing for your attention, you have to be careful not to add fuel to the fire. Stories featuring siblings who go from hating each other to re-discovering their underlying affection help to show kids that even the most antagonistic relationships can be pulled back from the brink.

It's rather shocking to hear how much the narrator of *My Rotten Redheaded Older Brother* hated her older brother, Richard. He looked, she says, like a 'weasel with glasses' and was always determined to prove he was better than her. The action-filled illustrations show a red-haired boy with a face full of freckles taunting his sister with ugly, jabbing fingers while her face clenches in antagonism. And there's blatant aggression in the way the two kids chomp through raw sticks of rhubarb in their babushka's garden, each determined to out-eat the other. Afterwards, belly aching, the younger child screams: 'I can't stand you, Richard Barber . . . I double dog can't stand you!' as the 'green-toothed' brother laughs and jeers. What snaps the pair of them out of their feud is an unexpected crisis involving a cracked head and a brother who carries his sister home. 'Looks like you finally did something special!' he teases – but the same could be said of him, too. The speed at which the relationship transforms leaves a big impression. We're left with an image of them snuggling up to their wrinkled babushka, a little girl in plaits and a little boy in pyjamas, both faces soft and yielding.

It's interference from the big, bad world that eventually shakes up Byron, older brother to ten-year-old Kenny in *The Watsons Go to Birmingham – 1963*. Byron is an even more challenging big brother to have than the weasel. Ganging up on Kenny with his friend Buphead, the two older boys are merciless with 'baby bruh', who lives his days in a state of constant anxiety about what to say and how to act in order to avoid another roasting. When the family make an epic trip to the Deep South in their 'turd brown' Plymouth with the idea of leaving Byron to tough-as-boots Grandma to sort out, it's the older boy's turn to be nervous. But Grandma has become too frail to intimidate anybody; and it's when Byron discovers his inner hero, saving Kenny from drowning, that things start to change. When their little sister is almost killed in a racist attack at their local church, Byron is shocked into full maturity. Nobody would wish such harrowing events on anyone, but this story helps to show how siblings ultimately look after each other in the face of bigger threats from beyond the family.

Girls can be highly competitive, and in *Summer and Bird* we see how the need to define themselves as distinct and separate individuals leads two sisters into conflict. Twelve-year-old Summer and nine-year-old Bird wake one morning to find their parents gone. A cryptic note urges them to go into the forest to look for them and – having always been encouraged by their parents to fend for themselves – they set off. The wilful Bird uses her powerful intuition to guide them and communicates with her namesakes via her flute, while the older Summer does her best to find food and drink. As they move deeper into the forest, Bird's magical side becomes more pronounced, and a wedge forms between them. When a mysterious 'puppet queen' appears in a dream, luring her with visions of a throne, Bird leaves her sister and follows its siren call. She's led to a mysterious, swan-shaped castle where, in the cellar, a giant swan-woman is cruelly tethered.

This, it transpires, is their mother – the true Swan Queen, back after thirteen years bringing up her human children; and the two girls work as a team to rescue her in the end. Being more avian than human, Bird assumes that she will inherit their mother's throne one day – and when it transpires that Summer is the rightful successor, the younger girl must swallow a bitter pill. The slow dawning of these two very different personalities as they struggle to find themselves offers an illuminating role model for what can be a complicated relationship.

SEE ALSO: **arguments, getting into** • **bullied, being** • **bully, being a** • **share, inability to**

sick, being

[PB] *Sometimes You Barf*
NANCY CARLSON

American writer Nancy Carlson steps into the breach here with a picture book that embraces what, for many, is a persistent taboo. There's nothing wrong with being sick, she says: it happens to us all – even aardvarks. Helping to soak up any embarrassment experienced by vomiting in front of others (the child in this story throws up, rather thrillingly, over her maths test at school), she allows herself just the right amount of yuckiness to make this book something kids will revel in (miraculously, the gleeful illustrations manage to make sick not look disgusting) without actually inciting more nausea. All the familiar stages of spewing are here: from feeling a little off-colour and being off your food, to feeling *very* off-colour and having to let it all come out – then, greenly, picking yourself off the floor and starting to feel well again. Use this book to show that some things – like a splinter, a bogey, a wobbly tooth, a swollen appendix, a hairball, and a microscopic but powerful tummy bug – are a lot better out than in.

SEE ALSO: **bed, having to stay in** • **car, being in the**

single parent, having a

CURE FOR GROWN-UPS *Danny the Champion of the World*
ROALD DAHL, ILLUSTRATED BY QUENTIN BLAKE

Shouldering the financial, practical and emotional responsibilities of raising a child by yourself requires you to be a multi-tasking model of inventiveness and resilience, especially if you're trying to do it on a budget, with no outside childcare, no relatives nearby, a full-time job – and no oven. This is what the father in *Danny the Champion of the World* has to do. It's perhaps somewhat galling, therefore, that he seems to be making such a good job of it. Because William, to give him his own name, has the sort of relationship with his son that anyone would envy: respectful, fun and one in which he's one hundred per cent adored. OK, so he's fictional, and we hear nothing about paying the bills . . . but we are not the types to let such a minor detail stand in our way. So, how does he do it?

First, by keeping expenses to a minimum. Danny and his dad live in a tiny gypsy caravan. At night, they light a gas lantern to see by. When they're hungry, they heat up a can of baked beans on a two-ring burner, or make a sandwich (especially if it's the middle of the night), or they pick a Cox's Orange Pippin off the tree. Yum! Mostly, though, they live off baked beans.*

Second, William works from home – and involves his child in his work. As soon as he's old enough, Danny operates the pump of their petrol station, takes the money, and hands back the change.† William also fixes cars in his workshop – which doubles as Danny's playroom.‡ By the age of seven, Danny can take a small engine to pieces and put it back together again.§

Third, he is creative. This is going to sound unhealthy, and perhaps it is, but

---

* Once they've saved up enough money, they're going to get an oven, and then they're going to make toad-in-the-hole, with the Yorkshire pudding very crisp and 'raised up in huge bubbly mountains'. You'll notice how big such a moment looms when you keep expectations low.

† This provides Danny with a lesson in basic arithmetic, social skills and responsibility all in one.

‡ Imagine all those lovely bits of exhaust pipe to look through, and nuts and bolts to put in your mouth! On second thoughts, don't.

§ In fact, Danny's father decides not to send him to school *until* he's learnt to do this, thus getting his vocational training in early and, potentially, removing the need to send him to college.

Danny never invites friends from school over to play – and not because he doesn't have any. He just doesn't feel the need. Why would he, when he has a father who gets as excitable as a ten-year-old – and is better with his hands? For Danny's most recent birthday, William made him a go-cart out of four bicycle wheels, a brake pedal, a steering wheel, a couple of wooden crates, a seat and a strong front bumper.* William's brilliant blue eyes are always flashing with a 'tiny little golden spark' when he's hatching a plan for something fun to make.

Fourth, he gives Danny time. Until he breaks his ankle falling into a trap while out poaching pheasants,† Danny's father has never missed a day walking Danny to school and picking him up in the afternoon. Danny loves these twice-daily walks with his father, because William always has interesting things to say about the hedgerows or birds they pass, or about the natural world in general.

Fifth, he listens. In fact, William does not only listen to Danny's ideas, taking them as seriously as if they were his own, but he runs with them – even when they involve slitting open two hundred raisins, filling them with sleeping pill powder, and sewing them up again with a needle and thread‡. *And* allowing Danny to take a day off school to do it. And, at night, when Danny's in his bunk, blissfully secure in the knowledge that his father will soon be sleeping in *his* bunk underneath, William tells Danny stories – wonderful stories, some of them involving characters who end up featuring in some Roald Dahl books.§

Danny knows, without the slightest doubt, that he has the 'most marvellous and exciting father any boy ever had'. As a role model for how to be a single parent – or indeed a parent of any description – he can't be beat.¶

SEE ALSO: **depressed parent, having a • things, wanting**

---

* OK, so we're not all car mechanics. But, before that, there was a homemade kite, a bow and arrow, stilts, a treehouse and a boomerang. You have YouTube; you can learn.

† Er, yes, you read it right. We probably should admit here that Danny's father has a relaxed attitude to helping himself to pheasants on Mr Hazell's land, Mr Hazell being the local landowner and a 'roaring snob' who drives around in an enormous silver Rolls-Royce and who once threatened to give Danny a good hiding with his riding crop if he dared to put his 'filthy little hands' on his paintwork. William did not let that one lie. Out of the workshop in a flash, he put his hands on the sill of the wound-down window, leant in and said, dangerously softly, 'I don't like you speaking to my son like that.' But we digress.

‡ This, by the way, is Danny's brilliant plan for how to poach the entire flock of pheasants, the night before Mr Hazell's annual shooting party. Yes, William teaches Danny some of his tricks.

§ We'd always wondered where Dahl's ideas came from.

¶ Roald Dahl thought so, too. At the end of the book, he included a message to children urging them to remember, when they grow up and have children of their own, that having a 'stodgy parent' is no fun at all. What everyone wants, he says, is a parent who is 'SPARKY!'*

*If you feel you are lacking in this particular quality, have a look at *The Novel Cure* (in particular: exhaustion; killjoy, being a; tired and emotional, being; zestlessness).

sister, having a

SEE: **sibling, having to look after a little** • **sibling rivalry**

sleep, unable to get to

PB *Llama Llama Red Pajama*
ANNA DEWDNEY

CB *Tom's Midnight Garden*
PHILIPPA PEARCE

The bedtime story has been read (see our list of The Ten Best Bedtime Reads for the Very Little, p.267), the goodnight kiss bestowed, the light has been put out, the exact degree at which the door should be left ajar has been measured, discussed and agreed upon . . . and although you still have the washing up to do, a laundry mountain the size of a small garden shed to process, and your 9am meeting tomorrow to prepare for – not to mention supper with your partner and an episode of your latest TV series addiction to watch (wait, did we say that out loud *again*?) – at least the hands-on element of your job as a parent is done for the day. But not so fast, our friend! Because the child still has to *get to sleep* . . . and as the first, thin, beseeching 'Mama/Dada/Grandma/Great-uncle Mervin?' drifts out the door, you know that *that* could take all night.

A picture book which gets to the heart of this fraught situation is *Llama Llama Red Pajama*. With her long lashes lowered in sleepy, loved-up contentment, Baby Llama looks set for a peaceful night once the bedtime story comes to a close. But no sooner has Mama Llama vacated the room than those eyes have snapped wide open. As Baby Llama notices how dark the bedroom is (see: dark, scared of the), and how terrible the absence of her mama is, her fretfulness gradually turns to upset. And when Mama fails to materialise immediately at her call (shock! horror!), her upset ratchets up the scale. Soon she is screaming in full-scale panic. This, of course, brings a terrified Mama racing up the stairs, heart in mouth, expecting to find a wild, sabre-toothed tiger in the room* and finds instead – well, nothing but a baby llama who's got herself all worked up. The acknowledgement of the little llama's panic and the sharing of the mollified moment in which she realises it was all somewhat unnecessary, is bonding stuff – and will help ensure a swift transition, with hugs, from tizzy to exhausted passing out, possibly for both of you. There goes the laundry again.

With older kids you need to approach the issue as you would for an adult

---

* Or whatever llamas most dread.

insomniac – with a story which absorbs without overly stimulating, and which lulls the reader into a dreamy state which can easily morph into sleep. *Tom's Midnight Garden* is ideal, being very much like a dream itself. To quarantine him from his measles-ridden brother Peter, Tom is sent to his aunt Gwen and uncle Alan for the summer holidays. This is appalling for many reasons. First, because Tom and Peter had been planning to build a treehouse in their garden and were looking forward to uninterrupted weeks of playing in it. And second, because this childless aunt and uncle have no garden at all, and live in an airless flat where there's nothing to do.

Bored and restless, Tom tries and tries to get to sleep, but in the end he gives up and starts prowling around the flat, raiding the larder first (as a matter of form), and then being lured out of his aunt and uncle's flat into the main house by the old grandfather clock in the downstairs hall. Tom has noticed that the grandfather clock seems to keep its own unique time, randomly striking numbers at all hours, and once even striking thirteen. So begins a whole summer of nightly adventures, in which Tom opens the front door to find a beautiful, boundless garden outside, where sometimes it's a lovely summer's day, and sometimes it's the middle of snow-bound winter. At times he emerges into dawn, at times at dusk, and once during a midnight storm. The garden itself is a wonder – and Tom is thrilled to have trees to climb, places to hide, and branches to whittle. But he also finds a playmate there, a lonely little orphan called Hatty who has been taken in by another unpleasant, superior aunt.

Always in his pyjamas, Tom leaves no imprints on snow, walks through doors, and feels no pain when in the garden – which is in part what gives the story its dream-like quality. And the magic from the garden seeps back into his daytimes, too. A pair of ice skates left for Tom under the floorboards of his present-day room allows him to skate from Castleford to Ely in the great cold snap of 1895. It is Hatty's nightly dreams, we slowly realise, that make it possible for Tom to visit her in the garden. Tom is living a dream within a dream – and through this story, your child can live it too.

CURE FOR GROWN-UPS PB *Go the F$#k to Sleep* ADAM MANSBACH, ILLUSTRATED BY RICARDO CORTÉS

Sometimes grown-ups need to laugh hysterically before they can get to sleep. The first time we came across this book, tired and emotional from baby-induced sleep deprivation as we both were at the time, we began chortling from page one (in our separate houses on either side of an ocean), and quickly found ourselves guffawing, unable to stop. Tears ran down our faces in such a flood of laughter (or was it crying? it was hard to be sure) that both our sofas still have salt-water stains. The book's cover, showing a sleeping child nestling up to a realistic family of tigers, says it all: it's a peaceful enough scene for now, with the little blonde head resting against a furry flank – but what's going to happen when the tigers wake up?

And so the story inside proceeds, first with the cutesy, innocent baby-talk lines: ('The cats nestle close to their kittens,/The lambs have laid down to sleep') and then the lines in which the latent aggression of the unendurably tired grown-up pierces through: 'You're cosy and warm in your bed, my dear./Please go the f$#k* to sleep.' Requests for one last story, a drink of water, a plea to use the bathroom – familiar ruses, one and all – are all met with zero tolerance: 'I know you're not thirsty. That's bullshit. You're lying.' Grown-up babes who used to go out, have a life, talk back, sleep exactly when and for as long as they wanted – and who cannot quite believe they're now being held hostage by a baby – will find much needed release in this combination of innocence and deranged delirium.

THE TEN BEST BEDTIME READS FOR THE VERY LITTLE

- PB *A Goodnight Kind of Feeling* TONY BRADMAN, ILLUSTRATED BY CLIVE SCRUTON
- PB *Tell Me Something Happy Before I Go to Sleep* JOYCE DUNBAR, ILLUSTRATED BY DEBI GLIORI
- PB *Time for Bed* MEM FOX, ILLUSTRATED BY JANE DYER
- PB *A Bed of Your Own* MIJ KELLY AND MARY MCQUILLAN
- PB *Can You See a Little Bear?* JAMES MAYHEW, ILLUSTRATED BY JACKIE MORRIS
- PB *A Book of Sleep* IL SUNG NA
- PB *Dr Seuss' Sleep Book* DR SEUSS
- PB *Sleep Tight, Little Bear* MARTIN WADDELL, ILLUSTRATED BY BARBARA FIRTH
- PB *Bear Snores On* KARMA WILSON, ILLUSTRATED BY JANE CHAPMAN
- PB *Goodnight Moon* MARGARET WISE BROWN, ILLUSTRATED BY CLEMENT HURD

SEE ALSO: **anxiety** • **bed, fear of what's under the** • **bed, wetting the** • **dark, scared of the** • **nightmares** • **worrying**

* But without the '$#'.

sleepovers

[CB] *Sleepovers*
JACQUELINE WILSON, ILLUSTRATED BY NICK SHARRATT

[PB] *Small*
CLARA VULLIAMY

Almost unremittingly awful for parents, sleepovers are the pinnacle of many a pre-teen's existence, defining and cementing friendships, setting the stage for pushing the grown-up/child boundaries, and providing opportunities for the sharing of secrets. But for those in charge, setting and enforcing curfews, dealing with night fears, friendship fallouts, pre-dawn hysteria and even which film to watch can be a trial for the most laidback of grown-ups. Forewarned is forearmed, however, and to help everyone prepare and avoid the worst of the pitfalls, we recommend the excellent *Sleepovers*.

Eight-year-old Daisy, a newcomer to school, is thrilled to find herself part of a gang of girls whose names, by chance, follow each other alphabetically. Sleepovers spread like shingles among these girls, and Amy, Bella, Chloe, Daisy and Emily – aka the Alphabet Club – are soon bedding down at each other's houses every couple of weeks. And though Daisy very much wants to have the others over to her house at some point, she's filled with anxiety about how her eleven-year-old sister will go down (see: anxiety; worrying). Daisy's sister, Lily, has special needs and can't form proper words – and her grunts and tendency to drool can be unnerving for those who aren't used to her. She's particularly nervous about Chloe who, she's increasingly aware, has it in her to be mean and selfish.

Sure enough, when she comes to Daisy's house, Chloe turns out to be a poisonous little toad who will do anything to be top cat (see: in charge, wanting to be). She boasts about how her parents will let her do whatever she likes, and deliberately brings an inappropriately scary film for them all to watch – disguising it behind an innocuous cover, then mocking the other girls for being too wet to watch it. She complains that the alphabet-related games Daisy has cleverly invented are boring. But Daisy's dad has Chloe's number in an instant, and colludes in Daisy's attempts to bring the girl down a peg. When Lily unintentionally impersonates a ghost with her 'ur ur urs', she unwittingly helps too. All ends happily: Chloe goes off with a new gang of girls, and Daisy loves Lily all the more for scaring her unpleasant friend off. Grown-ups will take heart in the simple joys discovered by the girls in their sleepover shenanigans, and tweens will relate to the complex friendship issues that can so often get in the way.

For those embarking on sleepovers when still very young – perhaps by staying over at a relative's house – pre-prepare with *Small*. When Tom stays over at Granny's for the first time, he forgets the most important thing – his toy mouse, Small. But he didn't count on how much Small would miss *him*, too. Bereft, Small bravely makes his way down the drainpipe and across town to arrive, sodden, beneath Granny's mailbox. Phew! This warm blanket of a tale, with nostalgic, sepia-and-blue watercolour illustrations, will ensure your child doesn't make the same packing mistake.

SEE ALSO: **best friend, falling out with your** • **over-tired, being** • **peer pressure** • **routine, unable to cope with a change in the** • **share, inability to**

small, being

PB *The Gruffalo*
JULIA DONALDSON, ILLUSTRATED BY AXEL SCHEFFLER

ER *Teeny-Tiny and the Witch-Woman*
BARBARA WALKER, ILLUSTRATED BY MICHAEL FOREMAN

Being tiny can be enormous fun, and a lot of children are aware of the advantages – spying on the grown-ups from under the table, getting out of carrying the groceries, and doing all the rescuing when playing stuck-in-the-mud, just for starters. But it becomes tough for the child left behind when their peers start to rocket skywards, especially if they find themselves overlooked in the choosing of teams (see: fair, it's not), or petted and cooed over more than is pleasurable for someone their age (see: grannies, having to kiss). Children's literature is full of examples of how the vertically challenged develop other qualities, however; and kids on the short side can select from a wide range of role models to find the one that best fits.

The diminutive mouse in *The Gruffalo* is hard to beat for sheer gumption; and with the force of Donaldson's irresistibly catchy rhyming couplets behind him, the mouse's journey from prey to predator is one of the most dramatic character trajectories in literature. 'A mouse took a stroll through the deep dark wood./A fox saw the mouse and the mouse looked good,' the tale begins and, amongst the soothing stripes of Scheffler's ramrod-straight brown trees, the mouse meets a series of animals who would like to eat him up. The quick-thinking mouse manages to convince each of them in turn that he is on his way to visit a terrifying gruffalo, and as he turns the (dinner) tables on them one by one, they flee in fright. We can't help but delight in the mouse's victory in the face of seemingly insurmountable odds – especially when the gruffalo itself comes out of the forest baring its claws, tusks, wart and deliciously horrible black tongue. Whatever their age, encourage your child to quicken their wits to give themselves extra heft.

Of the three brothers kidnapped by the witch in the frankly terrifying

Teeny-Tiny and the Witch-Woman, it is, of course, the littlest that saves the day. Another celebration of guile over size, it is while his two older brothers are tucking hungrily into their supper at the witch's house – wondering vaguely why she owns a cage just their size – that Teeny-Tiny devises a series of clever ruses to keep her occupied while he plans their escape. 'My mother always cooks me an egg before I go to bed!' he bleats. 'My mother gives me popcorn and raisins!' His final demand is for her to fetch him some water from the well with a sieve . . . Your ankle-biter will love identifying with Teeny-Tiny, as nimble in brain as in body, while he maxes out on the bedtime rituals. Older children will enjoy this book too, but we urge you to read it aloud rather than leave them to face the chilling paintings by the ever-versatile Michael Foreman alone.

SEE ALSO: **anxiety** • **different, feeling** • **tall, being**

small, feeling

PB *Mr Big*
ED VERE

How big or small you feel has nothing to do with how high your latest notch is on the door jamb. No one knows this better than the enormous gorilla in *Mr Big*. With his broad shoulders filling out his dark pinstripe and dwarfing his tiny trilby, Mr Big has to duck to sit on the bus – and indeed to fit on the cover of the book. But inside he feels very small. On his lonely way down the street one day, scattering the frightened passers-by just by being there, he sees a piano for sale and carries it home. That night, his sad, plaintive notes drift out the open window and over the rooftops of central Manhattan. Everyone comes to their windows wondering who could be playing so beautifully – including the members of a band due to appear at The Blue Note. 'Hey man, that cat can play!' says a monkey with a similar trilby. Children will enjoy acting out the snatches of dialogue that pop from different mouths – especially once this loveable gorilla, now in a bright yellow stripe, becomes famous ('Groovy man!' 'Let's hear it for Mr Big!') and finds a queue of adoring fans outside his dressing-room door ('Like . . . er . . . is it really *you*?'). Kids who feel small will take comfort from the fact that even someone as big as Mr Big needs friends who value him in order to fill out his skin.

SEE ALSO: **anxiety** • **confidence, lack of** • **shyness** • **worrying**

smelly, being

SEE: **bath, not wanting to have a**

smelly friend, having a

PB *Smelly Bill*
DANIEL POSTGATE

CB *Mr Stink*
DAVID WALLIAMS, ILLUSTRATED BY QUENTIN BLAKE

What do you do about a whiffy friend? Tell them to their face and risk causing offence, or hold both your tongue and your nose? In *Smelly Bill*, the pongy one is a dog, which makes verbal acknowledgement easier but action harder: 'His family would cry,/'You stink!'/ And try to get him in the sink.' Luckily, zealous Aunt Bleach is left with Bill for a day when the rest of the family go to the beach, and she has a fabulous time putting not only the house but Bill to rights. By the time they're back, Bill is all fluffed-up and smelling of roses – though Bleach herself is not. Mischievous rhymes (pairing 'faster' with 'dashed straight past her' and 'he knew exactly what to go for' with 'He scrambled underneath the sofa') combine with energetic pictures to make this as much a laugh to read aloud as to hear, and provides varied scope for a chat about what makes people (or animals) smell – and what you might do about it.

Broach the issue of unpleasant-smelling friends with slightly older kids with the fabulous *Mr Stink*. Twelve-year-old Chlöe feels so sorry for the tramp in her neighbourhood – who emits a pong so extreme that he uses it to clear a café when he needs some peace and quiet – that she offers him the use of her family's garden shed for the winter. And Mr Stink, an eccentric soul who chooses to go by that name, graciously accepts. He moves in and makes it surprisingly homely – even drawing mock portraits around the walls with chalk, as if it were a miniature stately home. Chlöe's parents are blissfully unaware of the development, which is perhaps just as well. Chlöe's mother is standing for local government, and a major part of her agenda is to crack down on homelessness.

One day Chlöe empties the pockets of the vagabond's coat, aiming to sneak it into the wash, and discovers that Mr Stink is actually Lord Darlington, a local aristocrat who took to the streets when his wife and baby were burnt to death in a fire at the family pile. Understanding the tragedy that brought him to his present pass makes Chlöe all the more keen to help him, and there ensues a comedic plot twist whereby Mr Stink invades a press conference held by Chlöe's mother at her house . . . Thus begins Mr Stink's unexpected rise to notoriety, even making it to Number 10 Downing Street, which creates much helpful publicity for the homeless. Smelly friends may be unpleasant to sit next to, but kids should try and find out the reason they don't get to wash before they write them off.

SEE ALSO: **body odour** • **embarrassment** • **secret, having a**

social media, hooked on

Remember what it was like living in the *actual* world – where you could smell, taste and touch? These books will remind you of the dangers of virtual living – and how great life can be when there isn't a screen in the way.

THE TEN BEST BOOKS TO CURE AN ADDICTION TO SOCIAL MEDIA

PB *Chicken Clicking* JEANNE WILLIS, ILLUSTRATED BY TONY ROSS
PB *Dot.* RANDI ZUCKERBERG, ILLUSTRATED BY JOE BERGER
CB *Goodbye Stranger* REBECCA STEAD
YA *Feed* MT ANDERSON
YA *The Future of Us* JAY ASHER AND CAROLYN MACKLER
YA *Need* JOELLE CHARBONNEAU
YA *Little Brother* CORY DOCTOROW
YA *Queen of Likes* HILLARY HOMZIE
YA *Unison Spark* ANDY MARINO
YA *More Than This* PATRICK NESS

SEE ALSO: **best friend, falling out with your** • **indoors, spending too much time** • **screen, glued to the**

sore throat

SEE: **bed, having to stay in** • **pain, being in**

soup, hating

CB *The Tale of Despereaux* KATE DICAMILLO, ILLUSTRATED BY TIMOTHY BASIL ERING

There are few foods more nutritious – and less appealing to children – than soup. Of course, babies have no choice and pretty much live off the stuff. But something seems to happen to kids when they turn two that makes them turn their noses up at hot, vegetable-rich liquid. The charming *Tale of Despereaux* will convert them. In a fairytale land, soup has been banned by the King – his beloved Queen having died while eating it. And in case anyone is tempted to make it, he has banned spoons and kettles, too. When a courageous mouse named Despereaux falls in love with the princess Pea and determines to rescue her from a rat-infested dungeon – armed only with a needle and a spool of red thread – he meets a brave cook who has thrown caution to the wind and brewed up the Queen's own favourite broth. 'There ain't a body, be it mouse or man, that ain't made better by a little soup,' she breathes, giving him a life-saving dollop in a saucer. With one mouthful, Despereaux is infused with strength – and the conviction and courage to achieve his quest. What child can resist such powerful evidence for this fortifying stuff?

SEE ALSO: **fussy eater, being a**

space, invasion of your personal

SEE: **alone, wanting to be left**

space, obsession with outer

SEE: **obsessions**

speech impediment

PB *Who-who-who Goes Hoo-hoo-hoo?*
PETER SCHNEIDER, ILLUSTRATED BY GISELA SCHARTMANN

CB *The Paperboy*
VINCE VAWTER

It's hard enough for kids learning how and when and with what words to communicate in life without having to worry about whether the words will come out. Speech therapists stress the importance of patience, giving the child as much time as he or she needs to say what they want to say – and to encourage them not to let the stares or discomfort of others knock them off course. Stories featuring characters who stammer or stutter are welcome, too, for showing both children and their grown-ups that they're not alone with their impediment, that others experience the same sort of emotions when their words refuse to come, and that good listening – when it's done right – can make a world of difference.

In *Who-who-who Goes Hoo-hoo-hoo?* we meet a young hedgehog who lives in the woods surrounded by friendly animal and insect life. The sumptuous watercolour illustrations show a group of insects playing cards and Chinese lanterns hanging prettily from the trees in this appealing world. In the middle of the night, the hedgehog is woken by a strange sound – 'Hoo hoo hoo!' it goes. 'Who-who-who was that?' he wonders. The hedgehog's mother tucks him back under his blanket of leaves, but in the morning the little hedgehog sets off to find out who was responsible for this sound that so reminds him of himself. As he makes enquiries among the other animals, we notice that they all have an interesting quirk of their own – the squirrel has a bald tail; and the snake a knot in her tongue. But this doesn't stop the animals being impatient with the hedgehog for *his* quirk. 'Learn to speak properly,' they demand, and refuse to answer his questions. But when the hedgehog finds a mouse who also stutters, a solidarity develops, and with the help of the owl they teach the other animals a lesson. This book is a great encouragement to those who stutter to insist that others learn to listen to them as they would to anyone else.

Older kids with a speech impediment will identify with the eleven-year-old boy in *Paperboy*, who agrees to cover his friend Rat's paper round. Throwing the papers onto the porches from his bicycle is easy, but Little Man – as he's referred to by his nanny, Mam – is sick with dread at the thought of having to ring the doorbell and ask for money at the end of each week. Little Man never knows what's going to come out of his mouth – or, more precisely, what's *not* going to come out – and is used to people either getting embarrassed or concluding he's 'not right in the head'.

Set in 1959 when speech therapy was in its infancy, Little Man deploys various tricks for trying to 'sneak up' on a word: making a hissing sound before difficult words, tossing a pencil in the air to distract himself, and changing the one troubling letter to something else – a tactic that doesn't always go well. But it's being listened to by the gentle, patient Mr Spiro, one of his customers, that makes the real difference. 'Our goal is dialogue, Messenger,' he says, refusing the piece of paper on which Little Man has written down his questions. 'That takes two. I have all the time we need so I would like to hear you ask.' By the time Rat comes back, Little Man has begun to hold his ground, and aims to say what he wants to say rather than just what he *can* say. Readers are left with the firm and uplifting conviction that what we say is more important than how we say it.

SEE ALSO: **anxiety** • **confidence, lack of** • **different, feeling** • **embarrassment** • **feelings, unable to express your** • **shyness** • **stand up for yourself, not feeling able to** • **worrying**

spiders, fear of

SEE: **animals, fear of**

spilling things

SEE: **clumsiness**

spoiling a picture

SEE: **mistake, frightened of making a**

spoilsport, being a

SEE: **loser, being a bad**

spoilt, being

Charlie and the Chocolate Factory
ROALD DAHL, ILLUSTRATED BY QUENTIN BLAKE

It's more or less impossible to imagine anyone coming away from Roald Dahl's most famous story with their spoilt-child tendencies intact. Who can meet the repulsive Augustus Gloop with his 'great flabby folds of fat', a boy who has never been denied a chocolate bar in his life; or the despicable Veruca Salt, who lies on the floor and kicks and yells until her daddy gets her what she wants; or the beastly, gum-chewing Violet Beauregard, who finds it funny to stick her chewed gum on the buttons in lifts; or the pistol-toting Mike Teavee, who spends his life glued to the television and shouts at anybody who dares interrupt – and not want to be absolutely nothing like them? What they all have in common, of course, is over-indulgent parents, wrapped like gum round their children's sticky fingers. The next time you refuse a child something they do not need, you cannot afford, or they have not earned, let Roald Dahl do the explaining for you.

SEE ALSO: **beastly, being** • **only child, being an** • **share, inability to** • **things, wanting**

sport, being a bad

SEE: **loser, being a bad**

sport, being no good at

SEE: **good at anything, feeling like you're no** • **school, not wanting to go to**

spots, having

SEE: **acne** • **zits**

spy, wanting to be a

SEE: **obsessions**

stammer

SEE: **speech impediment**

stand up for yourself, not feeling able to

PB *That Rabbit Belongs to Emily Brown*
CRESSIDA COWELL, ILLUSTRATED BY NEAL LAYTON

CB *Emil and the Detectives*
ERICH KÄSTNER

YA *What I Was*
MEG ROSOFF

There are lots of things that can stop a child standing up for themselves – shyness, the worry that others won't like them, that they'll be thought rude, or that they'll start an argument (see: arguments, always getting into). And when the person they need to stand up to is older or seemingly more important than them, they're even more likely not to feel able to do it. No one could be harder to stand up to than the Queen; yet Emily Brown does just that, fearlessly and resolutely, in *That Rabbit Belongs to Emily Brown.*

The Queen, it seems, has taken a fancy to Emily's stuffed rabbit, Stanley – a much-loved creature with a bare patch on his bottom and an unravelling stitch for a smile. But when the covetous monarch sends her Chief Footman to collect the 'Bunnywunny', offering a brand new teddy bear in return, Emily takes one look at the nasty, stiff teddy with his shocked, unmoving eyes and tells the Chief Footman, politely, no. The Queen, of course, is not used to being turned down. And so an escalating stand-off ensues, with the Queen sending in increasingly hefty henchmen and scaling up the bribe each time.

Emily Brown does not waver. She repeats her 'no' a little more firmly each time, and Neal Layton's fabulous sketchy pictures of Emily with her pudding-bowl haircut and flowery pinafore dress showing the pompous military grown-ups the door are deliciously satisfying. She only gets really cross when the Queen sends in her Special Commandos, who steal Stanley while she's asleep – at which point Emily storms the palace herself and tells the 'silly Queen' what's what. For the child who lets others take advantage, this story shows that nobody – not even the Queen – has a right to push them around.

A great suggestion for how kids can wield more weight in the world is offered by Emil Tischbein in *Emil and the Detectives*. When Emil takes a train to Berlin to spend a week with his cousin Pony – giving his hairdresser mother a chance to do overtime – he takes 160 marks with him to pay his way.* He pins this precious money into his pocket for safe-keeping, but when he wakes up to find both the money and his sinister fellow passenger gone, there seems to be only one conclusion.

Emil allows himself to feel trampled on for only as long as it takes to ponder the invasion of his body space while he slept. Then he sets about orchestrating a massive manhunt, rallying most of the under-twelves of Berlin to help him. The confidence with which he moves from victim to judge to hunter – and his refusal to let the thief get away with it – infects his helpers, and one of them, the delightful Gustav, has a motor-horn that he toots both randomly and with purpose. Together they chase the luckless Herr Grundeis through trams, into banks, out of hotels – and all the way to the city gaol. Children reading this will feel empowered to rally their peers and honk their horns whenever they need a bit of help fighting their corner.

Teens who find themselves always being picked on need a story that helps them take pride in who they are. The narrator of *What I Was* does his best to keep his head down when he starts at a new school on the bleak Norfolk coast (see: school, being the new kid at) – he has a history of being bullied and then taking the rap (see: fair, it's not). But when he comes across a boy named Finn

---

* The equivalent of his mother's monthly salary.

who lives alone on a nearby beach, he is entranced. Finn is entirely self-sufficient, cooking fish that he catches himself and living in tune with the seasons (see: loner, being a). He even built his own house. It turns out that Finn has his own reasons to live away from the madding crowd and for learning to be so capable. It's clear from the start that some kind of a tragedy awaits, but meanwhile Finn stands as an inspiring role model for not giving in to a world all too eager to punish those that don't conform.

SEE ALSO: **confidence, lack of • heard, not feeling • shyness • small, feeling**

stepparent, having a

CB *Sarah, Plain and Tall*
PATRICIA MACLACHLAN

CB *Half Magic*
EDWARD EAGER

Accepting a new parent-figure into the family can be tough for children, and it's a good idea to introduce some positive fictional examples into the household in advance of a stepparent moving in. When it comes to stepmothers, this is easier said than done, the breed having got such rotten press in traditional fairytales that anyone finding themselves in the position of being one might be tempted to banish those books from the house completely, starting, of course, with Cinderella, Snow White, and Hansel and Gretel. Thank goodness for *Sarah, Plain and Tall*. This slim little volume tells the story of a widower who places a thinly veiled advert in the paper for a wife, his own having died when the children were small. 'Ask her if she sings,' Anna suggests to her father when they hear back from the potential new 'help'. When Sarah arrives, she not only sings but braids hair, bakes bread, and is even game enough to climb onto the roof to nail down loose planks before a storm – which, when you live a subsistence life on the prairies, adds significantly to your assets. The children are sensible enough to see this – but what they really like is that she gets their father singing again himself for the first time in years. 'Will she stay?' becomes Caleb's anxious refrain. The children still miss their mama but they know that if Sarah stays, all their lives will be richer and happier for it.

Stories about loving stepfathers are easier to find. One such, which also allows for the fear that the stepparent will replace or dishonour an absent parent, is *Half Magic*. As far as three of the four children in this family are concerned, the small, bearded Mr Smith is a welcome addition to their lives. Unusually for a grown-up, he listens politely and with genuine interest to their stories of being transported by a 'half-magic' coin to other eras and other countries. 'This is the first magic thing that ever happened to me, though I always hoped something would,' he remarks quietly, endearing himself to us, too. Mr Smith drives them around in his motor car – which is in itself magical for these car-less kids – and proves to be an adept card player. He's also full of enthralling tales about his travels in 'Darkest Australia'. But Jane, the only one old enough to remember their dead father, can't accept that another man might be about to take his place. 'Has everyone in this family gone utterly and completely *insane*?' she cries in anguish when the others reveal their plan to bring Mr Smith with them the next time they travel with their magic coin. 'Haven't you seen the way he and Mother keep looking at each other? Do you want some old *stepfather* moving in here and changing everything?' She exhorts them to remember Mr Murdstone – the evil stepfather in *David Copperfield** (literary references abound in this book) – and, in a fit of pique, she wishes she belonged to a different family. Which, suddenly, she does – because she was holding the coin when she said it. It's Mr Smith who rescues her back, and wins her over in the process.

SEE ALSO: **arguments, always getting into** • **parents, having** • **single parent, having a**

still, unable to sit

SEE: **fidgety to read, being too** • **short attention span**

storms, fear of

PB *Thunder Cake*
PATRICIA POLACCO

If you're sheltering from a storm with a child who's afraid of thunder and lightning, follow the cure described in *Thunder Cake*. First, get them to come out from under the bed. Then get them to count the seconds between the lightning and the thunder to find out how long you've got. Ask them to fetch eggs from the hen, milk from the cow (you might have other sources), and a 'secret' ingredient† from the larder. Mix them together. Bake. If you've got the timing

* Which, by the way, is a great read for kids, and an ideal introduction to Dickens. We recommend treating the entire works of Dickens as children's chapter books, rollicking reads as they are – although you may want to wait until the stepparent in your household has been around long enough that you can all shudder at the horrors of Murdstone together.

† The recipe's in the back of the book.

right, your thunder cake will be coming out of the oven just as the thunder booms overhead and the lightning lights up the kitchen – and your child will realise how brave they've been not to have spent the whole time hiding. Don't be tempted to leave out the secret ingredient,* which, though bizarre, really works.

SEE ALSO: **anxiety • scared, being • sleep, not being able to get to**

strangers, talking to

PB *The Cat in the Hat*
DR SEUSS

We all tell children not to talk to strangers. But have you ever tried explaining *why* they shouldn't talk to strangers without a) scaring the living daylights out of them, b) inadvertently injecting a sense of intrigue into the idea or c) encouraging them to be cold and surly to everyone they meet? With Dr Seuss's timeless *The Cat in the Hat* and its equally enjoyable sequel,† you can show them the sort of stranger that they might need to be on the lookout for in a way they will understand.

The Cat always turns up just as the boy (our narrator) and his sister, Sally, need a distraction – on a rainy day when they have nothing to do (see: rainy day), or when they're grudgingly shovelling snow for their mother. 'I know it is wet/And the sun is not sunny./But we can have/Lots of good fun that is funny!' says the Cat, bewitching the children with promises of the various tricks he can do. He assures them that their mother 'will not mind at all' – which is how all strangers with malevolent intentions inveigle their way into the confidence (and houses) of their victims.

While there is something a little bit creepy about the Cat, with his button-bright eyes and his habit of closing his eyes as he talks, there is nothing ultimately sinister about him. In fact, we have always liked the Cat, with his red-and-white striped hat, his expressive, white-gloved hands and his tendency to inspire anarchy wherever he goes. He really does just want to have 'good fun that is funny'. But by now, the Cat is through the door and, with Seuss's irresistible rhythm and rhyming scheme behind him, it's nigh on impossible to get him out. Soon the Cat, with the help of accomplices Thing One and Thing Two, has ruined a perfect iced cake, bent a new rake, and generally created a mess that is 'so big/And so deep and so tall' that there's no way the boy and his sister can hope to clear it up by themselves before their mother gets home.

---

* Oh, all right then. It's tomato purée.

† *The Cat in the Hat Comes Back.*

As readers, we're glad that the Cat talked his way into the house; and, frankly, the kids in the story are, too. But not all strange cats, with or without hats, are as harmless. Tell the kids you look after never to let one persuade them to get into their car or house or, for that matter, to come uninvited into theirs – even one who says that their parents won't mind.

SEE ALSO: **trusting, being too**

stuck

CB *The Fastest Boy in the World*
ELIZABETH LAIRD

YA *Fat Boy Swim*
CATHERINE FORDE

Whether a child is stuck up a tree, stuck inside, or is stuck on a particularly pesky piece of homework (see: homework, reluctance to do), the feeling is exactly the same: frustration and the sense that nothing is ever going to change. The trick is to teach children to be resourceful. There may be no obvious way down – or out – but there may be a not-so-obvious one.

For children of chapter-book age, bring in *The Fastest Boy in the World.* Solomon, an eleven-year-old boy living in rural Ethiopia, harbours a dream of running in the Olympics. But in order to receive the standard of coaching required to have even a hope of achieving his dream, he'd need to go to a school half a day's bus ride away. His father won't even countenance the idea: Solomon is needed on the family farm.

One day, he accompanies his grandfather on the twenty-mile walk to Addis Ababa to visit a friend. There, they have the good fortune to witness the Olympic athletes returning home from the recent Games. But when his grandfather falls ill and has to be taken to hospital, Solomon knows he must get home as fast as he can. That way, his father can come back to Addis and see the old man before it's too late. Solomon has no choice but to run the twenty miles home.

His epic race – more or less a marathon – turns out to be the turning point of his life. With the internalised voice of his grandfather reminding him to keep a nice, steady pace, he realises that running isn't just about your arms and legs but about what's going on inside your head. He reaches home just in time for his father to make it back to the capital. Soon word is spreading of his extraordinary run, and it's not long before the talent scouts have scooped him up and found him the expert help he needs. Brimming with hope and exhilaration, this story will bring great heart to the child who feels that their dream lies out of reach.

A different sort of stuckness can strike in adolescence – that of being stuck inside a body you don't like. Fourteen-year-old Jimmy in *Fat Boy Swim* is a case in point. A binge-eater with a penchant for crisps, fizzy drinks and chocolate, Jimmy is in denial about his weight – and neither his mother nor his aunt Pol mention it either. Once he managed fifteen Mars bars and three Irn-Brus in one sitting; and even mild exercise leaves him panting. But one Friday night his mother comes back from Bingo with 'GI Joe' – the tough sports coach from school – in tow. GI Joe has heard of Jimmy's flair for cooking – a genuine talent he indulges every Friday with his aunt Pol – and makes him a deal. If Jimmy will cook for the upcoming school fundraiser, he'll help Jimmy lose all that extra weight.

At first, Jimmy is appalled to have his body talked about in this way, but a childhood dream in which he's swimming keeps prodding at his subconscious. And from the minute he gets into the pool, he discovers he loves it as much as cooking. Where before he was all layers of blubber, now he's a being of grace and power. Soon, he's liberated from the family-size bags of chocolate – and the body that came with them. This is a marvellously rallying, confidence-boosting story that could be just the thing to get your teen out of their hole.

SEE ALSO: **confidence, lack of** • **fair, it's not** • **overweight, being** • **small, feeling**

stuck in a book rut

READING AILMENTS

EMBRACE THE RUT

Grown-up (breezily, pretending innocence): So, what shall we read tonight? Shall we have a new story? Let's read one of these great looking *new* books we got at the library today. Look, what about this one? We've never read it before!

Child: No, I want [insert title of book here that you, the grown-up, have read 1,000 times already, possibly even 5,000 times. This is title A].

Grown-up (pretending surprise): But wouldn't you like a *new* story?

Child: No, I want [insert title A].

Grown-up (pretending deafness): Oh my goodness – have you forgotten that we got *this* one out of the library today? See how thrilling, and funny and *brilliant* this one looks?

Child: (becoming fierce): I want [insert title A].

Grown-up (whimsically): You know, when I was your age, I was really into [insert any title that is not title A].

Child (becoming agitated): But I want [insert title A].

Grown-up (desperately): How about this. We'll read [insert title A] tomorrow, first thing, when we wake up. But tonight we'll read this new one. What do you say? Deal? [Gets into bed with a book that is not title A.]

Child (furious): BUT I WANT [INSERT TITLE A]. I ONLY WANT [INSERT TITLE A]. WHY WON'T YOU READ ME [INSERT TITLE A]? WHY DO YOU HATE [INSERT TITLE A]? I THOUGHT YOU LOVED [INSERT TITLE A]! (Cries.)

Long pause, during which grown-up experiences complex emotions, the predominant one being guilt.

Grown-up: You really want [insert title A], huh?

Child (between sobs): I just want [insert title A].

Grown-up (experiencing a small death of the soul, but also understanding that this is love): OK. We'll have [insert title A].

Child: Yay! [Insert title A]! [Pause.] Can we have it twice?

CURE FOR GROWN-UPS [PB] *But Excuse Me That Is My Book* (Charlie and Lola) **LAUREN CHILD**

You are not alone. When Lola goes to the library with Charlie and wants to get out *Beetles, Bugs and Butterflies* – the book she borrowed on the last two occasions – she is horrified to discover that it's on loan to somebody else. Charlie points out all the other enticing books there are to choose from – from spy books and scary books to books about mountains and books about monsters – but Lola's having none of it. She wants *her* book. Finally, thanks to Charlie's persistence, she does try a new book – and decides that now *this* is her book. Reading this story will make you a little more forgiving of your child for being so entrenched in their book rut; and if your child catches you reading it – no doubt with a wry smile on your face – they may even be intrigued enough to step out of their rut to hear it.

stutter

SEE: **speech impediment**

suicidal thoughts

We may wish that suicide did not exist as a concept in any child's brain. But even quite young children can entertain hopeless and self-destructive thoughts (see: depression; self-harm). While professional help is imperative in any situation where such thoughts are in any way suspected, stories which deal sensitively with the subject can help everyone become more aware of the warning signs – and encourage a child experiencing such disturbing feelings to confide in a responsible grown-up.

THE TEN BEST BOOKS DEALING WITH SUICIDE

- YA *Thirteen Reasons Why* JAY ASHER
- YA *Grover* VERA AND BILL CLEAVER
- YA *Whirligig* PAUL FLEISCHMAN
- YA *If I Stay* GAYLE FORMAN
- YA *I Was Here* GAYLE FORMAN
- YA *Looking for Alaska* JOHN GREEN
- YA *All the Bright Places* JENNIFER NIVEN
- YA *This Song Will Save Your Life* LEILA SALES
- YA *It's Kind of a Funny Story* NED VIZZINI
- YA *My Heart and Other Black Holes* JASMINE WARGA

SEE ALSO: **anxiety** • **body image** • **depression** • **friends, feeling that you have no** • **nightmares** • **sadness** • **self-harm** • **stuck** • **worrying**

sulking

CB *The Little White Horse*
ELIZABETH GOUDGE

Everyone knows how tempting it is to punish others with a stony silence – and teens are especially good at it. But though sulking is understandable in someone still learning to articulate their emotions, it doesn't fix anything – and indeed runs the risk of digging the sulker more deeply in (see: stuck). *The Little White Horse*, featuring as it does a mega sulk that lasts twenty years and causes anguish not just to the individuals concerned but to an entire community, will nip the tendency in the bud before it becomes too much of a habit.

When she comes to live at Moonacre Manor with her spirited, three-chinned uncle Sir Benjamin Merryweather, thirteen-year-old Maria is delighted by everything: her turret bedroom with its unseen servant who lays out new clothes for her every morning; Periwinkle, the dapple-grey pony she discovers she already knows how to ride; and the glimpse, one moonlit night, of a little white horse with flowing mane running through the woods, then halting mid-flight 'as though it had seen her and was glad'. But something discordant lurks beneath this idyll. Why does the old parson's beautiful housekeeper, Loveday, not want Sir Benjamin to know where she lives? And why have no women set foot in Moonacre Manor for so long?

Gradually Maria pieces the puzzle together: a great passion, an impending wedding, a midnight quarrel – and a woman stalking off in a huff. 'Looking back, I really don't know how we could,' says Loveday, when Maria points out how silly the whole thing was. 'But . . . that's the way with quarrels . . . they begin over some quite little thing, like pink geraniums, and then the little thing seems to grow and grow until it fills the whole world.' This enchanting story will show a child how absurd it is to sink into an intractable sulk – and how much better things become as soon as they start looking for a way to reconcile.

SEE ALSO: **adolescence** • **moodiness** • **obstinate, being** • **stuck**

summer holidays

Whether it's about mucking around with boats, or cracking the mystery of an ancient treasure map, no July or August is complete without a summer-holiday adventure story to fire the imagination – and inspire a child's own escapade.

THE TEN BEST SUMMER HOLIDAY ADVENTURES

- [PB] *Time of Wonder* ROBERT MCCLOSKEY
- [ER] *Dead Man's Cove* (Laura Marlin Mysteries) LAUREN ST JOHN
- [CB] *The Penderwicks* JEANNE BIRDSALL
- [CB] *Over Sea, Under Stone* (The Dark Is Rising) SUSAN COOPER
- [CB] *Eating Things on Sticks* ANNE FINE
- [CB] *Moominsummer Madness* TOVE JANSSON
- [CB] *Minnow on the Say* PHILIPPA PEARCE
- [CB] *Swallows and Amazons* ARTHUR RANSOME

[CB] *Mighty Fizz Chilla* PHILIP RIDLEY
[YA] *This One Summer* MARIKO TAMAKI, ILLUSTRATED BY JILLIAN TAMAKI

SEE ALSO: **adventure, needing an** • **bored, being** • **car, being in the** • **laziness** • **rainy day** • **sibling rivalry**

superhero, wanting to be a

Some dreams come true. And some, like this one, can only ever be lived vicariously.

THE TEN BEST BOOKS FOR WANNABE SUPERHEROES

[PB] *The Astonishing Secret of Awesome Man* MICHAEL CHABON, ILLUSTRATED BY JAKE PARKER
[PB] *Eliot, Midnight Superhero* ANNE COTTRINGER, ILLUSTRATED BY ALEX T SMITH
[PB] *Max* BOB GRAHAM
[PB] *Super Daisy* KES GRAY, ILLUSTRATED BY NICK SHARRATT
[ER] *The Petrifying Plot of the Plummeting Pants* (Boy Zero Wannabe Hero) PETER MILLETT
[CB] *Powerless* MATTHEW CODY
[CB] *My Brother Is a Superhero* DAVID SOLOMONS
[CB] *The Shadow Hero* GENE LUEN YANG, ILLUSTRATED BY SONNY LIEW
[YA] *Steelheart* (Reckoners) BRANDON SANDERSON
[YA] *Nimona* NOELLE STEVENSON

SEE ALSO: **celebrity, wanting to be a** • **different, feeling** • **praise, seeking**

swearing

[PB] *Poo Bum*
STEPHANIE BLAKE

[CB] *The BFG*
ROALD DAHL, ILLUSTRATED BY QUENTIN BLAKE

[YA] *The Maze Runner*
JAMES DASHNER

Bad words hold great fascination for kids – not least because of the dramatic effect they seem to have on their grown-ups. Up to the age of six or so, scatological words and bodily parts are generally thrilling enough to suffice. *Poo Bum* – featuring a rabbit who responds with these two words to everything – will make a child laugh so much that you'll both, probably, cry; while also ensuring that the words 'poo' and 'bum' wear themselves out with overuse.

Until about seven (older, if you're lucky), grown-ups can often successfully dupe their children into using some juicy-sounding but actually meaningless coinages of their own, thus fulfilling a child's desire to be edgy *and* get that eyebrow of yours to hitch up (while providing you with some surreptitious entertainment). For inspiration, turn to the big, friendly giant in *The BFG*, that loveable macerator of the English language who, having never been to school, speaks the 'most terrible wigglish'. As he explains to Sophie, the little girl he steals one night from her orphanage dormitory, he knows exactly which words he wants to say, but they always get 'squiff-squiddled around'. Try passing off your own coinages first, and once the child gets wise to your ruse, encourage them to 'gobblefunk' their own with this marvellous story – one of our personal Dahl favourites – as their inspiration.

Teens will find it almost impossible not to swear, but some manage to get away with it more than others. Here again, creativity is key. If kids can be encouraged to twist their tongues around some madcap expletives rather than just the boring old usual ones, they may make people laugh rather than cringe. The unique swearing in *The Maze Runner* – in which a boy and his friends are attacked by giant, armoured caterpillars every night – comes satisfyingly close to the obscenities we all know and do our best to avoid⊛ without being actively offensive. Drop it in the pathway of your experimental crew and see how they run with it.*

CURE FOR GROWN-UPS CB *The Vicar of Nibbleswicke* **ROALD DAHL, ILLUSTRATED BY QUENTIN BLAKE**

It's important to remember that you are probably not immune to this ailment yourself. Indeed, you are probably the one who passed it on to the children in the first place. We defy you not to smile at the mess the poor vicar of Nibbleswicke makes of the word 'park' when he's tense – because he suffers from an unfortunate speech impediment that causes him to say things backwards. Dahl wrote the book to raise money for the Dyslexia Institute in London,† though the vicar's

---

* For instance: 'Hey, good morning, Newbie. Or should I say good afternoon? Forgive me for saying it, but you appear to be jacked in the head. Are you? Yes, you, Greenie! Don't tell me you're planning on breakfast? Shank! We're about to have lunch. Oh, and listen up! These walls moved when you came home last night. Ain't nobody allowed to come home and make that sort of racket. Your gaming time is doomed, you might as well face that now. The Creators had some kind of crazy plan for you this weekend, but it seems like none of us is getting out alive now. At least Frypan here can cook. You want to be a late-night Runner? Fine, just as long as it don't let the Grievers get in here. Blabber it, Greenie; we need to solve the Maze.'

† Now Dyslexia Action.

idiosyncratic ailment really has nothing to do with dyslexia, nor is it particularly helpful to the public's understanding of dyslexia, as far as we can see.* Nevertheless, it's a funny book – and once it's made you laugh, you'll have to get down off that high horse of yours, or at least whenever you're around an innocent, clean-mouthed child.

SEE ALSO: **bully, being a** • **manners, bad**

swim, inability to

PB *The Boy Who Wouldn't Swim*
DEB LUCKE

CB *The Sea Egg*
LUCY M BOSTON

Start them young enough and most children take to water with a fish-like ease. But leave it too long, and fear and reason may take the chance to jump in. Eric, in *The Boy Who Wouldn't Swim* – based on the author's own brother – spends a whole fearful summer on the side of the pool, refusing to go in. It's a particularly hot summer, too, and he becomes increasingly uncomfortable. Lucke's acrylic illustrations show the whole town lying in their deck chairs around the pool – and the inviting view from the high diving board. When his younger sister, Jess, ends up taking the swimming lessons meant for him, his shame hardens like a sweet left out in the sun.

When Eric does, eventually, get in the water, it's when nobody's looking. Try reading this story to your reluctant swimmer, then letting them test the water when your back is (ever so slightly) turned.†

Few authors have made swimming as appealing as Lucy M Boston in *The Sea Egg*, her lyrical story about two brothers on a Cornish holiday who develop a new relationship with the water thanks to a magical companion. One morning, with the tide going out and the sea smooth and blue and overlain with a silence 'like all the secrets in the world', the boys run down to the water's edge, stones 'skidding and clattering' under their feet, and find a lobster fisherman bringing in his catch. The man shows them a mysterious egg-shaped stone that 'fetched up' in his lobster pot. The brothers want it immediately. And though they're suddenly nervous of what it might contain – a sea ogre? a

* Dahl enjoyed this back-to-front impediment so much, however, that he gave it to himself when writing *Esio Trot.*

† And see: scared, being, for more on how to help children not let their fear take hold.

terrible storm that will claw down the cliffs? – they take it to a secluded rock pool which can only be reached via a tunnel that fills at high tide and wait to see what happens.

To tell you what hatches from the sea egg would spoil the wonder of this slow-building story. Suffice to say that with their sea-given companion, the two boys learn to swim like sea creatures themselves, drawing just enough air into their lungs to plunge without thought into the rearing waves and open their eyes in the salty, bubbled world beneath. Their secret – and the knowledge that they made the most of it – makes this a profound motivation to live life to the full, and be daring. Read this one aloud to the whole family, and they'll be inspired to aim for a whole new ease in the water.

SEE ALSO: **confidence, lack of** • **scared, being**

T IS FOR . . .

tall, being

Cosmic
FRANK COTTRELL BOYCE

Being tall for your age is a mixed blessing. On the upside you can reach the sweetie jar, see at concerts, and you're more likely to be picked for the basketball team. On the downside, it's harder to go unobserved when up to no good, you can feel gauche compared to your peers, and other people assume you're older than you are (and then wonder why you're not more capable/better behaved/ more intelligent than you're yet ready to be).

Children to whom this sounds familiar will appreciate meeting young Liam in *Cosmic*, Boyce's chapter-book extravaganza set in Manchester, China and Outer Space. Six feet tall and only twelve years old, Liam enjoys maintaining the illusion that he's already an adult. It helps that he's precociously sporting facial hair. One day he's asked to teach a class at school by someone who assumes he's another staff member, and from there it's only a matter of time before he's taking a brand new Porsche for a test drive . . . One thing leads to another, and when he finds himself in space posing as a dad in charge of four kids – all relying on him to look after them – he realises he's in rather deep. Can his height alone give him the authority he needs to get his charges safely back to Earth?

We're not necessarily suggesting tall kids abscond with unaccompanied minors into the blue, but we do applaud the way Liam rises to the challenge his stature invites. It's not just the length but the steeliness of his backbone that ensures a triumphant ending. Enjoy showing your immature six-footer what they could get away with if they tried.

SEE ALSO: **different, feeling** • **small, being**

tantrums

[PB] *Knuffle Bunny*
MO WILLEMS

'Tantrum: an uncontrolled outburst of anger and frustration, typically in a young child' (OED) – and whether they're rare, regular, triggered only by an extreme crisis or whenever someone says the word 'no', cures are as crucial for the grown-up in attendance as for the child that's having them. The best picture book for both is *Knuffle Bunny*, an urban tale set amongst the brownstones of Brooklyn.

Trixie is at the perfect tantruming age: feisty personality all intact but unable as yet to speak in a recognisable language. So when her daddy – a nicely witty, glasses-wearing hipster type – takes Trixie to the laundrette on Saturday morning, leaving Mum a moment of peace on their shady stoop, they communicate with affectionate looks and smiles. Down the block they go, Trixie holding her dad's hand, and gripping her Knuffle Bunny lovingly round its neck, through the park and past the school. At the laundrette Trixie 'helps' by swinging a bra around like a lasso and putting the coins in the slot; and soon, Daddy's whistling as they wend their way home. But then Trixie comes to a stop – and in an up-close image we see her eyes go huge and the line of her mouth begin to wobble. 'Aggle flaggel klabble!' she cries. *We* know what she's trying to say, Trixie herself knows what she's trying to say, but Daddy . . . well, poor Daddy hasn't the faintest idea. He endures a full-on tantrum on the side of the road, complete with tonsil-revealing 'WAAAA!'s, tears, gulps, frantic gesticulations and a limp and boneless body that refuses to move of its own accord before he finally makes it home, jagged lines emanating from his own frazzled head. Gallingly, Trixie's mum sees what's wrong in a flash, and when Knuffle Bunny is finally recovered, dripping wet and somewhat in shock itself, Trixie's joy will have everyone's hearts singing. Read it in the calm after the storm, and it'll help all concerned feel understood.

SEE ALSO: **arguments, getting into • heard, not feeling • over-tired • spoilt, being • understood, not being**

tattoo, wanting a

[YA] *Divergent*
VERONICA ROTH

A tattoo is a powerful and far-reaching thing, and whether it's tucked away on the inside of the wrist or covering the body in a Samoan-style swathe, it to some extent defines who we are. Stories featuring characters with tattoos can help remind a teen that choosing to have one means sticking with it, and all that it signifies, for the rest of their life.

Identity is very much the theme of *Divergent* and indeed the other two books in Roth's trilogy. The members of this dystopian American community must declare allegiance to one of five 'factions' when they turn sixteen: Dauntless, Candor, Erudite, Amity or Abnegation. Our heroine, Beatrice, receives no clear indication as to which faction she belongs to – which makes her by default a Divergent. And though the rest of her family belong to Abnegation, she decides on an impulse to join Dauntless – a tribe of brave, fearless warriors known for heavily inking themselves. In a moment of bonding with her new friend Christina, Tris (as Beatrice renames herself) has three ravens engraved on her collarbone, representing the parents and brother she left behind. Later she adds a feisty flame, the tribal symbol of the Dauntless, to one shoulder, and two clasped hands – the Abnegation symbol – to her other shoulder, so that she does not forget where she came from.

Tris's love-interest, Four, is also richly tattooed with meaningful images, creating a map of his past and his future. Indeed, tattoos of all kinds are applied and discussed repeatedly in this series. Readers are left keenly aware that identity is an ever-shifting thing. Whoever they feel themselves to be at sixteen, they can be sure they'll feel different at twenty-one.

SEE ALSO: **body image** • **gang, being in a** • **peer pressure**

teenager, being a

SEE: **adolescence**

temper, losing your

SEE: **anger**

thank you letter, having to write a

[PB] *The Jolly Postman*
ALLAN AHLBERG, ILLUSTRATED BY JANET AHLBERG

[CB] *Daddy Long-Legs*
JEAN WEBSTER

To the child, they're an onerous task – the curse of Christmas and birthdays – and can make them wish they hadn't had any presents in the first place. But to the grown-up, the thank you letter is the best bit: the gangly, spindly letters striding boldly across the page only to bunch up at the other side where the writer has run out of space. For that reason – and the opportunity it gives for reflecting on the kindness of others – it's worth trying to imbue the children in your household with an appreciation of the old-fashioned accoutrements of letter writing: paper, ink, envelope and stamp – as well, of course, as the choosing of what to say and how to say it.

Start with *The Jolly Postman,* coming as it so miraculously does with stamped, addressed envelopes containing real letters and cards to pull out. The story threads together a familiar cast of characters – Goldilocks, the giant from Jack and the Beanstalk and the wolf from Little Red Riding Hood among them – whose letters are delivered by a uniformed postman on a red bicycle who can sometimes be persuaded to stay for a cup of tea. The trademark Ahlberg pastel-coloured characters in pretty English landscapes all add to the sense that letters unite people, bring a moment of quiet pleasure to someone's face, and herald exciting news.

The best letters, of course, are those that reveal their writer's personality, such as those written by seventeen-year-old orphan Jerusha Abbott in *Daddy Long-Legs*. Addressed to a mysterious benefactor who is paying Jerusha's way through college on the condition that she write to him once a month, the letters show that she knows nothing about 'Daddy Long-Legs' except that he's rich, dislikes girls and has long legs – she having once glimpsed his shadow on a wall.

Perhaps it's precisely because she knows so little about him that Judy (as she now calls herself) feels so free to be herself. Chatty and exuberant, strewn with insights into school life and dotted with little stick-figure drawings, Judy's letters are appreciative of the unexpected chance to rise above her lowly beginnings, and she's as unafraid to gush as she is to speak her mind. 'Why couldn't you have picked out a name with a little personality?' she asks, having been instructed to call him Mr Smith. 'I might as well write letters to . . . Dear Clothes-Pole.' After a book full of letters like these – and those in the list of epistolary stories that follows – the reluctant letter-writer in your midst will see how much fun letters can be as a way to 'get acquainted' – not just with the person they're writing to, but with themselves.

THE TEN BEST EPISTOLARY BOOKS

- PB *The Day the Crayons Quit* **DREW DAYWALT, ILLUSTRATED BY OLIVER JEFFERS**
- PB *Dear Greenpeace* **SIMON JAMES**
- CB *Love from Paddington* **MICHAEL BOND, ILLUSTRATED BY PEGGY FORTNUM AND RW ALLEY**
- CB *Dear Mr Henshaw* **BEVERLY CLEARY, ILLUSTRATED BY PAUL O ZELINSKY**
- CB *Ella Minnow Pea* **MARK DUNN**
- CB *Letters to Leo* **AMY HEST, ILLUSTRATED BY JULIA DENOS**
- CB *Simone's Letters* **HELENA PIELICHATY, ILLUSTRATED BY SUE HEAP**
- YA *13 Little Blue Envelopes* **MAUREEN JOHNSON**
- YA *Finding Cassie Crazy* **JACLYN MORIARTY**
- YA *Because You'll Never Meet Me* **LEAH THOMAS**

SEE ALSO: **disappointment** • **grannies, having to kiss** • **manners, bad** • **presents**

things, wanting

PB *Just Enough and Not Too Much*
KAETHE ZEMACH

CB *Millions*
FRANK COTTRELL BOYCE

CB *Shine*
KATE MARYON

Most children are magpies at heart – drawn to shiny things that they then have an urge to possess. And unless they've been raised in the manner of Mowgli or Tarzan, they probably hanker after the latest new gadget or must-have accessory along with everyone else. A great story to go to for a lesson in being happy with what you have is *Just Enough and Not Too Much.* Simon the Fiddler has everything he needs in his cosy little house: a chair to sit on, a bed to sleep in, a hat and one beloved toy. Together with his clothes and his friends, what more could a man want? But then he starts to wonder if another chair (or ten) might be nice, and a choice of toys and hats, and soon his sun-yellow house is so crammed that it's no longer a nice place to be. The reader is as relieved as he is when he finds an ingenious way to get back to the purity of his former, uncluttered existence.

Encourage older kids to think about what's really worth spending money on and what's not with the excellent *Millions*. Brothers Damian and Anthony have been struggling to make sense of the world since their mother died and their father became depressed (see: depressed parent, having a). Damian, obsessed with the saints he's reading about, has taken to living in a card-board-box hermitage at the bottom of the garden. The older, more pragmatic Anthony has set his sights on improving his material lot in life. So when a suitcase containing £230,000 lands in Damian's hands while he's praying, they have different ideas about how best to use it. Damian considers it a gift from God, and thinks they should spend it to help the poor or look after animals, like St Francis of Assisi. Anthony thinks they should buy a new house. Their friends at school launch in with their own agendas. One thing's for sure: however they decide to spend it, they should spend it fast – because 'euro day' is approaching, and soon British currency won't be worth anything at all.

As Damian prays to the saints for guidance (and wonders if his mum, Maureen, is among them), the question of what is really worth £230K becomes one for the reader, too. We're presented with a stream of suggestions – from houses, phones and TVs to wells in Africa and shelters for the homeless – and we're shown how the presence of riches can affect our relationships, too. We won't reveal what becomes of the money in the end. Let's just say that the saints – and particularly Saint Maureen – would be proud. Give a kid this book, then ask them what they'd do if a similar windfall landed in their lap.

For a story that shows that things, in themselves, don't make you happy, see *Shine*. Twelve-year-old Tiffany's mum, Carla, has a serious shopping addiction. She buys everything she covets, from plasma TVs to a new laptop for Tiffany and, most recently, a handbag-sized dog called Chardonnay, footing the bill with 'borrowed' cards. But then, one night, the face of Carla's 'business partner' Mike is plastered all over *Crimewatch*, along with the red convertible they recently acquired. The next thing Tiffany knows, her mum's in gaol, Chardonnay's in the kennels and she's facing the prospect of foster care.

To avoid this, Tiffany opts to go and live with her auntie Cass on the island of Sark – even though her mother, who grew up there, has always described it as the 'most boring place on the planet'. And life on Sark does indeed turn out to be very different to what Cassie's used to in London. Here, everyone gets around by bike or pony, and it's safe to go wherever you want. Little by little, Tiff is won over by the simplicity she finds there – and she experiences a joy far deeper than anything ever triggered by one of the shiny products her mum brought home. Young readers will see that the temporary pleasure of new things – even a suitcase full of money – would pale in comparison with happiness of this sort.

SEE ALSO: **job, wanting a Saturday** • **spoilt, being**

tidy up, having to

SEE: **chores, having to do**

timid

SEE: **shyness**

toddler, being a

SEE: **potty training • questions, asking too many • small, being • tantrums • told, never doing what you're**

told, always doing what you're

[PB] *Miss Bridie Chose a Shovel*
LESLIE CONNOR, ILLUSTRATED BY MARY AZARIAN

[CB] *Lara's Gift*
ANNEMARIE O'BRIEN

The ultra-obedient child is a doddle to look after. But unquestioning obedience isn't necessarily a wholly positive trait. Waiting to be told what to do all the time can become, in adulthood, a failure to think for oneself. The importance of acting on your own initiative is the message behind *Miss Bridie Chose a Shovel,* the story of a young emigré to America in the late 19th century. Given the choice of a chiming clock, a porcelain figurine or a shovel to take with her on her voyage, Miss Bridie sensibly opts for the shovel. And, as we see in the charming woodcuts by Mary Azarian which capture the period beautifully, the shovel comes in very handy. Not only does she use it to earn enough money on the side to live where she wants, but also to clear – literally – a path to the man she will marry. This story shows kids that they're more likely to achieve the things that matter to them in their lives if they learn to think for themselves.

Children of chapter-book age will enjoy the example of Lara, the peasant girl in *Lara's Gift* who learns to question authority. Though it's clear to everyone that Lara has a special way with the borzoi – the powerful hunting dogs her father breeds on Count Vorontsov's country estate – she can never hope to inherit the role of chief kennel steward from her father. The position has always been held by a man; and when her mother gives birth to a little boy, her Papa reminds her she and Zar – the runt of the litter she raised herself – will no more hunt wolves than will Countess Vorontsova's lapdog.

But when Lara has a vision of Zar with a dead wolf at his feet, surrounded by blood-soaked snow, she realises she must break one of her father's golden rules in order to save them all. Amid snowy blizzards, packs of wolves and the lonely call of the hunting horn, we see that Lara's loyalty to her family remains as true as Zar's devotion to her, even when she is blatantly flouting the rules. Sometimes even good girls must disobey.

SEE ALSO: **stand up for yourself, not feeling able to**

told, never doing what you're

[PB] *Mr Gumpy's Outing*
JOHN BURNINGHAM

On the other hand,* kids can take thinking for themselves too far. Small children must learn to do what they're told for their own safety, if nothing else. For a gentle 'I told you so', turn to the ever-calm Mr Gumpy. To each of the children and animals on the riverbank asking to come on board as he punts lazily downstream, he says 'yes' – on condition that they don't squabble (the children), hop (the rabbit) or chase the rabbit (the cat).

For a while Burningham's cross-hatched drawings, overlain with a dreamy haze of colour, are the very definition of serenity. But of course it doesn't last. Soon everybody is doing exactly the thing they were told not to do and no prizes for guessing where they all end up. The wonderful thing is that although Mr Gumpy looks a little surprised by his sudden plunge into the ice-cold river, he never gets as far as needing an 'R' in his name – making this as good a cure for the exasperated grown-up as for the children it gently chastises.

SEE ALSO: **arguments, getting into** • **manners, bad** • **naughtiness** • **swearing**

told off, being

SEE: **punished, being**

* If you didn't catch what the first hand was, see previous ailment.

told what to read, not liking being

TRICK THEM INTO THINKING THEY HAVE CHOSEN THE BOOK THEMSELVES

Boy: I'm not reading *that*.

Dad: (peers at the cover of the book in his hand) What's wrong with it?

Boy: Isn't it obvious?

Dad: (frowns at the book) Is it too easy?

Boy: No.

Dad: Too hard?

Boy: No.

Dad: You want pictures?

Boy: *No*.

Dad: (turns book over and back again) Is the author the wrong gender?

Boy: (shrugs)

Dad: Wait, have you already read it?

Boy: *No*.

Dad: (pause) Everyone *else* has already read it . . .?

Boy: (irritated) It's just not my sort of book, Dad.

Dad: Oh. (Pause.) What is your sort of book?

Boy: I don't know.

Dad: Well then, how do you know it's not this?

Boy: I don't know. I just know.

Dad: Is it wrong because I gave it to you? Would it be better if you just sort of found it, lying around, and picked it up and started reading it . . .?

Boy: (considers this for a while) Maybe. I don't know.

Dad: . . . Because I could just go and leave it on that bench over there, and then just wander away. We could pretend we'd never met.

Boy: That's ridiculous.

Dad: I know. Well, I guess you're just going to have to watch the football lesson, then. (Dad tosses the book into an open bag. A referee's whistle blows. Dad gets another book out and starts reading. Boy kicks his heels against the bench legs. Dad turns the page.)

Boy: What's that one?

Dad: This? Oh, just a bit of rubbish.

Boy: What's it about?

Dad: Oh, you know . . . short guy with hairy feet. Sets off on a really long journey and has a lot of views about breakfast. It's really long and there are lots of trolls and elves and other small fellows with weird names. You wouldn't like it. They're forever breaking into song.

Boy: (sits up) Where are they going?

Dad: To the Mountain to retrieve the stolen gold from the dragon.

Boy: I tell you what. You read *this* one (pulls the first book out the bag), and I'll read that one.

Dad: But I'd just got to a really great creepy bit with this slimy –

Boy: (takes the father's book. Opens it, starts reading, falls into a deep hole . . .)

(Dad picks up first book. Turns it over to read the blurb on the back. Tosses it back in the bag. Referee's whistle blows. Dad looks at child and gives a small smile. Boy turns page.)

tonsillitis

SEE: ***The Novel Cure***

tooth, wobbly

[PB] *Madlenka*
PETER SÍS

'In the universe, on a planet, on a continent, in a country, in a city, on a block . . .' a little girl named Madlenka discovers her first wiggly tooth – and the enormity of the moment is thus acknowledged with appropriate splendour and solemnity. Peter Sís's intricate line drawings, splashed with resplendent colour, zoom in to Madlenka's apartment in Manhattan's Lower East Side before taking us on a tour of her multicultural block as she tells all her friends the big news. First there's Mr Gaston, the French baker ('Hello, Mr Gaston, my tooth is loose! I am a big girl now,' say the letters marching around the edge, dodging croissants and madeleines), then Mr Singh, a Sikh in a turban, and Mr Ciao, the ice-cream man, and Miss Grimm, who knows lots of German fairytales. Make it a ritual to read the book to mark the departure of each milk tooth, taking your child on a spin around the world as you do so.

SEE ALSO: **grow up, impatient to • grow up, not wanting to • tooth fairy, non-appearance of the**

tooth fairy, non-appearance of the

[YA] *Lady Cottington's Pressed Fairy Book*
TERRY JONES, ILLUSTRATED BY BRIAN FROUD

Milk teeth have a way of falling out when children are least prepared to catch them. And tooth fairies have a way of not turning up when a child most eagerly anticipates them. In the advent of a tooth fairy no-show, assuage the disappointment of the gap-toothed child – and any burgeoning doubts about the existence of fairies that such a blow might invite – with the remarkable document that is *Lady Cottington's Pressed Fairy Book*.

Supposedly copied from the original diary of a Victorian girl growing up on her family estate and told in her own childish hand – the sepia-brown, quaintly spelled letters large and ink-splodged to begin with – the first entry is recorded on 6 July 1865: 'Nanna wuldnt bleive me. Ettie wuldnt bleive me. Auntie Mercie wuldnt bleive me. But I got one. Now theyve got to bleive me.' And there, between the pages, we see them – pointy-eared, green-skinned fairies squashed flat and oozing with bodily fluids and the occasional popped-out eyeball.* Early on, the 'inkwizitf' young Angelica reveals a merciless streak as she 'SPLAT's and 'SQUISH'es whenever the fairies flutter too close. But as she grows up, the elfin creatures become more savvy and start to have fun with her, taking on lewd poses and revelling in their nudity. Gorgeously rendered in watercolour with natural pigments of fuchsia pink, apple green and hyacinth against faux-aged pages, the illustrations steer a fine and sometimes wobbly line between mildly disgusting and blackly funny.† An invaluable tool for prolonging the tooth-fairy years and diverting attention whenever the fairy gold fails to materialise, we suggest that grown-ups show selected fairy 'impressions' to their young, gap-toothed charges, and hold back on the rest until the years of experience allow. This taster, combined with the promise of more to be seen in later years, will add to the mystery and thrill of the conceit.

SEE ALSO: **disappointment** • **magic, loss of belief in** • **obsessions** • **parents, too busy**

toy, losing your favourite

Almost every child undergoes this calamity – and it's worth stocking yourself up in advance with a cure or two. They may not bring the loved toy back, but they may help to soften the blow.

THE TEN‡ BEST PICTURE BOOKS FOR LOSING YOUR FAVOURITE TOY

- PB *The Mitten* JAN BRETT
- PB *Tatty Ratty* HELEN COOPER
- PB *A Pocket for Corduroy* DON FREEMAN
- PB *Toys in Space* MINI GREY
- PB *Dogger* SHIRLEY HUGHES
- PB *Pete the Cat and His Four Groovy Buttons* ERIC LITWIN, CREATED AND ILLUSTRATED BY JAMES DEAN
- PB *Elmer and the Lost Teddy* DAVID MCKEE
- PB *The Velveteen Rabbit* MARGERY WILLIAMS, ILLUSTRATED BY WILLIAM NICHOLSON
- PB *Flotsam* DAVID WIESNER

SEE ALSO: **cheering up, needing** • **sadness** • **tantrums** • **trauma**

---

* Apparently, these are not their mortal remains but the '*psychic impressions*' left behind. The RSPCF* assures us, via a publisher's note, that no fairies were harmed during the making of the book.

*The Royal Society for the Prevention of Cruelty to Fairies, for those who don't know.

† This is Terry Jones of Monty Python fame, after all.

‡ We did have ten, but we lost one. We were inconsolable at first, but then we re-read the other nine books on the list and feel much better now.

transgender, feeling you are

[CB] *George*
ALEX GINO

[YA] *The Art of Being Normal*
LISA WILLIAMSON

The feeling of being trapped inside a body of the wrong sex starts young in transgender people (see: stuck). But without the right words to explain what it feels like – and an understanding audience willing to hear it – an isolating confusion can reign. This difficult phase is captured simply but effectively in *George*. To all outward appearances, ten-year-old George is the younger brother of Scott; but George has always known, at some deep level, that she's a girl – and from the start the story is told using the female pronoun.

When her teacher at school announces they're putting on a stage play of *Charlotte's Web*, George is overwhelmed by the desire to play the (female) spider – not just for the experience of acting as a girl, but so that her mother can finally see her for who she is. Of course, there are too many girls in the class for the bemused teacher to agree, but with the help of her best friend Kelly, George fulfils her dream. The moment at which George's mother finally registers what her daughter has been trying to tell her for a long time (see: heard, not feeling) is a moving one. This illuminating, from-the-heart story offers empathy and reassurance to anyone of George's age (and their grown-ups) who think they may be transgender, too.

Teens struggling to 'out' the issue with their grown-ups will find a kindred spirit in fourteen-year-old David, who has always known he's a girl. His parents think he's gay – and try to be supportive; but David shares his real feelings only with the scrapbook in which he notes down facts about his changing body and sticks pictures of Audrey Hepburn, Elizabeth Taylor and the beautiful things he's found – peacock feathers, sweet wrappers, a tissue with a lipstick kiss. When this scrapbook gets into the wrong hands at school, a merciless persecution begins (see: bullied, being) but a well-timed punch from a new boy, Leo, changes everything.

Told from the alternate viewpoints of David and Leo, the gradual friendship between these two boys makes for a moving story. Leo turns out to be undergoing treatment to change his girl's body into a man's, with flattened breasts strapped beneath a binder around his chest. When the two spend a weekend together, David makes a big step forward in embracing his sexual identity. His journey toward openness and self-acceptance will give anyone facing similar trials a huge confidence boost.

SEE ALSO: **gay, not sure if you are**

trashing the house while your parents are out

[ER] *The Dragonsitter*
JOSH LACEY, ILLUSTRATED BY GARRY PARSONS

[YA] *Doing It*
MELVIN BURGESS

Instil in your children a sense of how shocking it is to come home to find your house trashed when they're still young and impressionable with the enjoyable Dragonsitter series. Irresponsible Uncle Morton has left his fully grown, fire-breathing pet dragon for Eddie to look after while he jets off on holiday. But almost immediately the dragon eats little sister Emily's rabbit. As piles of steaming dragon poo accumulate on the carpet, the curtains catch fire and a hole appears in the door of the fridge where the dragon tried to get at the leftover cauliflower cheese, things quickly descend into mayhem. Told in the form of increasingly frantic emails in which Eddie begs Uncle Morton to come back and sort out the mess, and brought to vivid life by Garry Parsons's energetic illustrations, the thrilling sense of a family teetering on the brink of disaster is bonding stuff for a grown-up and child. Surely this enormous and unpredictable creature loafing around on the sofa, puffing black smoke and giving everyone the evil eye* can't behave like this with Uncle Morton? Luckily a one-word tip from Uncle Morton saves the house – and Eddie's mother – from total carnage. Make the most of the fact that Eddie and his mother are on the same side – and that once they know how to win the dragon over, they turn him (or her, as it later turns out) into a docile, loveable house-guest overnight.

It's pretty much a given that, at some point during the adolescent years, the grown-ups will leave their trusted teen in charge while they fly off for a well-earned city break – and that said trusted teen will invite all their friends to a massive house party. This is exactly what seventeen-year-old Dino does in *Doing It*. Cut to the scene at 2am when the parental bed is full of puke, teenagers are sprawled in the bath, cigarette ash is trodden into the carpet, and a stray girl who calls herself Siobhan (but is actually Zöe) is helping Dino lose his virginity (see: virginity, loss of) after having already helped herself to the cash in the pockets of the coats hanging in the hall. And then everyone starts throwing empty bottles out the window.

Somehow, someone has to clear the mess up. And, much to Dino's delight, his actual girlfriend (Jackie) turns up at 2pm the next day and works wonders with bin bags, vacuum and Pledge, all just in time to welcome his parents back. They're just about to realise that something a bit fishy is going

* An adolescent in disguise, if ever there was one.

on – the house seems a bit *too* clean, after all – when Dino usefully remembers that his mother is having an affair. His well-timed (though outrageous) bombshell ensures they never actually get to notice the weirdly put-on sheets on their bed . . . Teens will learn all the tips they need from this story,* and be able to throw the party, trash the house – and get away with it. As, of course, they should.

SEE ALSO: **adolescence** • **parents, strict** • **told, never doing what you're**

trauma

PB *A Terrible Thing Happened*
MARGARET M HOLMES, ILLUSTRATED BY CARY PILLO

CB *The Last Wild*
PIERS TORDAY

Any violent or threatening episode can leave a child traumatised – from a car accident or a natural disaster to a suicide, or physical abuse in the home – whether the child was involved directly or a passive witness. Though professional help must be sought in cases of suspected or obvious trauma, sharing a book can help to reach a child who finds it hard to talk.

We never find out what 'terrible thing' Sherman Smith – the little raccoon in Margaret M Holmes's made-to-measure picture book – has seen, portrayed as it is by dark scribbles in a muddled thought cloud above his head. But a great sadness is apparent in the downward drift of his eye markings and the way he slumps at the table, head resting on his arm; and whatever it is, it's bad enough that he feels the need to push the memory away. Soon Sherman is showing other signs of trauma: not wanting to eat, having bad dreams, feeling sad without knowing why and playing up at school. He's encouraged to recreate his feelings in drawings and, eventually, to draw the terrible thing itself, which is presented as the first step to his recovery. Because of the non-specified nature of the trauma, this is a book that can be used for a wide variety of situations. We suggest it as an adjunct to getting help from a professional therapist.

For older kids, fiction taking a more circumspect route can help open a door to communication when none yet exists. *The Last Wild* is about a boy of eleven, Kester Jaynes, who hasn't spoken since his mother died five years before. Told that his father has abandoned him, he lives at Spectrum Hall – ostensibly a home for 'troubled children', but really a kind of prison. He still holds out hope that his father – an animal lover and great scientist who, Kester

---

* And some they shouldn't ever use.

believes, had been trying to save the animals from being wiped out by the deadly Red Eye virus – will come back for him one day. Now the virus has run its course, leaving only insects in the natural world, and though insects are strictly banned at Spectrum Hall, Kester befriends a moth and a cockroach who visit him in his cell. When Kester discovers that his tiny friends are speaking to him – and that he's able to talk back – he breaks out of Spectrum Hall with their help. There are, it seems, a few animals still left in the world after all and, joined by a stag and a pigeon, this motley crew pick up the baton of Kester's father's conservation work.

Kester's unexpected new friendships, and his gradual awakening to his unusual powers, help to prise him slowly open from his molluscan state. Traumatised kids and teens who have turned in on themselves will find him a wonderful companion – and, perhaps, an encouragement to open up themselves.

SEE ALSO: **abuse** • **nightmares** • **violence** • **war, worrying about**

truancy

SEE: **school, not wanting to go to**

trusting, being too

CB *The Wolves of Willoughby Chase*
JOAN AIKEN

Much as we might wish to present the world as a safe place, one of the jobs of a responsible adult is to gradually disabuse their naive charges of the assumption that all other grown-ups have a child's best interests at heart. Bring in this story of two young cousins, Bonnie and Sylvia, to help.

Bonnie is thrilled that her cousin Sylvia is coming to live with her at Willoughby Chase. By day, the estate is a beautiful snowscape complete with horses, a frozen stream and Simon, the hermit boy who lives in the woods and tends to the geese. But by night it is a bleak and ominous place, filled with the howls of hungry wolves and red eyes shining out from between the trees. Bonnie's parents, Lady Green and Sir Willoughby, are preparing to go overseas and will be leaving the girls in the care of the dreadful Miss Slighcarp, the governess.

Miss Slighcarp shows her true colours within minutes of her arrival, when she wallops Bonnie's much-loved maid, Pattern, around the head with a hair-brush. The loyal, spirited Bonnie is quick to jump to Pattern's defence, sploshing a basin of water over her governess which, gloriously, displaces her wig. Bonnie's parents, predisposed to giving others the benefit of the doubt, laugh the incident off – and when the wolfish man that cousin Sylvia met on the train is brought in with her, apparently knocked unconscious by his own suitcase, they blithely agree to let him stay, too. But no sooner have the senior Willoughbys left the scene than Miss Slighcarp and her roguish cohort are rooting through the family papers, helping themselves to Bonnie's parents' clothes, and locking Bonnie in the schoolroom closet.

Luckily the girls have Simon and the redoubtable Pattern to come to their rescue – but not before they've received a harsh lesson in trusting too much. Not all grown-ups are forces for good, and this story will introduce the importance of learning to tell who can be trusted, and who should be sent straight out to the wolves.

SEE ALSO: **betrayal** • **strangers, talking to**

tummy ache

ER *Max Archer, Kid Detective: The Case of the Recurring Stomachaches*
HOWARD J BENNETT, ILLUSTRATED BY SPIKE GERRELL

According to Max Archer, kid detective – the creation of paediatrician Howard J Bennett – there are three main causes of tummy ache: lactose intolerance, constipation and stress. Let your child play detective along with Max, working out what might be the cause of theirs – and what they might do to cure it. Yes, this is medical self-help for kids, and the veil of fiction is thin. But the overall concept is excellent and Spike Gerrell's Scooby-Doo-ish cartoon illustrations bring a touch of levity that makes it all the more palatable.

SEE ALSO: **constipation** • **fussy eater, being a**

twin, being a

The Parent Trap
ERICH KÄSTNER, ILLUSTRATED BY WALTER TRIER

The special relationship shared by twins is legendary, and non-twins are often envious of it. We certainly admire how Thomson and Thompson, the identical twins in *Tintin*, share their charming tendency to switch the beginnings and ends of their sentences around, such as 'This man has apologised to us, and we demand an insult!' The twins in William Golding's *Lord of the Flies* are so alike that no one can tell them apart, and they gradually collide in both name and flesh, becoming 'Samneric'. The red-haired Weasley twins in *Harry Potter* work so well as a double-act when they're playing their practical jokes that their tragic separation towards the end of the seventh book haunts each new generation. But what if the twins you know tire of their tedious similarities – or fail to live up to the expectation that they will think and act as one?

For twins with this issue, we prescribe *The Parent Trap** – a story that has become well known since the Hollywood film. Two nine-year-old girls arrive at summer camp to find, to their mutual horror, that they have a doppelgänger in each other. Luise's friends sympathise with her dismay. 'What a nerve, turning up here with your face!' they mutter about Lottie. But when the girls discover that they were born on the same day and in the same town, and that one lives with her mother and one with her father, they are forced to admit the obvious.

The emotions that follow are mixed: anger at being misled by their respective parents, and curiosity about the parent they don't yet know – and with this fuelling their motivation, they pull off one of the best identity heists in fiction. Luise, going back to Lottie's house, has to learn how to cook and clean and buy groceries for the newspaper-editor mother she has never met; and Lottie must learn to talk about French and music and stay out of the way of her composer father. It's not, of course, plain sailing for either of them, and their plan to get their parents to meet and marry each other again hits an unexpected obstacle when their father reveals his engagement to the slim and elegant Irene. But as they learn to impersonate each other with increasing success and are both beset by powerful dreams in which they are separated, cut in half and put back together again – with one half Luise and the other Lottie – their identities start to merge. By the time their parents have sussed the hoax, the girls are almost as bewildered as they are. 'I am both!' they each cry, when asked which one they are. We won't give away the ending, but we

---

* Originally published as *Lottie and Lisa*.

will say that Kästner, unlike his Hollywood counterpart, doesn't go in for cheesiness . . . Twins who have lost sight of their mutual connection will be struck by the freshness of Lottie and Luise's discovery of how life makes more sense when two halves of a whole are joined up.

twin, wanting to be a

SEE: **loneliness**

two, being a terrible

SEE: **beastly, being** • **bed, not wanting to go to** • **over-tired, being** • **questions, asking too many** • **tantrums**

umbrage, taking

The Miraculous Journey of Edward Tulane
KATE DICAMILLO, ILLUSTRATED BY BAGRAM IBATOULLINE

A child's rightful place is at the centre of the universe, basking in adoration. Right? Of course; but if that child is so convinced of their own importance that they take umbrage at the slightest thing their grown-up minions get wrong, you'll want to bring in *The Miraculous Journey of Edward Tulane*. A child who takes umbrage too easily may know that they're loved, but not know how to love in return.

Edward Tulane, a china rabbit with a real fur tail, jointed limbs and large, expressive ears, is the prize possession of ten-year-old Abilene. She loves him so much that she changes his outfit each day, and he gets his own place at the table. There's only one person who thinks more highly of Edward than Abilene does – and that's Edward himself.

During a transatlantic voyage on the *Queen Mary*, Edward (dressed, by the way, in a handsome straw boater and with a silk scarf billowing in the wind) is accidentally knocked overboard and sinks to the bottom of the ocean while the ocean liner sails blithely on. He can't believe that something so appalling could have happened to someone as fine as him. Face-down in the muck of the seabed, he experiences his first genuine emotion. What if Abilene doesn't come for him . . .? This calamity turns out to be only the first of many humiliating adventures – in the course of which the rabbit discovers, at last, how to feel gratitude and love. Once his china heart has been broken and put back together several times, he turns into the sort of rabbit worth having – one who can allow a small misdemeanour to be shrugged off in the light of the greater bond.

SEE ALSO: **feelings, hurt** • **forgive, reluctance to** • **spoilt, being** • **sulking**

underachiever, being an

SEE: **good at anything, feeling like you're no**

understood, not being

[PB] *Slow Loris*
ALEXIS DEACON

[CB] *Miss Happiness and Miss Flower*
RUMER GODDEN

For babies, the problem is a literal one. By the time their grown-ups have learnt to decipher their wails, burbles and exclamations,* the exasperated infant has given up and switched to using language instead. But of course the problem still doesn't go away. A child can know all the words in the *OED* and still fail to get their feelings across.

A child who feels misunderstood will find great solace in Alexis Deacon's story of a slow loris who takes ten minutes to eat a satsuma, and a whole hour to scratch his bottom. Not surprisingly, visitors to the zoo conclude that he's slow and boring – as do all the other animals – and don't spend very long at his cage.

But Slow Loris isn't boring – and he isn't slow. Every night, when no one's looking, his real self comes out to play – and oh, does he know how to play! Deacon's beautiful watercolour illustrations of the little creature, with his bottomless black eyes and stealthy, sinuous body, manage to capture both his night-time hyperactivity and his daytime lethargy with the subtlest of angle shifts. The lovely thing about this story is that Slow Loris doesn't care that he's so fundamentally misunderstood – at least for now. In a way, it gives him the chance to get on with being himself. This story will encourage your misunderstood child to do likewise while you work a little harder to suss them out.

Older children will take comfort from the story of eight-year-old Nona in *Miss Happiness and Miss Flower*. When the dark-haired, pale-skinned Nona is sent from her home in India to live with her ruddy-cheeked, fair-headed cousins in England, everything feels strange and different. It's terribly cold for a start, and Nona doesn't like the porridge, or the puddings, or the sausages. She has never ridden a bicycle before, nor roller-skated, nor played ping-pong, or hide and seek, or even Snap – for which her cousins think *she's* strange.

---

* Unless they're Sunny, the baby in *A Series of Unfortunate Events*, whose one-word utterances are deciphered with ease by her older siblings (and her author, Lemony Snicket). When she says the word 'Bax!', for instance, what she is trying to say, according to her sister Violet, is 'I'm nervous about meeting a new relative.' If only all babies had siblings like hers.

When two Japanese dolls arrive from a distant aunt, Nona immediately sees that they, too, aren't understood here – especially by cousin Belinda, who shoves them roughly into her already crammed-full doll's house. With their beautiful kimonos and ability to bow at the waist, Nona can see that Miss Happiness and Miss Flower need cushions instead of chairs, chopsticks instead of spoons, quilts they can roll out on the floor, and a clean, uncluttered house – and she makes it her mission to create for them just such a place.

The story of how she does this takes up the bulk of the book, and there are even footnotes taking us to working architectural plans at the back and a glossary of Japanese terms. Gradually the other children start to appreciate what she's doing – and through Nona's understanding of Miss Happiness and Miss Flower they see how they might understand Nona too. A quiet, unusual story with a Zen calm emanating from the architectural project at its heart, this book will encourage misunderstood children not to try to become like everyone else but to find a way to show others who they are.

CURE FOR GROWN-UPS CB *Finn Family Moomintroll* **TOVE JANSSON**

Some people feel misunderstood all their lives. One such is Moominpappa in *Finn Family Moomintroll.* So tragic do his memories of childhood seem to him now, and so misunderstood did he always feel, that the father troll's efforts to write his memoirs are constantly thwarted by his tendency to burst into tears. These feelings have followed him into adulthood, where he has 'had a frightful time in every way' – although one would never know it, given the idyllic existence he shares with his adoring wife Moominmamma and their delightful son, Moomintroll. Moominpappa spends a lot of time imagining how sorry everyone will be when they read his story and understand how much he has suffered at last. Grown-ups will see that it's often best to focus on understanding others* rather than trying to make others understand you – which generally has the happy circular effect of making you understood in return.

SEE ALSO: **adolescence • baby, being a • deafness • different, feeling • feelings, not able to express your • heard, not feeling • language, having to learn another • parents who can't talk about emotions, having • speech impediment • stand up for yourself, not feeling able to**

* As does Moominpappa's dear missus, Moominmamma.

unfairness

SEE: **fair, it's not**

unfriendliness

[PB] *Beegu*
ALEXIS DEACON

[CB] *Bridge to Terabithia*
KATHERINE PATERSON

If you're in the habit of greeting others with a grin and an upbeat opening gambit, the kids in your orbit won't need this cure. But if you're the type that hangs back, sussing out a new person from the sidelines before extending a welcoming hand, you may want to stock up on some stories which model the art of being friendly better than you do. *Beegu* never fails to make a child want to be friendly. The sole survivor of a space-craft crash on planet Earth, Beegu – an appealing, yellow rabbitty creature with long, expressive ears and three eyes – is met with blank stares from the two-eyed rabbits she meets, and though she stretches out one of her soft, tentative ears to a passer-by with a briefcase, he doesn't even grace her with a glance. Eventually she finds a playground full of children who are eager to include her in their games – and her long, flexible ears prove adept at spinning a hoop. But then an unfriendly grown-up steps in and warns the children away (see: outsiders, distrust of) . . .

Luckily Beegu is whisked off this unfriendly planet by her own kind in the end – and we're thrilled to see her being hugged by two bigger three-eyed rabbitty creatures in the rescue spaceship. But as she looks back at the shrinking orb of Earth, she remembers 'those small ones' who were nice to her. Painted in tasteful sepia shades, with poppy-red and turquoise-blue highlights, this picture book shows friendliness as a quality which, with a bit of encouragement, comes very naturally to kids.

Being brave enough to befriend the unpopular kid gets harder as children get older, and when ten-year-old Jesse Aarons befriends his new neighbour in *Bridge to Terabithia*, we are aware of the risk to his status he's taking. Already known as the 'sensitive' boy who likes drawing, Jesse has been practising sprinting all summer in the hope of winning the favour of his peers. So when new girl Leslie moves in to the next-door farm – and then, to his alarm, pitches up in his class too – Jesse does his best to ignore her. She's wearing the wrong sort of clothes for the first day of term (faded cut-off jeans and trainers without socks in a place where everyone wears their stiff Sunday best) and she doesn't even seem to care. On the school bus, Jesse plants his little sister May Belle on the seat beside him to make sure Leslie can't sit there. But one day, swept up in the joy of singing with his favourite teacher, Miss Edmunds, Jesse's eyes meet Leslie's. 'What the heck?' he thinks, and smiles. And from that moment on, the two are inseparable, inventing their own secret land of 'Terabithia' in the woods next to Jesse's house – a land where the bullies from school can't find them.

Tragedy intervenes all too soon: be warned, this story has a kick. But Jesse knows that he would never have discovered his 'other, more exciting self' if it hadn't been for the friend he risked his fragile reputation to make. Kids will see that sticking your neck out to be friendly is not only the right thing to do but is likely to make life more fun.

SEE ALSO: **bossiness** • **bullied, being** • **bully, being a** • **friends, feeling that you have no** • **friends, finding it hard to make**

unhappiness

SEE: **sadness**

unwell parent, having an

PB *Brave Irene*
WILLIAM STEIG

It goes against the natural order of things for a young child to have to look after a sick grown-up; but sometimes there's nothing anyone can do to avoid it. William Steig – never one to shy away from dropping characters into desperate situations – offers a refreshing take on the subject in *Brave Irene*. Irene's seamstress mother is too unwell to take the gown she's been stitching to the duchess, even though the ball is to be held that very night; so her valiant daughter Irene offers to deliver it instead. Taking her mother tea and tucking her up in bed before she goes, Irene sets off just as it begins to snow.

Soon poor Irene, with her big, cumbersome box, is caught in a violent snowstorm. Steig's uninhibited pen-and-wash illustrations show Irene's body being buffeted one way then the other as a blizzard of fat, white flakes blows from the left and then the right. Things go from bad to worse when the box is whipped from her hands, and the gown itself hoisted aloft, the delicate fabric spreading out its arms in a flutter of pink and grey. She then twists her ankle, loses her way, and starts to turn grey in the face. At one point she even ends up buried in a snowdrift, with only her hands and the top of her hat peeking out.

Somehow, Steig manages to stop himself sending poor Irene to an early grave – and things turn out OK in the end. But the shocked child to whom you read this book will see that, compared to Irene's act of heroism, being a tiny bit nice to an unwell grown-up – perhaps even reading them a nourishing story or two (see: cheering up, needing) – might not be too much to ask, after all.

SEE ALSO: **chores, having to do • depressed parent, having a**

useless, feeling

SEE: **good at anything, feeling like you're no**

V IS FOR . . .

vampires, obsessed by

SEE: **obsessions**

vegetables, fear of

SEE: **fussy eater, being a**

violence

[YA] *The Knife That Killed Me*
ANTHONY MCGOWAN

[PB] *The Story of Ferdinand*
MUNRO LEAF, ILLUSTRATED BY ROBERT LAWSON

We all hope that the children we know will never see a real knife or gun being used with the intention of causing harm. At the same time, it's helpful to understand the causes and effects of violence – and to think with our children about ways to deal with and help dissipate violence should they ever encounter it. Fiction is an ideal way to explore the issue, and there are many excellent delvings into the mindset behind violence to be found – from Dickens' Bill Sykes in *Oliver Twist* to the agitating teens in Catherine Bruton's edgy *I Predict a Riot*. Some of the most thought-provoking YA novels featuring weapons focus on how what starts as a playground skirmish can rapidly escalate into something far more serious, conveying the message that the sensible thing to do is to steer clear of weapons altogether. One of the most powerful and effective such novels is the artery-sapping *The Knife That Killed Me*.

It opens with a meditation on what the titular knife *ought* to look like:

inscribed with ancient runes, imbued with magical power, and handed down from generation to generation. The reality, of course, is that it's a cheap knife from Woolworth's with a blade that 'wobbled like a loose tooth' in its handle. When the action begins, the knife is poised to fatally stab our narrator, Paul – but we are held suspended in a Zeno's paradox-inspired moment for the duration of the story, in which Paul anticipates the cut of the blade and his subsequent death while taking us back to the events that led to this point.

The story is a familiar one: school kids divided into factions (bullies and geeks); teachers failing to keep control; parents too far in the background. Neither a bully nor a geek, Paul is attracted to the 'freaks' who hover on the edge of the playground, ignored by the malevolent gang led by Roth, but also shunned by everyone else. He is bright but undirected, and when he's inadvertently involved in the delivery of a parcelled-up dog's head – belonging to the beloved pet of the leader of the gang at their rival school, the Templars – and receives a knife in return, we know he's in trouble. We watch with mounting sorrow as Paul turns his back on more sensible paths. The final twist – one that cuts deep for the reader and kills any last glimmers of glory they may have seen in the fight – is unforgettable. This clever, hard-hitting novel makes a potent case to teens of both genders for avoiding all contact with violence from the moment they turn the last page.

Instil a preference for pacifism with children of all ages with the iconic *Ferdinand*. Ferdinand the bull doesn't ask much from life. While his brothers and sisters prance and preen, butt and challenge, Ferdinand is perfectly content sitting in the shade of a cork tree, inhaling the summer breeze and the scent of flowers. When, one day, 'five men in funny hats' come to their field to collect the fiercest bull, Ferdinand knows it won't be him. But just at that moment he's stung on his rump by a bee. Seeing him butt and paw and leap with pain, the five men are thrilled. The next thing he knows, he's being carted off to Madrid for the biggest bullfight of the year.

Of course, once in the flower-bedecked arena, packed with spectators, all Ferdinand wants to do is stand and sniff the perfumed air. The proud, moustachioed matador resplendent with cape and sword, is unable to get so much as a twitch out of him. Soon the humans are the ones stamping in fury. In the face of their bloodlust, Ferdinand's unwavering stance brings kids a clear and resounding message: nobody can force you to be violent if you don't want to be. Encourage kids to remember Ferdinand and stand firm on the side of peace.

SEE ALSO: **abuse** • **bullied, being** • **bully, being a** • **gang, being in a** • **pornography** • **stand up for yourself, not feeling able to** • **trauma** • **war, worrying about**

virginity, loss of

[YA] *Lobsters*
TOM ELLEN AND LUCY IVISON

Some young adults are happy to take the arrival of sex in their lives whensoever it comes. Others feel pressured to find a consenting partner at the same time as their peers, if only so that they can say they've done it. Hannah is somewhere in between. 'I just need to get sex over with so I can get on with living my life,' the eighteen-year-old says at the start of this heart-warming story about a pair of heterosexual teens going through this ultimate rite of passage. *Lobsters* is an excellent companion piece for teens to whom the issue is a current concern.

It's the summer of waiting for A-level results and before heading off to university, and Hannah has decided that tonight, at Stella's party, is the night. The boy she's earmarked for the job is Freddie – who is not her 'lobster', a term coined by Hannah and her friends, believing that lobsters mate for life,* but handsome and popular and perfectly adequate. Meanwhile Sam, also eighteen, is preoccupied by whether he'll get into Cambridge; but he feels it's not helping his self-esteem to still be a virgin, and he wants to reinvent himself – perhaps as a Samuel, like Beckett or Samuel L Jackson. 'You won't find many virgins called Samuel, that's for sure,' he thinks. When he meets Hannah outside the aubergine-coloured bathroom at Stella's party, and finds himself engaged in a surreal but hilarious conversation, he's shaken by the intensity of their connection. They share, they discover, a love of hot Ribena – and have a great time giggling at their fellow revellers down in the garden fumbling the social kissing routine (once on each cheek, or twice?). When Freddie finally turns up, drunk and entertaining the notion that the proposed deflowering take place on the trampoline, Hannah realises she's no longer very keen on the idea – or, for that matter, him. Freddie then seals the deal by puking up all over her in the kitchen.

It's clear from the bathroom conversation onwards that Hannah and Sam are each other's 'lobsters', but pride and the complex negotiations of friendship prevent them from getting together until the end of the novel – which makes this a highly satisfying romantic comedy. Stella proves an excellent foil to Hannah and Sam's mutual naivety and generosity of spirit, conniving and engineering in the background while our two innocents step around each other delicately. The hotly anticipated moment is – at first – a failure. 'I know for a fact that his willy will not fit in,' Hannah tells us, and: 'Maybe we will break up because I have a thimble fanny.' But Sam is quite delighted by the words, 'It's too big. I'm sorry.'

---

* An erroneous assumption, as it turns out. Male lobsters are in hot demand on the seabed and queues sometimes form for their services. But we digress.

And when they try again later, it works. It's not a blast of angels' trumpets, or a cascade of pure joy, but they feel completely comfortable with each other, and Sam happily goes off to make them both hot Ribena in the morning.

Written from the alternating points of view of both Hannah and Sam, the actual dual authorship of the novel gives the book a remarkable sense of authenticity. The treatment of teen sex in all its awkward, bumbling reality, with plenty of humour thrown in, is hugely welcome – as is the touching romantic love they share. *Lobsters* shows that losing your virginity is not necessarily the heavenly moment it's cracked up to be, but it's also not something to feel anxious about – especially if experienced with someone you really like.

SEE ALSO: **adolescence • first kiss • first love • gay, not sure if you are • masturbation, embarrassment about • peer pressure • pregnancy, teenage • sex, having questions about • transgender, feeling you are • wet dreams**

visual impairment

Reading aloud, playing audiobooks and sharing books with highly contrasting images are all important for visually impaired and blind children – as are books featuring other people who depend on touch and sound over sight. For infants, see also our list of The Ten Best Touchy-Feely Books (p.28).

THE TEN BEST BOOKS FOR VISUALLY IMPAIRED AND BLIND KIDS

- PB *Dan and Diesel* CHARLOTTE HUDSON, ILLUSTRATED BY LINDSEY GARDINER
- PB *The Snow Tree* CAROLINE REPCHUK, ILLUSTRATED BY JOSEPHINE MARTIN
- PB *The Blind Hunter* KRISTINA RODANAS
- PB *Andy Warhol's Colors* SUSAN GOLDMAN RUBIN
- PB *Mole's Sunrise* JEANNE WILLIS, ILLUSTRATED BY SARAH FOX-DAVIES
- PB *The Seeing Stick* JANE YOLEN, ILLUSTRATED BY DANIELA JAGLENKA TERRAZZINI
- CB *Peter Nimble and His Fantastic Eyes* JONATHAN AUXIER
- YA *Blind Spot* LAURA ELLEN
- YA *The Heart of Applebutter Hill* DONNA W HILL*
- YA *She Is Not Invisible* MARCUS SEDGWICK†

SEE ALSO: **bullied, being • different, feeling • disability, coping with • glasses, having to wear**

---

* Available also in Braille, DAISY and audio versions.

† Available also in Braille, DAISY and audio, read from Braille by Anna Cannings.

W IS FOR . . .

walk, not wanting to go on a

[PB] *Owl Moon*
JANE YOLEN, ILLUSTRATED BY JOHN SCHOENHERR

[CB] *The Incredible Journey*
SHEILA BURNFORD

[CB] *From the Mixed-up Files of Mrs Basil E Frankweiler*
EL KONIGSBURG

Trying to muster enthusiasm among kids for a walk is the bane of many an energetic, fresh-air-loving grown-up's existence. Even once you've managed to get them out the house with their wellies on, you still have to keep them pepped up and moving, diverting and deflecting the complaints as best you can. Inject some mystery into the experience by initiating walks at unusual times of day or night – as modelled so beautifully in *Owl Moon*, a sensual picture book about a father and a child going 'owling'. The child narrator (of indeterminate gender) and his or her pa, bundled up in hats and scarves, set off into the snow-bound landscape 'long past' bedtime – and the strange quality of the moonlit night makes for an immediately heightened event: 'There was no wind. The trees stood still as giant statues.' In Schoenherr's pen-and-wash illustrations, we see the father and child's shadows stretching over the snow behind them. Ears sharpened, they hear the crunch of the snow underfoot, the whistle of a faraway train, 'long and low,/like a sad, sad song' – and a couple of farm dogs giving each other answering barks. Soon the woods rise up tall and dark, and in they go, Pa holding up a hand every now and then for silence. When the father tilts his face up and makes a 'Whoo-whoo-who-who-who-whooooooo' between cupped hands – the call of the Great Horned Owl – there is no answer at first. 'I was not disappointed,' the child is quick to tell us. 'My brothers all said/sometimes there's an owl/and sometimes there isn't' – revealing how this special walk has been anticipated and discussed in advance. The moment an owl does appear, lifting itself off a branch to reveal itself as a separate thing, will take everyone's breath away. Use this book to inspire and generate a similar sense of occasion around the special walks you like to do, and you'll begin to make walks appealing.

To give kids a sense of what is a long way and what is really not a long way at all, share a blast from the past with *The Incredible Journey*. Three household pets – a Labrador named Luath, an old bull terrier named Bodger, and a Siamese cat named Tao – are left with a family friend when their owners go on a trip to England. But when the friend himself disappears on a fishing expedition, Luath decides to try and make it back home on foot – and the other two follow. Heading west by instinct, their journey takes them through woods, across rivers and around the lakes of north-west Ontario, and they have to fight off bears and lynxes as well as find food, often working as a team. They've covered 400km by the time they're reunited with their owners again. Getting everyone familiar with this story will help you recruit your brood to different roles on a family walk – one to map-read, one to hand out the provisions, one to befriend the passers-by.* And if they dare complain about the distance, you'll be able to remind them what a long journey is.

For those attempting to explore a city on foot with kids, we prescribe *From the Mixed-up Files of Mrs Basil E Frankweiler*. When eleven-year-old Claudia and her younger brother Jamie decide to run away to the Metropolitan Museum of Art in New York, it's not through any unhappiness but rather to have an adventure (see: adventure, needing an). While they successfully hide out in the museum for a week, sleeping in a 16th-century canopy bed, Jamie's job is to keep control of their purse strings and, a natural miser, he insists they walk instead of taking a bus or taxi whenever they need to go to the laundrette or find something to eat. And so they schlep many blocks in each direction and get to know the surrounding streets pretty well.

They notice all sorts of interesting things on these walks, from skaters in Central Park to a forgotten copy of the *New York Times* in which they read about the Met's intriguing statue known as 'Angel'. Most importantly, they spot a typewriter bolted to a stand outside the Olivetti building, and use it to type a letter alerting the museum's director to the statue's provenance. Had the children not walked, they wouldn't have seen the typewriter and written the letter – or, eventually, met Mrs Basil E Frankweiler, the linchpin to their adventure. Reading this paean to the joys of pounding the streets of a city full of treasures will convince reluctant walkers that the best adventures are the ones you find on foot.

SEE ALSO: **indoors, spending too much time • laziness**

---

* If you only have one child in tow, give them all the roles at once.

war, worrying about

Just as the Cold War hung over our childhoods, the threat of random terrorist attacks and a Third World War looms over children today. Ensure a child is not left alone with their fears by exploring why wars break out, how they might end, and why resolving conflicts through negotiation will always be better than fighting.

THE TEN BEST BOOKS TO HELP CHILDREN UNDERSTAND WAR

- PB *The Enemy* DAVIDE CALI, ILLUSTRATED BY SERGE BLOCH
- PB *Where the Poppies Now Grow* HILARY ROBINSON, ILLUSTRATED BY MARTIN IMPEY
- CB *The Summer of My German Soldier* BETTE GREENE
- CB *Number the Stars* LOIS LOWRY
- ER *War Horse* MICHAEL MORPURGO
- CB *Five Children on the Western Front* KATE SAUNDERS
- CB *My Name's Not Friday* JON WALTER
- YA *The Ask and the Answer* and *Monsters of Men* (Chaos Walking) PATRICK NESS
- YA *The Complete Maus* ART SPIEGELMAN
- YA *The Book Thief* MARKUS ZUSAK

SEE ALSO: **anxiety** • **planet, fearing for the future of the** • **trauma** • **violence** • **worrying**

wash, reluctant to

SEE: **bath, not wanting to have a** • **body odour** • **hands, not wanting to wash your**

washing up, having to do the

SEE: **chores, having to do**

watch the film first, wanting to

INSIST ON THE BOOK-FIRST RULE

Take a hard line. They read the book first, and then – and only then – do they get to watch the film. When they do, make it a movie night with the full works – popcorn (salty *and* sweet), hot chocolate (with squirty cream, sprinkles and marshmallows on top), and friends to watch it with.* Evidence that they've read the whole book (in the form of answering random questions about the characters/events in the story) must be provided to gain entrance.†

If it goes on till late, see: sleepovers.

werewolves, obsessed by

SEE: **obsessions**

wet dreams

Then Again, Maybe I Won't
JUDY BLUME

Ejaculations during sleep occur in many boys when puberty begins‡ (sometimes as early as nine), leaving surprising stains in the morning. For boys waking to this intriguing but potentially embarrassing phenomenon for the first time, Judy Blume offers reassurance and some practical advice.

When thirteen-year-old Tony Miglione in *Then Again, Maybe I Won't* moves to a new neighbourhood with his family, he finds himself living next door to the overly well-mannered Joe. But Joe has a swimming pool in his backyard – and, Tony soon discovers, an older sister, Lisa, with 'curves all over', which makes his neighbour a much more interesting prospect. Tony finds himself

* Only those who have read the book first, too, of course.

† For which you'll have to read the book yourself.

‡ Girls can also experience orgasms in dreams as they enter puberty. We encourage grown-ups to give this book to girls too, both for helping to understand the phenomenon, and so that they can know about what might be going on in the heads – and other parts – of boys.

having to deal with hard-ons at awkward moments: when reading his brother's racy paperbacks while at home with his family, and in front of his entire maths class (he just about conceals it with a book). When he wakes up to find his sheets wet for the first time, he worries that there's something wrong with him. But he soon realises it's perfectly natural, his gym teacher having told him about 'nocturnal emissions', and his concern switches to how to deal with the sheets, given that he doesn't want to discuss them with his family.* When he discovers he can see Lisa undressing from his bedroom window, the wet dreams occur more often and, not one to turn down such an opportunity, he persuades his parents to get him a pair of binoculars – purportedly for bird-watching . . . Effectively a boy's equivalent of Blume's *Are You There, God? It's Me, Margaret,* Tony's frank first-person narrative is perfect for quelling anxieties about wet dreams – how they happen, what causes them and how to side-step embarrassment. Leave it by the bedside of boys when it all begins.

SEE ALSO: **adolescence** • **anxiety** • **gay, not sure if you are** • **masturbation**

why, wanting to know

SEE: **questions, asking too many**

witches, fear of

[PB] *Meg and Mog*
HELEN NICOLL, ILLUSTRATED BY JAN PIEŃKOWSKI

[ER] *The Worst Witch*
JILL MURPHY

Children scared of witches need to befriend a couple who show their human side. What better place to start than Meg, the witch brought to life by Helen Nicoll and the blocks of colour and strong black lines of Jan Pieńkowski in the Meg and Mog books. The first in this series shows Meg waking at midnight and looking suitably harmless and bedraggled in her white nightie. Gradually, she puts herself together out of her constituent witchy parts – black stockings, big black shoes, long black cloak and tall black hat. So far, so unthreatening. The fact that she treads on poor Mog's tail as she goes downstairs, and throws a delightfully weird combination of ingredients into her breakfast cauldron (three eggs, bread, cocoa, jam and a kipper) makes

* He stuffs them into his laundry basket along with a wet flannel to make everything else seem damp, too. Way to go!

her approachable, too. Off she goes on her broomstick to meet her friends and cast a witchy spell on top of a hill where – oops! – she accidentally turns her friends into something unexpected . . . It's hard to be frightened of someone as bad at being a witch as this.

Move on at early-reader stage to Mildred Hubble in the Worst Witch series. A trainee at Miss Cackle's Academy for Witches, Mildred has much in common with Meg. She is so bad at steering her broomstick and casting spells that she's under constant threat of being expelled; and her tabby cat resolutely resists sitting on her broom. Instead Mildred is forced to carry the animal around in a bag, much to her teachers' distress. Each of the six books in the series takes place during the course of a school term and, in every one, Mildred gets into a succession of scrapes, aided and abetted by her friends Enid and Maud. Murphy's exuberant, schoolgirlish humour is infectious; and her drawings of the feisty witches in their splendidly ungirly uniform (hob-nailed boots, gym slips with ties, as well as the regulation witches' hats and cloaks) are guaranteed to dispel any lingering fears.

SEE ALSO: **bed, fear of what's under the • nightmares • sleep, unable to get to**

words, fascination with naughty

SEE: **swearing**

worrying

ER *Wilf the Mighty Worrier Saves the World*
GEORGIA PRITCHETT, ILLUSTRATED BY JAMIE LITTLER

CB *Comet in Moominland*
TOVE JANSSON

YA *The 10pm Question*
KATE DE GOLDI

As many of us take a lifetime to learn, the best way to stop fretting about something is to turn and face that thing head on. This, however, is easier said than done. In her delightful series that begins with *Wilf the Mighty Worrier Saves the World* (a pun all children will enjoy), Georgia Pritchett gives us a character that manages to face his fears despite being a bigger worrier than most.

Wilf worries about a lot of things, and keeps a running list. Some of them are things a lot of people worry about: creepy-crawlies with lots of legs, for example, and elevators. But some of them are more surprising – like stuffed animals, and peanut butter getting stuck to the roof his mouth. Wilf has a system for how to stop worrying which involves drawing his worst-case scenario, then preparing an action plan for what he'd do if it should occur.

He's not particularly worried when a man named Alan moves in next door and admits to being an evil lunatic out to destroy the world. But when Wilf and his baby sister, Dot, go down to Alan's evil lair and discover Mark III, the robot Alan built to obey his every command*– plus Alan's 'Big Gun Thingy' and his miraculous flying machine – Wilf has the urge to crawl under something, have a 'big old worry', and knit. But instead, Wilf draws his worst-case scenarios, comes up with various action plans and, with Dot on his shoulders and his trusty pet woodlouse, Stuart, in his pocket – plus a few extra gadgets of his own – plunges straight towards them. When he finds he's come through unscathed – and saved the world in the process – he realises they're not worries any more. Full of perfectly pitched, age-appropriate humour and lovely scratchy illustrations by Jamie Littler, Wilf is fictional proof that confronting one's fears really works.

Worriers will find blissful respite in the pools of calm, wit and wonder that are the Moomin books by Tove Jansson. In *Comet in Moominland*, there's an unseasonal chill to the air; and when the inhabitants of Moominvalley find pearls on the forest floor arranged into the shape of a star with a tail, a sense of unease sets in. Only the Muskrat is clever enough to know what these portents mean – but, being convinced of the meaningless of everything, he doesn't care. Sniff, the Snork Maiden and the Hemulen are all worried, but Moomintroll retains the presence of mind to try to find out more, taking Sniff with him to the Observatory in the high mountains where the professors observe the sky.

After several adventures and some hazardous climbs, they discover that a comet will land in Moominvalley at precisely 8.42pm on 7 October or 'Possibly four seconds later'. Moomintroll realises he must get home as quickly as possible, and though he begins to worry about all the things he loves that will be lost if the comet destroys their valley – 'the forest and the sea, the rain and the wind, the sunshine, the grass and the moss' – he stops worrying after a while because 'Mamma will know what to do.'† Keep the whole set of Moomin books to hand for reassurance whenever worry levels run high.

Teens will find a similarly reassuring mother figure in *The 10pm Question* – albeit one with issues. Frankie's ma runs a successful cake-making business from home. But she also, for reasons of her own, refuses to *leave* that home.

* Except that it doesn't, because it's got the mindset of a teenager.

† Which is true: she does. This is in fact true of Moominmamma in all the Moomin books, whether she's facing a flood or flattened cakes.

This leaves twelve-year-old Frankie to do the grocery shopping and deliver the cakes himself. As if this wasn't burden enough, Frankie's head spins with worries about earthquakes, bird flu and his own mental health as he lies in bed at night. And so, at 10pm, he visits Ma to get the worries off his chest.

Ma always takes his worries seriously – even when it's whether the rash on his chest means he has a 'galloping cancer' – and always has something helpful to offer. But it's only when he meets Sydney, the dreadlocked new girl at school, that he can talk about the biggest worry of all. His worries feel less significant when he's around Sydney – partly because she's so fearless, partly because she's so accepting of 'sad endings', and partly because her own mother is something of a fruitcake, too. But what will he do if Sydney moves away? Will he have to ask his own mother the ultimate 10pm question?

It's impossible not to fall in love with Frankie; and though young readers will sense that things will never be completely straightforward for this boy, they'll see that his ma is determined to help him succeed in the world, even though it's a place she no longer goes. Along with Frankie, inveterate worriers will pick up some new worry-shifting tricks to add to their armoury.

CURE FOR GROWN-UPS: *Pollyanna* ELEANOR H PORTER

The second-best way is to talk yourself into believing your worries are not, in fact, worries at all. For this, we prescribe *Pollyanna*. When the eleven-year-old Pollyanna and her father open a charity box in which they had hoped to find a doll but instead find a pair of crutches her father refuses to let it disappoint his daughter. 'Why, just be glad because you don't – need – 'em!' is his delightful response. And so the 'glad game' is born.

Shortly afterwards Pollyanna's father dies, and it's much harder to turn negatives into positives. But Pollyanna valiantly tries nonetheless. She can try to be glad, perhaps, that her father is now with her mother and the angels, for instance. And when Pollyanna goes to live with her aunt Polly, who puts her in a room at the top of the house so that she'll hardly see her, Pollyanna decides to be glad of the view. When Aunt Polly punishes her by giving her bread and milk in the kitchen with Nancy, the maid, she's glad because Nancy is nice. When she manages to engineer the revitalisation of her aunt's love affair with Doctor Chilton, Aunt Polly sees the point of the glad game at last – and enters into the spirit. The philosophy may seem a little strained these days, but we predict you'll be playing the game on your worries by the end, too.

SEE ALSO: **anxiety • confidence, lack of • small, feeling • stand up for yourself, not feeling able to**

wrong, everything's going

[PB] *Alexander and the Terrible, Horrible, No Good, Very Bad Day*
JUDITH VIORST, ILLUSTRATED BY RAY CRUZ

[YA] *Seconds*
BRYAN LEE O'MALLEY

Sometimes when one thing goes wrong, everything starts going wrong, and bedtime is the only sure way to halt the disaster domino-effect. Children prone to days like these will take comfort from meeting Judith Viorst's mop-haired Alexander, whose bad day tops all bad days.

It all starts going wrong for Alexander when he wakes up in the morning to find chewing gum stuck in his hair. Then he trips over his skateboard, drops his sweater under the tap and can't find a free toy in his cereal box, even though there's one for both his brothers in theirs. In the car to school, everyone else gets a window seat but him. Soon Alexander starts to feel as if the world has it in for him. As in real life, there's no happy ending to this day – and Ray Cruz's black-and-white illustrations show Alexander experiencing various types of distress, from frustration and fury to the miserable realisation that life's unfair (see: fair, it's not). As Mum says at the end, some days are 'just like that', but tomorrow will bring a whole fresh start. Any child struggling to maintain their composure at the end of a difficult day will feel less alone for this story.

If, as a child becomes a teen, the feeling that everything always goes wrong starts to occur with regularity, they may need encouragement to examine why it might be happening. The attractive but difficult Katie in the surreal graphic novel *Seconds* has always been a go-getting type, with her clumpy boots and cute, figure-hugging jeans. At twenty-nine, she's got her own restaurant, Seconds, which she started four years ago with some friends, and she has a second restaurant in development. She loves to cook and knows her food is the best in town. But her friends have since moved on – including Max, her handsome, stubbled boyfriend – and the renovations on the new building are taking too long and draining her finances too quickly. When Max shows up at Seconds with a lovely new girl at his side and Hazel, the awkward new waitress, spills hot oil on her arms, Katie's fragile composure starts to crack.

This is when she remembers the creepy 'house spirit' she encountered in her dream, hunched on the dresser in a black furry coat and offering her a 'second chance'. In the dresser drawer Katie finds a box containing a mushroom – and a list of instructions. '1: Write your mistake. 2: Ingest one mushroom. 3. Go to sleep. 4. Wake anew.' With nothing to lose, she tries it, throwing the little red-and-white mushroom down her throat – and, to her amazement, she finds herself sitting down to a meal with her stubbled boyfriend – and, it seems, they are still going out. She can hardly believe her luck.

Even with the second chances Katie messes up again – and, as reality becomes increasingly confusing (for her as well as us), she starts to look at herself in a more critical light. Eventually she realises it's not so much events that need to change, but her. With its pacy frames and complex kaleidoscope of stories-within-stories, this is a wonderfully original wake-up call for accepting that the buck, in the end, stops with you. Read it alongside your teen and discuss.

SEE ALSO: **confidence, lack of • good at anything, feeling like you're no • loser, feeling like a • mistake, frightened of making a**

WRONG, EVERYTHING'S GOING

X-rated films, wanting to watch

Offer up some risqué fiction instead. Books offer a safe space in which to explore sex, drugs and the darker side of life.

THE TEN BEST RISQUÉ BOOKS

- YA *Sydney Bridge Upside Down* DAVID BALLANTYNE
- YA *Candy* KEVIN BROOKS
- YA *I Predict a Riot* CATHERINE BRUTON
- YA *The Accident Season* MOÏRA FOWLEY-DOYLE
- YA *Rumble Fish* SE HINTON
- YA *Ugly Girls* LINDSAY HUNTER
- YA *The Summer Prince* ALAYA DAWN JOHNSON
- YA *The Spectacular Now* TIM THARP
- YA *Maresi* (The Red Abbey Chronicles) MARIA TURTSCHANINOFF
- YA *Liccle Bit* ALEX WHEATLE

SEE ALSO: **peer pressure** • **pornography**

young, impatient with being

SEE: **frustration • grow up, impatient to**

youngest, being the

SEE: **grow up, impatient to • heard, not feeling • sibling rivalry • spoilt, being**

Z IS FOR . . .

zits

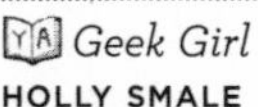

Geek Girl
HOLLY SMALE

Lucky is the adolescent who never has to contend with a spot. They always erupt at the worst possible moment; and no amount of fussing with exfoliants, creams or cover-ups will make them disappear. Next time the teen in your household complains of a blemish, give them *Geek Girl*. Few have been worse than the one that turns up on the forehead of geek-turned-supermodel, Harriet Manners.

Long-legged and red-haired, fifteen-year-old Harriet never wanted to be a supermodel. The only reason she'd gone to the Clothes Show was to support her best friend, Nat. But it's Harriet who catches the eye of a talent scout and who now finds herself standing in front of the Kremlin, holding hands with Nick, the world's hottest male model, and wearing nothing but a Baylee coat that only just covers her bottom, a pair of shorts and heels so high she'd needed a wheelchair to get here from her hotel. Oh, and with an enormous zit in the middle of her forehead.

Her dad isn't helping matters. He's talking to her zit as if it were capable of intelligent thought, ordering it drinks and generally making merry over it. Nor does the fact that Harriet is practically swooning from standing so close to Nick. But despite the zit and her inability to walk, Harriet does indeed take the fashion world by storm – and it's not her looks but an act of kindness that does it. Give this one to teens to remind them that spots come and go, but generosity of spirit, honesty and good friends stick around.

SEE ALSO: **acne** • **adolescence** • **body image** • **confidence, lack of**

INDEX OF AILMENTS

INDEX OF READING AILMENTS

INDEX OF LISTS

INDEX OF AUTHORS, BOOKS AND ILLUSTRATORS

LIST OF ILLUSTRATIONS

ACKNOWLEDGEMENTS

This book is in itself a tribute, drawing as it does its life force from the many extraordinary children's stories to which it so freely refers, quotes from and, at times, gets thoroughly carried away with re-telling. We acknowledge our debt to every author and illustrator featured in these pages, past and present, and thank them for the immeasurable gift of their books. Little did they know the uses to which we would put them.

Many people helped us in the making of this book. A very special thanks goes to Martin Berthoud, Ella's dad, who, like the very hungry caterpillar, chomped his way gleefully through every story that was sent his way, from tales of samurai to YA love stories of every era and persuasion to adventures on the high seas. Frankly, without his dedicated reading, we'd probably still be on M. Special thanks go also to Doreen Elderkin, Suse's mum, for transatlantic love and being a stickler for the bedtime-story ritual from the beginning; and to Bill and Jennie Thomas, and Saroja Ranpura, for flying in at a moment's notice to hunt for our forgotten children and give them something to eat.

We are hugely grateful to Charlotte Raby, whose knowledge of children's literature and children's reading issues has been invaluable.

Adult readers have been wonderful, including Becky Adams, Natalie Avella, Andy Bennett, Gael Cassidy, Sarah Cassidy, Chris Berthoud, Clare Berthoud, Coky Giedroyc, Mel Giedroyc, Kevin Harvey, Averil Hudson, Sharen McKay, Anna McNamee, Sam Nixon, Kate Shanahan, Katie Sollohub, Selma Stafford, Claire Usiskin, Claire Westgate and Rachel Wykes.

Younger readers have been essential, including Ava Berthoud, Charles Berthoud, Eric Berthoud, George Berthoud, Isla Berthoud, Lai Ling Berthoud, Lois Berthoud, Nick Berthoud, Felix Bes, Catherine Bethell, Iris Bethell, Isidora Bethell, Laurence Bethell, Andreas Bougheas, Petros Bougheas, Rosie Bowyer, Hamish Bromley, Monty Bromley, Rufus Bromley, Sophie Chapman, Toby Chapman, Casper Davidson, Mary Davidson, Daniel Elderkin, Isabelle Elderkin, Ariella Glaser, Noa Glaser, Cal Gorvy, Leela Guha, Anna Harries, Jess Henshall (from Delve into Dystopia), Coco Heppner, Daisy Heppner, Sam Heppner, Olivia Horner, Eve James, Finn James, Vita Jones, Esther Lacey, Rosalind Lacey, Harry Lindfield, Rowan Macy,

Agnes Malin, Evie Malin, Robin Malin, Ava Maralani, Roxana Maralani, Sian Messenger, Flossie Morris, Hannah Morris, Vita Morris, Darcey Nixon, Cyrus Noushin, Lucy Okonkwo, Felix Partridge, Ella Papenfus, James Platt, Olivia Potter, Zac Prosser, Ella Raby, Herb Raby, Lettie Raby, Inigo Serjeant, Otto Serjeant, Theodora Spufford, Nancy Turner, Benji Wells, Lizzie Wells, Noah Wells, Ollie Withers, Leila Wyrtzen and Nora Wyrtzen. Thanks to the pupils of Cold Spring School, New Haven, the pupils of Downlands Community School, Hassocks, and the pupils of St Lawrence Primary School, Hurstpierpoint; and to the enlightened teaching staff at all three schools who let us raid their libraries and their knowledge of children's literature.

Thanks too for guidance and recommendations from Child and Adolescent Psychiatrist Ethel C Bullitt, MD; Pam Sayre LCSW; English tutor to deaf kids William Davidson; Amy Soule, the special needs teacher from Ontario we've never met but who emailed us with suggestions on a monthly basis, unasked; Marilyn Brocklehurst of the Norfolk Children's Book Centre; Damian Barr for his general championing; Jo Unwin for her inspiration; and Juliet Bromley, Bruce Coffin, Maria Coffin, Sarah Constantinides, Susan Cunningham, Anne Dearle, our fantastic Facebook friends, Alex Finer, Annie Harper, Mimi Houston, Alison Huntingdon, Josh Lacey, Doug McKee, Vida Maralani, Heather Millar, Bonnie Powell (and her fantastic Facebook friends), Joanna Quinn, Gael Gorvy Robertson, Dr Kristina Rath (and daughter Jane), Anne Watkins and Charmaine Yabsley. Moody Khan and Jyoti Prajapati were hugely generous with their ideas and sharing of booky love. Special thanks go to Maureen McKeon Armstrong and her team at the Whitneyville branch of Hamden Public Libraries, and to the Connecticut public libraries system for tirelessly shipping in books from all corners of the state at, seemingly, the murmur of an author's name. Thanks to all at The School of Life for their continued advocacy; and to Simona Lyons, our London lynchpin, who valiantly kept our bibliotherapy service running, often at full pelt, while we were held captive by children's books.

Huge thanks to Jamie Byng and the team at Canongate who continue to bring their unique sparkle to everything they do. We are indebted in particular to our editor, Jenny Lord, who has become as integral to our process as shared Google docs, Skype and Hendrick's* gin. Thanks, also, to our Gandalf (aka our agent) Clare Alexander; to our practice nurse (aka our publicist) Jaz Lacey-Campbell; our enormously patient managing editor Vicki Rutherford, our sub-editor Debs Warner (who we think may, like Beegu, be blessed with an extra eye); our art director Rafi Romaya, and Rohan Eason, whose extraordinary illustrations tread that exhilarating line between darkness and joy.

Last, but not least, thank you to Carl for being Ella's living, breathing, polyphonic audiobook; to Ash for showing Suse that sometimes jumping in with two feet, especially from a great height, and probably head-first, can do you good even when it means having to put a book down to do it; and to our children, Morgan, Calypso, Harper and Kirin, for leading us back to once-upon-a-time in the first place.

* Broker's for Suse.

Ella Berthoud and Susan Elderkin met as English Literature students at Cambridge University, where they began giving novels to each other whenever one of them seemed in need of a boost. Ella went on to study fine art and become an artist. Susan became a novelist. In 2008 they set up a bibliotherapy service through The School of Life in London, and since then have been prescribing books either virtually or in person to clients all over the world. With four children, two husbands, various cats, dogs, mice and tortoises (some of them imaginary) between them, they created their first book, *The Novel Cure*, together in 2013, followed up by *The Story Cure* in 2016.

thestorycure.com

Design by Rafaela Romaya
Illustrations by Rohan Eason